POETS OF THE NEW CENTURY

POETS
OF THE NEW CENTURY

EDITED BY ROGER WEINGARTEN

AND RICHARD HIGGERSON

INTRODUCTION BY JACK MYERS

DAVID R. GODINE

PUBLISHER · BOSTON

First published in 2001 by

DAVID R. GODINE, PUBLISHER, INC.
Post Office Box 450
Jaffrey, New Hampshire 03452
www.godine.com

LIBRARY OF CONGRESS CATALOGING-IN-PUBLICATION DATA

Poets of the new century /
edited by Roger Weingarten and Richard Higgerson ;
introduction by Jack Myers.—1st. ed.
p. cm.
ISBN 1-56792-177-9 (hardcover : alk. paper) —
ISBN 1-56792-178-7 (softcover : alk. paper)
1. American poetry—21st century.
I. Weingarten, Roger. II. Higgerson, Richard.

PS615.P6237 2001
811'.608—dc21 2001040394

FIRST EDITION
Printed in the United States of America

Contents

Introduction

. . . moments of pure air and light.
Isn't that what missing is?

A MAN WENT OUT to bring back what was missing, what he felt he missed. That was the plan, to hold himself open for as long as he could to what he missed.

He didn't think, "How silly to bring a sprig of pine to a barroom, a mushroom to a 3rd-floor walkup, a mockingbird to Los Angeles, a rusted miner's pan to a college class, an ant to an executive's desk," for his errand was about what finding what wasn't there, what was missing.

He knew, of course, when he got back some would question by what authority he had been sent; how ridiculous it is to think one could recognize what wasn't there; how throughout the whole spillage of history, the way things were done was to bring things that were done to the wilderness; and, finally, in any case, what possible use could starlight be to a cop, the chthonic odor of earth to a woman flipping burgers, an ant to a man facing an elephantine task?

The man paid no mind to this, and focused only on his quest, from which he didn't look up until what was not done was finished and he had sent back what was missed. A man at a bar, who had been gnawing on the gristle of a domestic argument, smelled the bright sprig of pine and bought jewelry for his wife who miraculously conceived that night; the mockingbird that landed in Los Angeles, a kind of living mirror, repeated to the people who they were but hadn't heard; seminars in dance were conceived around a rusty tin pan; and in the dark of a small bedroom, the little mushroom told The Story of Being Different to some nuyorican children in a 3rd-floor walkup. In other words, wherever What Was Missing landed, people suddenly felt what they missed.

But still there was something missing. Finally, a man was appointed and asked to introduce what was missing. He dutifully numbered, described, and classified what was there: a breeze, an ant, a mushroom, an old tin pan, a sprig of pine — but in his heart he knew something larger than that was there, there was something missing. He summoned up the Great 5 W's of the story: Who, What, Why, When, and Where, but, of course, he only got back what was already there. Finally, at a loss for words, and despairing, he saw an ant introduce itself, feel its way like miniscule handwriting out of the pile of what was missing, writing out, without knowledge of writing, what wasn't there, the very kind of thing the man who was appointed to introduce the thing that was missing had missed.

— JACK MYERS

Ralph Angel

Twilight

That he might just snap again was part of it, blind himself, and, well,
you're there.
You'd climb the wooden stairs again, lock the bathroom door behind
you, will yourself away.
Maybe get it right this time, I don't know,
the card I thought to send, a thousand crows on a Chinese screen, a
light from down below somewhere, everything.

Among schools of flashing fish, a shadow and its camera, we've all been
there before.
Among the fruit and praying figures, his latest medication, his threatening,
stupid call, each dangerous time.
You talk to him, put aside a little money for somebody else, pen messages
and stay. Move again.
And it's a better story there,

it must be. The beginning of a street, a slant of houses. Glint and shimmerings,
porches, and leaves. And now the twilight,
instantaneous. The tables, and the chairs. How the unseen break bread
together, carefully.

Twice Removed

Not even sleep (though I'm ashamed of that too).
Or watching my sleeping self drift out and kick harder, burst awake, and
then the nothing,
leaf-shadow, a shave and
black coffee, I know how a dream sounds.

This ease. This difficulty. The brain that lives on a little longer. The long
commute (not even what happened back then — this sort of
giving up with no one around and therefore
no charge for anything).

No word. No feeling
when a feeling wells up and is that much further.

Most Recent Book: *Neither World* (Miami University Press Poetry Series, 1995)

Cupola and drumming, from the inside, holes open up a sky no thicker
than cardboard.
You, the one I'd step over. You, whom I care for

and lie to, who doesn't want to, either, not even this failure
(having grown so used to it), the wreck that still
seeps from a stone, sinks down among the roots and, in that perfect
darkness, such bloom.
No name for it. No place inscribed with its own grief,

where the grass resists, and I too
resist.
No place to get to. No place to leave from. No place where those times,
and times like these, are allowed to die.

Months Later

Where? In the black trees that lay down and drown here? In the drowned clouds? — and no one to hold them back. Rhododendron, the night never ends. A still life and a way to get home again. A moss-dark photograph turned holy in his memory.

It's anyone against the wind tonight. In the eyes of a child who looks up at us from the bottom of a well, or across the table, the uninvited guest taking the oranges we intended to eat.

In these very hands. A window of the soul already open to the sea. An hour outside of itself. A name that's repeated over and over until it's just noise.

River of ashes. River and flame, the small vibration we set in motion there. I wouldn't know how to find you or anyone.

Searchlights and choppers. With cats on the rooftops and moths-turned-to-dust on the sill. Pillar, and bell tower. Wall, and earlier than that, the peaceful cities.

Calm, without talking. In our oldest clothes. From the balcony, on the fire escape — just leaning on the railings above the flooded streets.

Untitled

Or as along the river buildings brighten and grow dim again.
As a distant bridge repeats itself, and the domes above, and that much further, the city reassembled there.

Easy as listening, or choosing not to. A breeze comes up, a door glides through its own perfect outline. Halyards and traffic. In a courtyard the puddles of last night's rain.

I watched my pain ease between spaces of the air itself.
Watched a waiter fidget with his apron, a woman selling lilacs, arranging cans. Strangers, their footsteps, as if

the soul were buoyed there, moist and leafy, a shadowed street where fruit rots in a wooden crate.
A pile of bricks. A ladder. Packages and papers, I miss everyone.

As in this quiet, always. My body. A whispered song.
As if, in this quiet, a man turns away and with a pole a shopkeeper lowers the awnings.

My body. In time. And the hour passes.

Robin Becker

Why We Fear the Amish

Because they are secretly Jewish and eat matzoh on Saturday.
Because they smell us in fellowship with the dead works
of darkness and technology. Because we doubt ourselves.
We find their clothing remorseless; we find their beards unsanitary.
Who among us is not ashamed, speeding, to come upon a poor
horse pulling a cart uphill, everyone dressed the same?
We believe in the state and they believe in the button.

With their fellow Pennsylvanians, the Quakers, they hold noisy pep rallies.
They know the quilting bee, the honey bee and the husking bee
are the only proper activities for women.
Even their horses are thrifty and willing to starve for Christ.
In the Poconos, the men vacation with Hassidim and try on

Most Recent Book: *After Leaping Upriver* (University of Pittsburgh Press, 1999)

each other's coats. Back home, no tractors with pneumatic tires.
Pity the child who wants a radio and must settle for a thermos.

When the world shifts to Daylight Savings Time, there's no time
like slow time, to stay out of step. In Standard Time
their horses trot faster than ours, for the Amish
set their clocks ahead. In January, they slaughter the animals.
In March, they go to the sales. In April, they plant potatoes.
In June, they cut alfalfa. In August, they cut alfalfa again.
In October they dig potatoes. In December they butcher and marry.

They modify the milk machine to suit the church, they change
the church to fit the chassis, amending their lives with hooks-and-eyes.
Their dress is a leisurely protest against chairmindedness.
We know their frugality in our corpulence. We know their sacrifice
for the group in our love for the individual. Our gods are
cross-dressers, nerds, beach-bums, and poets. They know it.
By their pure walk and practice do they eye us from their carts.

Midnight at the Third Street Sculpture Garden

Calcified looms, the rib cages
of giant cats
shine in the moonlight.

This is how the dead
return: costumed children knock at your door,
bones transparent.

Plaster spinal columns —
fused mid-motion, Pompeian —
expose a violent

city's burial. Someone has pillaged the headstones,
urns, pot sherds, coins, ash and left
only the vertebrae to guide

the urban anthropologist.
Like her, I stand at the bars,
drawn to the white

throne on the black grass,
a phosphorescent
electric chair.

Above me, a lunette ornaments the gates,
the sculptor punning the lunacy
of walking at an hour when the gypsum skeletons

become a spectral zoo —
creatures firked and flensed until
this part of Third Street appears

funereal, a ghost town
of shades and phantoms.
And I'm a headless traveler

galloping home, one hand cold
on my wallet of illusions, the other
frozen to the heavy bag of hope.

Sisters in Perpetual Motion

Urban wanderers,
        unhoused and unhinged, they are rapt in
                a perpetual motion of paraphernalia

trundling from Kendall to Central, Harvard to Porter.
        One in a gentleman's greatcoat —
                worsted gabardine and fur collar —

holds a sidebar conference with herself, pushes her metal
        shopping cart, argues with the invisible
                censorious judge of Mass Ave.

Parallel to traffic, she retains a centrifugal
        relationship to the lanes she occupies, strides
                away from the main, parent axis of rotation,

abjures public transportation or charity and returns,
        early evening, cold, coincident with those of us
                not charged with a conundrum of streets.

She sleeps in undocumented doorways and on grates and
        in neighborhood parks on benches and propped
                on soiled cushions she pushes,

and even her sleep toboggans through the cantonments
        of temporary habitation. I wake in a white Victorian.
                She wheels her cart in time-lapse storefront glare.

Sponge of pocked foam bedding. Torn lining of a brown coat.
        Thus I remember my sister, her unbuilt days
                of compulsive walking before she decamped

to clinics and psych wards. Her walkabouts. Her unfettered speech.
        Her terrorist phone calls and the tyranny
                of her jurisdiction: thus, beleaguered,

she engineered a siege and won. *Timber up a frame dwelling,*
        I said. *Explain yourself to yourself.* In the end,
                the cops broke down the door of an empty house to find her.

Rustic Portrait

for Carolyn Sachs

Here is the woodpile, listing a bit under its tarp, a few logs fallen
and the stump to which she goes, sometimes after dark, with an axe.
Here is the kitchen of cast iron pans, history of garlic, tomatoes and oil.
Here is the midnight mouse, the moon moving across linoleum.

Here is her morning of dogs on the road of corn and winter wheat.

From her hand pours seed that draws grosbeak and bunting,
chickadee who will not go home but sits in her hair.
Now the downy woodpecker arrives for his cage of suet
and now the nuthatch who sees the world upside-down.

Here is her garden, where the spring toad leaps from lettuce to peas,
where she goes to pick dinner, kneels against everyday
torpor before herbs in their fragrant circle of stone,
florets in blue mantles, flourishing.

Here the brief lilacs, there the peonies with their essential ants,
the hungry day lilies, open-mouthed and singing, the delphiniums
scaling the season where trillium
and lady-slipper grow at the edge of a clearing.

Here is the owl who belongs to herself, sending the dark news
of her succession from forest to house.

Here is the rake with its long afternoons of labor
in the gathering dark, the mower that knows retirement is near
when the neighbors set out their harvest of gourds and pumpkins.
Sunflowers feed the finches long after she mulches the rest.

In winter, she enters the white field on long skis, one dog
trotting in her tracks. Small animals have dragged the last corncobs

to the edge of the wood, where a frozen deer haunch sprawls in the snow.
Chickadee and titmouse alone now at the feeders.

Here is the woodpile, listing a bit under its tarp, a few logs fallen
and the stump to which she goes, sometimes after dark, with an axe.

Robin Behn

Interlude: Still Still

Inside the hole, where it's yellow,
the boy has dropped a quarter
so that the guitar rattles

when he shakes it by the neck.
Knocks, scrapes, scars.
So this is what music is.

The wooden body is no longer
bigger than his body.
The strings, which, when

he strums them,
go on forever are forever
wound around small pegs

that creak like the ones
they wrap the ropes around,
there being an absence of

able-bodied mourners
to lower, with the softer machines
of their bodies, the coffin down.

It was a cold day.
The boy had not been born yet,
but stood among us

warm in his round place.
Then, from the distance,
the bagpiper who'd been found

in the yellow pages
extracted the horizon note
like a red needle from the sky.

Most Recent Book: *Red Hour* (Harper Collins, 1993)

And so it was not with nothing
human our friend was lowered.
This is what music is.

But how did it sound to the boy,
the bladder of cries squeezed
through the slit throat

when there had not been anything
yet to cry about?
The solace of music is

not that we recognize it.
It is that the hearing
comes from before and is wound

around after. Between,
our bad singing a stranger
dozed, then bulldozed, to.

At home, in its case, the guitar
was hunkered inside the dark
into which music goes,

and the more particular dark
from which music comes
was inside of it.

The sound hole swallowed and passed back
buckets of silence
until the inner and outer dark

had the same yellow smell.
This, while the song the boy
would pay for waited, still still.

Whether or Not There Are Apples

I like to take the dress off the line,
the heat still in it.
The heat comes from the whole dress into me,
and the smell of apples,
whether or not there are apples.
It comes into me it comes into me it solves
a simple coldness.

All these years I still unpin you from the air
when I feel the other, unfathomable, cold.
You are your same shape
and weightless as a photograph
and I can find you any old where, my darling, my
direction. There is a moment when the heat is finally
gone out of the dress so that
it disappears till I think *dress*
and then it's there, and spent.
It is like the little dead space, blue hinge
at the switchback of breathing.
Then the dead air comes out.
Every time I've needed you you
let me dress in your old soul and smell you.
Since you died I've taken you,
I've taken you in, just in.
But I am getting old.
And so I need to ask you.
Maybe I'll be able to cross
the quick blue shift without you.
But will you be wanting to take me
in colorless windrows of wind
instead of my long brown hair?

Elegy for Lessons

When I have reached the point of no return, I return
    to the girl and her indelible mascara of sadness
that came from her knowing her fate
    and the words for her fate, but not
the rhythm of the words, not
    the dance inside them, when I recall

her strength that had nowhere to go,
    that chewed upon itself like a bone,
like a muscle chewing on its own bone,
    that knows the taste of chalk inside, but not
what can be written, not what will not
    wash off, when I follow

the string of time back
    to where it splays into five lines

full of notes someone else
    has written, and watch her lift the finger
of the flute and point it
    away from the page, when I hear

her try to proclaim
    in a language crowded with tone and tones
and rhythm, yes, and pure flying, yes,
    and dancing, yes, and shape-in-air but not
the *what* or *who* or *why* or *where*
    of the life inside it, when I see her

on her bicycle trolling
    the vicinity of her flute teacher's house
because, after all, he has told her
    she must exercise her lungs,
the bicycle itself like three flutes
    lashed together, when I smell

the omen-odor of diesel fuel
    flare up and feel the truck mirror sever
her handlebar an inch
    from the finger that works
the flute A-flat key or typewriter *a*
    if she survives, when I think

of her face rising moon-slow in the ditch
    to shine across the field into the back room
in that house where music
    and kindness were boiled and distilled
once, unbearably once,
    in the crucible of the body, when I feel

her resurrect herself
    thumb by gear by hair, tube by
wind by limb into a whole girl dizzy
    in the rank ranks and haze
of towering, terrifying corn,
    once, just once, let me say:

    You've had a long ride filled with longing
but you can brush yourself off now,
    the blood and grease are only
blood and grease and you still have
    ten fingers you can fashion into
something or other that flies, when I see

myself look back then as at
    a house on fire, no shoulder left
to lean on, go ahead and say that,
    no shoulder left to lean on,
boy's or man's or road's,
    then, in the corn, it's there: power:

the miniature, chain-linked,
    buzzing, bolted city of volts
from which the nerves branch to the populus.
    Behind, in the ditch, the fire music is.
And unspoken misery thereunto pertaining.
    Ahead, some sort of life among people.

The way out is either to marry the source of power
    or to move in the direction of its uses on the earth.

Dark Yellow Poem

Slice of yellow wind in yellow curtains
I sewed although the house was never mine
except where the rod went through.
Breeze does it.
                Or snow on pines. Faint clink
of yellowing spoons. Or crow-call piercing snow-pine
reflected in the spoon-shaped past,
its wing its crescent moon. Seeking any equally
black thing.
            There, in my high rooms.
The landlord's piano and arpeggios of dust.
The angles of three rooms and constant
vectoring. Every tangent outward
curving back in.
                But the man from Africa
coming up the stairs. Admiring, imagine,
the curtains. Coming up. Which made for stairs
which made for going down. To the world.
Him teaching me to loosen earth the
Zimbabwe way, small patches of stubbornness
and the single hoe.
                    What does the Other do?
I must have known at one point how to wait

upon the ground, smiling and watching.
I must have known the swing as of an ax
and then the boot, and then the bearing down.
The seeds and finally blossoming. The bearing
baring.
        This squash.
                It is the color of
those strands of golden fur caught
in the grain of wood — his cat liked
the top drawer, soft among my softest things.
What we left there has been allowed
its daily audience with light
as long as someone else lives there.
Dressing in the mornings.
Opening and closing things.
His dark yell my yellow tears these
twenty years.

Stephen Berg

The Chair

When he told me about the breakup of his marriage, about his wife fucking other men now, (that's what he believed), that he wanted to die because she wouldn't take him back,

Then, a year later, about being caught in the parking lot minutes after he squeezed the metal and wood office chair into the trunk of his Honda Prelude,

About not understanding why he stole it, why, even after he knew security guards were watching, he continued to fit the chair into his trunk,

When the chair became the main theme of his suicidal shame, his helplessness, his endless daily calls, I felt some clue to the secret of his cure had been revealed, though I had no idea what it was.

He needed to be forgiven, redeemed, but for what, after all? Surely not for something as common as divorce, surely not for stealing a cheap chair from the addiction clinic he ran.

Most Recent Book: *Halo* (University Press of New England, 2000)

I try to see him in the parking lot, lugging the worthless object to his car, setting it down, unlocking the trunk, wrestling it in until he saw he couldn't close it, jumping into the car, and a guard appears and asks what he's doing.

"All I wanted, really, was to sit down, to rest . . ." I hear him say, and it's crazy, it makes no sense — chairs are everywhere. Why steal a rickety old chair from your employer?

Poor friend, what could have soothed your infinite need? Last night, in a dream, bearded, disheveled, drained, exactly as you were, you sat so close your breath and hair smelled real, you were hoping for a word, and I yelled, "Go away! You're dead."

The guard's hand thrust through the car window, grabbing your shoulder, the transfixed menacing glare of glass and painted metal through the windshield at that instant, wild with detail. . . .

But you can't describe the event, its textures and traits, shapes, gestures, light. You can only sketch auras of mood. Jeff, I'd ask you, and you'd be silent. You thought your confusion meant you had no right to speak. You believed words betrayed you, even in your poems where you grieve for an unnamed woman, for your soul infected with the silent wish to die, with the necessary theft of the chair. You equated silence with truth. I'd sit with you, day after day, helpless in your silence.

Two years after your wife demands you leave, hours after you slave all weekend to start a Japanese garden behind your new house, your heart stops, then the monthlong coma before the tubes are pulled and you dissolve.

Sit in it, feel it under you, relax; stand next to it, place your hand on its backrest; kneel, rest your head on its seat. Cool green steel legs, rivets, laminated wood.

The chair is an afterimage, a thing smoldering in the air.

Your final silence hums on the air.

December. Gray sun. Bamboo seedlings, grass, sky. Squatting to a rock that weighs much more than you do, your face crammed against it, you stretch your arms and hands around it; for the hundredth time, try to lift it, lean, kneel, clutch it tighter, squash your cheek and chest against it, grunt, jam your fingers under it, half-stand, push, hold your breath. Your life is like the darkness inside the rock, inside your brain.

The chair is a blindness that will kill you.

Nights at The Cedar

Blue points, sawdust, youth, white wine,
when I was writing ad copy
9 to 5 for a refrigerator company
forty years ago. de Kooning died yesterday.
He'd sit with Kline at the bar a few feet away from me,
a slight jovial man beside his black-mustachioed friend,
each downing martini after martini
until they'd wobble out smashed to the gills,
leaning against each other. Naomi,
voluptuous Jewess, hung out there.
She led me to a nearby Village cemetery,
leaned back on a tombstone, lifted her skirt,
received me in that ominous darkness — we did it everywhere —
at her folks' Fire Island house, under a sheet on the sand…
and a few years ago she phoned from London
raving about how Motherwell, Pollock, Johns
stole "millions of my best ideas."
Time moves like a mason's arm smoothing cement
Backyard bucolics, bombed in a lawn chair.
Peeled birch limbs, pop-up daffodils, rich air
birdies pecking gravel, first soft March rain
jittering leaves, what was, what is,
stark undeniability, and — who knows? — soon
the serene proof that one never was here.

All I Can Say

Lately that's how it's been for me, living in the wish, hearing it inflect the late night silence often like isolated street noise so clear it isn't simply a voice recurring but a steady gentle whisper next to my ear — *I want to die now* or *Please let me die, okay?* That's how my father must have felt the night of his last, massive heart attack: so weary, wanting it because it was the only way he could solve himself. I was told he gulped down two quart cans of Campbell's tomato juice, went back to bed, then woke with chest pain, jaw pain, pain down his arm, stumbled to the kitchen and vomited until the ambulance my mother called came and took him off, unconscious. Then the delirium in ICU, tubes and monitors, two weeks of raving he's on a plane to Miami captured by the Nazis; then back to life; sitting in bed, real food, TV, and finally, miraculously, home, the family calling visiting, waiting, the air each day seared a little by the peril of this dying man, this father, this origin who should share some kind of wisdom before he dies, but can't. The nice thing is it can give survivors a kind of passionate secret song to try when they can't say where their pain's coming from, why their lives are the way they are, how and what to change, a song of infinite consolation, it probably seems, much much deeper than grief. It doesn't have words or sounds you can actually modulate with lips and teeth and tongue, like a song. It comes by itself at odd times when you've stopped thinking, are sure you never want to be touched again, wonder who caused what and why. Your mouth opens. You can't tell whose lips move. Your face in the darkness breathes. Space breathes. Like that luminous gray wall in the Vermeer — a young woman sits at a table or desk, turned toward us, toward a maid who's handing her a letter. The expression on her face — cautiously poised, veiled apprehension, not quite fear — says what's inside the envelope could change the placid room, her placid life, instantaneously, by igniting the straw of pain that's always susceptible to a treacherous fact or the scope of another's will or unearned unavoidable bad news. Behind her, soaked in mellow pearly light, the wall looks like the light is welling out of it, though a window fills the left edge of the painting. The wall seems one solid yet absolutely ephemeral plane the viewer or the woman could pass through without the least effort. That's it — it's a zone of grace and silence, a holiness of pure color, safe, fair and unconcerned, endlessly itself, the place we look for in ourselves as the source of faith, the always accessible otherness that is not personal or even human. And, yes, it breathes like your face in a room on one of those hard nights when thought exhausts itself. Lying alone, seeing it, you want to kiss the wall, then lean all of yourself against it, run your hands across its fine-grained, plaster skin, warm with sun, then press your cheek to its huge body, shut your eyes, stay.

LINDA BIERDS

Burning the Fields

1.

In the windless late sunlight of August,
my father set fire to a globe of twine. At his back,
the harvested acres of bluegrass and timothy

Most Recent Book: *The Profile Makers* (Henry Holt, 1997)

rippled. I watched from a shallow hill
as the globe, chained to the flank of his pickup truck,
galloped and bucked down a yellow row, arced
at the fire trench, circled back,
arced again, the flames behind
sketching first a *C*, then closing to *O* — a word
or wreath, a flapping, slack-based heart,

gradually filling. To me at least. To the mare
beside me, my father dragged a gleaming fence,
some cinch-corral she might have known,
the way the walls moved rhythmically,
in and in. And to the crows, manic
on the thermals? A crescent of their planet,

gone to sudden sun. I watched one stutter
past the fence line, then settle
on a Hereford's tufted nape,
as if to peck some safer grain, as if
the red-cast back it rode
contained no transformations.

2.

A seepage, then, from the fire's edge: there
and there, the russet flood of rabbits.
Over the sounds of burning, their haunted calls
began, shrill and wavering, as if
their dormant voice strings
had tightened into threads of glass.

In an instant they were gone — the rabbits,
their voices — over the fire trench,
into the fallows. My father walked
near the burn line, waved up to me, and from
that wave, or the rippled film of heat,

I remembered our porch in an August wind,
how he stepped through the weathered doorway,
his hand outstretched with some
book-pressed flower, orchid or lily, withered
to a parchment brown. Here, he said, but
as he spoke it atomized before us —
pulp and stem, the pollened tongue,
dreadful in the dancing air.

3.

Scummed and boxcar thin,
six glass-walled houses stretched beside our fields.
Inside them, lilies, lilies —

a thousand shades of white, I think.
Eggshell, oyster, parchment, flax.

Far down the black-mulched beds, they seemed
ancestral to me, the fluted heads of
dowagers, their meaty, groping,
silent tongues. They seemed
to form perspective's chain:
cinder, bone, divinity. . .

4.

My father waved. The crows set down.
By evening, our fields took the texture
of freshened clay, a sleek
and water-bloated sheen, although no water
rested there — just heat and ash
united in a slick mirage. I crossed the fence line,
circled closer, the grasses all around me
collapsing into tufts of smoke. Then as I bent
I saw the shapes, rows and rows of tougher stems —

brittle, black, metallic wisps, like something grown
to echo grass. The soot was warm,
the sky held smoke in a jaundiced wing,
and as a breeze crossed slowly through,
stems glowed — then ebbed —
consecutively. And so revealed a kind of path,
and then a kind of journey.

The Lacemaker's Condenser

Two globes — clear glass, water-filled, the size
of early melons. And placed between them, a single,
burning candle. For the women sitting left and right,
the globes have cast toward their lace-filled hands
two beams of light, yellow and singular,
condensed on the stitchwork like egg-shaped ponds.

And that is enough, one woman thinks, to ask of
fire, water — that the candle's glow on the cloaks and hearth
is drawn, down and down into perfect O's,

as breath is drawn into little words.
Noose, she says then. *Lace* is from Latin's *noose*.
And this is a *bride*. Her blunt finger strokes
through the light, traces one thread of background net.
At the window, now, the moon has emerged
from a shallow rain, and throws to her apron and pale shoe
the lengthening shadows of raindrops.
Noose. *Snare*. And why, she wonders,
is the bride the tether, the steadfast thread, and not,
growing in cirrous-thin needlepoint, the pattern?
The blossom? The filigreed leaf and whorl? Why is the bride
the *ground*? De-flowered? Then her quick laughter

troubles the candle, and its errant light
sends jittery shadows, a circular flapping, to the ceiling,
walls. Like a net of birds, the woman thinks,
or, in reverse, white over white, an ermine
trapped in a rabbit snare. She remembers sun then,
a brilliant snow. The dangling body, white, fluttering.
How, as she watched, the glare pulled down
to one hairless foot, clenched in the noose loop, one
glistening, umber bead.

Then the ermine pulled free, its light tracks
sinking a little, in the sun, the snow,
toe and claw prints moistening, lessening.
Enough to ask of fire, water:
to hold while releasing. Of the tether, the ground:
to have, and to hold the slow letting-go.
That a body might circle, this side and that.
Or a moment, circle. That the day,
like the ermine, might gradually darken.

The Suicide of Clover Adams: 1885

All the bodies like fallen cattle.
And the snubbed-brimmed caps. The war. Civil.
Brady's shadow, at times, rinses a photograph
with its black pond. But the image I keep

is a blasted meadow. Burdock, bloated sacs

of lungwort. And up from the earth's fresh trough,
I think, the mineral scent of ripped grasses.

Henry slumps in the grip of a toothache.

If I were real, I would help him. But I
am the fabric of well-water — slick and transparent —
my voice a bird where my shoulder should be.

In the Doctrine of Signatures, each plant
cures the body it mimics.
So the liver-shaped leaves of hepatica
temper the liver's jaundice, and snuff
from the snapdragon's tapered neckline
heals the tubular body of the human throat.

Heart leaf and toothwort.

Steam from the kettle
has cast a late dew on the ladles.
And a privacy to each of the windows.
In print after print, Brady centered the men
facing east. The sandbags and cannons.
One midday, I centered our cousins with an eastward
glance, fresh for the incoming hour.
In the darkroom musk, they
rose through potassium baths
with the languorous ripples of flounders...

Steam. Its simmering mist.
If I were real, I would offer a flower. But I

have taken a body of water, stirred
through with cyanide salts. Slick and transparent,
they stroke their signature to the echoing self.
Which is nothing. And from which
nothing rises at all.

Marianne Boruch

The Vietnam Birthday Lottery, 1970

Not winter still, but not
quite spring, and any hope narrowed

Most Recent Book: *A Stick That Breaks and Breaks* (Oberlin College Press, 1997)

to the dorm's TV
in the lounge downstairs, the official
gravel of its voice. And girls
in scattered chairs, not languid or wise-ass for once,
not distracted. Such a little screen: black
and white, and men who moved only
their mouths, in suits that made them
bigger. But the girls kept track,
and each had a birthday
hidden in that quiet like a flame
you'd cup a hand around,
in wind. The wind
was history and its filthy sweep, whatever
rots like that, in one head
or a thousand. Or this day, all days
turned a tragic swift ballet. And thinking as I did
no *what if*, no boyfriend, nothing
staked directly in the heart to stay
and stay, I thought merely
a kind of cloud
filled the room, or smoke. You could see it
and smell it: everyone dark-dreaming there alone
though — what? — twenty, thirty of us?
The only light
was dread, one small window of it, with its
vacant men on the other side
poised above the spinning box like those
cheap quiz shows, and you could get
a gleaming washer or a spiffy car, an Oldsmobile
with any luck. Of course
you could. Of course, sobbed my friend
whose boy was suddenly born all wrong,
right on target, though, that moment, illegal
as an angel, already half
stupefied by visions
on a fake i.d. in some bar downtown. The whole
night like that: sobbing
or relief, dead drunk either way.
I fell asleep late to the boys'
roaring home, broken
wayward lines of them, the marked
and the saved, by moonlight or streetlight
I can't remember which.

Piano Tuning

Of course I left it, the tuning hammer
on the piano, and walked straight to the kitchen.
Left the old guy out there poised, bent
over it. Such a private thing
between them, the wooden panel open, hammer
to it, twin shafts on a maple handle. Something
about it — I couldn't watch — major,
not minor, then what the hell, back
to minor again, that underwater rush
going sharp and flat.

But I could feel it
in my chest. All morning, the pure
ache of it. And I did nothing in the kitchen,
that listening nothing, where you just
look out a window and watch for anything — birds,
grass bent at an angle. Because the whole time
it was the slow weight of the tuning hammer,
the metal strings that don't know
what music is, sweet
dumb narrowest expanse
of the deepest ore, singing out
its genius anyway.

I thought to do
other things — some cleaning up
or fixing a cold supper
for later. But I kept picturing
how it was out there, the tuning hammer
at the ancient upright. The old guy,
a genius himself in how he bent into it.
Again and again that private thing between them,
hammer to the strings, twin shafts, wooden handle.
I heard the turn and counterturn. It wasn't
love. But I heard
a shape — god, to know
what I was hearing — up, then down, forgiveness,
no forgiveness at all. . . .

X-ray Vision

is what my brother longed for, clipping out
his coupon from the screwy comic,
longed for and paid for, one solid
quarter beneath the cellophane tape.
Then he waited day and night
for sight. *Right through clothes*: oh monstrous,
miniature scope in the hand to set the eye
to all things in the world
delicious and forbidden, under something
vastly, boringly
not. *Allow six weeks*, he
kept intoning. Hope, not litany
though certainly it was prayer. (I can
see, cried the trembling
blind man in the movie for our Catholic
fifth grade, our teacher half
weeping as the projector
spit and smoked and nearly burned up. . . .)

At home it was simply
any mail? Week after week my brother
sailing through the door. Our poor mother
with her *no* aimed at his back,
exact. I said, could you see through cats' fur? Through a door
of steel? Something quick like an eyelid,
quicker, like a bird,
like the wing, down to its bones
and glue? *Anything, moron* — he
forever patient, still
patient. O invincible
country, where childhood is,
and faith, a little
masterpiece.

Smoking

I don't regret it, not smoking,
though times in my twenties, I couldn't sit
through a movie whole. Halfway,
at the crucial second that weird sucked-up

feeling would come over me, and I'd bolt
to the lobby, find one of those ancient
nubby couches, smoke
going clear for the interior, down every
unlit passage until I was
normal again, fit for all those strangers
on the screen. But still out there, still sunk
to that pleasure, I'd drift into the great
boredom of the popcorn boy and the ticket girl,
that languid ache
of a place when everyone's
elsewhere — if only the next room —
stalled, distracted into themselves. I'd sit
and smoke quietly, and they'd talk
to each other, flirt even. The popcorn boy
always had a trick he'd do, stacking
Dots or Milk Duds until one box, quick,
would vanish. And the ticket girl would
lean into his counter, just so,
amused, disbelieving. *Sure*, she'd say,
and I'm Yoko Ono. Those little dramas of pure smoke,
I miss them — two real voices in those old
wedding cake theaters of the 20s, Chicago, 1973,
before they were razed for a thing
gleaming, steel and glass, when everyone
in the next room kept looking
one way, and by the bad light above me, I was
looking in, or looking down, or looking toward
these two, the dearest nothing
suspended between them.

Marcus Cafagña

The Cockroaches of Tuol Sleng Museum

To this day the hallways smell
    worse than wet dogs, and bristle
        with the concertina wire

Most Recent Book: *Roman Holiday* (Invisible Cities Press, 2001)

used against Buddhists
    or the ones who wore glasses.
        One thousand skulls

hang in the shape of Cambodia,
    and so sicken my sister
        as she thinks what a land mine

or Khmer Rouge rebel boy
    could do to a junior U. S. envoy
        like her. Even at the Beauty Inn,

the distant clatter of Kalashnikovs
    turn her fear to water which drips
        down temples and around ears

as if her forehead were stone
    and worry had washed it smooth.
        Within this breathless sweat

she swims, trades her dreams
    for mosquito netting and kerosene
        lanterns that frazzle her shadow

over shades, an awkward limbo
    between darkness and enough
        light to keep the cockroaches

from her long American hair.
    Then furious for sleep,
        she traps them in overturned jars

they cannot topple but nudge
    upright over tile, sealed under
        their prison-domes of glass

as if they are the lost souls of Buddha
    touching all night
        in cold-blooded clinks.

Gloomy Sunday

If the instrument of your beloved's suicide is within your reach, get rid of it.
— Traditional

This was the time of year, this gloomy Sunday
in October when I descended
our basement steps to the bottom of hell
and found my wife hanging
as if the lord mayor
had lured her to the other side.

Don't let me forget that Lansing place,
and wonder who lives there now
and what they make of our cracked foundation.
Let it be clear, but small, through a lens,
my wife's cropped hair, the chairs
so torn with fabric stripped from their arms.

She had promised she'd stay in this poor little world
and redeem the diamond ring,
but the ulcers in her colon did not stop
bleeding and the facelift seared her scalp
to the stitches and the manic depression
coiled her throat like a necklace,

burning pearl by pearl. But she could not
avenge the first husband's fist, or the CMT
in Fort Myers who left her in restraints,
hospital gown on backwards.
Or the snapshot pose with her father
on prom night, the secret bristling

between them. Now the dolorous wind
swings branches sharp-edged and shadowed
with clouds. Now the radio wakes me
from a bathroom floor in Pittsburgh, the clamor
on every station a summons
through evening's wormy pomp —

acid guitar, sarabande whirling
under electric globes, the voice of an angel
blown to dust — as if from my wife's
dying breath the germ I've caught
will self-inflict. Ridiculous thought,
but I'm throwing my extension cords away.

Haldol

I wear a long-sleeve shirt with cuffs
for protection – and try
never to restrain an escalated girl alone –
since that night the Haldol
wore so thin one of them sputtered saliva
and flung her weight
against each lock on the ward I'd bolted. The door
to seclusion only opening out
so they can't kick it shut and trap us in.

That night her teeth chewed the skin up
and down my arms, leaving
ragged welts and contusions
the doctors in Emergency merely stitched.
Now the rattle of old casters
sends me deeper into what
fluorescent light refracts, the tick
and jump of dayroom walls.
Now another new foster father

hugs the girl, whose posture we've perfected
over years with straitjackets.
The dorsal horn of her spinal cord
is so medicated he can't imagine
bandages like mine might ever wrap
his arms. I'll remind her
how to slip her hands
willingly into the satin
sleeves of a warm coat,
watch her button it tight.

Crack

The speed and lactose have burned away
and this blueshift of stars
pinwheels the man's brain with pure crack,
not like the peep show
marquees that blindfold Morningside Heights,
but as if vapor light inside
a train tripped the 9th Avenue El
with sparks that spike
my shadow toward destination

and open double doors
to tow me through the surface of fear,
the space any man
could fill at gunpoint, so amped
under hooded sweats
his pupils and vessels crisscross
a bloody map
to the brownstone below, where my friends
huddle behind bars on windows,
behind eyes like mine that skirt the blazing
fixity of his, these wire rims
he knocks from my temples, icing my skin
with blue steel, juking me, tapped out,
to the purse of a lady
pulled inside out, until unglued
I lurch the platform,
my spine braced for the shot,
yet I am so full of life
I wonder if the stairway
plunging to the street, the next block down,
the beveled glass
of my friends' locked door, will be memory's
last detail.

Billy Collins

Genius

is standing by the stove in a bathrobe
stirring the soup with a long wooden spoon.

Earlier in the afternoon he was busy
in the margins of a heavy book

and tonight he will step inside a molecule
or wade into the deep pool of calculus.

But now there is only the pot of vegetable soup,
the circling of the spoon,

the easy rotation of the wrist
and the aroma of onion, bay, and rosemary —

Most Recent Book: *Sailing Alone Around the Room: New and Selected Poems* (Random House, 2001)

just the kind of moment when a brainstorm
might roll in over the ridge of the valley.

Not when you are holding your head in your hands,
but when you are cutting carrots,

troweling soil into a clay pot,
or washing a glass in the sink.

You look up and see a cloud in the window
and then there is only you,

the glass underwater, and the cloud —
now clearly in the shape of an astonishing idea.

The Country

I wondered about you
when you told me never to leave
a box of wooden, strike-anywhere matches
lying around the house because the mice

might get into them and start a fire.
But your Face was absolutely straight
when you twisted the lid down on the round tin
where the matches, you said, are always stowed.

Who could sleep that night?
Who could whisk away the thought
of the one unlikely mouse
padding along a cold water pipe

behind the floral wallpaper
gripping a single wooden match
between the needles of his teeth?
Who could not see him rounding a corner,

the blue tip scratching against a rough-hewn beam,
the sudden flare, and the creature
for one bright, shining moment
suddenly thrust ahead of his time —

now a fire-starter, now a torch-bearer
in a forgotten ritual, little brown druid
illuminating some ancient night.
Who could fail to notice,

lit up in the blazing insulation,
the tiny looks of wonderment on the faces
of his fellow mice, one-time inhabitants
of what once was your house in the country?

Absence

This morning as low clouds
skidded over the spires of the city

I found next to a bench
in a park an ivory chess piece —

the white knight as it turned out —
and in the pigeon-ruffling wind

I wondered where all the others were,
lined up somewhere

on their red and black squares,
many of them feeling uneasy

about the salt shaker
that was taking his place,

and all of them secretly longing
for the moment

when the white horse
would reappear our of nowhere

and advance toward the board
with his distinctive motion,

stepping forward, then sideways
before advancing again —

the moves I was making him do
over and over in the sunny field of my palm.

Velocity

In the club car that morning I had my notebook
open on my lap and my pen uncapped,

looking every inch the writer
right down to the little writer's frown on my face,

but there was nothing to write about
except life and death
and the low warning sound of the train whistle.

I did not want to write about the scenery
that was flashing past, cows spread over a pasture,
hay rolled up meticulously —
things you see once and will never see again.

But I kept my pen moving by drawing
over and over again
the face of a motorcyclist in profile —

for no reason I can think of —
a biker with sunglasses and a weak chin,
leaning forward, helmetless,
his long thin hair trailing behind him in the wind.

I also drew many lines to indicate speed,
to show the air becoming visible
as it broke over the biker's face

the way it was breaking over the face
of the locomotive that was pulling me
toward Omaha and whatever lay beyond Omaha
for me, all the other stops to make

before the time would arrive to stop for good.
We must always look at things
from the point of view of eternity,

the college theologians used to insist,
from which, I imagine, we would all
appear to have speed lines trailing behind us
as we rushed along the road of the world,

as we rushed down the long tunnel of time —
the biker, of course, drunk on the wind,
but also the man reading by a fire,

speed lines coming off his shoulders and his book,
and the woman standing on a beach
studying the curve of horizon,
even the child asleep on a summer night,

speed lines flying from the posters of her bed,
from the white tips of the pillow cases,
and from the edges of her perfectly motionless body.

Today

If ever there were a spring day so perfect,
so uplifted by a warm intermittent breeze

that it made you want to throw
open all the windows in the house

and unlatch the door to the canary's cage,
indeed, rip the little door from its jamb,

a day when the cool brick paths
and the garden bursting with peonies

seemed so etched in sunlight
that you felt like taking

a hammer to the glass paperweight
on the living room end table,

releasing the inhabitants
from their snow-covered cottage

so they could walk out,
holding hands and squinting

into this larger dome of blue and white,
well, today is just that kind of day.

Peter Cooley

A Place Made of Starlight

This is the woman I know to be my sister.
Wizened, apple-sallow, she likes her room dark
inside the nursing home's glare. She barely sees me,

Most Recent Book: *Sacred Conversations* (Carnegie Mellon University Press, 1998)

black shades drawn against the radiant autumn day,
purple, hectic yellow streaming from the trees.
I stand and stare. One of us has to speak.

How are you? FINE. Why did I try to speak
as if we could talk, a brother and a sister
perched on the same branch of the family tree?
We share our parents. But the forest, suddenly dark,
dwarfs me always, now I'm here, where I see me,
ten years younger, shrinking beside her every day.

She is a raven, I some tiny winged thing, me
she shouts down, I-me longing to speak,
to tell my parents how she beats me every day,
dark wings claiming she will be my sister
no matter what I suffer in the darkening dark.
I scramble out farther on the family tree.

Where are my father, my mother on the tree?
I am growing smaller inside myself each day
while my body lengthens, climbing larger in the dark
toward a moment when I will finally speak
about the wounds inflicted, purpling, by my sister.
Who will believe someone small as me?

Sometimes I think the silence contains me
even today, knowing I leaped from the tree,
discovering I could fly away from my sister
to land in a clearing in the woods that day,
a place made of starlight I could finally speak.
Released by telling others, I can wear the violet dark

luminous around me now, standing in the dark,
staring at my sister who is staring back at me,
neither of us knowing how or what to speak.
Does she remember what happened on that tree?
I screamed, jumping the branch snapped on the day
I showed my parents the bruises from my sister

and the secret toppled, falling with the tree.
And bruised truth came home to belong to me:
Never, never speak up against your sister.

For Jude the Obscure

Sometimes I am brought so low
in my melancholy I know only you

can restore me: I turn to your book
in which Hardy has doomed you, line by line.

Taking you down, I have only to touch
the gold-embossed title: now

my transport lifts me as if I had drunk
salvation's cup, eaten its bread.

Then, as I wander the day,
all I pass through are shadows

who would be my wife and children, students
I talk to, spectral, tenebrous,

so consumed as I with guilt
that I must devour you for myself,

take you in as a living sacrifice
who are not Christ but just a man

living only in small print
and then my memory. In his image Hardy made you

to set free someone you will never know
from the cage of himself that hunger

failing, to be for others
solace, respite, or a friend in need

himself of consolation, all of us
one beneath that wheel night and day

turning throughout the sky, imperceptible
pitiless, rolling over us.

Brothers' Keepers

When my brother the rat dies tonight
spasming in fulfillment, hacking bubbling blood
while his heart snaps above the bait box

I set out this afternoon in the attic,
will I be entering the gates of sleep, God-given
like this life I take, or will I be up, pacing

my floor as he paced, looking for I-don't-know-what?
A rat is born, he fattens, learns the art
of scavenging on our lives, the trash we set out

Sunday nights after praying, of running down
spaces between us we missed the last minute
to take his refuge in the rat-dark, some crevice,

fissure or crack we never plugged in time
and discover only as I did this afternoon, his eyes
taking me in, terrified, nameless, like any one of us

without the other we talk to. And you,
reader, riding the rat-skin
of daily breath, this silence between us when I speak

bloating longer each word, your tail my own
saying this, your eyes remembering mine
as I always reflected yours, ruddier, more magnificent

which of us set out to kill the other, running,
you to some cross-beam, I to the room below
and, therefore, who deserves the more to die,

devourer or devoured, free of all devouring?
Rat: you are probably still living, scared off
my house, or, dead, have already awakened before morning

in your new body, prepared to meet rat women at your tomb
which I can never visit or give words to, ever,
Brother, in the world we divided up, this morning, rising.

To My Hypocrite Reader

Every day in motion, these wheels under me,
the city swarming around me, every season
another summer surrounding my glassed-in world,
this cool sarcophagus urging me on.
And at the edge of my eyes, the multitudes,
the poor always with us, wandering the roadsides,
those who beg at intersections or forage uncut grass
for a bottle, a tin can, to sell back at dinner time.

Reader, come with me, guide my hand,
I need directions, turning. I need
to keep my words steady going down.

New Orleans, unreal city. . . I have nowhere to be
myself, no room can bear my body's hunger
for taking down the shadows, the armatures of all I see:
the three-legged dog in heat on the churchsteps;
the whores letting down straps of pastel sundresses
tanning their breasts across the balcony of their motel.
Yawning, they wave to me, always plying their trade.

And now, street after street of houses abandoned
to those with no house, windows knocked out.
Nausea: the wheels spin me on.

Reader, without you, I have no one.
This sickness quickens me. I feed on it.
I am thrilled by my own illness. Be my friend.

Vertigo: the wheels spin me on:
crows, gulls, bent over patches of black water
between cracks in the road; a pelican,
lost inland, wanders, one leg broken, a used car lot,
flapping and stumbling, passed over by a man
of the cloth, white collar riding a rusted motorbike,
a sign on his chest, another on his back,
HAVE YOU BEEN WASHED IN THE BLOOD OF THE LAMB?

Reader, drive for me. I have nothing
here to hold me as, rung by rung,
I go down the old ladder of terror
attaching itself to a stone wall, shaking
the foundations of despair which may,
any step, give out as I straddle the blind air,
rising at morning to wander, to pass the day in transit
out of doors, feeding on this city, its liver, heart and brain,
no other way to satiate this need to leave myself.

God Comes in a Dream to Cure a Suppliant

After they stripped me, they tied me in my chair
I love to come home to, the frayed rocker we keep
since my wife bought it for me, "an old man's resting place,"
when I was thirty. All right, I'm stalling, here it is,

what happened next: they lifted black hoods
from two cages, slid up the doors of each. I screamed,
the rat and cottonmouth were at it in a second.
The rat clawed the snake, I saw insides spurting out.
They were milky, I started to cry in the dream
which I knew was a dream and knowing made no difference
even when I got hard: the snake caught the rat
at the scruff of the neck and broke it and began
after the rat's scream to eat it, inch by inch.
I told you: I was hard. I came. This was my night.

Robert Cording

Gratitude

In his prison letters, Bonhoeffer is thankful
for a hairbrush, for a pipe and tobacco,
for cigarettes and Schelling's *Morals* Vol. II.
Thankful for stain remover, laxatives,
collar studs, bottled fruit and cooling salts.
For his Bible and hymns praising what is
fearful, which he sings, pacing in circles
for exercise, to his cell walls where he's hung
a reproduction of Durer's *Apocalypse*.

He's thankful for letters from his parents
and friends that lead him back home,
and for the pain of memory's arrival,
his orderly room of books and prints too far
from the nightly sobs of a prisoner
in the next cell whom Bonhoeffer does not know
how to comfort, though he believes religion
begins with a neighbor who is within reach.

He's thankful for the few hours outside
in the prison yard, and for the half-strangled
laughter between inmates as they sit together
under a chestnut tree. He's thankful even
for a small ant hill, and for the ants that are

Most Recent Book: *Heavy Grace* (Alice James, 1996)

all purpose and clear decision. For the two
lime trees that mumble audibly with the workings
of bees in June and especially for the warm
laying on of sun that tells him he's a man
created of earth and not of air and thoughts.

He's thankful for minutes when his reading
and writing fill up the emptiness of time,
and for those moments when he sees himself
as a small figure in a vast, unrolling scroll,
though mostly he looks out over the plains
of ignorance inside himself. And for that,
too, he's thankful: for the self who asks,
Who am I? – the man who steps cheerfully
from this cell and speaks easily to his jailers,

or the man who is restless and trembling
with anger and despair as cities burn and Jews
are herded into railroad cars – can
without an answer, say finally, *I am thine*,
to a God who lives each day,
as Bonhoeffer must, in the knowledge
of what has been done, is still being done,
his gift a refusal to leave his suffering, for which,
even as the rope is placed around his neck
and pulled tight, Bonhoeffer is utterly grateful.

Fashion Shoot, Frijoles Canyon

Where did they come from? – suddenly, among the Anasazi
ruins: two models, a photographer, two hair stylists,
a smiling entourage. Racks of dresses and skirts,
of blouses and vests and accessories. Across the canyon,
in the emptied rooms of a pueblo, I had been pretending
to piece together dusty traces of the past. I couldn't
imagine the effort required to cut dwellings out of cliffs.
I watched them through binoculars: flutter of hands,
sweep of skirts, a loose blouse luffing in hot breezes –
and the faces, changing expressions as the photographer
moved right then left, as he kneeled and lay down,
the rest following, as if wherever the models were going,
desire would be satisfied. He waved his arm

and the wind covered or revealed a face, the sun imparted
its fashionable radiance and shadings, and soon enough
I imagined the pages of the magazine taking shape,
its glossy attractions like a vague desire enlarging itself,
each new item turning into a necessity, its cost
and possession always larger and more elusive,
and always promising a greater satisfaction, the glory
of a different future alive in those clothes, in those two
models who went on posing long into the afternoon
in a world where the Anasazi scratched deer and running
men into the million-year-old-canyon walls and then
vanished, leaving us to ask all these years, where did they go?

Memorial Day

Like a mockingbird lunatic with repeating,
he cursed Jesus to kingdom come, his harangue
in the tongues of the Old Testament,
and then fumed to me, a passerby too young
to ignore him, and demanded, *Tell me
about Jesus*, his emphasis making clear
he knew too much of a world never washed
clean enough by anyone's blood. *What's good
about this world?* he asked again and again.

That was almost forty years ago, in a city
where sirens were always wailing a new disaster.
A question lost for a time, now resumed,
asking to be fit to this moment at May's end
as I read about two brothers who shot their parents,
the jury hung, unable to understand their motive.
My father wouldn't get my brother a cell phone,
one brother calmly explained. The other said,
my mother always asked if our homework was done.

The day they shot their parents, they believed
the future's rich venues opened before them:
one played basketball, the other made some money,
had some beers, spent the night with his girlfriend.
Who *could* understand? This morning, survivors
of three wars gathered on our village green.
Speeches, rifle volleys, taps, the chronicle of church bells

in the empty sunlight and, like a trapdoor
opening, the vast, deserted silences of the dead.

Outside, the late May light hangs on,
the day long and warm. Summer smells in the air.
The sky's a glorious bloom of pinks and reds —
the result many would say of what we've done
to the air. Yet, just now, I'm struck by how
this light-soaked moment seems to absorb
the pain of what goes unanswered, and I want
to ask why the clement light, no matter how
we cut it off, or pollute it, still keeps coming.

Moths

I woke to the flutter of all
their wings over the screen
as, slowly, they assembled
themselves out of the dusty
half-light of morning —
thirty-four moths,
their small gray-brown bodies
covering the screen like lichen.
At noon, they basked
in what little sun there was,
the pale September light
resting briefly on wings
that moved hardly at all
yet never stopped moving
until the moths began
to die. Even then they
seemed more composed
than exhausted, taking
the time they needed,
as if they were dreaming
their death into being.
They simply became their end,
death so naturally wrought,
I needed to touch each one
to be certain. Where
I placed my finger, they broke
out of their bodies

f dust, leaving
rint
By then
ntered
he sky, dense
l colors,
collapsed in on itself,
the low clouds igniting
in a bonfire of last light.
And I felt suddenly
the slow, irreversible moment-
to-moment passion
of every thing to keep
moving — and I leaned close
to the screen and blew
my breath on what remained
until nothing was there,
then stood a while listening
to the wind in the leaves
while the plush dark freed
a scattering of stars and the moon
broke clear of the trees.

Mark Cox

Red Lead, 1978

The way a boy might kick a can,
or a field goal, or a stone to skip
down one long empty street
toward a home that held no warmth for him;
as if putting on a sock or unbuckling a belt,
some small gesture shared by all of us,
he kicked him in the face. Then,
standing like a hunter over his trophy,
one foot on the tailgate,
he dabbed the blood from his boot
with a napkin.

Behind us, clouds muddied the horizon,
pigeons peered from their nests in the girders,

Most Recent Book: *Thirty-Seven Years from the Stone* (Pitt, 1997)

and the latticed shadows of the bridge
lay like a puzzle on the ground.
To the east, the broken-toothed St. Louis skyline
yawned up into haze. It is a trial, the stanchions said,
bound here as we are, our sadnesses given us
so we won't float toward heaven too soon.

Spot primer, finish coat, blood, dust and asphalt,
squabs laid gingerly down to die
by bottle caps full of water. For miles
that paper napkin, rode the Missouri,
getting darker and darker, going under,
being pulled apart and into
the fierce, filthy river of everyone.

After the Sea Parts, My Daughter Walks Among Gravestones

Don't be fooled. Though the ocean would give anything to lie down
fully for one moment, completely relaxed, across the whole earth,
a dry towel on its forehead, the sea floor is just another shore.

And what a slathering the sea makes of it: the weeds, the driftwoods,
all the night's dead washed back and forth. Imagine the pressure of that
sky in your ears, that deep a blue in you, that useless plea to all
the pleasure craft bobbing above the drowned.

This deep, we can barely hear the motors' throbbing, the keen of riggings
and maneuverings along shallow reefs. This deep, the intensity of last things
puts its shine on the coffin handles, the sunlight of the fifties slants
across windshields, casts storm doors in bronze, and the warped antennae
are twisted until the grainy blue black ocean of interference pales with the news.

You could say the dead keep choosing for us and choosing badly, puddles of
family history the living step over and around. You'd be right. The ship
tacks back to where the little lapdog yelps in circles on the manicured lawn,
to where the porcelain dolphins assume their postures on shelves, to where
your grandmother's embroidered cushions served as pedestal for her feet.

Like a Simile

Fell into bed like a tree
slept like boiling water
got up from bed like a camel
and showered like a tin roof.
Went down stairs like a slinky
drove to work like a water skier
entered the trailer like a bad smell
where I changed clothes like a burn victim
drank my coffee like a mosquito
and waited like a bus stop.
A whistle blew.
Then I painted like I was in a knife fight for eight hours
drank like a burning building
drove home like a bank shot
unlocked the door like a jeweler
and entered the house like an argument next door.
The dog smiled like a chain saw.
The wife pretended to be asleep
I pretended to eat.
She lay on the bed like a mattress
I sat at the table like a chair.
Until I inched along the stair rail like a sprinkler
entered like smoke from a fire in the next room
and apologized like a toaster.
The covers did *not* open like I was an envelope
and she was a 24-hour teller
so I undressed like an apprentice matador
discovering bullshit on his shoes.

Joyland

Here, between teen lovers spooning each other ice cream,
and the press of a five-putting family of four,
along the slippery graded slopings
to Rapunzel, Snow White and Sleeping Beauty
there will be no playing through.

Soon lights will appear
in the windows of the windmill,
the tree house, the coastal beacon.

Soon the synchronized fountains will fall and rise
reminding us it has always boiled down to precision timing
and score cards that tell us little
about those myths by which we've lived.

That mini-villa, is that the famed artist's colony,
snow painted on its roofs, tinsel icicles dripping from its eaves,
spiritual haven for the single or soon to be divorced?
Beside you and your silent wife,
on the surface of the manmade lagoon
its waters laced with blue food dye,
a real rain begins to fall, rings appearing,
as if invisible range balls were plunging from heaven.

There is, at the heart of the matter,
some wiring, a weak motor and a two 60 watt bulbs.
Sure, the little drawbridge goes up and down
and the moat indifferently returns each ball to your instep,
but you know what's going on
behind the saloon's teensy swinging doors;
you should have been able to say no, should have
returned your watch to your wrist and your keys to your hand,
and the ice bucket to its plastic tray on the toilet tank.

And it doesn't matter whether she knows or just suspects,
you have felt the pointed tap of her putter
square on your heart saying
nothing will ever be the same.

Smoke chuffs from the teepee.
A few leaves curl at the igloo door.
You could swear you saw a field mouse in the chapel's spire.
Meanwhile, your wife is perfecting her stance,
aligning her shoulders and feet, distributing evenly
the new weight of having smelled another woman
on your clothing. Let the warning lights of the water tower
blink off and on all night, let the planes traverse the sky,
there are these holes you have dug for yourselves,
these emptinesses that need be aimed at, filled.

Craig Crist-Evans

Heat

All day we've watched the hushed Atlantic waves and left
so much unsaid, but she tugs my hand until
we hover just outside a group of Cuban boys,
circling on the packed sand near the water,
their knotted shoulders brown with sun,
poking at a shark they've speared
and dragged up from the sea.

The tallest one moves in, a long thin
fish knife balanced in his hand. The rest
fall back, chanting *¡Cortalo! Cortalo! Cortalo!*
He thrusts the blade and saws the belly open.
She leans and presses fingers to the wound.

Wordlessly the boys reach in, yank out
the heart and guts; they empty it of everything,
then carve thick slabs of meat and build
a driftwood fire. Clouds
drift in and rain begins,
our tongues cool, our fingers
barely touching as we turn to go.
But they gesture toward us: *Stay*,
and then they wash the pale flesh in seawater.

As the fire burns to coals, they turn
the meat on sticks until fat drips and sizzles.

And when it's cooked, we do what they do:
we eat it with our fingers, hungrily,
surprised how sweet it is,
eating like we've never
had enough of anything.

Morphine

Once the pain subsided, he would
drift again from sleep to consciousness,
catching snippets from the nurse's station,

Most Recent Book: *Moon Over Tennessee* (Houghton Mifflin, 1999)

a few stray words, a phrase, nothing
he could call a story. Still, there were
colors in the air around him, the smell
of fresh-cut flowers and an antiseptic
hum that came, he guessed, from
thin fluorescent tubes that hung above him.

If there's a place that offers anything like solace,
it must be here, where the body accepts the drug,
gives in to timelessness, forgets its urge to move.

When the nurses in their soft white blouses
bend to touch him gently,
to move would be to interfere.

And when they push the needle
like a beam of light beneath his skin,
the humming starts again as loud,
as wonderful as the first time
he made love, in his mother's bed,
with a girl who wanted,
when she graduated,
to join the Peace Corps,
and live where no one
could speak English.

First Solo Flight

The earth a broken trampoline,
the sky a synonym for death. This
is why the airplane drops and crumbles
into sheared aluminum and scraps of Plexiglas.

The air is sudden and particular.
No one moves for seconds. There is
a sound and then there is nothing:
This is how the end arrives.

I was young and didn't know
the varied permutations of death. I didn't
know that sometimes it will fall
without warning – *bam* – in the heart

of your world. But then, why not?
After all, I'd seen my grandfather

laid out in his coffin, smiling
and unmoving in his best clothes.

But this is different. Here, a young
man on his first foray into clear blue
heaven loses control for just a second,
and it's the end of everything. I am

actually not home when it happens. I
return from a birthday party to find
the pieces of his death like confetti
scattered in the yard, where summers

I chase fireflies, or play little games of war.
But it's impossible to equate the truth
of this death with platoons of plastic
soldiers dying. Perhaps this is why

I change my mind about the small violence of pretend,
insisting instead on the unflinching truth of poems.
Here, finally, is the last cargo of reluctance:
how we learn to love, how we learn to be alone.

Clown Prince

Idling at the corner of State and Main, I'm waiting
for the light to change this frog-soaked sky

to Prince Charming with a weather map. Later,
at the Fourth of July Town Bash, she asks me for a dance.

On all the hills, crickets rub their noisy legs together. An old
man on a Harley hits a pothole and careens into a ditch.

The golden bear in Maxwell's Traveling Circus breaks
his chain and swims the reservoir. Two school kids kidnap

Tolkein's cardboard hobbits where they're propped and smoking
stogies by the Bijou. If there's moonlight, it's wet and shines

upon her teeth. If there is wind, it lifts her words up
over distant kingdoms and a haunted wood. I watch

the sky for signs: an owl, three stars in a crooked line,
a comet dragging ice around the sun. It's all there:

the wicked witch with false teeth licking apples,
snakes and buddhas leaning on a corner selling dope.

She bullies me against a culvert, holds my tongue with hers
until I cannot speak my name without her name caught up in it.

The crickets fiddle wildly. Cars out in the street chew gravel.
The light goes green. *So this is love*, I think, and everything

starts moving. The quick embrace, her words like tender
knives. Almost anything I wish for, I can have.

Jim Daniels

The Day After

the worst snowstorm in years,
a horn blares — a stuck cab
blocks the street, the guy
in the car behind leans on his horn
then stomps out and starts pounding
on the cabbie's door shouting move it
move your fucking car and the cabbie's
saying I'm stuck and the guy's screaming
try it you're not stuck and the cabbie opens
his door and the guy hits him in the face
and throws snow at him and the cabbie says
he's gonna call the cops and the guy says
call the cops fucking call the cops
and the cabbie says I'm gonna get my gun
and he goes around to his back door
and the other guy starts running
back to his car until it occurs to him
that the cabbie's bluffing because he's stopped
with his hand on his back door
so the guy charges back saying
get your gun get your fucking gun
but the cabbie don't move
because he ain't got a gun so the guy starts
throwing snow at him again and shouting

Most Recent Book: *Blue Jesus* (Carnegie Mellon University Press, 2000)

move, motherfucker, let's see your gun
but he ain't got no gun
so the guy keeps taunting him
let's see your fucking gun
and punches the cabbie in the face
then gets in his car and rear ends
the cab till it's out of his way
and speeds off and the cabbie's alone
in the street shouting next time
I'll have a gun
next time I'll have a fucking gun.

My Mother's See-Through Blouse

A rare night out, my older brother
babysitting the rest of us.
My mother emerged from their bedroom
in a see-through blouse,
her plain white bra
clearly visible.

What was she thinking? To wake up
my father's numb shuffle, I guess.

What was she thinking?
My father looked up, jumped,
spilled his coffee.
I was thirteen and couldn't look.

My father didn't yell —
he paced and shook his head
he opened his mouth
he closed his eyes
he made fists.

He sent us to our rooms.
What were you thinking?
He asked her.

I can pile up the facts:
My father was never home.
They were both forty.
She cried. They went nowhere.

We never saw the blouse again.
It was rose colored.

My mother had one of her
dizzy spells — she lay in bed
all weekend.

My father made us pancakes
the next morning, and they
weren't bad.

He didn't say much.
Kept looking at his watch.
Your mother's sick, he said
and we knew.

Through the cracked door
I saw him sitting on the edge
of their bed. I couldn't see
her. Nobody said a thing.

Something might have happened,
but the next day it was back
to work, and overtime.

Brown's Farm

I drive past the orchard, then swerve off
the road to circle back. Sunday morning,
everyone in church except us and Mr. Brown.
We are on a drive to nowhere, our two children
strapped in behind us, eyes wide with silence.

The sign says Open 2-5, but she tells me
to ask the man behind us mending fences.
We've been fighting over what's wrong with her.
The doctors can't find anything —
asthma? MS? Ulcers? She studies
her hands for signs. They tremble.

What we're left with
spins while we await the latest test results.
Mr. Brown, he doesn't say
We're closed. Can't you read?

He says, *Yes, but we don't have much*
right now. We must look like
people who need some apples.
We enter the barn, the dark
smell of apples. He flips on lights
as he leads us to the cooler
where the apples are stored until two.

We shiver. He's talking about apples,
which ones are ready this early
in the season. We buy a peck,
and a jug of frozen cider from last year —
all they have.

We drive off, waving, our fake smiles
turning real. She passes out apples
and we start crunching. My daughter
is one. I bite the skin off for her.
The car fills with the music of crunching.
Chew it up, don't choke, we both say.

I can't know her body, the insides,
though in good moments I have claimed to.
The insides, what are they telling her
beneath the skin?

The cider thaws in the sun
filling the squares of our windows.
I imagine its cool pleasure.
How are we going to eat all these apples?
she asks. I love her face
in this light, its soft glow.

I squint into the sun and turn the wheel
as the road curves toward gentle hills, and home.
I want to say, *I'll see you through this, whatever it is*.

I say, *One at a time*.

Night-Light

for Mrs. Nesta

Up late again, I sit on the toilet
flicking your night-light
on and off in the little pink bathroom
under the stairs. I am writing
on the little scraps of paper
you left by the phone.
We do not use the night-lights
you left to dot these halls.

We are taking care
of your old house. Last week
we bought a bedroom set from an old widow
moving in with her brother. Cherry wood.
Maybe you know her? Mrs. Santoro.
A scapular hung over the bedpost —
it must have been her husband's.
I gently lifted it, draped it
over a stack of boxes.

I wanted to put that scapular on.
Can you understand that? I wanted
to drape it over my neck
and say a few prayers for him,
for you, for old people everywhere
selling off their goods.

Are you done with the treatments,
has your hair grown back in?
Will it ever? I worship everywhere.
In the kitchen I pray to the vase you left,
the ceramic woman's head. Her earrings
have dropped off. I have made her
a pair of sunglasses and taped them on
so she will not see us scuff your floors.

Sometimes we still come across a note
you left us — instructions for the stove,
the furnace, the floodlights, the locks.
I heard how the gypsies robbed you
when you let them use your phone.
But that's not why you sold this
for a prayer.

The absence of your grandfather clock
ticks in the hallway. You called to ask
for the catalogs you use to shop.
We'd thrown them out. We are young
and small in this big house
but we will fill it up with our dust and sins.

In this tiny room under the stairs
I flick off the light and step out
into the dark hall, feeling my way.
It is time again to dump the bag of keys
you left, to finger your old bones.

Greg Delanty

The Bindi Mirror

> *The small patch which a married woman places on her forehead is known as a bindi ('zero'). These are usually bought ready-made from the market and have become almost a fashion accessory, with every imaginable shape and colour to match the occasion. You'll also come across a wide variety of used bindis stuck around the mirrors in hotel bathrooms!*
>
> — *India*, Lonely Planet Travel Survival

Here we are, ringed by the circular mirror, you in front,
        head bowed, brushing rats' nests and static
in hair that's the long, sable-silk of Indian women.
        We're oblivious of each other in that married way
that some call oneness, others call blindness. Your O
        snaps us out of our morning motions
as you spot the various bindis round our mirror.
        The index finger of your wedding-band hand traces
from one to another, connecting confetti zeros
        that are red as the razor-nick on my Adam's apple;
others are inlaid with pearls as if with love itself.
        Who wore that God's teardrop, that bloody arrowhead,
or those joyful signposts, gay-coloured as saris?
        O women of such third eyes, did any of you grow
weary of the SOLD stickers on your brows, the zeros

Most Recent Book: *The Blind Stitch* (Oxford University/Carcanet Press, 2001)

of your vows? While your men slept did you vanish
into the immense Ravana dark of the Indian night?
Could you have slipped them off like wedding rings
in hotels on our side of the faithless globe?
Below our moving reflection are rows
of crimson bindis like tiers of shimmering votive flames.

Ululu

After the crossfire of words we lay in bed under cover of dark.
I think you dropped into an obliterating sleep. Hearing the strange
banshee sound
— a curious mixture of a crying cat and the keen of a loon —
I figured it must be the monkey of these parts you told me of.
It had to be trapped and hurt, perhaps in its final throes.
Asleep, I dreamed my body was washed up by the ocean's procession of
waves that I'd lost myself in
after our latest tempest, and my soul had entered this creature high in
the trees, ululating to the emptiness of the night.

The Stilt Fisherman

How glad I am to
have come to this out-of-the-way island
— ditching the hubbub of the city
with its pubs and cafés and my literati buddies —
seeking enlightenment by way of a woman.

And even if that's out of the question,
even if we can't know the world through each other,
going our separate ways, I understand why
Muslim sailors called this the Isle of Serendip
as I come upon a stilt fisherman
simply clad in a white lunghi
sitting on the perch of his stilt,
steadfast among the breakers.

*

He swings the lasso of his line
and waves me away as I swim to him,
scaring off the fish, buoyant in my stupidity.

*

Now he winds in a shimmering seerfish
and dunks it into his stilt's mesh bag.
He gives thanks and asks forgiveness of the seer.
The ocean in the swell of a wave
washes in around him.

*

I too am supplicant,
having wasted so much time,
all my life it seems,
fishing to be known.
Combers furl and fall
around him, the boom
of tall drums played in the Temple
by bowing, anonymous men.

Tagging the Stealer

to David Cavanagh

So much of it I hadn't a bull's notion of
and like the usual ignoramus who casts his eyes
at, say, a Jackson Pollock or 'This is just to say,'
I scoffed at it. I didn't twig how it was as close
to art as art itself with its pre-game ballyhoo,
antics, rhubarbs, scheming, luck; its look
as if little or nothing is going on.
How often have we waited for the magic
in the hands of some flipper throwing a slider,
sinker, jug-handle, submarine, knuckle or screwball?
If we're lucky, the slugger hits a daisy cutter
with a choke-up or connects with a Baltimore chop
and a ball hawk catches a can of corn
with a basket catch and the ball rounds the horn —
Oh, look, Davo, how I'm sent sailing
right out of the ball park just by its lingo.

But I swear the most memorable play I witnessed
was with you on our highstools in the Daily Planet
as we slugged our Saturday night elixirs.
The Yankees were playing your Toronto Blue Jays.
They were tied at the top of the 9th.
I can't now for the life of me remember
who won, nor the name of the catcher, except
he was an unknown, yet no rookie.
Suddenly behind the pinch hitter's back he signalled
the pitcher, though no one copped until seconds later
as the catcher fireballed the potato to the first baseman,
tagging the stealer. It doesn't sound like much,
but everyone stood up round the house Ruth built
like hairs on the back of the neck, because the magic
was scary too. Jesus, give each of us just once
a poem the equal of that unknown man's talking hand.

Alison Hawthorne Deming

Biophilia

On the day I found the snakemouth orchids,
little explosions of organic joy,
blooming in the spaghnum bog, you were walking

a thousand miles away and found a half-grown
gopher tortoise, head collapsed on dozer-paws,
asleep beside the trail. "No dreams to dream,"

you wrote, "just evolved too soon." And there it lay
in the awful smoulder of wildfire and
summer heat, waiting for its mind to change.

But I was dreaming about you, a closeness that distance
didn't erase but underscored, as if something
had been written in our meeting that I needed

to read over and over, reading myself awake.
Some days I wonder if I should trust how quickly
my mind has changed from hermitage to love nest,

Most Recent Book: *The Edges of the Civilized World* (Picador, 1999)

as if I could explain the marriage of my solitary ways
with the hopes for love that I still harbor. I want everything with you
to be new. My birthday today — fifty-two. Number of

cards in the deck, weeks in the year — a completeness
in the number reminds me of that holy ratio the mystics quote
to convince skeptics that the universe wants order

and proves its desire in pattern and form. I walked today
across the breakwater — granite blocks that encumber
and gentle the tide — to swim in the reed-lined channel

where I love feeling the gentle tug of planetary
motion, my arms pulling with or against it
in the silky brine. A busload of kids from the city

arrived, parading out along the great stones,
dressed in bright yellow T-shirts that made them
look like daisies blooming for a mile across

the water to the distant curl of sand. The girls
screamed at spiderwebs spanning the rocky gaps,
and the boys said, Man, that water feels good.

Last in line came a boy who was stupid or blind
or just incomplete, his senses slow, movements timid,
every step a challenge to the fear that kept him

closed so tightly inside his awkward body
he could not move freely even in the open air
of the beautiful world — sea glittering like fish scales,

marsh grass electric green in sunlight, the gulls
and the children singing formless cantatas. An older boy
walked the slow one along, instructing him —

Step here, now lift your body up — and listening to the
unfinished words the other spoke, saying back to him
their meaning; patiently, so patiently, one child

led another, just held that hand and looked around
enjoying the day, his kindness bringing him into
the joy of it. "Has anyone known a sorrow like mine?"

asks the old hymn, and everyone knows the answer
is supposed to be, No, because every sorrow known
is solitary woe, until one hears the words

sung to melody, and a roomful of strangers
begins to weep, at first in sorrow, but then, seeing
others weep, knowing that the answer is, Yes,

and in the form of that sharing the tears are for joy.
When you wrote me about the tortoise — how it lay
in a forest that had been the bottom of an ocean,

only the ghosts of fishes for company — I knew
you loved the world's beauty and mystery in a way
that made me love you, and I knew I was finished

waiting for my life to catch up with my art — all that love
dispersed to bog orchid, butterfly and
eucalyptus bursting its bark; all that cultivated

wonder at the earth's dizzy recapitulation of the theme
no sorrows can stop; all that paying attention
to the beauty of the small, teaching me it's in our nature

to love, just as it's in the blackberry's woody canes
to bear fruit, in the black-throated green warbler's breast
to sing its certain patterned song, every mystery

of planet or heart, every longing that ever led you
where you needed to go in spite of your best intentions,
every act of bearing witness, lament or praise,

adding up to knowing that *what* we love — hard-wired,
generative, biologic power — could teach us *how* to love,
bright and awake to each other, alive under the surprising sun.

God

God was bored with everything
being the same and so
He created difference, everything
cracking, splitting, splaying,
crumbling, and God said,
It is good, a planet that splinters
into light. My animal, God said,
comes when I call, my animal
speaks to me when hungry,
my animal sleeps off the kill,
licks what tastes strong, takes love
when it's there, and God said,
It is good, progress, the plane gone down
in the enemy's forest, two armies,
one bent on murder and one
bent on grace, racing toward

the collision where the pilot lies
wounded. God wonders how
to be gentle with His dominance,
the late paradise a ruin, golden
monkeys and rats snacking and
leaving their stains in the sanctuary,
and God says, It is good, the galaxy
spinning like water down a drain,
difference longing for sameness and
killing itself to get there. There
you are, says God, arms opening,
I missed you. And all of it is so good,
the universe of hydrogen and eyes,
engines, hunger and prophylactic pain.

Toi Derricotte

Clitoris

This time with your mouth on my clitoris, I will not think
he does not like the taste of me. I lift the purplish hood back
from the pale white berry. It stands alone on its thousand branches.
I lift the skin like the layers of taffeta of a lady's skirt.
How shy the clitoris is, like a young girl
who must be coaxed by tenderness.

Dead Baby Speaks

i am taking in   taking in
like a lump of a dead baby
on the floor   mama kicks me
i don't feel anything

---

i am taking in   taking in
i am reading newspapers
i am seeing films
i am reading poetry
i am listening to psychiatrists, friends

Most Recent Book: *Natural Birth* (Firebrand Books, 2000)

someone knows the way
someone will be my mother
& tell me what to think

---

the dead baby wants to scream
the dead baby wants to drink warm milk
the dead baby wants to go to lunch with her mother, woman to
    woman, say,
i can't always say the right thing
sometimes i've got to say what feels best
i'm not perfect
but i will not be a lump on the floor
the dead baby wants to kick her mother
the dead baby wants her mother to lie down & let herself be kicked
why not   she let father do it

---

how to separate
me from the dead baby
my mother from me
my mother from the dead baby

---

nothing is expected
nothing is expected
of you
you don't have to do this or say that
nothing is known
just be   be who you are
a little defiance   a little defense
say, if you want
i lifted up a little

---

there is that stunned moment when she shuts up & lets me speak
i have nothing to say

---

then i say
rotten mother who opened your legs
like iron gates & forced me into this prison

who lay among lilies & pressed me to your breasts, saying i will never be alone again
who wanted my soul for company, used my body in the place of your soul
who brought me up to the surface by straining off the rich dark broth
until what remained was as vaporous as the shadow of a shadow
whose breasts were bruised fruits
whose legs were swollen tree trunks, but when you were shaken, only one red apple fell
whose genitals hold me tethered, a string like a primate's tail, so that i am your monkey in the red hat, you are my organ grinder

if you say do not write about me
i will write more
there are many more mouths to feed
than yours
my life is juice pouring
out of me
let it find a channel

---

i could knuckle under & be good
i could pray for her & turn the other cheek
i could live in her house with her sickness like a stinking body in the stairwell
i could bake bread until my hands puff off
i could sweep the floor
i could suck misery out of my teeth like stringy meat
i could poison her with a plate of sorrow
i could leave the door open on her corpse so that no breath would warm her back to resurrection
i could throw myself at her feet
i could languish like a whore in colored rags
i could lie as still as a still life
i could be cut up & served on her table
i could go to my father & beg for her life
i could dance the seven veils while she escapes
i could give to the poor
i could close my legs like a hardened corpse
i could grow into a hag & compare myself to her pictures
i could eat her while she's sleeping
i could put her in the oven & burn her into a lace cookie
i could roar like a gored dragon
i could come crawling like a sexless husband

i could beg her to touch that scratch between my legs which should open in a flower

---

every time i question myself, i say
mother did not believe me
she thought i was making up my life to torture her
i take off the layers of pain for her to see the teeth marks in my soul
she thinks i can be born fresh once my rotten desires are removed

the desire to touch
the desire to speak

i could clean house until it is empty
i could put everything in the right place
but what about the one mistake i always make

---

i could love her
i could love her every time she is mistreated
i could love her every time someone forgets to pick up a plate from the table
i could love her weeping in church with a light on her face
i could love her stinking on the cot of ben gay waiting for my father to come
i could love her roaming from room to room in the dark with a blanket on, trying to be quiet
i could love her eating at night, hungrily, slowly, going back for seconds
i could love her white breasts
i could love her belly of scars what remains in her — half of a woman
i could love her with the dead baby in her
i could love her though the dead baby could be me
i could love her even if she wants some part of me dead
some part that invades her with sorrow she never understands

for the mystery of her childhood
for being too white & too black
for being robbed of a father
for wearing the cast-off clothes of the rich
for eating figs & cream on silver that wasn't hers
for putting the comb & brush neatly in place because they were the only things she owned
for learning to make up lies & make everything pretty

(she never believed her own body)
i could love her ocean black hair
i could love it in a braid like a long black chain
i could love her kneeling over the tub cleaning the scum out with a rag
i could love her trying to hit the flying roach with a shoe
i could love her standing in the doorway, thinking she's made the wrong
choice
as frail as i
as strange to herself as i
as beautiful as i
as ugly as i
i could love her as i love myself, imperfect mother

---

worse was done to me she said & *i never told*
i always told
in the body out the mouth
everything from insults to penises
needed words to make it real
be still   you make me suffer
i thought it was me who would die
I thought silence was a blessing
& i was its saint
i was prepared for
a higher calling

---

my mother is on my mouth
like a frog
be good be good
she points her finger, that old spinster teacher
she points her stick at my tongue
she knocks some sense into it across its red knuckle
half of my tongue hangs like a limp dick
a flag of my mother's country
half rises like a bridge
words might leap across that great divide, a daredevil driver
but i am the driver
& my mother is peeping out of the back like a baby
her eyes big & black with fear

---

my mother is on my mouth
like a gold frog
she is sparkling & quick as sin
with terrible humped breasts
that nothing can suck at
the black spots on her are universes you could walk on
if she were flat & sound as a board
i take her on my tongue like a lozenge
& roll her around
then i bite down

Deborah Digges

Two of the Lost Five Foolish Virgins

I'd climb the ladder,
my eyes trained above
her head where the rope's
lashed to the harness
hook, and cut her down –
weep at the privilege.
My tears would not prevent
me from the task at hand.
I've lived, myself, this year
as long as she. The poetry's
no longer the vessel
it once was. Now it's
the mooring rope
fugitives grasp, hand over hand,
under cover of night
near launching, followed
by rats from dock to ship
who live on ballast grain,
grow strong through the long
crossing. But I'd rather
be the one to hold Tsvetaeva
as the rope is cut,
my strength tried awfully,

Most Recent Book: *The Stardust Lounge: Stories from a Boy's Adolescence* (Doubleday, 2001)

my arms around her
waist, my ear pressed against
her dead heart, breathing
her in. I'm old enough.
I have reason to imagine
we might recognize each other
and embrace, say in a flower
shop or walking by a river,
embrace as women do inside
the aftermath of youth,
its strange, enduring dust,
like two of the lost
five foolish virgins, once
so surprised at our delight
that we were turned away from
the bridegroom's door,
the oil in our lamps enough
to rub light into our faces,
gleeful in our sacrilege.
Delighted, oh yes — laughing
together at the memory,
pleased with ourselves —
that we were locked out,
turned back to the night
and its night people. I'd
rather be the one to hold
Marina as the rope's released,
as men suspend their women
in the dance and spin them
above the robbers' fires, the one
who holds her, heaves her
as the rope is cut, the one —
her age— who lays her down
and holds her head and rubs
the bloat out of her face
and smoothes her months
worn smock over her knees.
Takes off her shoes. The one
who readies her and disappears,
leaving the burial to others.

The Rainbow Bridge in the Painting of the Sung Dynasty

For the tying together of two ends of the hemp cord
and the harvesting of bamboo forests,
for the month of rains,

the river flooding,
and the scaffolding reflected in the water,

for the ghost-of-what-had-been departing

and the brush fires doused
with opium and urine,

for the poles that found the bottom of the river
and the colors in their order nine times braided,

for the hundred roses fed into the pyre
and the foot bridge strung on shore to learn the netting,
for the crush of berries,
blood, and coal, and two boats

anchored in the middle of the river,
for the boar's hair brushes
dipped into the water and the greater rise and thrust
of the abutments, for the finger-stitch

from beam to arch,
and the centuries of mornings stealing pigment,
for the float of granite

boat-shaped pilings, and the counter-law in which redundancy
is safety, for time locked in a circle

on the ground and the boat springing a leak
that held the frame,

for the trapeze of hammocks wafting between willows

and the hands knit closer by their weaving,

for the circle of fires that kept away the tigers
and the certain bleed of earth's three colors,
for the spaces between characters
inked right to left

and the other shore each day by dusk
foreshortened, for the distance
inside the years of letters written
and the warp of the reverse-curve's arch dismantled,

for the moths enclosed,
their wing-dust finger-printed
and the charting of the light, season by season,

for the weeds
sprouting in the clefs between the pilings
and the dragon's shadow in the keystone lengthening,
for the shift in clouds,

the bridges disappearing
and the strength of the rope of grasses nine times
braided, for the divinities

whereby the four horizons gathered
and the toe of the dragon fixing latitude at sea,

for the spinning of the webs broken each morning

and time looking back from the middle of the river,

for four hands
touching in the shuttling of the string bridge
and the ox led out across the rainbow.

Guillotine Windows

Fifty brief summers, fifty northeastern
winters have close to petrified the frames
once carefully recessed and rigged with pulleys, though the ropes
have frayed,
the weights like clappers dropped inside the walls.

They're called "eight over twelves," my guillotine windows,
that slam themselves on spring,
and the wooden spoons that prop them up belly like yew bows,
and the empty shampoo bottles *woo*, and the knives, hair brushes,
shoe trees, books, and jewelry boxes,
all will be ruined soon.

Ring the house that wants it to be winter,
a house for wintering, warn the spirits they'll lose a hand,
a tail sailing in and out of the bell tower

above rue festering, the huge moonlight scotch broom,
above my rabid gardens, my complicated gardens.

If the body is a temple, surely one's garden is like a mind,
half-seeded by the wind, ready to slip into its own peculiar
madness,

the Russian sage awash over the beech roots strangling my pipes,
and the bellwort rampant, foxglove, violets
banked by my Grecian stones, and blue glass totem toads
and china figs, beheaded angels, and shells I've carried back

from different coasts fashioned like Sapphic cliffs.
Someday they'll think this was a lovers' leap,

the floor of a crossroads wishing well
into which those passing threw what weighed them down —

hair in a locket, keys, rings, bibles and the flowers pressed
in the Psalms, a doll's head, funeral lace:

preserved in the historic leaf-rot of a willow,
plum and apple, oak, and two white pines, two sycamores.

I love to imagine someone, say when I'm transplanting
at midnight, finding the remnants of this place.

On my knees in the garden in the dark I can look in the windows
and see fields that will be glaciers,
hillsides on which the headstones dwarf and pitch

above a woods from which my floors came flying
in clouds of animal fur and dust and human hair and ash from a
thousand fires
swept from the hearth, saved until spring — tamped down,
drawn up as color into lilacs.

Once I watched a house taken out to sea. From that distance it
looked like the earth bent down to crown
the ocean and the ocean, rising, thus received the crown
of the house that deified the waves a while.

Imagine standing alone there at the threshold,
having an ocean as one's garden for a moment, a garden
of enormous green-blue rollers, sea birds, all four winds,
countless clouds!

You can have a good life and not know it.
You can claim that seeing far means seeing into the future,
into the time ahead of you.

But it was all right to have believed in something —
that those you loved, they would outlive you
or simply be here always from time to time,
and you would recognize each other,

take hands and walk through a garden, have a meal together,
talk late into the evening and fall asleep in separate rooms.

See those young selves waving back at shore,
see them running, calling to you as the walls of the house
break up, pulling from the foundation while the roof
slides sideways, gone, and the windows shatter,

and some float in their frames, float shining whole,
carried out, drifting, windows on the sea.

STEPHEN DOBYNS

Unexpected Holiday

In the story of Orpheus and Lot's wife
each looks back, but they look at each other:
in such a way do eternal themes get entangled.

Lot's wife, expecting to find the blazing
cities on the plain, sees instead a handsome
young man with a lyre, wearing a lion skin.

Orpheus instead of discovering Eurydice,
his beloved, sees an older woman, the mother
of two grown daughters. Perhaps she is fifty.

Both are surprised. Pardon me, says Orpheus,
I was expecting to meet somebody else.
Lot's wife scans the horizon. Where are

Sodom and Gomorra, she asks, those fun towns?
Neither can answer the question of the other.
Distracted, Orpheus wanders back. Recently,

he says, I've been depressed. Lot's wife sighs:
If you knew how dull it is to share the bed
of a virtuous man. They sit upon warm rocks

Most Recent Book: *Pallbearers Envying the One Who Rides* (Penguin, 1999)

beside a rippling stream. Being strangers
to one another, each brings an objective eye
to the other's difficulties. Perhaps you're

lucky to be free of her, says Lot's wife.
Orpheus makes a similar remark about Lot.
A pious type, he calls him: they always think

they know best. Released from their passions,
they begin to notice the world around them:
the lark's song, light shimmering on clear water.

Orpheus takes comfort in this amiable older woman.
Lot's wife is pleased by this polite young man.
Tomorrow perhaps new problems will arise,

but not yet. Orpheus leans against a stone
and begins to sing nothing too amusing,
nothing too sad. A song about sunlight

glistening on the white bark of birch trees
on the first warm evening in early spring.
It is one of his better songs. Years later

new words are added about lost love and bloodshed,
the usual themes, but not today. Lot's wife
raises her face to the setting sun and behind

closed lids the world turns pink. Tentatively,
she touches her tongue to her lips to discover
the slightest hint but still distinct taste of salt.

(Often, In Dreams, He Moved)

Often, in dreams, he moved through a city not found in the real world. From one dream to the next he charted its streets, the texture of its neighborhoods. From one to the next, he recalled what lay to the north or south, its subways and bus lines, until the city became the place he knew best: morning light upon storefronts, the bridges over the river, the rush of traffic on a hill through the park. But although he found the city beautiful, it wasn't unique. Not like Paris or London. It was just a place in his dreams. Yet its making became one of his major tasks: its crowds, its rain or sunlight, its rich facades, even a piano heard through an open window, even the statues of city fathers in swallow-tail coats, until its details and geography could fill several books — a dream city, all swept away when he departed from the other, the one we call real.

(That Day He Spent Hours)

That day he spent hours on horseback, a wooden saddle with a layer of blankets, scrambling up and down hillsides on trails he would hesitate to take on foot. The sun burning through his shirt and hat; bristly thickets and cactus, sand, rock and red dirt: the path a faint track among darting lizards and dust-colored toads. Rising above them, mountains climbed past prickly pear, saguaro and organ pipe cactus to fields of snow so peaceful that he kept riding only to reach them as the trail rose toward distant passes. Then among the peaks he saw a bird but so high that he realized it must be immense, riding the air currents with a slight stirring of wings, tilting and sliding, a dark hardly discernible color as it dipped and soared. How did they appear from that alien freedom — a man and woman on horseback, creeping earthbound creatures, hauling themselves inch by inch toward ever vanishing horizons?

Mystery, So Long

At first, it filled the space around us with holes,
the mystery. It was scary. People fell through them.
There goes Og, people might say. They sang hymns
to the mystery. They pounded on drums. They fed
the mystery both friends and strangers. It seemed
a good idea. The mystery hungered for human flesh.
Oh, implacable and mysterious mystery.
But bit by bit people began to cover over the holes —
first with mud and sticks, then with bricks and mortar.
You get the idea. Some holes vanished, others got smaller.
Time passed. The mystery stopped being such a big deal.
As for the remaining holes, people knew their time was coming.
Scientists still got excited, but politicians started playing golf.
The mystery began to disappear just as giants and ogres
had disappeared — the ones who had terrified villages,
wore animal skins and never washed. They had kept
getting smaller, until they were nearly indistinguishable
from homeless people, living in alleys or under bridges.
In the winter they went to Phoenix or Tampa, warm places.
The only people they continued to frighten were children,
until their mothers told them not to stare — the mystery
was like that: unwashed and undependable, a security risk.
My neighbor complains, My car won't start, it's a mystery.

My friend scratches his head, My wife left me, it's a mystery.
People publish their memoirs: It's a mystery how I got
from my dysfunctional roots to the success of my present life.
Sometimes it's a mystery why I don't hurt myself laughing.
This morning I'm stuck in traffic — for miles in front stretches
a mass of parked cars. I don't know what's wrong, it's a mystery.
Then up above a biplane begins to shoot out puffs of smoke
into the immaculate blue sky: an emissary from the past
with help for the future. I roll down my window and lift my head
to the heavens. I'm ready for even the smallest revelation.
These cottony white morsels of smoke, their tender solicitude
nearly breaks my heart — What is the balance between too much
mystery and too little? — Dominic's Diner for Tired Travelers.

Mark Doty

At the Gym

This salt-stain spot
marks the place where men
lay down their heads,
back to the bench,

and hoist nothing
which need be lifted
but some burden they've chosen
this time: more reps,

more weight, the upward shove
of it leaving, collectively,
this sign of where we've been:
shroud-stain, negative

flashed onto the vinyl
where we push something
unyielding skyward,
gaining some power

at least over flesh,
which goads with desire,

Most Recent Book: *Firebird* (HarperPerrenial, 2000)

and terrifies with frailty.
Who could say who's

added his heat to the nimbus
of our intent, here where
we make ourselves:
something difficult

lifted, pressed or curled,
Power over beauty,
power over power!
Is muscle truth then,

and all you need to know?
There's something more
tender, beneath our vanity,
our will to become objects

of desire: we sweat the mark
of our presence onto the cloth.
Here is some halo
the living made together.

Fish-R-Us

Clear sac
of coppery eyebrows
suspended in amnion,
not one moving –

A Mars,
composed entirely
of single lips,
each of them gleaming –

this bag of fish
(have they actually
traveled here like this?)
bulges while they

acclimate, presumably,
to the new terms
of the big tank
at Fish-R-Us. Soon

they'll swim out
into separate waters,
but for now they're
shoulder to shoulder

in this clear and
burnished orb, each fry
about the size of this line,
too many lines for any

bronzy antique epic,
a million of them,
a billion incipient citizens
of a goldfish Beijing,

a Sao Paolo,
a Mexico City.
They seem to have sense
not to move but hang

fire, suspended, held
at just a bit of distance
(a bit is all there is), all
facing outward, eyes

(they can't even blink)
turned toward the skin
of the sac they're in,
this swollen polyethylene.

And though nothing's
actually rippling but their gills,
it's still like looking up
into falling snow,

if all the flakes
were a dull, breathing gold,
as if they were
streaming toward —

not us, exactly,
but what they'll
be . . . Perhaps
they're small enough

— live sparks, for sale
at a nickel apiece —

that one can actually
see them transpiring:

they want to swim
forward, want to
eat, they want what
anyone wants:

to take place. Who's
going to feed or cherish
or even see them all?
They pulse in their golden ball.

FROM *An Island Sheaf*

1. SEA GRAPE VALENTINE

Loose leaf:
golden
fire-streams

branching into bayous
of darker flame,
breaking apart

near the rim
to finer, finer veins:
unnavigable Amazonia

in the shape of a heart
— a real heart, dear,
not the idealized kind,

and thus all throb
and trouble, and fallen
as if to remind us

we're fire at the core,
various heats.
Though everything

mottles,
at this latitude:
fruit and flower

and once-pink
porch columns,
even the puddle

between the bakery
and Kingdom Hall
giving up thunderhead

and rainbow, even
the concrete pier
a slow study

in corrosion's arts:
nothing unchecked
or unstippled,

(old pink taxi
rusting in the sun)
nothing simple or im-

pervious to decay:
why not
this fallen valentine,

candybox token
veined in hot gold,
its tropic wax

embalmed and blazing?

2. Watermelon Soda

Pink scuttle
(a roasted pink,
like pork

in Chinese restaurants):
these claws poke out
from the pull-top

opening
of an empty can
of watermelon soda,

which clicks along
the sidewalk,
wobbling cylindrical

and alarming
beneath weary palms
accustomed to

the homeless.
Strange island,
to yield a walking

hot-pink soda can
inhabited by a lucky,
Modernist crab,

carrying on his back
a tropic shelter
by Barragan

or Corbusier,
perennially modish
if not quite practical,

since the candy-pink
pop can tips
and gyros

as he proceeds,
unstable island
— housed in style,

or hobbled by it?
The pink metal
flashes in the sun,

and seems worth it.
Or did yesterday.
This morning, after

the all-night storm,
where's he gone,
our exile? Floated clean away.

Norman Dubie

On the Chinese Abduction of Tibet's Child Panchen Lama

The commandant, Black Chen, has walked
Across the pastures in his yellow thong
To bathe in a summer stream.

Most Recent Book: *Mercy Seat* (Copper Canyon, 2001)

Resting among the caliche waters,
In the roots of blasted trees,
He sleeps, a wild application
Of leeches
Claiming his face, chest and knees...

From behind a large gold cloud
With a thousand red eyes,
The noon sun warms the swollen leeches
Speckled with increased appetite.

Black Chen wheezes in the gnarl
Of bottom willow. The yaks, beyond scale
and perspective,
Like risen black rugs
Are moving over the field above him.

A boy lama and his small family
Were abducted among lanterns in the winter night
And are, perhaps, alive — huddled prisoners
Of a new superstition of rice.

The boy's uncle was shot
In the first year of famine. He was wrongfully accused
Of stealing a carburetor from a green tractor.

His wife was seen walking naked into trees.
Can still be seen
Praying in the foulest of cremation grounds —
Smoke rising from her hair and shoulders.
She is adorned in the full glamour of human bones.

Who contrives that like wild rice
Slugs have fallen to a stream
From a dark skirt of berries and scrub?

The cries of the commandant
Are now reaching his young guards
In the narrow ravine
Above the gate and checkpoint.

An old hag dressed in a necklace of bone, shaded
With age and lichen, reaches down
Lifting the commandant, mucous plug
Of hair and blood, out of the water.
Singing and with a heated stone, she howls
The leeches out of their absolute feeding.

The commandant, weak and angry, spits on the earth.
He crosses the field, his arms
Waving in sunlight,
Transparent body with blue ribs, sucked
Meat of an alien fruit. He is making vows

In the air with his hands. The men
Running to meet him drop their guns. In amazement, they are running
To welcome the Black Chen
Who is returning to them
From somewhere they believe they've never been.

A Genesis Text for Larry Levis, Who Died Alone

It will always happen — the death of a friend
That is the beginning of the end of everything
In a large generation of sharing
What was still mistaken
For the nearest middle of all things. So, by extension

I am surely dead, along with David, Phil, Sam,
Marvin, and, surely, we all stand
In a succession of etceteras
That is the sentimental, inexhaustible
Exhaustion of most men. It's like

That rainy night of your twenty-eighth birthday.
A strip-joint stuck in the cornfields
Of Coralville, Iowa.
Big teddy bear bikers and pig farmers who were
Not glad to see us: my long hair,
Your azure Hawaiian blouse and David
                    ordering gin — first in blank verse
And then in terza rima with an antique monocle.

The exotic dancer with "helicopter tits," or was
It "tits on stilts," was not coming — a flat on the interstate
From Des Moines; her breasts probably sore,
She sat out the storm in the ditch
Feeding white mice to the boa constrictor
Who shared her billing.

So you jumped onto the jukebox and began
A flamenco dance — all the sharp serifs showing a mast,

An erectness that was a happy middle finger
To all those unhappy gentlemen
Seated there in the dark with us.

I walked over to you, looked up –
Begged you to get down before they all
Just simply kicked the shit out of us.
You smiled, sweetly gone.
The song, I think, was called "Pipeline"
And the platform glass of the jukebox cracked.

I said that if you didn't get down
I'd kill you myself. You smiled again
While I aged. I said
The elegy I would write for you would be riddled with clichés!
You giggled.

So now you *are* dead. Surely, Larry, we've always
Thought that the good die young.
And life is a bitch, man.
But where was that woman and her snake when we needed them?

The Caste Wife Speaks to the Enigmatic Parabolas

The two stonebreakers in loincloths
Have put aside the pickaxe and iron broom,
Are rolling an oildrum weighted with cement
Over the immaculate orbits
Of a white feldspar accident, stone fields
Flung from the throat of Cygnus: a fire of hydrogen
Like ghosts of perfectly circumspect suns
Collapsing into oblivion. Holding

My husband's seed in my mouth I walk
Out to his mother's pond and sink to the bottom –
Seed rises slowly from between my teeth:
Cap of salted milk, dead lily
Above me, or the dried birth caul of skin
That a pilgrim carries with him
To fend off ghouls, influenza and the many
Sundry deaths by drowning.

Settled, my breasts lift with the green waters,
I am some rounded syllable lodged

In the brain of the contented sleeping child,
A trail of mother's milk drying on its shoulder
Lead to the fully opened cloak of a cobra
Motionless in shade
Who the now awakened child pokes at with a stick,
Laughing and dancing in her place. . .

My husband's prick is an instrument of inscription
That has brought us to this banyan shade

Where the child on her side breathes, flutters
Imperceptibly: dropped cypher of a race
Of lightly colored men who I now exchange
Glady like blood for wine, like water
For the rising cream that forms a golden brick of butter.

Elegy for My Brother

I'll walk awhile, maybe as high as the tree line—
The tick-infested heads of those deer, their silhouettes
Over the field, gave me courage somehow
To speak with you. I awoke, did
You know, just as you died. Later I was told
That it rained quietly all over Manhattan.
Neon, even in rain, is a crippled light.
I awoke from a dream of irregular snowfields
Where all the white lampshades
Were taken away; regained as blood-soaked orchids —
April's lady's slipper: labial, alien — these supernumerary
Flowers were being eaten by mule deer. Mozart's
Requiem K. 626 turning to snow
While being broadcast weakly from deep inside Canada. . .

The cold river has a lashing movement like cilia
And we can see our breath in the air. The lit rooms.
Robert, where are your shoes?
What was it that haunted Pierce House? All the way
Down that oak hall to an unheated bathroom
Which we were asked to share
With four other families of poor divinity students.
Who was it, me or you, who first realized
We could reach the kitchen sink and pee into it?
I have a memory where I am watching wind
Fall deliberately, at night, over the red carriage barn.
There is lightning sickness in the trees. Everything's thawing.

You're there, at the windowsill, with me. The storm windows
Begin rattling, great sheets of ice
Fall from the slate roof like blades.
We pretend the house is a guillotine.
You say we must save the life of an aristocrat's maid. You say,
Giggling, that she is knock-kneed.

Once we waited outside on the porch
Knowing our ears were badly frostbitten. Mother had
Warned us of how it would hurt
When eventually we returned to a warm place. You rubbed
Snow on both our ears and we just stared at the colored
shocks
Of Indian corn our father had nailed to the door.
You begged me to stay out longer.
I would have actually left you there...
but now
I am still preparing to leave, to return
To a heated kitchen where dried marigolds stab the ceiling.

We were just two boys contemplating a wooden door.
It's getting colder. Mozart's heavy Sanctus turning to snow.
Then you smile at your feet, laugh,
Run up into the orange light that spills
From the opening door. The requiems are melting back into music.
I stand in snow
And watch the door now being closed behind you...

Stephen Dunn

The Death of God

When the news filtered to the angels
they were overwhelmed by their sudden aloneness.
Long into the night they waited for instructions;
the night was quieter than any night they'd known.
I don't have a thought in my head, one angel lamented.
Others worried, Is there such a thing as an angel now?
New to questioning, dashed by the dry light
of reason, some fell into despair. Many disappeared.
A few wandered naturally toward power, were hired

Most Recent Book: *Riffs and Reciprocities* (W. W. Norton & Company, 1998)

by dictators who needed something like an angel
to represent them to the world.
These angels spoke the pure secular word.
They murdered sweetly and extolled the greater good.
The Dark Angel himself was simply amused.

The void grew, and was fabulously filled.
Vast stadiums and elaborate malls —
the new cathedrals — were built
where people cheered and consumed.
At the nostalgia shops angel trinkets
and plastic crucifixes lined the shelves.
The old churches were homes for the poor.

And yet before meals and at bedtime
and in the iconographies of dreams,
God took his invisible place in the kingdom of need.
Disaffected minstrels made and sang His songs.
The angels were given breath and brain.
This all went on while He was dead to the world.

The Dark Angel observed it, waiting as ever.
On these things his entire existence depended.

Nature

Spring's hesitant splendor had given way
to steady rains. The sky kept crumbling
and the laurels whitened and everywhere
a ripeness was visible. Nature was okay.
For me it had its place, scaffolding and
backdrop to the stage on which people
ruined and saved themselves, played out
who they were. I liked its animals best,
the big cats and the preposterous mad-God
creations like tapirs or rhinoceri.
A rose, well, a rose was
just a prom queen standing still
for a photo. Mountain sunsets,
waterfalls, they were postcards to send
to good friends who trusted happiness
occurred, if at all, in other places.

It had rained now for so many days
rain had become another form of silence.
Granted there was beauty to it as well,
gray against gray. If you stared long enough:
tiny shadings, as if someone had painted
the varieties of boredom.
And the rain made puddles on the tennis courts,
spoiling one of my pleasures.
It made some of us contemplative, soul-searching,
who had lives that couldn't bear scrutiny.
Summer was upon us. I could only hope
that it might contain enough contraries
to make it a season of plenty.
Soon I'd seek out someone not sad
to whom weather or beauty was a pretense
to get together, and drive to Cape May Point
where marshland and dune converge.
Last fall, there on the nature trail
in early morning fog, a lone man disappeared
and reappeared, in and out, until the fog
seemed to dissolve him, color him its own.
Gray, then, was the only truth in the world.

Different Hours

As the small plane descended through
the it's-all-over-now Sturm und Drang
I closed my eyes and saw myself
in waves of lucidity, a vanisher
in a long process of vanishing,
of solitary character, erotic eye,
too often truant in citizenship and heart.
When we landed, I flipped down
my daily mask, resumed my normal
dreamy life of uncommitted crimes.
I held nothing against me anymore.
And now, next day, I awake before
the sound of traffic, amazed
that the paper has been delivered,
that the world is up and working.
A dazed rabbit sits in the dewy grass.

The clematis has no aspirations
as it climbs its trestle.
I pour myself orange juice, Homestyle.
I say the hell with low fat cream cheese,
and slather the good stuff on my bagel.
The newspaper seems to be thinking
along with me: No Hope For Lost Men.
Relationship Between Laughter and Health.
It says scientists now know the neutrino
has mass, that one of them called it
the most ghostly particle in the universe.
No doubt other scientists are sad
who asked the wrong questions,
some small defect
in their lives pointing them astray.
No doubt, too, at this very moment
a snake is sunning itself in Calcutta.
And somewhere a philosopher is erasing
"time's empty passing" because he's seen
a woman in a ravishing dress.
In a different hour he'll put it back.

A Postmortem Guide

For my eulogist, in advance

Do not praise me for my exceptional serenity.
Can't you see I've turned away
from the large excitements,
and have accepted all the troubles?

Go down to the old cemetery; you'll see
there's nothing definitive to be said.
The dead once were all kinds —
boundary-breakers and scallywags,
martyrs of the flesh, and so many
dumbbunnies of duty, unbearably nice.

I've been a little of each.

And, please, resist the temptation
of speaking about virtue.
The seldom-tempted are too fond
of that word, the small-
spirited, the unburdened.

Know that I've admired in others
only the fraught straining to be good.

Adam's my man and Eve's not to blame.
He bit in. It made no sense to stop.

Still, for accuracy's sake you might say
I often stopped,
that I rarely went as far as I dreamed.

And if you're aware of my hardships,
understand they're mere bump and setback
against history's horror.
Remind those seated, perhaps weeping,
how obscene it is
for some of us to complain.

Tell them I had second chances.
I knew joy.
I was burned by books early
and kept sidling up to the flame.

I'd rather you didn't invoke God.
If you must, say he was a story
I loved, as I once loved monsters,
hide 'n seek, and the brothers Grimm.

Smile if you can.

Stuart Dybek

Inspiration

Finally, down an askew side street
of gingerbread houses held up by paint,
where bony kids crowded around the body
of a cripple who'd been trampled
when the shots rang out,
I spotted a taxi with a raised hood.
The driver was adding motor oil
which was leaking into the gutter
nearly as fast as he was pouring.
I threw in my suitcase and we started

Most Recent Book: *The Baby Can Sing and Other Stories* (Sarabande Books, 1999)

down the mobbed streets,
him laying on the horn, yelling in Creole,
driving, by necessity, with his head
craned out the window. Cracks
ran the length of the windshield
from where the old wound of a bullet
left a crater that vaguely resembled
the shape of a pineapple, and since a cabbie
could never afford to replace the glass,
he'd painted the crater instead —
pineapple yellow with the bullet hole
gleaming at its center like a worm hole
emitting another dimension.
And once he'd painted the pineapple,
wasn't it not only logical, but inspired
to see the cracks that ran from it
as vines, and so he'd painted them
a tangled green that transformed driving
through the streets of Port-au-Prince
into racing blindly through a jungle.
But he wasn't finished yet —
the vines grew flowers: rose red, orchid,
morning-glory blue, and to the flowers
came all manner of butterflies
and newly invented species of small,
colorful birds, twining serpents,
and deep in the shadows,
the mascaraed black-slit, golden eyes
of what may have been a jaguar.

Vigil

On a brick street slicked
with a ruby, spiritual neon,
I thought I saw you again,
bareheaded in damp weather.
I recognized the shape
of your breath in the cold.
To whom else could that shadow belong
when, by the flickered vigil light
of bums cupping a match

in radiant hands, you passed?
From the all-night laundromat
the great round sloshy eyes
of wash machines watched
through steamed windows.
With each rap of your heels,
your legs, distorted but still
beautiful, disappeared
down a chrome aisle of hubcaps,
and raising my arm, I remembered
the weight of your body
reflected along the length
of a silver-plated cuff link
cloudy with sweat.

Narcissus

Down on his hands and knees
outside the biker bar
as if searching the pavement
for his tooth; between the kick
that lacerated a kidney,
and the kick that cracked a rib,
my ex-pug uncle, Chino,
said he caught a look
he hadn't seen for years
on the distorted face
that lovingly gazed back at him
from a blood-spattered hubcap.

Overhead Fan

Beneath an overhead fan, a man and a woman,
slatted with light leaking through green shutters,
are unaware that they, too, are turning.
The shadow of the blades imparts a slow rotation
to each still object in this hazy room,
and the wobbling fan chirps at its mounting
as if the gecko doing pushups on the mirror

is counting time. Otherwise, it's quiet
but for the whir above the sweaty friction
of their skin. Her mouth gapes
as if emptied of speech, her closed eyes
can't see the shadow that plays
across her eyelids and breasts, and that later
will play across the man's memory.
And though their bodies now press
as if pinned together by centrifugal force,
they feel the spin as if they're hovering —
not like the souls of the newly dead
are said to hover above their abandoned bodies,
but like the hummingbird above the red lips
of the hibiscus just beyond the shutters,
or, high overhead, the black blades
of a frigate bird, circling on extended wings,
above the Gulf Stream's azure gyres.

NANCY EIMERS

Exam

Had any children? the doctor asks. I say *No*.
And close my lips — the other half of the answer.
If this were a party, I'd feel I had to go on,
even if the other person hadn't asked
Why not? or *Are you planning on having any?*
They feel free to ask. And almost always, I explain
something about wanting them but not enough,
or how I wish I had two lives: in one of them
I'd have a child by now. But it's no good,
not doing something never sounds as real
as doing it. I seem to stand in for reserve,
my life a keeping back, a state of being
not in active service. But I meant to talk here about time,
the way it passes us at different rates,
two people in the same room — parent and non-parent,
or doctor and patient in an examining room

Most Recent Book: *No Moon* (Purdue University Press, 1997)

just big enough for a desk, a table, and a curtain between them,
quite a squeeze with the nurse. For me, the moment has slowed
to simple sentences in present tense.
He asks. I answer. I lie back. She comes in.
They look inside. I answer. No one asked.
For him, the moment probably speeds along,
a paragraph of questions, then another paragraph
of looking with a flashlight. Then
a paragraph of silent writing down.
This doctor doesn't say much with his face.
I'm worried, he's evasive. It's his job
to stay just out of reach.
And crazily, there comes into my head
a job interview I was on once, in a hotel room,
a row of professors sitting on a bed.
One of them smiles and asks me, *Why do* you *think*
so many fiction writers use the present tense these days?
Some answer that the teaching job depends on
hangs in a cloud of thought inside his head.
I can't think, I make something stupid up.
Maybe I should have told him I was terrified
to find myself in that moment, present tense,
stuck in a simple sentence, having to ride it out
by talking and gesturing, hearing my voice in my ears
that sounds like it doesn't know what it thinks
it's talking about, and my hands move awkwardly
inside the gloves of hands.
I think that man despised the present tense,
and the fiction writers who those days were using it,
despised the shortsightedness of the moment,
any foolish groping in a tiny dark.
I close my eyes and still feel this cold table,
long as my life, and the doctor is gone
except for his gloved hands and the icecold
unseen instrument holding me open,
gone the ceiling and walls, just me and the table,
me inside the top half of my clothes,
bra and over it the blouse buttoned up to the top
to keep me safe at home,
and the opening of me between my legs
and the tiny beam of the flashlight
he plays around in me. He's in the dark too,
I guess — he just moves through it faster.

You're probably fine, but let's have an X-ray just in case —
make sure nothing sinister's going on.
He smiles a little then, to soften the *sinister*
or maybe just downshifting for an instant
into his natural personality.
As for me, I don't understand anything about time,
how it passes from your parents into you
then into your children, if you have any,
or where it goes to if you don't.
Keep me going, doc, I almost say.
And don't say, but he knows. And God knows what, inwardly, he answers.
Then his smile vanishes, it is no longer possible.
He draws the curtain around me,
I put on the bottom half of my clothes,
trying to rustle as little as I can
while, on the other side, he goes and sits down at his desk
and writes, I can *hear* it, another paragraph:
my paragraph. The one I'm rushing through.

Outer Space

Today I caught the feeling-tone of a voice on the street, though not the words —

someone was asking a question
of the silence and of the waiting

that live in things suburban and stationary:
windows, garage doors, sidewalks, unlit streetlights,
the bland topography of the lawns.

This was a daylight question,

not one you'd ask of glimmer or flight,
lit streetlights, star magnitudes, fireflies, TV snow.

Not the moonless night question
you'd ask of flowering bulbs
and vegetables that bear their crops below the ground.

Not a question that drives you out of Self
like a moth to its porchlight epipsychidion

but a question that drives you into Self
like the soul of a rock in torrential rains.

Not the question a roadside diner asks
of its empty parking lot.
Nothing a shadow could ask of a highway underpass.

This was a question mouthed by a man

not by the drone of an edger,
not by the blown trees gliding into place.
Not by the ants that follow their winding scent-paths through the
        blades of grass.

Asked by the visible, asked by the working lips and tongue.

What sounds and moves
was asking its question of what does not,

something to do with the peeling paint on the walls
and the crooked pitch of the roofs, the dampness creeping into the
        cinder-block basements

and soaking down the chimney flashings,
the festering of the gutters, the glandular swell of the wood,
the rust that lines the pipes that, linked together, would reach to outer
        space.

I don't remember an answering –

just the vertigo of ascent, just the looking over a cliff
that is any question.

The street didn't know there was anything wrong
with its shingles, flashings, sockets, anthills,
deferrals, lulls.

I heard the sound slide out of its words.
Not a full moon question asked of the windows that gorge
on the magnitudes of the stars

but a lifting up of a human voice
that could not lie and could not promise to lift us
out of disrepair

nor lift us in our waiting out of what we are waiting for.

Passing Things

When I hear the sound of someone talking I go to the window.
That's how quiet my house is,

everything holding still
like a rabbit hidden so deep inside itself you could miss it

trembling at the edge of the lawn,
while outside the rabbit, sound goes pretty quietly about its business,

a house finch singing its tangled string of song up in one of the
many thought-cloud trees.

And when a helicopter rips along like a roofer shucking tiles
or a jet unravels a sadness knit of steel wool

these are passing things. These are things taken out of a box
of planets and stars and put back again.

The cat across the street like a pale orange ghost or a puff of smoke
drifts in and out of bushes and stalks the difference

between what is private and what is a secret.
The mole and the thirteen-line ground squirrel tried all night to be secrets

even from themselves. But sometimes you have to live in the public eye,
which could be lonely or simply frightening.

A man, a tall man, looks back, talking over his shoulder
to a woman pushing a baby in a stroller.

But "something is wrong with the picture" in *this* coloring book —
no door in a tree trunk or a bird upside down in the sky —

no. I mean their pace is erratic, their gestures too wide. Free and open to
the public.
The two of them walking single file. The way he's calling back to her.

And how she jolts the stroller over a rut and shrieks,
lifting the baby oh so carefully by its foot.

Then the man stares at *me* — me at my window, bringing up the rear.
I see then he isn't the father. The child is a doll.

Its blank eyes and smile and hard cheekbones preset to happiness.
Its hair spun yellow

like a hank of what fills the room of a fairy tale by morning light,
once straw, now simmering gold.

She lowers it back down into the stroller. As if into bathwater.
And the loud, patient voice of the man keeps herding her on.

But no, she stopped. And stays stopped as a mother bending over a
stroller.
For all the world to see she leans into the task

required of a woman attended down a public street:
to tuck the secret in. To make it seaworthy. To smother it.

Lynn Emanuel

The Instruction Manual

How-to on how to read this? Listen.
For one thing, there is no you.
She owns you: you're the dog;
she's the leash you follow

through the plot opening into the dark city.
The pace is frisky. To your left — door, door,
window, woman in red dress. You want,
in your doggy way, to back up to that hydrant

for a sniff. And to your right the throb of traffic.
You like her, but she likes Chevies
with glass-pack mufflers, the rickety staccato
of spiked heels nailing down the sidewalk.

Who is it? Wouldn't you like to know.
Plot doesn't tell,
that's what description is for.
It's clothing and it's revealing.
Listen to this: "the lissome friction
of the red silk dress is like a sea; you can hear it glisten."

Etcetera. You see with your ears, but
you aren't listening. You're a dog.
And you're lost. Where is my street, you wonder. Gone.
And so are you, you restless-longing-for-more.
Aren't you sorry. There is no more. No place.
Just blank page, white space, void with a splash of voice.

Most Recent Book: *Then, Suddenly* (University of Pittsburgh Press, 1999)

The White Dress

What does it feel like to be this shroud
on a hanger, this storm cloud hanging
in the closet? We itch to feel it, it itches
to be felt, it feels like an itch —

encrusted with beading, it's an eczema
of sequins, rough, gullied, riven,
puckered with stitchery, a frosted window
against which we long to put our tongues,

a vase for holding the long-stemmed
bouquet of a woman's body.
Or it's armor and it fits like a glove.
The buttons run like rivets down the front.

When we're in it we're machinery,
a cutter nosing the ocean of a town.
Right now it's lonely locked up
in the closet; while we're busy

fussing at our vanity, it hangs there
in the drooping waterfall of itself,
a road with no one on it, bathed
in moonlight, rehearsing its lines.

She

The body has its own story   she said   Oh, yes?   I said.
The body   she insisted   doesn't care that it doesn't fit your theories
        no I said   I suppose not
flesh, too, has a voice   and is quite articulate   it says —
yes I say   I know what it says   it says the end   is the end no matter
        how you slice it
precisely   she said   she was herself quite eloquent   we were sitting in
        the café   the street
disappearing behind the rainy plate glass window   behind us hovered
        the waiter and the good smell
of coffee   she was beautiful   bookish   I loved her serious glasses   she was
trying to explain about the flesh   and I did not want to hear it
        but she persisted   your
stories   Yes?   utilize the latest methods   they disrupt everything!
strike out in new directions!   nothing is certain   death to tradition!
        why thank you I said

at her back the city wept with rain   and to the dominant paradigm I said
death to the dominant paradigm   of the beginning the middle
        all that sad etcetera
of course   she continued severely   the body is   I looked at her
        her hair was long and as dark
as the earth and I said   of course   the body is   a thing having a beginning
        and a middle and an end
and is what my text struggles against   and so the body and I are like
        two people in a café   arguing about
the way the story would go   I argue my position vis à vis
        the end and beginning   and the body argues
hers   yes   she said   but let's face it   no matter what you say   the
        body wins.

Walt, I Salute You!

From the Year Of Our Lord 19**,
from the Continent of the Amnesias,
from the back streets of Pittsburgh
from the little lit window in the attic
of my mind where I sit brooding and smoking
like a hot iron, Walt, I salute you!

Here we are. In Love! In a Poem!
Slouching toward rebirth in our hats and curls!
Walt, I'm just a woman, chaperoned, actual, vague and hysterical.
Outwardly, my life is one of irreproachable tedium;
inside, like you, I am in my hydroelectric mode.
The infinite and abstract current of my description
launches itself at the weakling grass. Walt, everything I see I am!
Nothing is too small for my interest in it.
I am undone in the multiplication
of my perceptions. Mine is a life alive with the radioactivity
of its former lives.

I am in every dog and hairpin. They are me! I am you!
All is connected in the great seethe of seeing and being,
the great oceans and beaches of speeding and knowing.

I groan and surge, I long for hatches and engine sumps,
for sailors in undershirts. Walt! You have me by the throat!
Everywhere I turn you rise up insurmountable and near.

You have already been every Conestoga headed to California
that broke down in a cul-de-sac of cannibalism in the Rockies.

You have been every sprouting metropolis re-routed
through three generations of industrialists.
You, the sweat of their workers' brows! You, their hatred of poets!

You have been women! Women with white legs, women with black
mustaches,
waitresses with their hands glued to their rags on the counter,
waitresses in Dacron who light up the room with their serious wattage.
Yes! You are magically filling up, like milk in a glass, the white
nylon uniform, the blocky shoes with their slab of rubber sole!
Your hair is a platinum helmet. At your breast, a bouquet of rayon
violets.

And you have been places! You have been junk yards with their rusted
Hoovers,
the pistils of wilted umbrellas.
And then, on the horizon (you have been the horizon!)
Walt, you are a whole small town erupting!
You are the drenched windows. The steaming gutters.
The streets black and slick as iron skillets.
The tawdry buildings. The rooms rented.
And now, in total hallucination and inhabitation, tired of being yourself —
Walt, the champ, the chump, the cheeky — you become me!
My every dark and slanderous thought. Walt, I salute you!
And therefore myself! In our enormous hats! In our huge mustaches!
We can't hide! We recognize ourselves!

Beth Ann Fennelly

Madame L. Describes the Siege of Paris

You say that you could never eat a snake?
Had you been here, mademoiselle, in seventy-one
this zoo would seem the freshest of buffets.
We too would have denied it of ourselves
but war is turpentine that strips the gloss.

We built a wall to keep the Prussians out
and barricaded Haussmann's boulevards.
We forged new guns, drilled soldiers for attack,

Most Recent Book: *A Different Kind of Hunger*
(Sam Houston University Press, 1998)

then waited for the shells. They never hit.
Too late we learned they meant to starve us out.
It seemed almost a joke those first few days,
our handsome soldiers yawning, playing chess.
When Bismarck sneered "The Paris bourgeoisie
will break after a day without éclairs,"
we laughed. Then had a day without éclairs.
The jokes, and children, thinned. The markets stalled —
we lost our fruit. We lost the beef and eggs.
Stale bread and unripe camembert were hawked
for sums — *Mon Dieu!* — that tripled overnight.
The first milk-hungry babies made their moans.
Flaubert bought braces, his first pair in years —
his belly couldn't hold his trousers up.
We thought it'd gotten bad. Then it got worse.
The *ville des lumiéres* went out — no light!
No oil for lamps! No coal to feed the stove!
November, and too cold to sit inside.
The poor huddled along the Champs Élysées
mobbed kiosks, tore up cherry trees for wood.
The staple cafe diet, God and art,
was jettisoned — they talked only of food.
The men got drunk and drunker — we had wine
and mustard in abundance all those months.

Le Journal left off printing world affairs,
gave recipes for cooking rotten peas.
Outside the barricade the Prussians drank
French wine, slept in French beds, and nibbled brie
from lips of well-fed maidens, also French.
Inside, the city withered, locust-stripped.
I was young like you and had a man,
an officer, but stationed in Angers.
The tracks were cut. Although I dreamt of him
and how he'd feed me *beurre et sucre crêpes*,
the weeks grew long. Soon I just dreamt of *crêpes*.
The plump girl he had loved discovered ribs
and collarbones and hips under her dress —
each day I molted memories like a snake.
There was a boy named Jacques who hunted crows
inside the Tuilleries — I dug for root
of dahlia, and we would picnic there.
Sometimes he put his hands inside my blouse,

a different kind of hunger. Afterwards
he'd tell how he would feed me if he could
madeleines and berries dipped in cream,
gorging me with words til I was full.

No help came from abroad. Always no news.
Shipwrecked, we tied our pleas to pigeons' legs
and ate the olive branches they returned.
We sent hot air balloons up from Montmartre
that blew into the Prussian's chubby hands,
our Grand Sortie laid bare for them to squelch.
The hundredth day of siege: I queued for bread
while baby coffins circled Pére Lachaise
like white ants choosing their last picnic spot.
A claustrophobic humor reigned the streets.
We all were single-minded: food; so speech
became superfluous, the same ideas
in every house. The cats, suspicious, felt
in stroking hands the butchers' greedy thumbs
appraising *embonpoint*. The dogs were dumb.
Meows and barks soon came from butchers' carts.
I ate a slice of Siamese at Maude's
that tasted just like chicken with her sauce;
the meatballs made of mice caused Maude to toast:
"To enemies made friends in cooking pots!"
Victor, my dog, was old; though it was *triste*
to fatten him for Christmas — what a roast!
A good dog, Victor, til the very end.

With Paris circumscribed, why keep a horse?
My father used his cane to beat the mobs
who tried to steal his mare, but acquiesced
to mother's frank "She's starving; why should we?"
The butcher stayed for *filet de cheval*
and courted me with eggs. The town dehorsed.
The soldiers used their strategy on rats;
they baited lines with wax and fished in sewers.
Then we ran out of rats. The city paused —
no howl, no cheep, no whinny in the streets —
and panicked. We turned upon the zoo inside
our zoo. Trumpetings and ape-cries from the ark:
The hippopotamus, the kangaroo,
wapiti, bear, and wolf — all mustard-doomed.
We killed them two by two. We cheered the boys

who drove the weeping zoo keeper away
and broke the locks made strong to keep us safe.
On fire, we roasted camel on a spit,
danced palm to bloody palm. The drinking troughs
were filled with wine. Two elephants, the pride
of town, Castor and Pollux — their trunks were sliced
over a barrel for blood. My torch revealed
two twin girls eating monkey from their hands,
a severed gazelle head atop a man's,
some boys working a bar loose for albino
koala skewers. While at the lion's cage
I felt a hand slip underneath my skirt.
Beard on my neck. Feathers and bones
were all we left to greet the stricken sun.
I threw that dress away, it was so stained.

Later that week Thiers proclaimed defeat,
ceded Alsace-Lorraine, our francs, our pride.
The walls came down and Paris could reworld.
The Brits sent mutton, pies, and currant jam.
And things returned to normal. Shelves restocked.
The butcher shop on Faubourg Saint-Germain
took down its rhino horns. And gardens grew.
Resuming lives, we fought amongst ourselves
a civil war — well, who would govern now?
Who pay the money owed? Who seek revenge?
We were reminded who was rich, who poor,
and so if the poor starved they could be blamed.

Well, that was years ago. Since then I've seen
more war — called "Great" — if what they say is true,
we'll see another here before too long.
I've stockpiled tins of flour, sugar, grain.
I eat well always now, though it seems bland.
Perhaps because I'm old. But my tongue holds
the taste of bear passed from a stranger's mouth.

So me, I settled down, bought Victor Deux.
I plumped up, took a husband and his cares.
My life grew dense: I bore him seven sons.
The four that live prepare themselves to fight
the grandsons of the ones my husband fought.
Jean — that was his name — is gone. I spend
my days on this bench in this zoo. I like

to watch the animals and think of things
and people I have known. It's strange how fresh
the siege is in my mind, as if my life's composed
of those eight months. I think we keep ourselves
so tightly wrapped we never see our spools.
We saw them, clear as skeletons, that time.
What's wrong? What's right? To live was right. To know
that you could take the heart and eat it raw.

Alice Fulton

Split the Lark

== Taste another snowflake, always flavored
with symmetry and quick. Taste it just by breathing.
Try the true north that is nothing
if not meat divine. He said

he'd seen a space shaped like a bowl
in the delicious snow, with brushmarks around it
as if someone had been sweeping
with a cypress limb. Some Mrs. Muskrat
from a golden book of storyland
where forest folk wear clothes.
Though these incisions were the work of wings.
And nearby, piled neatly on the crust, a lavish
moistly saturated maroon, were the intestines.
I guess it made him grasp enfleshment better,
the way flying glosses gravity
more vividly than lying down. It was something
about contrast, exotica, that livid turban on the snow.
"I want to kiss you but I feel nauseous,"

the poet gushed into the open mike,
and I quoted it later, amused and cruel.
I made it worse. Well, look
who's spilling now. At first he spared me
his discovery but I'm the kind who'd rather know.
It runs in the family. At least I've stopped thinking

Most Recent Book: *Felt* (W. W. Norton & Company, 2001)

knowledge is power and realized knowledge
is knowledge and power is
another thing entirely. Am I going to die?
my cousin asked her primary care physician.
It runs in the family. When Europeans visit
Michigan they sometimes ask

to feast on bear or moose. And there was that American
who went to France to eat a songbird, an ortolan,
which stands, they say, for the French soul.
The chef called them canaries, though ortolans
are buntings, a kind of bobolink, members
of the finch family, the size of
penises with gray-green heads. No two alike,
the snowflake platitude. The clouds' opacities
and glassy fields are textured as never
before, though on the whole, the winter
sky looks like the wrong side of a painting.
If I could only flip it, use my head or back to
lift it, if I had the eyes to
sift it, a proximate chromatic paradise
might come to light. The ortolans are caged in the dark

for weeks. Well, once upon a time
they were blinded with knives.
They feed constantly when deprived of day, you see.
After fattening, they're drowned
in cognac, plucked, fried, and presented
on their backs, swollen, shriveled delicacies
with wings folded and eyes bruised

open wide. *What's the Ugliest Part*
of Your Body as the old Mothers of Invention
tune asked. *Some say it's your nose —*
the celebrants drape large white cloths
over their heads for privacy and to enhance
the aroma of the liver and kidneys,
anus and brain becoming paste or pomade

　　= = When I opened the tiny bottle with my incisors
　　the frangipani essence, bile
　　yellow, spilled on my bitter orange skirt,
　　and what had been delectable
　　became a stink I couldn't stand or leave. Cruelty's

caused by ignorance, I used to think,
an unsolved riddle, like the one about the chicken
and the egg. Now I beg to differ. Now I think
you can prove the brutal
using split fields, fixed and moving
eyepieces, depth samples, horizon scans,
a wedge and a transparent plunger, you can shove
your fingers in the mess itself
and your mind will say but still and yet.
Will blend in white
until the visceral business turns pastel
then market it as peachy
patent leather edible bright wipes

and send you the nice invoice. Cruelty is convenient,
that's the thing. Ignorance is.
Bliss. I mean, I also have suffered
the sensational to die. "Make sure your own
oxygen mask is fastened
before assisting others." In Beijing,
we interviewed the old men who walk
their birds every morning, swinging the cages
to mimic the sensation of flight.
They held contests to decide whose thrush sang best.
When I asked how they got their pets to sing they said
"We beat them. With a little stick. And did the U.S. troops
in Vietnam eat babies? We've heard this

is what you did." The American
savored the last meadow gasp of pollen
in the ortolan's lungs, the grit of millet
in its bowels, its final swig of sun
before its tissues filled with night,
grinding small to smaller till his molars met
the resistant cartilage and sinew, when, well,
I want to kiss you but
I feel nauseous says it best. Split the Lark—

and you'll find the Music—Place the Crystal
Gizzard on my tongue. I'll melt
the gothic arches of the not-body,
dissolve its feather pixels. I'll clean its clock,
receive. Lettuce leaf grass ripe unripe tomato
orange chocolate

beetroot white and whiteman's face
are tones plotted on the tongue-shaped graph
in *Colour: Why the World Isn't Grey*. Though of course it is

sometimes. I said punch-biopsy me
till the juice runs down my leg,
and they cut a scrimption of flesh
like the hole in binder paper except
this hole had depth, it was a tiny well
with a wicked wine confetti at the bottom,
it had death, I said, it was unsettling
to see so far into myself, creepy, I said,
and the doctors tried to hide
their smiles. You are going to die. Keep it simple, stupid,
which abbreviates to KISS. Keep the blech and yum
and ick. *The Ugliest Part?*

Some say it's your toes, grippage,
the opposite of on the wing.
The sky's gray emphasized by contrast
the swelter on the crust and the quiet felt
compensatory, felt remembering of
the shriek followed by the lift
of the carnivorous thing, the digestion of
a heaven ruminant with all
it had absorbed. "All the colours
formed by mixing real lights lie inside
the area enclosed by the tongue . . ."

    = = When I got to the bottom of the dish,
    I saw what I'd taken
    for peppercorns was in fact
    ground glass. Did you know

any pigment ground infinitely small
will look sky blue? And isn't it cool
all snowflakes taste alike. Always flavored,
with no fat corners, with six-daggered ellipse.
Storm callus, blizzard skin, you taste
like death wish. Like marvelous
cold thing. That God does not apologize
is God's one sin. Well, it takes one

to make one, he said. It takes one
rooster and a million hens

to produce these free-range eggs.
The male chicks are suffocated, crushed,
decapitated, or gassed. He said this
at breakfast, provoking a loud
calm. Does the face look different
eating an ortolan, I wonder?
As it does speaking French
compared to, say, Chinese? As snowflakes
get their shape from water's shape
and the pigments in bile create
the blue of some birds' eggs.

"As the area outside the tongue
represents imaginary stimuli
we need not consider it further."
As long as I got a toehold, as long as I got
a piece of you. *Part of Your Body?*
I think it's your mind: where the moist and the warm meet
the cold and the pure snow forms.
The spring catalogues are full of hollow

chocolate hens and foiled chicks. Full of panoramic sugar
eggs with windows in their shells that let you see
the smiling Easter beast inside. See this
Baccarat bunny dish?
The head and spine lift off. The cover.
Yes, I see. Glass tastes like spring
water rising from a bed of chalk, flinty
without body or bouquet. Its microstructure
resembles rusted chicken wire. Going smaller,
at the quantum level, it's all oscillating

    == clouds. And I touched my lips
    to the tumbler, tuning out its flavor
    to relish what it held. The crystal

rabbit looked empty yet reflective:
you could catch your face in it.
Light turns incarnational upon entering
the brain. I filled mine with sweets and party favors.

Tess Gallagher

One Kiss

A man was given one kiss, one
mouth, one tongue, one early dawn, one boat
on the sea, lust of an indeterminate
amount under stars. He was happy
and well fitted for life until he met a man
with two cocks. Then a sense of futility
and of the great unfairness of life befell him.
He lay about all day like a teenaged girl dreaming,
practicing all the ways to be unconsciously beautiful.

Gradually his competitive spirit began to fade
and in its place a gigantic kiss rowed toward him.
It seemed to recognize him, to have intended itself
only for him. It's just a kiss, he thought,
I'll use it up. The kiss had the same thing
on its mind — 'I'll use up this man.'

But when two kisses kiss, it's like tigers
answering questions about infinity with their teeth.
Even if you are eaten, it's okay — you just become impossible
a new way — sleepless, stranger than fish, stranger
than some goofy man with two cocks. That's
what I meant about the hazards
of infinity. When you at last begin to seize those things
which don't exist,
how much longer will the night need to be?

When the Enemy Is Illiterate

You must speak as St. Francis more than
spoke to the birds — with your hands out, upturned
to show you mean no harm. And, borrowing
a little wisdom from the trees, receive
everything that comes — strange nestings,
exorbitant winds, blind syllables of lightning,

Most Recent Book: *My Black Horse: New & Selected Poems*
(Bloodaxe Books. Ltd., 2000)

tormented lovers carving their names
in the rough tablet of your lap.

Thus you will be obedient not to speech alone,
which is only the crude horizon upon which a mighty castle
was put to the torch and consumed
in a paralysis of over-exuberant, yet too solemn light.
Uncontending, you must yield intention so fully
that the template behind speech will sound
like a resplendent gong
above the aggrieved yet expectant face — its
closed radiance as the New Year confetti piles up
on your shoulders.

Finally, make yourself the site of a purposeful failure
to decipher harm in the frenzied economy
of any message. Remember virtue's unspoken strategy —
that we are put on earth as seriously as dreams,
as night and silence. The first star of the year
is always over our shoulders.
Take the splendid never-again path
which allows each clamped beak to divine
its surround of feathers.
Oh glad and fearful signs of bravest welcome.

Invaded by Souls

. . . but I'm always being invaded by others'
souls so I can't see my own soul very well.
— Shuntaro Tanikawa

One night you fall asleep with an ungiven kiss
on your lips, you fall asleep in your kiss.
It is like sending yourself on an all night errand
to interview echoes about where they think
they're coming from. Where did it come from
anyway, your falling-asleep kiss? your
good-for-eternity soul?
How do you know they aren't imposters,
your unclouded kiss, your sublimated-soul?

To kiss and return a kiss is to be invaded
by souls, like a dead artist or a living poet,

like the twin sails of a ship in its sky-filled
sex act with the wind. Sometimes
we are taken charge of by the freedom of all those stones
children threw at nothing into the sky or into
the ocean from the Stone Age onward. We are
invaded by souls. We can't hold ourselves back
from each other then.

And besides, you've fallen asleep in your kiss.
Suddenly you are in a railway station
in a state of undress, naked except for your kiss
which, like your soul, is invisible and ungiven.
A whistle blows like a missed rendezvous with
the rest of your life. Souls are rushing past and into
you out of the vast Everything.
There is a dark frame around this absence
called 'the dream'. You are trying to exit
the wrong way down a stairwell invaded by souls.

You'd like to kiss your way out of this like a gangster
of the Starry Moment, but there are too many of them,
these lonely, imperishable souls rushing at you
full of desire and paradox, with wide pockets
of illumination and, as if to prove this is an American
dream and these are American souls,
some are riddled with bullets, cosmetically
punctuated with a certain brutal frankness.

But our capacity for love belongs to the birdsong
of antiquity which cleanses our dream-eyes and
allows them to mix moonlight with starlight
in those phosphorescent kisses multitudes
of plankton give the night.
They kiss with their whole beings, invisibly
sucking the fingertips of the dream's halflife.
Your own soul is in there too
filling up its tank on Infinite Joy and Diversity.
I don't know what else to tell you, except
you'll know when it happens.
A certain restless undulation as with waves
under fog. It's the souls, moving in.

Laughter and Stars

I didn't make present
those days he didn't complain
but I knew he was sick, felt
sick, and a look would pass between us,
a doomed look that nonetheless
carried streamers of light like a comet
scratching light across the tablet of the night sky.
We looked into each other
and like the comfort a small branch is to a bird
on a long migration, we took comfort in
the two-way knowing of that look.

I didn't make present enough
his beautiful will as he went to his room
with the fireplace and heaped the fire up
to match the inner burning of his body's candle,
the cells igniting so fast by then
it kept him awake, pacing him wall to wall
in the cage of his body's luster like a panther
of the will, supple and searching its parameters.
He fed the fire; he wrote
                                        poems.

No, I couldn't make present
the tender way he took my body in the night
into his arms, holding his one radiance to me
like a wet match upon which one
dry spot remained and he turned just so and struck himself
against me and there was a blazing up, the way the night
ignites with more then lips and parted legs
when two souls
in their firefly selves
come together asking
to be buried in the no-song-left-but-this
                                                            dark.

Had I been able to give these things
I might have described his innocent laughter
with a friend and me the night before his death, laughter
at the clumsiness of the body, his body,
with the oxygen tank attached, making sure the tube
was in his mouth. His wanting to go out onto

the deck of the house to see the stars again. The wheelchair
catching on the rug, the oxygen tank
trying to jolt loose, but somehow everything jangling along
out the sliding glass doors, and the sky huge
with a madman's moon, huge as a man's heart on its last
breath-beat so we had to shield ourselves
and turn away to find the
stars.

Such a plaintive, farewell hissing
they made, like diamonds imbedded
in the blue-black breast of forever. But then
it was the night before my love's last morning,
and we were together, one body to another, laughter
and stars, laughter and stars.

Then he got up, stood up with everything still attached and we
helped him hack open a bright crevasse in the night, to hurl
his heart-beat like the red living fist it was
one more time
out across the sleeping thresholds
of the living.

Jody Gladding

Rooms and Their Airs (Camere et Aer Ipsius)

Air out the quilt. Down remembers
the wind.

Remake the bed. Down remembers
its nest.

Open a window for northerly winds
that have swept across sweet water.

Open a window. Rain falling
on good land is good for melancholy.

Prepare a fish. If the skin's not thick,
it lived in shallows that run among stones.

Most Recent Book: *Stone Crop* (Yale University Press, 1993)

Eat fish with wine and raisins. Your thirst,
too, might be derived from grapes.

Conserve the bones. Nothing you do here
will be forgotten.

White Asparagus

Like her brother, whose letters appear below, my mother left Germany after World War II, although she would refer to it as "her country" until she died. "Show me your face before you were born," demands the Zen master. My question is less enlightened: "Show me your face before I was born." And always her answer remains both a commonplace and an enigma.

White asparagus,
sweet, stringy mushroom you tend at night.
By moonlight, you reach under the ground to slice it clean.
The nights before the war,
my mother danced with barons who smoked short cigarettes,
and gypsies read her palm.
The shoes she wore shone silver like the moon.

. . . Baron Von Kutschenbach. He was Estonian. I remember the long Egyptian, or were they Russian, papyrossi. Five marks a day we had, either for cake or horseriding. The best hotel, etc., of course paid by our father. Though only lard for breakfast. Butter was already stored.

To protect from the light
by burying: this is different from innocence.

. . . When we left in August we saw from the train all the heavy guns and everything was ready and we did not really know for what. Barons in Germany mean little. They bought their titles. I remember the 16th of October, 1939, Margarete's 20th birthday. Poland was already taken.

Europeans prefer their asparagus white,
though any variety may be blanched.
As in, *to blanch with fear*.

. . . The parquet at Osterdeich was ideal for dancing. I had the honor to turn the spring on the gramophone. Once some British bombers came, forty of them.

Here, it's all grown green.
Predominantly male plants put their energy
completely into producing spears.

. . . It needed courage to drive a Ford in Germany in 1939. Our father would not drive the same car as Hitler. He did not like him. He sent my sister twice to England on the *Europa* and the *Bremen*. Beautiful ships. They held the Blue Ribbon.

To mutilate. To cultivate.
Same bed, different roots.

. . . I remember her time in a munitions factory when her hair turned green. I remember her in some Red Cross uniform. But I have seen Margarete very little.

The day my father calls to say
he's bought her cemetery lot,
I'm putting in asparagus.

. . . I remember the silver shoes.

My mother's wedding band was gold as butter.
Before each meal, she'd bow for grace,
hands poking up toward God.

. . . When did you travel with her on a train?

As if hilling up our ghosts
could keep them tender.

. . . Was it when you went together to Germany?

Give careful thought to where
you locate the planting
because it could be there a long time.

. . . I cannot remember.

The day stretches long, most of it spent on trains. We're rocking against our bags, traveling north in the country my mother still calls hers. It's fall. There isn't much to see — mounded earth, inedible moot points. "Look," she says, "asparagus." Her finger taps the window long after the view has changed.

Albert Goldbarth

What We're Used To

Or the woman who, after the seeped stink of her death
had slapped the neighbors into attentiveness and then the cops,
was found to have shared the dungeon-dark of her backlot shack
with (this was by actual clicker count) 548 rats, that
(who?) she'd made her confidants — had fed,
and built a gamy junkparts playground for, and nested with
in sleep (perhaps by then could *only* sleep with the familiar
tictac dance of their garbagey paws across her body). And
"familiar" *is* the keynote word: that dankness
was the comfy psyche-soup in which she lazied back
and happily dissolved at the end of a day. For her.
this was natural. In the Hanzai Valley, the villagers

*

live with ghosts around them as commonly as oxygen
is around them — ghosts, cospatially with the air
they breathe, the air that rides the blood, the air we'll all become
one day, one way or another. "Rounded [cosmos/sky-container]"
(their ritual greeting) they say on meeting any of this invisible
and thronging population. For them, it's natural. The spectral selves
of animals and plants attend the hunt and the fields. Stars,
the various intimacies that occur at night in those fields.
Ancestral spirits see through the dark, of course, and so
not even the fevery knots of the sexual union are secret
from them — if anything, their up-close sidelines cheering
is expected, is part of the order of things. In Rembrandt's

*

engraving *Het Ledekant*, of a couple in coitus (he's on top
between her legs, in a billowy, canopied four-poster), the woman pictured
in this otherwise realistically rendered bedtime scene is given
three arms; to this extent, the viewer is given two choices.
If we ask to accept the arm that laxly sprawls at her side
(presumably paired with one out of sight, on her other side), then
the woman's nearly asleep, or swoozled on too much wine.

Most Recent Book: *Saving Lives* (Ohio State University Press, 2001)

If we ask to accept the hands that clasp his ass in tightly,
the woman's actively passionate: dark lines beneath one hand say
fleshly pressure. Whichever. Neither reading's "wrong." Each
has a naturalness, depending on the lives, and on the thousand
constituent details of their time together. Once I loved

*

in the way I thought love worked: you made
life easier for someone: made it into a calm continuum,
sans burden or suspicion; you were free of frowst and bitterness.
and you trusted that life would buoy you in return. For her,
each day Creation started up from zero again, tough brick by brick,
and debt by debt: attack was ever immanent, defense was ever
hammered-on in thick emotional sheet metal. So it
didn't last. And both of us felt betrayed. I remember...
the sun through the bough, like a loading ramp into infinity...
I explained my idea of life, and I could see it wasn't material
at all, it was a phantom life, and she could put her hand right through me:
I was supernatural.

Imps

Fire isn't allowed, for the sake of the books.
The lean monk-copyist who scribes the books is slate-blue at his fingertips
this steely late-November day in the year 1000. Brother Ambrosio
huffs some perfunctory warmth on his stiffening hands,
then bends again to his goat's-horn of ink. For every line,
he believes, he's forgiven a sin. And now he's at his heavy
uncial letters, and will be for nine hours more,
until a slab of bread and a beet relieve his transcriptual ardor.
What he copies? — psalter, missal, hagiography:
the predetermined and sanctioned community passions
of a religious culture. Nothing like the twentieth century's
prevalent kneejerk "self-expression." Nothing like the priest,

excuse me: *former* priest, and former nun, on daytime talk TV,
who live, she tells us, in a "trinity of love" with the former
creator-of-tourist-ashtrays-out-of-catfish-heads. This is,
she insists, the final and jubilant stage of a lifelong "quest
to feel belongingness" initiated thirty years before
by parents skittering cross-country with the military: *they*

were wholly rootless, and so *she* grew up "unable to commit." The
following day,
a man confesses to pedophilia because of a lesbian aunt.
A woman says she robbed the Sack-N-Save of $13.42
"because of what they're dumping in the water supply, it makes me
go all freaky." Steve was bounced out from The Chicken Shack
"because I'm Scandinavian." The culture

of blame is *so* completely exterior in its search for cause,
some days I wake to think I'll find most people laboring
under the weight of sci-fi-style mind parasites, like fleshy turbans
spewing in, and feeding off, their brain blood. This (by "this"
I mean of course a recognition of the magic of objective correlative
boppin' about in the spotlight) is, to some length,
understandable: you can't beat the miniscule carry-along
convenience of a silicon chip invisibly set in something,
BUT for sheer persuasive visual power, *that* can't touch
a 1940s generating plant, its giant Alcatrazian shape
against the sky, and the enormous wrestling electrical crackles
snaking its rooftop pylon. In the scriptorium, even

— such an isolated unit of human endeavor, its limited range
of reactions surely is pure — when Brother Ambrosio
nods off, sleepy in his long day's long eighth hour
of thickly nibbed and careful letters, he knows
it's imps in league with Satan that keep pulling down his eyelids.
If in scratching his flea-measled thigh he spills
a hand's-expanse of ink across the vellum page, the fleas
are tiny devils on a guerilla mission from Hell.
And once a devilkin took lodging in his belly, and there
created "rumbling noises like a toad, and which, for hours,
spoiled the concentration of all of the other Brothers."
We find parchment scraps with appropriate exorcisms:

"Away! you flaming sow, you poisoned udder,
you arse of the arch-fiend, shit-fly, stinking he-goat,
out out out, away, back into thine infernal kitchen,
you bestial puke!" We also find
those charming marginal doodles (sprigs in flower,
unicorns, seemingly every songbird in Creation): such
diminutive external bodies given to the longings of these
cooped-up men. And when they came to drag my friend Jess
screaming to the ward, because he was beating his head
on the lawyer's steps, it was clear to us all that the chemicals

in his mind had turned against him. It was clear to Jess
that he was being hunted like prey by hounds from the moon.

Ancestored-Back *Is the Overpresiding Spirit of This Poem*

If only somebody would drill with a finger-long rig down
into my skull, and saw a tiny circle out of its bone,
so pools of acid antsiness and angst can steam away;
so all of the great in-gnarling, all of the bunched-up
broodiness can breathe; and so at least the day's
accumulated ephemera, its fenderbender squabbles,
its parade of petty heartache can evaporate in writhes
of sour mist — this spatting couple, for example,
in the booth across the aisle as I'm chowing on a burger
and their every more-than-whispered perturbation is,
this afternoon, a further furrow worked into my mind. . . .
You know I'm kvetching metaphorically. But literalist
Amanda Fielding, wielding a scalpel and electric drill.
bored a hole in her skull in 1970, filming that self-surgery,

*

and zealously thereafter promoting the benefits of this
third eye, finally "running for Parliament on a platform
of trepanation for national health." The operation
was successfully conducted in the Stone Age (72%
of the skulls we've found reveal that the patients far survived
that crisis moment), and the Chinese medico Thai Tshang Kung
(150 B.C.) was said "to cut open the skulls of the sick
and arrange their brains in order." A Roman physician's
effects from the second century A.D. include a trepanation kit
in bronze, its tooth-edged bit and driving-bow
as finely produced as any machine-tooled apparatus
a surgeon in 1996 would wish for — when the bow unfolds
it's as intricate in its simplicity as a line of true haiku.
I've read a book whose major pleasure is its breathlessness

*

in gasping at the ancientness of various devices,
flushing toilets(!) condoms(!) hand grenades(!) — the book
is a grove of invisible exclamation points. These

green glass beads like rain-splats on a leaf
— 4,000 years ago. Bone dice, the same. The ribbed vault
in this early Gothic church is a masterly hollowing-out
of space — but houses of *literal* ribs, of mammoth bones,
were sturdy dwellings 15,000 years ago. Rhinoplasty(!)
soccer(!) odometers(!) "Butter" (a favorite sentence)
"spread everywhere, once it was discovered." Though we don't know
poot about the urgent stirrings in our own hearts
or the dreams irrupting nightly in our own heads,
we've been diagramming stars on plaques
of tortoise plate and antler, we've made sky maps,

*

from before we even understood the link of sex
to birth. And if our coin-op slot machines
can be ancestored-back to that Greco-Egyptian
contrivance of Heron of Alexandria (by which
a dropped-in-place five-drachma bronze piece
starts the portioned flow of a worshiper's ablution-water)...
if *ancestored-back* is the overpresiding spirit
of this poem ... we *are* the progeny of stars,
we *are* their original core-born elements
in new recombination, densed and sizzled into
sentience and soul. I can't imagine the interior tumult
driving Amanda Fielding and her followers, but
I'm not surprised our smallest human units were created
in explosion, speed, and void. My friends

*

are not the kind to drill their heads and rid themselves
of troubles by decanting. Even so, I've seen them consider
their restless faces in the mirror and wish for *some* release.
Our daily dole of woe is unrelenting. In this burger joint,
in the Booth of a Thousand Sorrows across the aisle,
they're arguing still. Outside, the snow provides each tree
with a clerical collar — this couple is arguing. Outside,
the setting summer sun makes each tree a flambeau
— this couple is arguing, they'll never stop, their joys
have been prodigious and their anti-joy will balance this
or more, the hands with which they make their hard points
in the air are hands of oxygen and nitrogen and argon
older than dust or salt. It's midnight. How
emphatic we can be. How long they've been at it.

BECKIAN FRITZ GOLDBERG

Refugees

There are too many shoes in the world.
Let's burn them. There are too many
oceans, let's not accept
one more. And let water fend
for itself.

There are too many matches and horses and odometers.
Birds have begun to fly over in boats.
And whatever our hearts are full of they
are full.

Go back.

We have enough bread, terraces, and blue soap.
We have enough starlets.
Our brooms are populous and our roses
need to die. There is too much cupped
and unfolded. . .

There are too many shoes.

There are too many paintings of trees.
Deer have begun to surround New Hampshire.
And wherever our wine spills there's someone
to throw salt.

We have too many satellites and salons and pennies.
We have eyes in front and don't need them in back.
We have six million pianos —

And let windows find their own faces,
there is too much through them at night —

There are too many desires in the world.
Let's pass a law. Too many black ones
and brown ones, tight ones and pink.
We have too much velvet.
There are too many pomegranates.

Go home.

Most Recent Book: *Never Be the Horse* (University of Akron Press, 1999)

Twentieth-Century Children (5): Blood-Kissing

The boy in the girl's ear says, Kiss me until
    you draw blood.

And she's the hot thorn on his lip.

Stars wince and swell and wet,
    endless little cut-me's...

Through the night the great sponge of traffic,
    the oozy distance, the radios, the malls,
    the cat survivalists

living out of a hole in the library.
Someone

has to say it: Nail me
    to you.

The girl has always loved like suicide.

And the kiss wants to
    know, Am I deep enough —

Am I lord and cock-ring
    and ruby hammer,

spike and sundering thing?

The black place in the skull saying,
    Infect me. Be not only *Other*
    but *It*.

The way desire is —
    live rat sewed up inside us.

Torture Boy's Watch, Burn Boy's Boat of Souls

What kind of boy was this
watching over the Orchid Town swannery —

He was the kind, he'd marry a girl and then say,
"I hate your mother,
your sister too, and all the shitbirds
you came from." Oh, then
you'd know the ache of love...

But first he'd meet the boy at the wolf-rock
lighting gasoline rags
and they'd wonder together if the story
they were in was true,

the story where the burning rag floated
across the water, and the fat tantaras
of the swans set off

a knifing lamentation in the woods
as the rag boat lit the other shore
and died –

the shape of the wolf flared out
the shape of the boy flared out
dark,

weird as an accident in the Bible –
the chapter where God, having lost
his lover in the trees, stumbles

in verse 18
across forgetfulness...

Retro Lullaby

Sometimes I carry the smell of moist hay from my childhood.
    And sometimes I put down this burden, never
    without its consent. Long have I

known memory and willingness to be one fold,
    though I find it difficult to talk to my childhood
    since I had the flying dream – my robes

    bubbled over the desert –
And now all I have is a postcard of a little stranger.
If I drop the card in the hay-smell

her ear will plump up like a dried apricot in wine.
And her stupid white hands will come up like two
    white pages from the bottom of a lake

And I'll coo, It's ok, you can be my baby.
    My part.

I can never remember the whole day.

After all, my sister said I was a strange child, an
automaton.
My mother said if they talked idly in February
of going somewhere in June, I'd wake in June,
my suitcase packed.

Terrible she said to have a child who never forgot a thing.

But now, of course, I've slipped
my mind forever in some infeasible way, flown

stiff as a toy in my dream altitude and I remember
wondering even in my elation if I'd drop
suddenly and if I did

I don't remember. But if I did I'd say
It's ok, you can be my angel. You can be
my human kite

At any time, we might give in. Just a knuckle of us,
or a cheek. Because the
ferment of the hayfield unpacks on the side of a road
and one second

gets the Gone going again, her little hairs stand up.

And childhood stinks big in our lives as death,
And in between is willingness, her tongue comes out
speaking its *motherese* —

All right. You can be my lake, my June, my hay-fish.
Be my keen hound. My. Love of My Life.

BARRY GOLDENSOHN

Law and Sensibility

My mother understood that she only
was the model of true delicacy of feeling.
She remembered as a student, still a girl,
the foul mouth of the insane Nijinsky
and white asylum pitchers jammed full —
asters, purple loosestrife, fireweed, bracken.
He flew with one leap from the back wall

Most Recent Book: *Uncarving the Block* (Vermont Crossroads Press, 1978)

to the new electric footlights at the Met.
With precise care and curses that could kill
for her wavering pirouettes, he sent her
to Massine as a principal dancer. It mattered,
the view one took of wavering.

My sister and I learned at this difficult school
the principled boundary of love, its precise
irregular discriminations — the nuance
for giving and for listening and sweetness.
(Mother was good at the first two and wavered
on the third.) She taught us leaps of tough sympathy
for the flagrant outcast style. *Artists are mad.*
Love them! There ware even acceptable forms
of success at business. Those were her gifts to us.
We could not deserve it but the wave of her
generosity could break over us with wild
astonishment as when in a favorite sonnet the lines
that cut open the heart can inflict
their pain with a perpetual surprise.

The Bat

On the stump of a torn wing
it planted itself in the driveway
and screeched to keep me away
from doing the merciful thing
and crushing it under my foot.
I scooped it up in my cap
and hid it away in a yew
to save it from the cat.
It would starve in a day or two.
I once heard a chipmunk scream
for hours in the slow jaws
of a king snake under the house.
Gradual death is hell
but the human terrified dream
in the beast face of that thing
made me unable to kill
as it lingered in suffering.
Don' t test me on anything close.

Lao Tzu Rebuked

When Lao Tzu warns against the fetishism of commodities
He means to warn us against the false desires
Aroused by fancy food, cars, wine, fancy women, watches, men, trophy
    people
Aroused by women with bodies who must therefore cover themselves to
    their toes
And walk without making noise and forswear white socks
(Women without bodies may swim naked through the air),

Aroused by men muscled like ex-cons in tank tops, swaggering,
Inarticulate with sincerity, bold, tender,
slender, doe-eyed, articulate pattern-weavers
(Men without bodies may swim naked through the air),

About all which a Jewish divine remarked, that the scheme
Of satisfying our needs by lopping off our desires
Is like cutting off our feet when we need shoes,
Signifying that the revolution in desire will not occur among the Jews.

The Summer I Spent Screwing in the Back Seats of Station Wagons

was the last summer that lasted all summer.
This was not — do not misread the title —
screwing the seats in but climbing in
the back seats and screwing as fast as I could.
It was always the same, open the back and fling
in the power driver and the big tool
box with the braces and screws as the tall Pole
pressed the window firmly into place,
as I would drill the holes, line up the clamps,
and screw them in. If the clamps sat too tight
the window cracked and then a flurry of work
as we swarmed ahead of our spot on the line,
the tall Pole and I at Fisher Bodies
in Euclid, Ohio, and rushed to return to our place.
I kept bashing my hands and my nights were crushed,
and in all that soul exhausting work
the cars were as rotten as we could make them.
There was nothing of ourselves we wanted to see

in what we did to Chevy Kingswood and Nomad
and Pontiac Safari with pubescent tailfins.
This was in Euclid, who looked on Beauty bare,
Ohio, whose three long syllables danced
in only four letters, pronounced Ah-hah,
by my fellow workers who wrenched, torqued, and screwed
on the assembly line with me in Euclid, Ohio.
At the end of the day all we had was numbers
corporate totals. It brought to mind
the boast of Wilt the Stilt that he had fucked
twenty thousand women in his time,
and never, never, the same woman twice.
And as we looked, wearied, at our line of cars
we wondered, how could he tell?

Rest

There were real ducks in the pond, not fake ducks,
and even the Quakers tolerated music in the service
and I had such an intense nostalgia for the wrong history,
another self-deceiving dream order, as we gathered
around the casket of this slim young woman — even beautiful dead.
Her hair combed straight as always, but her eyelids strictly
closed. She reminded me always of a veiled Botticelli.
We exhausted our fear as we watched her struggle with cancer
everywhere that finally closed her lungs, though she lay
very still and tried to live without breathing the last few days
And now her body, her real body, with a cross in her hands
that beckons upward for the grand promise. And they sang
Mozart's *Requiem* that begins and ends with a prayer for *them*,
the dead, who need eternal rest, perpetual light,
and in the center a terrified soul pleading for mercy
from a judgment that frightens even the just and the virgins.
Salva me, fons pietatis, fountain of pity, save me.
It is the famous holy dread. We learned enough of dread
hoping for her, even thinking she beat it, that vital
body beat it. There was comfort in that hope for weeks
at a time, often longer. When I was young, my parents
warned me about the undertow at Coney Island beach,
but I could swim like a shark and was never overpowered
and never afraid of oceans. Now the cry of terror

after the real dread we suffered and saw come true
takes on a ritual fullness, *Salva me*, and we wished her
eternal rest in the arms of her torturer and killer.
How adequate for our grieving all those voices were and
the largeness of structure, and even the prayer, not abject,
not loose talk about the soul. With all the show of
theatrical emotion, there was dignity and understanding and
hope of generosity. The way we want ourself spoken of, sung of.

Eamon Grennan

Lesson

I was watching a robin fly after a finch, the smaller bird
chirping with excitement, the bigger — its breast blazing — silent
in lightwinged earnest chase, when out of nowhere

over the chimneys and the shivering front gardens
flashes a sparrowhawk headlong, a light brown burn
scorching the air from which it simply plucks

like a ripe fruit the stopped robin, whose two or three
cheeps of terminal surprise twinkle in the silence
closing over the empty street when the birds have gone

about their own business, and I began to understand
how a poem can happen: you have your eye on a small
elusive detail, pursuing its music, when a terrible truth

strikes and your heart cries out, being carried off.

Artist at Work

On slow wings the marsh hawk is patrolling
possibility — soaring, sliding down almost to ground level,
twisting suddenly at something in the marsh hay or dune grass,
their colours (old copper, strawgold) shining in his eye
where he finds the slightest aberration, any stir

Most Recent Book: *Relations: New & Selected Poems* (Graywolf Press, 1998)

that isn't the wind's doing, and abruptly plunges on it. Then,
if he's lucky, and that scuttling minutiae of skin and innards,
its hot pulse hammering, isn't, he will settle there
and take in what's happened — severing the head first,
then ripping the bright red strings that keep the blood in check,
then heart, gizzard, eyes, and so to the bones, cracking
and snapping each one, that moved so swift and silent
and sure of itself only a minute ago in the sheltering grass.

Heart Attack

1.

One minute the summer sun is warming
hands, hair, the nape of your neck,
the breeze making a familiar whisper
in your ear and the redwing blackbird
a clean note on the air where he balances
a cattail; just as his *chek! chek!* and
the growl of a car engine changing gears
are about to go out the other ear
a blaze of pain incinerates the knees, races
to inflame the belly, be a spring torrent
in the veins and lightning along the ridges
where shoulderblade and breastbone hope
to keep things together, and it's happened.

2.

If you lie very still, like a spotted newt in shadow,
maybe it won't know you're there, maybe
it will flap on over, maybe its eye will blink
at the right instant, maybe it will not smell your
fear, maybe the nervous waves of air will stay
unruffled, smooth, will not break over you,
not tell all there is to know by that sudden
spritz of foam they spit at any impediment. Don't
breathe, that's it, don't let the wind in your chest
set the whole heave of it waving the way grass
becomes a pale mane running under the hand of
any breeze that whispers to it. Be the girl who leans
in her horse's ear and whispers *Easy, now, easy*.

Approximation 7

Bite Marks

A landslide of palpitations and nothing to be done
except let go of themselves and go as directed.

First, bite into the heart of it and feel the spurt
of sweetness under tongue and teeth. Then

the picture shifts, and two halves are howling
over the word *asunder* that someone's written

in crimson on the bedroom mirror. Another
flick of the wrist: the child is pressing against

a door that's swollen after days of rain and won't
open, the wood blindly sensing wetness, pining

for its buried roots and how, earthed as it was,
it stretched to its heart's content in the soft weather,

although the child knows nothing of this, only
her own votive need, the safe arms of rooms, voices

taking her in, explaining everything. But here
is a string of kisses, a scarlet bite-mark

where a fall of hair barely covers the skin
between earlobe and neckbone, the eager air

alive with talk, tireless phrases flying about
like swallows that flash the semaphore of wing and belly

in city windows. But here is the bristle
of rage, pain lying out in all weathers, slowly

eroding even memory. They have seen it
and turned away, letting it happen as if

someone else were living their lives, making
the known space strange, the heart stranger,

the open wound close enough to see beating,
but breathing into it spit and vinegar, silence, salt.

Mark Halliday

Wrong Poem

Not *this* poem, *your* poem, your poem is the one,
not this poem, this is not what you want,
though it seemed refreshing for a second
this poem will not feed you but only
increase your hunger. Already you don't quite like it
and this trend will only intensify.
Is intensify the right verb?
Is hunger the right metaphor?
Neither feels quite right to you, of course not, because
the poem you need is yours. Stop reading this

now before the frustration turns sticky and black
like tar on your shoes. That's a simile
you wouldn't have chosen and it chews on you
like a drooling gerbil, because it spoils the tone
or the momentum or the focus, naturally, since
the focus for you is on another page. Discard this

now if not before, discard seems too tame a verb,
you got the point anyway much earlier, why do I
in my brutal moist gerbil avarice persist in filling
up your world with my unwanted repetitious tropes?
Trope is not as funny a word as it used to be and filling
up is an atrocious line break. Well then, if that's
how you feel then quit already!
                                                            You owe me nothing
and if
we meet
you can easily pretend to have read the whole thing
and I probably won't test whether you noticed certain lively images
near the end, dark pantry tall brunette short skirt warm
tongue which you would sternly judge gratuitous in any case.
This is not what you want,
                                                    wet little adventures of my heart
— heart is such a cheap overused word even among sophisticates
but it's yours that counts, isn't it, yours, your heart
so very unique (gauche phrase) yet always hunting,

Most Recent Book: *Selfwolf* (University of Chicago Press, 1999)

it's sad, hunting insatiably for some mythic deep-bonded
compadre, as if anyone could make your poem
save lonely old you.

Frankfort Laundromat

Plastic chair, my eyes closed, my father walked in,
he had his bag of laundry. My laundry was in a machine
already, thirty-eight years prior to my death. Like me
my father was alive, he was eighty-one. We were both
sunburned and tired, this was after hours on the beach,
after the picnic, after when the Honda got stuck in sand,
this was after, then came the laundry; my father said
"Did you get burned much?" I said "Not too bad" and
he put his clothes in a machine. Small box of Tide.
My eyes closed over *The Burden of the Past* by W. J. Bate
and my eyes opened, hot room smell of soap and hot fabric,
and my father's shirt was dark pink, like a heart.
But my eyes closed, after the hours in the sun and
buying the stuff for sandwiches for everybody and
making sure Nick and the girls didn't really hurt the seagulls
and after Asa felt sick at lunch and after the humid tennis
so my eyes closed. Then opened apparently for more living,
I put my laundry in a dryer and my father was reading
The New Republic — concentrating, with his reading glasses,
and caring about the truth, despite all the sun and
all the sandwiches and tennis and driving, and I loved
him reading there in his dark pink shirt. But my head was
gravitational to the floor, my chin to my neck, I tried
The Burden of the Past and closed my eyes thirty-eight years
before my death unless it comes sooner, and a fly shifted
from *People* magazine to my father's shirt to a Certs wrapper
and the fly was the word "and." Then my clothes were dry
and awfully hot and I held my face to a hot dry towel.
I wanted to live — to live enough; but to live all day —
the sunburn and the gravitation — but my father was still
reading. Therefore with the normal courage of
any son or any daughter I folded my laundry and carried it
out to the Honda for more living, as my father went on
reading for truth in his shirt dark pink like a heart.

Your Visit to Drettinghob

Welcome to Drettinghob and welcome more specifically
to the North Transept of Smegma Manor which once formed
the warm-weather dalrymple for the Prince's consort's gardeners
when the East Winkle of the castle was still standing.
So much here will engage your interest you may wish
to linger till the evening shuttle! Notice for example
those high windows overlooking the Glorn: they are
trypanneis windows (recall your Chaucer!) as can be seen
by the smecked tarnwork of the crundle stones
around the marble brayton of each. If the tarnwork were brass
and unsmecked and if a mock-Greek kleptudorus were dremmled
around each corner, we would have Neo-klepchordly windows,
not trypanneis windows, but in this case we don't.
To have come to Drettinghob is thus to have seen
one sort and not another, whereas in death,
as the Duke of Flinch once said, all names have the same sound.
This castle of course was built in 1581
by the Duke's huffingmeisters with help from yancies
hired by the Earl of Drettinghob, who by 1594 had completed
the spamming of Smegma Manor. It was the Earl's morridgemen
who worked the clench-ovens in which these trouted bottles
were shreamed with scatgurry oil to deepen the morlseed flavor
of the local hooch called Dretbrof. Try a sip! Ah,
that's the true Dretbrof. These round pollytreat humberbun cakes
were invented by the Earl's niece Lady Nudgehope;
they are made of plum spofford which requires
a full night of slow joiling over a gribbed and mountebanked fire,
and the chob sputtles on top are laced with peach purfle
and the melted brist from Leontine brown dankle.
Your caring about all this is so facilitated, so somehow
substantiated by your caring about the names and terms
that you might almost make the error

of caring solely or primarily about the names and terms
were it not for the painful beauty of
the actuality which comes (not the actuality but its painful
beauty) in through
the high windows of your head late late at night
always with that slight
fabulous fragrance of peach, or cilantro, or something else.

Parkersburg

I will arise now and put on a black baseball cap and go
to Parkersburg. It will fit me,
the cap will, and it will be black,
the sneakers on my feet will be purple,
and I will not have shaved for three days.
The day will be rainy and cool
and I will wear an old jacket of pale wool
that was once my Uncle Lew's.
And go to Parkersburg.

On a bus I may go
or in an old car full of tapes —
Elmore James. Fred McDowell.
The Kinks. Into the town of Parkersburg
on a day so rainy and cool. And I will be
terrifically untroubled if anyone thinks I am strange,
in fact everything about this day will be a ratification
of how I am not them; and my manner, though courteous,
will tend to make them suspect that they are boring.
They will wonder why they have no purple sneakers. Cool

and lightly rainy in Parkersburg
and me all day there exactly as if my belief
had long been firm; not forgetting for one minute
how I felt listening to "I'm Different" by Randy Newman
years ago and the sacred tears in my eyes at that time.
I and my black baseball cap will enter a tavern

and there we will read a French poet with such concentration
it will be like I *am* that guy. Then pretty soon
in another tavern it is a Spanish poet whom I read
with similar effect. Parkersburg!
Oh my Parkersburg . . . And I swear,
though I might not meet a lonely marvelous slim woman
with black hair, it will still be as if I did.

Daniel Halpern

Zeno's Lemur

Isn't he the man with crimson socks
        and the slow loris climbing
                like the hour hand from his shoulder,
        over his ear and up
to the pale dome of his head?

The man's face shines with affection.
        He's an honest man and his pet,
                lackadaisical but not dispassionate,
        is devoted and clear about the nature
of their relationship. There are times

to eat and times to climb, the two things
        a loris is always in the act of.
                As the man turns, nearly in slow motion,
        the slow loris peers
from behind his left ear and a smile

begins to spread like a sunrise
        on his face. A word
                takes shape in his mouth as his hands
        reach into the air — reach out
as the word moves forward,

a word of arrival, recognition hovering before him.

Desperados

We were desperate. No, we were beyond desperation.
We were beside ourselves. At wit's end.
We said we could slip outside, that was it.
Get in the car and just keep on driving. Never look back.
No second thoughts. No chance of posing as salt.

But they'd find us, you said. *They'd bring us back
and it would begin again*. We could start a new life.
We could begin again, trying the something new.

Most Recent Book: *Something Shining* (Knopf, 1999)

The road ahead again untrod, winding beyond the next curve
with speed and assurance. Did I say we were desperate?

The lightning took over and revealed the night.
The landscape looked altered — rocks and trees
no longer where they had been hours before.
We hadn't made a move, but we were desperate.
Desperate still — Oh, desperate beyond description.

But they'd find us, you said. *They'd bring us back*.
We said we could slip outside, that was it.
Never look back. No second thoughts.
We were desperate. At wits end. Beside ourselves.
The landscape looked altered, beyond description.

We could begin again. Something new.
The landscape looked altered. Never look back.
Did I say desperate to try something new?
A new life? The road ahead untrod, winding beyond.
We hadn't made a move — just kept on driving.

Her Body

The Fingers

They are small enough to find and care for a tiny stone.
        To lift it with wobbly concentration from the ground,
                from the family of stones, up past the pursed mouth —

for this we are thankful — to a place level with her eyes
        to take a close look, a look into the nature of stone.
                Like everything, it is for the first time: first stone,

chilly cube of ice, soft rise of warm flesh, hard
        surface of table leg, first and lasting scent of grass
                rubbed between the tiny pincer fingers. And there is

the smallest finger poking the air, pointing toward the first heat
        of the single sun, pointing toward the friendly angels
                who sent her, letting them know contact's made.

The Eyes

We believe their color makes some kind of difference,
the cast of it played off the color of hair and face.

But it makes no difference, blue or brown,
hazel, green, or gray, pale sky or sand.

When sleep-burdened they'll turn up into her,
close back down upon her sizable will.

But when she's ready for the yet-to-come —
oh, they widen, grow a deep cool sheen

to catch the available light and shine
with the intensity of the newly arrived.

If they find you they'll hold on relentlessly
without guile, the gaze no less than interrogatory,

fixed, immediate, bringing to bear what there's been
to date. Call her name and perhaps they'll turn to you,

or they might be engaged, looking deeply into the nature
of other things — the affect of wall, the texture of rug,

into something very small that's fallen to the floor
and needs to be isolated and controlled. Maybe

an afternoon reflection, an insect moving *slowly*,
maybe just looking with loyalty into the eyes of another.

The Toes

Who went to market?
Who stayed home?
This one goes,
this one doesn't.
This one eats

the flesh
of grass-eating mammals,
this one does not.
In the 17th century
Basho — delicate master

of the vagaries of who
went where —
wrote to one he loved
not of market
and not of meat,

but something brief,
abbreviated,

like five unburdened toes
fluttering like cilia
in the joy of a drafty room,

You go,
I stay.
Two autumns.

The Signature

Who knows how they get here,
beyond the obvious.
Who packaged the code

that provided the slate for her eyes,
and what about the workmanship
that went into the fingers

allowing such intricate movement
just months from the other side? —
Who placed with such exactness

the minute nails on each
of the ten unpainted toes?
And what remains

beyond eye and ear, the thing
most deeply rooted in her body —
the thing that endlessly blossoms

but doesn't age, in time
shows greater vitality? The thing
unlike the body that so quickly

reaches its highest moment only
to begin, with little hesitation,
the long roll back, slowing all the way

until movement is administered
by devices other than those devised
by divine design. The ageless thing

without a name, like air, both resident
and owner of the body's estate.
But this thing, only partially

unpackaged, sings
through the slate that guards it,
contacts those of us waiting here

with a splay of its soft,
scrutinizing fingers.
Her spirit is a sapling thing,

something green, still damp
but resolute, entering this world
with an angel's thumb pressed

to her unformed body at the very last,
a template affixed to her body
when they decided it was time

to let her go, for her to come to us
and their good work was done.
An angel's thumbprint, a signature.

The Eternal Light of Talk

for Bill

That's one way to look at it, I thought,
without naming it, leaving the thing
unnamed, without definition — still,
just beyond, breathing but silently.

Well, he would have thought of it that way
too. A passing on of language, like the gift
of one of his beloved oxymorons, like
famous poet or *living will* or *sure thing*,

or a bottle of his favorite bargain Bordeaux
to accompany one of his famously elaborate meals
compiled of unlikely ingredients —
like his palette of language.

Or late into the evening, to himself,
it might have been a passing *through*
language to the other side, a landscape
no longer requiring hip and knee for transport.

And over there if there's *foie gras* he's found it,
and when he found it he found a way
to import the right chardonnay to keep it company.
I never met a sweetbread I didn't love, he would say

sipping slyly on a rare, woody white isolated
on a sudden mission to the west coast.

He had a life he kept even from himself.
I never heard him utter an interrogative.

Why be surprised by the unknown?
We made it a point to toast the life
we seemed to be leading
wherever we found ourselves.

Who else would so intuitively name a cat Velcro?
Or love Mingus and Donizetti with equal vigor?
The vocabulary for solace is impoverished.
To be sure, his was a living will.

Joy Harjo

The Path to the Milky Way Leads Through Los Angeles

There are strangers above me, below me and all around me and we are all strange in this place of recent invention.
This city named for angels appears naked and stripped of anything resembling
the shaking of turtle shells, the songs of human voices on a summer night outside Okmulgee.
Yet, it's perpetually summer here, and beautiful. The shimmer of gods is easier
to perceive at sunrise or dusk,
when those who remember us here in the illusion of the marketplace
turn toward the changing of the sun and say our names.
We matter to somebody,
We must matter to the strange god who imagines us as we revolve together in
the dark sky on the path to the Milky Way.
We can't easily see that starry road from the perspective of the crossing of boulevards, can't hear it in the whine of civilization or taste the minerals of planets in hamburgers.
But we can buy a map here of the stars' homes, dial a tone for dangerous love,
choose from several brands of water or a hiss of oxygen for gentle rejuvenation.

Most Recent Book: *A Map to the Next World* (W. W. Norton & Company, 2000)

Everyone knows you can't buy love but you can still sell your soul for less
than a song to a stranger who will sell it to someone else for a profit
until you're owned by a company of strangers
in the city of the strange and getting stranger.
I'd rather understand how to sing from a crow
who was never good at singing or much of anything
but finding gold in the trash of humans.
So what are we doing here I ask the crow parading on the ledge of
falling that
hangs over this precarious city?
Crow just laughs and says *wait, wait and see* and I am waiting and
not seeing
anything, not just yet.
But like crow I collect the shine of anything beautiful I can find.

Songs from the House of Death, or How to Make It Through to the End of a Relationship

for Donald Hall

1.

From the house of death there is a rain.
From rain is flood and flowers.
And flowers emerge through the ruins
of those who left behind
stores of corn and dishes,
turquoise and bruises
from the passion
of fierce love.

2.

I run my tongue over the skeleton
jutting from my jaw. I taste
the grit of heartbreak.

3.

The procession of spirits
who walk out of their bodies
is ongoing. Just as the procession
of those who have loved us

will go about their business
of making a new house
with someone else who smells
like the dust of a strange country.

4.

The weight of rain is unbearable to the sky
eventually. Just as desire will
burn a hole through the sky
and fall to earth.

5.

I was surprised by the sweet embrace
of the perfume of desert flowers after the rain
though after all these seasons
I shouldn't be surprised.

6.

All cities will be built and then destroyed.
We built too near the house of the gods of lightning,
too close to the edge of a century.
What could I expect,
my bittersweet.

7.

Even death who is the chief of everything
on this earth (all undertakings, all matters of human
form) will wash his hands, stop to rest under
the cottonwood before taking you from me
on the back of his horse.

8.

Nothing I can sing
will bring you back.
Not the songs of a hundred horses running
until they become wind
Not the personal song of the rain
who makes love to the earth.

9.

I will never forget you. Your nakedness
haunts me in the dawn when I cannot distinguish your

flushed brown skin from the burning horizon, or my hands.
The smell of chaos lingers in the clothes
you left behind. I hold you
there.

This Is My Heart

This is my heart. It is a good heart.
Bones and a membrane of mist and fire.
are the woven cover.
When we make love in the flower world
my heart is close enough to sing
to yours in a language that has no use
for clumsy human words.

My head, is a good head, but it is a hard head
and it whirrs insider with a swarm of worries.
What is the source of this singing, it asks
and if there is a source why can't I see it
right here, right now
as real as these hands hammering
the world together
with nails and sinew?

This is my soul. It is a good soul.
It tells me, "come here forgetful one."
And we sit together with a lilt of small winds
who rattle the scrub oak.
We cook a little something
to eat: a rabbit, some sofkey
then a sip of something sweet
for memory.

This is my song. It is a good song.
It walked forever the border of fire and water
climbed ribs of desire to my lips to sing to you.
Its new wings quiver with
vulnerability.

Come lie next to me, says my heart.
Put your head here.
It is a good thing, says my soul.

The End

(Pol Pot, infamous leader of the Khmer Rouge, responsible for the killing of thousands, died peacefully in his sleep April 1998. His body was burned on a stack of old tires, tended to by a few exhausted soldiers. In the midst of the burning the fist of the corpse saluted.)

The dark was thicker than dark. I was a stranger there. It was a room
of ten thousand strangers, in a city of millions more.

The park across the street was heavy with new leaves
with an unbearable sensual drift.

I had been sleeping for a few hours, and the room was thick with cedar
and root medicine. I wasn't dead though I was traveling

through the dark. The lower gods pounded the pipes for my
attention, the bed swayed with the impact of unseen

energy. No one saw it. No one saw anything
because it was dark and in the middle of the night and it was just

a hotel room, one of millions of hotel rooms all over
the world, filled with strangers looking for refuge,

sleep, for sex or love. We were a blur of distinctions,
made a fragrance like a glut of flowers or piss on concrete.

Every detail mattered
utterly, especially in the dark, when I began traveling.

And I was alone though the myth of the lonely stranger is a lie
by those who think they own everything, even the earth

and the entrails and breath of the earth. This was the end.
It was Cambodia or some place like it, and the sun

was coming up, barely over the green in the restless shiver of
a million singing birds. Humans were wrapping

a body for burial. It stank of formaldehyde. It was a failed clay
thing, disheveled and ordinary. They rolled it

into a box and dragged it to a stack of trash. Why have I come here
I asked the dark, whose voice is the roar of history as it travels

with the thoughts of humans who have made the monster.
The fire was lit

fed with a wicker chair, a walking cane and several busted
tires to make it hot. What I had

feared in the dark was betrayal, so I found myself there
in the power of wreckage. There was no pause

in the fighting. The killer's charred fist pointed toward the sky,
gave an order though no one heard it

for the crackle and groan of grease. The fire was dark
in its brightness and could be seen by anyone

on the journey, the black smoke a dragon in the sky.
This was not the end.

I was attracted by a city, by a park heavy with new leaves,
by a particular flower burning in the dark.

I was not a stranger there.

Jeffrey Harrison

Our Other Sister

The cruelest thing I did to my younger sister
wasn't shooting a homemade blowdart into her knee,
where it dangled for a breathless second

before dropping off, but telling her we had
another, older sister who'd gone away.
What my motives were I can't recall: a whim,

or was it some need of mine to toy with loss,
to probe the ache of imaginary wounds?
But that first sentence was like a strand of DNA

that replicated itself in coiling lies
when my sister began asking her desperate questions.
I called our older sister Isabel

and gave her hazel eyes and long blonde hair.
I had her run away to California
where she took drugs and made hippie jewelry.

Most Recent Book: *Signs of Arrival* (Copper Beach Press, 1996)

Before I knew it, she'd moved to Santa Fe
and opened a shop. She sent a postcard
every year or so, but she'd stopped calling.

I can still see my younger sister staring at me,
her eyes widening with desolation
then filling with tears. I can still remember

how thrilled and horrified I was
that something I'd just made up
had that kind of power, and I can still feel

the blowdart of remorse stabbing me in the heart
as I rushed to tell her none of it was true.
But it was too late. Our other sister

had already taken shape, and we could not
call her back from her life far away
or tell her how badly we missed her.

Sex and Poetry

(After a friend asked me why
I didn't write more poems about sex)

For one thing, it's hard to get away with,
caught as we are red-handed in the Chamber
of Mimesis, one of those kinky rooms
with mirrors all over the walls and ceiling
where we hope to satisfy our unspeakable needs
but get instead an abyss of dwindling reflections.
Also, it's less like being in bed with a lover
than standing alone in front of a copy machine
xeroxing her panties and bra. Snaps and garters
give way to the block and tackle of narrative,
which no amount of fumbling will undo.
Now tell me, does that sound like fun to you?

Sometimes, however, while we are looking
elsewhere, the green-gold dust of pollen falls
and begins to settle over everything
like an idea that takes over without our knowing
and adds a glow to whatever we see,
and we find ourselves in the middle of a sentence,

we want to keep going, clause after clause,
as if the sinuosities of syntax were
the suave unfolding of limbs and skin
and language a seduction to which we love
to succumb, feeling the words take shape in our mouths
and tasting them on someone else's tongue.

Rowing

How many years have we been doing this together,
me in the bow rowing, you in the stern
lying back, dragging your hands in the water —
or, as now, the other way around, your body
moving toward me and away, your dark hair swinging
forward and back, your face flushed and lovely
against the green hills, the blues of lake and sky.

Soon nothing else matters but this pleasure,
your green eyes looking past me, far away,
then at me, then away, your lips I want to kiss
each time they come near me, your arms that reach
toward me gripping the handles as the blades
swing back dripping, two arcs of droplets
pearling on the surface before disappearing.

Sometimes I think we could do this forever,
like part of the vow we share, the rhythm
we find, the pull of each stroke on the muscles
of your arched back, your neck gorged and pulsing
with the work of it, your body rocking
more rapidly now, your face straining with something
like pain you can hardly stand — then letting go,

the two of us gliding out over the water.

A Shave by the Ganges

Sleepwalking from one ghat to the next,
I came to the place where the barbers
all hunkered down, their bony knees akimbo,
dhotis bunched around their loins like diapers,

the tools of their trade laid out on burlap mats:
straight razors, scissors, combs, battered brass bowls.

Not once in my life had I been shaved by a barber,
but I sat down then to wait my turn.
I'd come this far, I'd just seen a foot
twisting up like a flag from a cremation,
I wanted to be shaved in that holy city
as if I were part of a daily ritual.

So I was happy to pay my two rupees
and surrender my face to those dark skilled hands
that slapped the foam on with a shaving brush
and worked the razor quickly across my cheek.
Sitting there as he turned my head this way
and that, I saw the crowds of bathers

in the river below, the temple stupas
looming overhead, as if about to fall,
a skeletal umbrella, a legless beggar
lolling on a dolly — all at angles odd enough
to make me see them finally, and feel
the rusty razor's edge against my throat.

My Double Non-Conversion

NYC, 1976

I must have been looking up at the stars
on the vaulted ceiling, that simulacrum of heaven,
as the muffled bustle of arrivals and departures
washed over me like surf. I must have looked
so young and unstreetwise in my wonder,
standing like that in Grand Central's concourse,
a perfect target for the skinhead in saffron robe
who greeted me and pushed into my hands
a garish edition of the *Bhagavad-gita*.
And I must have been a very different person
from the one I later became, to stay
and talk with him, and even buy the book.

I'm trying to remember what it felt like
to be that person, a novitiate to the city
open to any approach. Less than a minute

after leaving the Hare Krishna, still inside
the basilical concourse, I allowed myself
to be waylaid by a young man with a Bible,
listened to the passages he quoted,
then (this is the part I can hardly believe)
knelt down with him in a bank of phone booths
and prayed, delirious with self-consciousness
as if God Himself were watching. Afterwards,
he said a seed had been planted inside me.

That copy of the *Bhagavad-gita* has slipped
into the gulf of twenty years between then and now,
and that seed has gone untended just as long.
When I left the Born-Again, I took the subway
uptown to Columbia, where I was a freshman,
then the dingy elevator up to my monk-like cell:
one bed, one desk, one chair, one dresser, one window
facing a roofscape to the south, and open sky.
Also, a fern I'd bought my first day there
in front of St. John the Divine, from an old woman
who told me, with a look of crazed belief,
that someday it would grow into a tree.

Swifts at Evening

The whoosh of rush hour traffic washes through my head
as I cross the bridge through the treetops into my neighborhood
and what's left of my thoughts is sucked up suddenly
by a huge whirlwind of birds, thousands of chimney swifts
wheeling crazily overhead against a sky just beginning
to deepen into evening — turning round and round
in their erratic spiral ragged at the edges
where more chittering birds join in the circling
flock from every direction, having spent all
day on the wing scattered for miles across
September skies and now pulled into the
great vortex that funnels into the air-
shaft of the library, the whole day
going like water down a drain with
the sucking sound of traffic and
the birds swirling like specks
of living sediment drawn from
the world into the whirlpool
into the word-pool flapping
like bats at the last
moment diving and
turning into
words.

Bob Hicock

The Party

Bugs are chewed by the blue light into something
like the excrement of ghosts. We are still
drinking at forty for the same reasons as 21
only our shirts are better, our hands
are less inclined to destroy the elegant
shrubbery, now we own
the elegant shrubbery and suckle it
on Saturdays before the ascent

Most Recent Book: *Animal Soul* (Invisible Cities Press, 2001)

of white balls dimpled for aero-dynamic
zest. Finally there's no shame
in drinking domestic wine, it's a matter
of degree, of vintner and how much,
the ratio between pattée and chardonnay
sip and chug, and do your gestures
become menacing like a windmill
or trenchant like the chop-chop of Julia
Child? At 21 a car was necessary
for the mobility of its loneliness
and the basic philosophy of speed, zoom
goes the head, zoom the body and why not
peppermint Schnapps, why not blotter
together with the shattered stars,
and when hips were involved, when
two mouths whispered along the pinker
joints of flesh, the river drummed
its broken fingers, the shards of glass
cultivated by gravel stared at the moon
with the moon's own eyes. At 40
a well-moored veranda's better backdrop
for rapture, maybe three drinks, maybe
by the fifth someone will remember
the rudiments of dancing, another
will begin to eat her napkin, just
nibbling as she talks of the chalks
she put away, the notebooks
she used to fill with bodies that looked
like anemones praised by an up-draft
of wind. Bugs perish until someone
throws a hamburger at the light
and the light goes nova and thereafter
mosquitos find the booming veins
wherein the sustaining music flows.
What we see of each other in the dark
is what fish at the core of the ocean
make a pact with, so much movement,
the gestures of creatures
slowly abraded by the fluid
that gives them life. This is when
someone begins a song we all know
but can't fully remember, when new verses
are invented that bear the shape

of the original but move lurch-stop
like crutches, like tumbleweeds
taking an inventory of the bruised land.

Miscarriage and Echo

He or she let go of my wife and me.
The doctor said *it*, stressing objectivity.
Blood on denim looks like water at first.
Water interprets wind subjectively.

The child returned their face to the wind.
If I repeat myself I should say something new.
The doctor's smile was a weak cup of tea.
Blood on tile's a form of clarity.

When I say something new I repeat myself.
A child would repeat and erase ourselves.
We had a list of names, column girl, column boy.
We waited for the face to decide itself.

She stood in the door with blood on her jeans.
I was reading a book I won't read again.
My wife thinks her genes let go of the child.
The doctor said no, stressing his certainty.

The nurse almost tiptoed around the room.
Wind takes a broom to water, repeating its name.
My wife and I slept awake in different rooms.
We each let go and have never explained.

It's hard to prove by flesh you give no blame.
Blood unlike water never truly goes away.
Each name carried a different clarity.
We repeat to each other *it's impossible to explain*.

The doctor hoped we would try again.
When we touch she moves like water under wind.
In her flesh I hear the names repeat themselves.
Blood on her hands will never be new.

It's impossible to stop wanting to repeat ourselves.
We slept in different rooms with our shame.
It's impossible to bury names under wind.
Blood disappears into water without blame.

Birth of a Saint

If there's a gun in her theory of Heaven it's unloaded,
pearl-handled, graced with the feel of flesh
extending from hand to steel, the confidence
of her palm radiating to the man
behind the counter and converting sullen
to smile, making him wet, making him stammer that she
can have anything she wants, bounty of Slim Jims
& Newports, all the cocks in all the Playgirls
and enough money to make her car zoom
across the whisper of Kansas and Nebraska.
Even as she flees, her Impala moving from 80 to 100
to 127 at full stride, the gun's weight, the drop-forged
mass would hold her down, keep her moving
through mists of Del Shannon and Nirvanna,
she could think back to the Twelve
Interlocking Lectures on Heaven, could remember
the SUNY professor speaking to the bulb
of the microphone as he said *Heaven is not a place*
but the refusal of place, not a wish
but the ability to confuse all wishes. This
would allow her to close her eyes and will
away the State Troopers' triangulation, evade
the appetite of law-enforcement technology. This
would compel her to meditate a second body,
a third self, to drive to the desert, to count
the broken grains of sand and kiss every scorpion
full on the lips they don't have. This is what
dopamine and the synaptic cleft and too much
Scoobie Doo made of her thoughts in the few
seconds after she asked for a pack
of Beemans and was basically ignored
basically spit at by the clerk if we can spit
with our eyes didn't Ollie North
sit in the senate sending fuck-you
vibes laced with dribble out to our little
screens. And that she says nothing but thank you
when he finally moves his hands in the pattern
we call making change: that she doesn't
kick the Hostess display or cop a few dozen
Bazooka Joes: that even her dreams of revenge
have her holding an unloaded gun:

have her thinking please be kind please
let there be dignity in the small moments
grace in the graceless acts let me live
through this day not wanting to hate
not wanting to kill: that she wonders
driving away in her cloud of a car
if she didn't do something wrong if there isn't
something cataclysmic in her face something
offensive in the architecture of her nose
makes her a saint a stupid saint a saint
who'll get no holiday no entry in the Emerald
Book of Saints so you and I must agree
on a name that she'll be known
as the Stop-n-Go Saint the Burger King
Saint that as we wait in line we'll grind
our teeth in prayer tap our feet in homage
that when we lean in and grab
a fist of shirt a fist of hair and scream
give me the goddamn burger now we'll say
please we'll chant thank you we'll pick up
our condiments and slip them neatly
into the trash.

Neither Here nor There

Again with the gunfire, vague pops that suggest
we live in a bowl of Rice Krispies. The earth

moves at 18 miles per second and the sound
clings, the sound travels as if menace were clawed.

Here it is at my door, knocking, being upstaged
by the more evolved gunfire on TV. Kids ask

Why don't we slip off, not knowing we do. Kids
ask older kids how to release the safety, reload,

when to shoot. Always is one common answer.
The gunfire's there, I am here. Here and there

are words I've forgotten in German, I even knew
for an afternoon how to say to a small boy

in French, *I am a teapot, short and stout, here
is my handle, there is my spout*. That small boy

laughed, which is the service French provides
when administered by an American tongue. Pluto

moves at 3 miles per second though without
benefit of gunfire. Maybe everyone's shooting

at Pluto because it blocks our view of eternity.
Maybe a hole in a body is the equivalent

of a conference on Derrida, a way of exchanging
information, a way of breaking everything down

into bitesize, into blood-soaked bits. Here
becomes more there all the time. For instance

the growth of bars on windows like crystals
in a beaker after a catalyst is introduced.

Catalyst fear. Catalyst the bleeding of money
to and fro. Here green trees make a tent,

the density of the earth is 344 pounds per cubic
foot, lawnmowers debate each other on Saturdays

and guns are pets. Everything's the same
there except leisure is hunger

and hunger the artifact of an unflinching
weather. Slowly the dead kids there

matriculate into the dead kids here. This
is progress if you consider that graves

are no longer dug by hand or caskets lowered
by wailing relatives, instead motors are used,

instead a back-hoe grumbles through a few
ravenous bites. Then a chunk of stone's

thrown down that was cut from the zooming earth,
the heavy earth, then someone chisels

Here Lies and we go home and listen to the sky
chatter like the rivets are popping out.

Richard Higgerson

The Strong Yet Hollow Life Force of Hot Tub Jesus

Put a small, hairless dog in the microwave,
shake and bake the neighbor's Persian cat,
pour a tall measure of the water of life, no ice,
and prepare thirteen seats at the last long table –
we're going to celebrate the teachings and life
of Hot Tub Jesus. Lord, his Holy Father knows,

that boy knows how to fratboy party, even all-knows
how to eat bugs whole, testified over FCC airwaves
about big bugs, big as bird bugs, like roaches, half-life
two-thousand year bugs. Man, this wispbearded hepcat
could really blow. Seen him sit with snake handlers at the table
they're still calling his altar, palming aces, cool as ice:

even while camping out in the desert he shit ice
cream, swear to God – chained silver spoon up his nose –
40 days and nights living in temptation. He tabled
a motion to abolish the Ten Commandments, waved
a hand, commanded silence & shimmied down the cat
walk. He pissed morning into a babyfoodjar, lived

the fantasy, drank deep from his own purged liver
like all other holy men. Irreverent? Check the icy
stare he throws me when I sin. Hell Yeah! He goes cat-
atonic. I think that cross-biz was a-cut-off-his-nose-
to-spite-his-face and I bathed his pierced feet in waves
at the river after he puked in his shoes under the table –

too much damn holy wine in his blood – sprayed a tableau
vivant over K Street's graffiti, memento mori of his life,
and signed the dead one's tag in red and black on a wave
of cold concrete. Three A.M., stumbled home drunk, up an icy-
hill from Georgetown, climbed four flights then nose-
dived to tile, filled up the hot tub, turned on the jets – let the cat-

abolism commence! He rumbled like a hog, purred like a fat cat
bathing in milk, crazy about living on this earth, the table
hopping in exotic cities, generating a buzz like he never knew.

Most Recent Book: *Poets of the New Century* (David R. Godine, 2001)

Second Coming? Come again? Come and gone in the departure lounge of life
after death, flight delayed by bad weather. We got him on ice
quick as we could the night he drowned but he never waved

goodbye. We were ice, didn't even call the police. Can you imagine giving the four-11
on the Son of God, are you crazy? His life was our table money, we knew he'd be back –
supercat has nine lives and I don't need that light shining in my fucked-up face.

Evel Knievel; The Fountain at Caesar's Palace, (151 feet, 6 inches) Las Vegas, Nevada, September 4, 1968

1.

The TV audience smoked
& prayed a silent patriotic pledge
of allegiance to a burning patch
Of rubber left on the ramp. Even

in China Nixon never wore a cape
& after Zapruder's Kennedy
assassination footage, everything
seemed like the thinnest edge

of the impossible, like the liminal
verge, like the amped-up tingle
of broken promise. But Evel hung
his heroic parabola up there for us,

for that dreambirth all our flying
desires portend. The grainy photo
has him soaring over spread feathers
of winged victory, pondering

the hard kiss just an inch off course,
an instant before the careening bike
upends. Thirty years later his oft-snapped
wrists now bandaged in ticking

gold, each hash the second hand
passes marks a minute of hang time
remembered, his tresses crowned
with the braided brim of nylon laurel,

the embroidery reads *STP,* a brand so old
it's become a geared cipher, a legend,
a dragon's black blood. But I say
that for every time Knievel pounded

his knobby body back into this world
he took a shot at rebirth & who
among us would not, to see him fly,
have given blood for the spectacle?

2.

Watch closely & you can see
the blood fly as he rolls, a splayed
ragdoll pinwheeling the pavement
towards unconsciousness — (thirty-five

broken bones) — (twenty-nine days
in coma) — rewarded with five hours
of darkness for every foot of flight.
He gave blood to cover the house line,

a fraction of five to one against
the invisible hand of the wind
as he approached the jump, the limit
check, the impossibility of coercing

pieces of flinted bike out of flesh, massaging
gouged asphalt from his back and legs,
gravel, clumped gravel, dirty constellations
in his palms. We all secretly hoped

for the crash. He can still ride the fat-
piped custom-chrome hogs & I've seen
him swing a crooked thighbone over
the tooled black saddle, pocket stuffed

with six million cold cash earned
launching a skycycle halfway across
an obscure canyon, the Daredevil King
who claimed he'd crossed an eternity

only to be blown back by something
unseen, defeated but clutching
the starred helmet of his crown,
still soaring on promise.

After the promised interview
I walk with Evel, out from under
the cool canopy of his air-conditioned
Winnebago, out into the heat of Utah's

black sun, our beers abandoned, beading
pools of sweat on the galley's custom
Formica banquet. I walk out with Evel
across historic miles of etched speed,

across the furrowed tracks of records
left by the reinvention of the wheel,
across the memories of gold cups
melted down for cash, for oil. I float

in the rising heat, cast a long shadow
across his back as he drops to kneel
in the salt of Bonneville's crumbling
temple, running his hands over the veined

porphyry, over the gems and fossilized
shells, the burnt grain of the oven floor,
his blue eyes searching, flashing silver
the way he might scan the gut-felt physics

of the imagined trajectory of a jump
over fourteen Greyhounds before
praying over the powdery coat of flight
rising from a brittle desert moth's wings.

Blanket on Grass

I don't need to say that there was fruit
or that everyday she paints herself on me.

I've seen the way ivy grows
on just the sun and air and this is not that.

Half-hidden in tall grasses, we hovered over the warm dirt
of the construction site, the freshly poured foundation, our new home
rising

like a promise.
This is it.

And I know it's right from the wind
between our bare legs, the tree bowered with fruit,

the figs and tender leaves hung to touch.
And it was as if part of her was raining and nothing to hold us but the
distant trees,

the unexacting sky flying out to us,
the sun heaving light in spears around us

in this perfection, the script of the clouds,
outlines of the wind's brief fluid travel,

vapor, sparks, rust, rock on rock, glyphs and handprints
in the flattened grass. And I remember as a child running

my hand around the pitted mouth of an ancient cannon again
and again, the limestone ramparts and a light from the sea.

This is not that.

This is three plucked notes, their cycling reverberation, and the taut curve
of kite string to the middle of her, soaring naked above, me flying in
her flesh.

And this is a bliss that doesn't mock us our capacity.
a few stray lines of verse written on paper

napkins we use to clean ourselves with after,
smearing fresh black ink and sticky

and worth the sacrifice.
No baby

yet between us, when we had become
unstoppable, the celebration of glistening emptiness,

the hollow world waiting to be filled.
This is the one hole in the earth we celebrated.

This is exactly it.
This is the way she held the world

in her mouth, cool and smooth
like a single small pebble plucked from the tongue

of the brook, her thigh sweet
with spilled wine, the sun all over us

and something dark
rolling in the valley.

Lullaby Rub

When I watch my wife kneel nightly
by the tub the capitoline of bones

in her spine pressing flesh up
in a chain of small hills left

unconquered and see the spidered,
branching blue highway of veins

run in her back, a sight withheld
from her forever, I imagine the tight

and tortured route these two
children must have swum. I've

bumrushed that narrow hall. I've already heard
the echo of a million cells pinging

in the dark. What does it do to me
to tell you that the secret of this love

affair might be our mutual fear or
that I've seen the first room of their growth

laid out haphazard, like something
beautiful I swore was her heart carved out

of her beating on her knifed
and gory stomach while she lay under gas,

the sweat on my lip beading like a gift
of pearls come unstrung? I embraced

swooning amazement. I heard
myself saying *This is a galaxy* then all the air

left me. They'd made a small room
at sheets around her middle. The nurse whispered

she would catch me. The surgical specialist — who
the night before had stitched a ditch-rolled

stray dog on my aunt's
kitchen table — gleamed a smile

and stuck her hand inside my wife to make
room for the room that had held our sleeping

wet child she'd just removed. It has happened
twice this way. Kind strangers patted our children

dry. So this nightly ritual of the bath,
the suds likes halos ringing them, I love. I don't

question why water beads the way it beads
and prisms itself in the mirrored light into more

colors than there are words for. We
collect it. We make a city of it. We stake

our lives on it running clear. So when
I die children, I promise to fly out of all this

water and to walk back across
the air to you. But for now I promise to watch you

come clean from the tub, breaking the tense
surface water, this reborn amnion, amazed

at the commotion of small lights
in your eyes before I ferry you away

like ancient philosophers in terry cloth togas
headed for the fluid republic of dreams.

BRENDA HILLMAN

FROM *Thicket Group*

. . . a burning liquid that was called the original force of Nature.
— anonymous tenth-century alchemist

A Power

For some reason it's likely to think of the insides of a thicket
as a five-pointed liquid star.

Most Recent Book: *Loose Sugar* (Wesleyan University Press, 1997)

A group of us, not knowing how to stand in nature, in the
sixties; each breath sponsored by that.

Possible friends nearby smelled like hemp, white tortillas
and twelve-oz. Coca-Colas; the fire in their fingers
talked back, had feelings.

Locating consciousness, where would you say it is;
"it was the happiest moment in the first twenty years."

And, why do we seek to destroy it by changing?

mottled doves
garnets

Empty Spires

Magic fought with the ideal, time
curved the barren glow, and animals called from their
nests at the center of the world.

I had been a child being guessed at by onyx, fresh
from nothing. Dimension's pawn.

My brother okayed the ground with sticks; when
something called, we answered it. With a drop or two
more of that inherited chemical we would have been
a schizophrenic.

Empty spines of sticks filled up with liquid fire; they had done this
before, we just hadn't been quiet enough to mention it.

Making theories of creation is about repetition, though even
the infinite happens just once.

XX sticks
cross-referencing
each other

A Window

Had intended to climb out a window, but intended is not
what makes it happen. Delicious to climb out a window.
The weather was not the window's fault.

Smears on chrome fenders like pet clouds between which
they might see a body coming curved to them. Before
the thicket your mouth stopped off at a boy.

Going back a little: nearing them was faster; that which
owned the thicket also owned the flower.

Either tell the story or don't. Narrative is such an either/or
situation, like a window, just as sex is a metaphor for
not getting it.

You have changed the assignment to Swirl: voice from
a thicket; surfaces meet where you live into things.
A body is a place missed specifically. They met you
in your body, where you couldn't go alone.

The spell:
unable
unable
unable
pretty soon

The Thicket

A power came up; it was in between the voices.
It said you could stop making sense.

Have you seen it? Of course you have. Based on
what? A red bird that caught fire on the alchemist's
table.

The girls stood around in long paisley dresses, coyote cries
coming through them, something frightened and
being canceled. We weren't on drugs then.
The thicket looked like a star of pub(l)ic hair.

You always wane to control how everything will turn out,
is the problem.

Suburban kids — on the edge of change — give up hope of being
understood. Why did the fire need to rest in us after
that fluttery little absolute terror of childhood.

(wands being
on fire)

Edward Hirsch

Ethics of Twilight

As it leaves dawn behind and advances into day, light prostitutes itself and is redeemed — ethics of twilight — at the moment it vanishes.
— E. M. Cioran

Ethics of secrets and vanishings,
of sunny downfalls and cloudy cover-ups.

The reign of commonsense has ended
and strangeness floats through the air.

Deceptive moonlight, dusky erasures —
night welcomes us with open blue arms

to its plots and betrayals, desires
wafting like music through our bodies.

We go forth to our furtive daydreams —
our unaccountable, inadmissible motives —

and come home to lie down again
alone or together, drifting obliviously

into the vacant coffins of sleep.
Ethics of nightmares and dawn advancing. . .

Colette

My mother used to say, "Sit down, dear,
and don't cry. The worst thing for a woman
is her first man — the one who kills you.
After that, marriage becomes a long career."
Poor Sido! She never had another career
and she knew firsthand how love ruins you.
The seducer doesn't care about his woman,
even as he whispers endearments in her ear.

Never let anyone destroy your inner spirit.
Among all the forms of truly absurd courage

Most Recent Book: *For the Sleepwalkers* (Carnegie Mellon University Press, 1998)

the recklessness of young girls is outstanding.
Otherwise there would be far fewer marriages
and even fewer affairs that overwhelm marriages.
Look at me: it's amazing I'm still standing
after what I went through with ridiculous courage.
I was made to suffer, but no one broke my spirit.

Every woman wants her adventure to be a feast
of ripening cherries and peaches, Marseilles figs,
hot-house grapes, champagne shuddering in crystal.
Happiness, we believe, is on sumptuous display.
But unhappiness writes a different kind of play.
The gypsy gazes down into a clear blue crystal
and sees rotten cherries and withered figs.
Trust me: loneliness, too, can be a feast.

Ardor is delicious, but keep your own room.
One of my husbands said: is it impossible
for you to write a book that isn't about love,
adultery, semi-incestuous relations, separation?
(Of course, this was before our own separation.)
He never understood the natural law of love,
the arc from the possible to the impossible...
I have extolled the tragedy of the bedroom.

We need exact descriptions of the first passion,
so pay attention to whatever happens to you.
Observe everything: love is greedy and forgetful.
By all means fling yourself wildly into life
(though sometimes you will be flung back by life)
but don't let experience make you forgetful
and be surprised by everything that happens to you.
We are creative creatures fueled by passion.

One final thought about the nature of love.
Freedom should be the first condition of love
and work is liberating (*a novel about love
cannot be written while you are making love*).
Never underestimate the mysteries of love,
the eminent dignity of not talking about love.
Passionate attention is prayer, prayer is love.
Savor the world. Consume the feast with love.

Days of 1968

She came to me with a mind like fire
and a name written in smoky letters on the wind.

She came to me with the grief of a fallen angel,
with white arms that should have been wings

and skinny legs sadly rooted to the ground.
She came to me barefoot in a sleeveless dress,

playing air guitar and talking about the gods
who said she never should have been saddled

with a body in the first place, with a human
past and a disembodied voice flickering

like a small candle in the endless dark.
"I believe in being reincarnated," she declared –

my pure psyche, my haunted half-girl turning
back into the spirit she wanted to become.

Ocean of Grass

The ground was holy, but the wind was harsh
and unbroken prairie stretched for hundreds of miles
so that all she could see was an ocean of grass.

Some days she got so lonely she went outside
and nestled among the sheep, for company.
The ground was holy, but the wind was harsh

and prairie fires swept across the plains,
lighting up the country like a vast tinderbox
until all she could see was an ocean of flames.

She went three years without viewing a tree.
When her husband finally took her on a timber run
she called the ground holy and the wind harsh

and got down on her knees and wept inconsolably,
and lived in a sod hut for thirty more years
until the world dissolved in an ocean of grass.

Think of her sometimes when you pace the earth,
our mother, where she was laid to rest.
The ground was holy, but the wind was harsh
for those who drowned in an ocean of grass.

Tony Hoagland

Windchime

She goes out to hang the windchime
in her nightie and her workboots.
It's six-thirty in the morning
and she's standing on the plastic ice chest
tiptoe to reach the crossbeam of the porch,

windchime in her left hand,
hammer in her right, the nail
gripped tight between her teeth
but nothing happens next because
she's trying to figure out
how to switch #1 with #3.

She must have been standing in the kitchen,
coffee in her hand, asleep,
when she heard it — the wind blowing
through the sound the windchime
wasn't making
because it wasn't there.

No one including me especially anymore believes
till death do us part,
but I can see what I would miss in leaving —
the way her ankles go into the workboots
as she stands upon the ice chest;
the problem scrunched into her forehead;
the little kissable mouth
with the nail in it.

Lawrence

On two occasions in the past twelve months
I have failed, when someone at a party
spoke of him with a dismissive scorn,
to stand up for D. H. Lawrence,

a man who burned like an acetylene torch
from one end to the other of his life.

Most Recent Book: *Donkey Gospel* (Graywolf Press, 1998)

These individuals, whose relationship to literature
is approximately that of a tree shredder

to stands of old-growth forest,
these people leaned back in their chairs,
bellies full of dry white wine and the ova of some foreign fish,
and casually dropped his name

the way that pygmies with their little poison spears
strut around the carcass of a fallen elephant.
"O Elephant," they say,
"you are not so big and brave today!"

It's a bad day when people speak of their superiors
with a contempt they haven't earned,
and it's a sorry thing when certain other people

don't defend the great dead ones
who have opened up the world before them.
And though, in the catalogue of my betrayals,
this is a fairly minor entry,

I resolve, if the occasion should recur,
to uncheck my tongue and say, "I love the spectacle
of maggots condescending to a corpse,"
or, "You should be so lucky in your brainy, bloodless life

as to deserve to lift
just one of D. H. Lawrence's urine samples
to your arid psychobiographic
theory-tainted lips."

Or maybe I'll just take the shortcut
between the spirit and the flesh,
and punch someone in the face,
because human beings haven't come that far

in their effort to subdue the body,
and we still walk around like zombies
in our dying, burning world,
able to do little more

than fight, and fuck, and crow:
something Lawrence wrote about
in such a manner
as to make us seem magnificent.

Benevolence

When my father dies and comes back as a dog,
I already know what his favorite sound will be:
the soft, almost inaudible gasp
as the rubber lips of the refrigerator door
unstick, followed by that arctic

exhalation of cold air;
then the cracking of the ice-cube tray above the sink
and the quiet *ching* the cubes make
when dropped into a glass.

Unable to pronounce the name of his favorite drink, or to express
his preference for single malt,
he will utter one sharp bark
and point the wet black arrow of his nose
imperatively up
at the bottle on the shelf,

then seat himself before me,
trembling, expectant, water pouring
down the long pink dangle of his tongue
as the memory of pleasure from his former life
shakes him like a tail.

What I'll remember as I tower over him,
holding a dripping, whiskey-flavored cube
above his open mouth,
relishing the power rushing through my veins
the way it rushed through his,

what I'll remember as I stand there
is the hundred clever tricks
I taught myself to please him,
and for how long I mistakenly believed
that it was love he held concealed in his closed hand.

How It Adds Up

There was the day we swam in a river, a lake, and an ocean.
And the day I quit the job my father got me,
and the day I stood outside a door and listened

to my girlfriend making love to someone obviously
not me, inside, and I felt strange because I didn't care.
There was the morning I was born, and the year

I was a loser, and the night I was the winner of the prize
for which the audience applauded. Then there
was someone else I met, whose face and voice

I can't forget, and the memory of her is like a jail
I'm trapped inside, or maybe she is something
I just use to hold my real life at a distance.

    Happiness, Joe says, is a wild red flower
plucked from a river of lava and held aloft
on a tightrope strung between two scrawny trees
above a canyon in a manic-depressive windstorm.

Don't drop it, don't drop it, don't drop it,

and when you do, you will keep looking for it
everywhere, for years, while
right behind you, the footprints you are leaving

will look like notes of a crazy song.

Jonathan Holden

Teaching My Son to Drive

The Wareham Cemetery seems the safest place,
a miniature town of children's blocks,
a place so harmless
the baby rabbit squatting in the drive
doesn't know enough
to move. We're alone.
The only policemen on duty are trees
holding over us the shelter of their quiet.
I climb out. My son
sets our phone book on my seat,
gets in my place, sits down, releases
the brake, shifts into first, lets out

Most Recent Book: *Knowing: New and Selected Poems*
(University of Arkansas Press, 2000)

the clutch. The car jerks and stammers,
fighting off a stroke, totters forward,
and we're creaking like a toy train up its track
in this toy world, we're a joke.
Slow is comic when it's slow enough.
We crawl around the loop
past the little buildings without doors,
my son peering over the wheel,
his face grim,
determined not to stall, pretending
to steer the enormous thing
that's steering him.

Integrals

Erect, arched in disdain,
the integrals drift from left
across white windless pages
to the right,
serene as swans.
Tall,
beautiful seen from afar
on the wavering water, each
curves with the balanced severity
of a fine tool weighed in the palm.

Gaining energy now, they
break into a canter — stallions
bobbing the great crests of their manes.
No one suspects their power
who has not seen them rampage.
Like bulldozers, they build
by adding
dirt to dirt to stumps added
to boulders to broken glass added
to live trees by the roots added
to hillsides, to whole
housing developments
that roll, foaming before them,
the tumbling end of a broken wave
in one mangled sum: dandelions, old
beer-cans and broken

windows — gravestones all
rolled into one.

Yes, with the use of tables
integration is as easy as that:
the mere squeeze of a trigger, no
second thought. The swans
cannot feel the pain
it happens so fast.

The Third Party

Her mind
was so much more than she —
it was a third party.
Like some large instrument
at the love-bed,
it made an exotic guest: able
to decide on its own
whether or not to participate.

Hurt people bear with them
a slightly puzzled look,
a scar between the eyes
where their grief is lodged,
a lead plummet.
I'd seen her, a scientist, delve
into a differential
equation like a boy rudely
unlocking an orange by
forcing the seams from the lobes
to spring it open.
But as she analyzed her rotten marriage
she was plain stupid.

There is no one, I think,
whose private life isn't more
or less unlovely than daily weather.
It's the country where our friends
all speak the same tongue.
Whatever you do,
every angle of the bones,
has been tried before.

and the speech of grief,
a dead end in itself,
so satisfying, so useless,
is the same tautology, the last
cliché, the one area of expertise
in which, sooner or later,
we get as good as anybody.

As she talked, her hand on mine,
heavy, opaque, and sad,
her heartbeat a mute syllable
typed out in code,
her beautiful mind — so
much better than she — could no more
save her than the pure
scaffolding of chamber music
as it goes up
can save the four, short
scholarly men huddled under it,
a quartet of carpenters
with too much on their hands,
measuring, filing, conferring
like mad to assemble
another section of an intelligence
almost too plausible.

Like a calculated smile, it,
too, might break
a man's heart or save
his life,
but is, indeed, heartless,
better than we are,
hardly any help at all.

Such Beauty

It has long been known
that the ideal mortar positions
are pine groves and dappled sunlight,
ski-slopes rated "Expert" —
the prettiest places in the world
above the quaintest towns.

How can we talk of such beauty
as the landscape above Sarajevo
without lapsing into easy
semi-automatic irony.
A bored American boy
with my family's woods to hide in,
I owned the largest collection
of cap guns on Pleasantville Road.
Like a flinty-eyed U. S. Marshall,
my idol, Randolph Scott,
I would routinely evaluate
every quarry or cluster of boulders
as a potential position
from which to ambush a posse.
Most grown-up American boys
know how the Bosnian Serbs
must delight in their hilltop positions
like spectators with the choicest seats.
They have the best view of the action –
puffs blossoming, sprouting tendrils
of phosphorus, frosty pistils
in the village below.
As I watch on TV, in technicolor
the soldiers busying themselves
like boy scouts earning merit badges,
like squirrels in films by Walt Disney,
I remember my friend Irma
recalling her experiences
in the French Resistance:
plots, bombs, disguises,
tales more fascinating than the movies.
It's not for beauty that we do it.
Just as one's hand may return
compulsively to a bruise
again pawing at its pain,
I think that we humans
find pain interesting, that's all,
and warfare by far the most
interesting activity
that we have ever devised.

David Huddle

Model Father

Now when I say my father
— meaning his smell of carbide
and cigarettes, his curtain
of opened and held-up
newspaper, the red dents
at either side of the bridge
of his nose, the parchment skin
on the backs of his hands,
and his thick thumb that to me
meant he was a grown man
and that has in recent years
attached itself to my hand —

I'm really saying my father isn't
in my life any more, except
in just this way — when I choose
words to assemble him,
as when he and I sometimes chose
to spend a Saturday afternoon
at a newspaper-covered card table
gluing together small pieces
of balsa, keeping quiet
company without much regard
for whether or not what
we made would fly.

Ooly Pop a Cow

for Bess and Molly

My brother Charles
brought home the news
the kids were saying
take a flying leap
and eat me raw
and be bop a lula.

Most Recent Book: *Summer Lake: New and Selected Poems*
(Louisiana State University Press, 1999)

Forty miles he rode
the bus there and back.
The dog and I met him
at the door, panting
for hoke poke, hoke
de waddy waddy hoke poke.

In Cu Chi, Vietnam,
I heard tapes somebody's
sister sent of wild thing,
I think I love you
and hey now, what's that
sound, everybody look what's. . .

Now it's my daughters
bringing home no-duh,
rock out, whatever,
like I totally
paused, and like
I'm like. . .

I'm like Mother, her hands
in biscuit dough,
her ears turning red
from ain' nothin butta,
blue monday, and
tutti fruiti, aw rooty!

Crossing New River

I'd seen two fifth-grade friends pulled up by hooks
and flopped into rescue squad boats — blue shirts,
dark jeans, heavy high-top shoes streaming mud-
darkened water.
                    And if I remember
that so clearly after forty-eight years —
and if I've never been a strong swimmer,
always been fearful of water,
                                        then why
did I — even just this once! — choose to swim
across with Eddie Wolcott, my high school
pal? (He's long dead now, natural causes,
of course.)

Well, I don' t think there' s an answer
to that question. I could say it was dog
days weather, school would start in a couple
of weeks, Eddie and I were bored, downstream
toward Austinville, no one else around,
the fish totally uninterested
in what we had to offer, and the water —
that old coffee & cream living creature
of a New River, steadily flowing north
— got us in the trance of watching its swirls
and ripples.

That' s when Eddie asked, "Want to?"
and I said, "No." Then he said "Oh come on,"
and so I did. The two of us stripped down,
waded out, and swam across. Harder was
getting back. The current had carried us
downstream, and so, naked as savages,
we had to walk the rocky bank upstream
half a mile or so to aim ourselves back
down to our clothes and fishing gear.

I must
have been tired that day, and probably glad
to be alive, but I'm only guessing.
What I do remember is how strange it felt
to be naked on the far bank, scraping
bare feet, shins, and ankles on the mean rocks
over there, and how we talked as we made
our tedious way — muddy to the knees —
about how really cool it would be if
Velma Williams and Bonnie Demers were there
with us, bare-ass naked — as we'd never
seen them — on the other side of the world.

Cynthia Huntington

Home Fires

It's late; I've finished cleaning up
the kitchen; our son is asleep.

In the quiet the house settles;
the furnace kicks on, forcing heat
up through the walls.
I fold laundry in the living room.

You left so quickly this time
your clothes still turn up in the wash.
I pick out your old blue shirt,
tangled in Sam's pajamas,

and lay it across my knees to fold.
Still warm from the dryer, the nap
lifts under my fingers, soft.

I must have washed this shirt
two hundred times. Folded it,
put it away in a drawer.
It's mine now; everything here is mine.

This old house breathing
fire into the night,
the dishwasher grinding and groaning.

Our bedroom, where the grain
of old wood shows through
four layers of paint.
These shadows on the carpet

where footsteps lifted and fell.
Smoke, ash, cinders. . .
Anything you want here

you better come and get.
This house is burning

soundlessly. Everything we know
is being translated
into flame. I can forget you.

Most Recent Book: *The Salt House* (University Press of New England, 1999)

For Love

I would not go there again for money;
for the way the sky closes over you there,
for months without sun, for the beaten look
of those streets, heaved brick, painted storefronts,
and stark fronts of houses, for streets where the day
goes to die in gutters heaped with old black snow,
and for what people have known about each other forever
and will not amend. I would not go there even
to die, to add one single ounce of sacrifice
to the tombs of Main Street, graveyards of old farmland,
the cursed diesel factory, whose machinery crushed
my grandfather's spine when its cables snapped overhead,
stretched thin, made weak by overuse and uncaring.
I would not give another death, another curse
to that sorry history. Enough that it has eaten,
mangled and eaten, my grandfather, worn out
my grandmother, who was a silvered ghost weaving nests
of her own white hair for the birds, stopped my lucky father
whose luck ran out, and hauled him back, and caught
his quick, nervy brothers, who went to war and came home
and subsided into wisecracks and darkening philosophies.
Enough that my father's sisters have gone mad,
leaning over the oilcloth to read their fortunes in the cards,
their sweet, worried faces grown old. I would not go there,
even to satisfy my wish to join them, my longing to be there
in the long afternoons beside them, when the snow
hangs in the empty air, whirled about, driven sideways,
like the souls of my family given for nothing. Not for my need
to give a name to our lives, to be again, most truly, myself —
even to save myself, I would not give satisfaction to that angry ground.
I would not go there again. For love, I would not go.

For Dora Maar

My neck is sunburned
just on the right side, where the sun
shone from the east all morning.
I lay on the Picasso towel,
right on the face of his "Weeping Woman"
who never stopped weeping, who died
last week at eighty-nine

and every newspaper called her his lover
and talked, in one way or another,
of how she was broken by him
and went mad, and ended
the events of her life there,
but lived on fifty years more.

I read the obituary, sitting right on her face.
The paper blew in a hot wind;
the print was dancing, yellow and purple
dots in a compensatory strobe; she had a green
tear on her cheek, a blue nostril.
I thought nothing could touch me like that,
that I knew how to master need,
so I lay down and ground my body
into that weeping woman; the hot sand
under us was moving with my hipbones,
shifting, sifting, but never soft,
always rock; however fine,

however mutable, at the beach you lie on rock
that presses back and makes you ache
if you lie still, that is only soft
if you keep moving it, making it give way
under you. The sun was all over me,
glinting off my oiled and lathered skin,
harmlessly hot, and that one place
the unguent missed, the white curve of my neck
behind my ear, above my shoulder,
silently burning though I could not feel it,
taking the sun's primitive beating
down to the bone.

Today I can barely turn my head;
it's like wearing a garment that's too tight,
which is my burned skin trying to repair
itself, the spot where my hand
keeps going, too late, to protect,
to hide or soothe, or simply to acknowledge
the branding the sun gave me,
in the one place where I was not protected
when I lay on the burning rock I made yield
beneath me, on the face of that weeping woman
I said I would never become.

The Rapture

I was standing in the kitchen, stirring bones for soup,
and in that moment I became another person.

It was an early spring evening, the air California mild.
Outside, the eucalyptus was bowing compulsively

over the neighbors' motor home parked in the driveway.
The street was quiet for once, and all the windows were open.

Then my right arm tingled, a fluttering under the skin.
Fire charged down the nerve of my leg; my scalp exploded

in pricks of light. I shuddered and felt like laughing;
it was exhilarating as an earthquake. A city on fire

after an earthquake. Then I trembled and my legs shook,
and every muscle gripped so I fell and lay on my side,

a bolt driven down my skull into my spine. My legs were
swimming against the linoleum, and I looked up at the underside

of the stove, the dirty places where the sponge didn't reach.
Everything settled there in one place, one flash of time.

There in my body. In the kitchen at six in the evening, April.
A wooden spoon clutched in my hand, the smell of chicken broth.

And in that moment I knew everything that would come after:
the vision was complete as it seized me. Without diagnosis,

without history, I knew that my life was changed.
I seemed to have become entirely myself in that instant.

Not the tests, examinations in specialists' offices, not
the laboratory procedures: MRI, lumbar puncture, electrodes

pasted to my scalp, the needle scraped along the sole of my foot,
following one finger with the eyes, EEG, CAT scan, myelogram.

Not the falling down or the blindness and tremors, the stumble
and hiss in the blood, not the lying in bed in the afternoons.

Not phenobarbitol, amitriptilene, prednisone, amantadine, ACTH,
cortisone, cytoxan, copolymer, baclofen, tegretol, but this:

Six o'clock in the evening in April, stirring a pot of soup.
An event whose knowledge arrived whole, its meaning taking years

to open, to seem a destiny. It lasted thirty seconds, no more,
then my muscles unlocked, the surge and shaking left my body

and I lay still beneath the white high ceiling. Then I got up
and stood there, quiet, alone, just beginning to be afraid.

Richard Jackson

Do Not Duplicate This Key

It is not commonly understood why my love is so deadly.
At the very least it uproots the trees of your heart.
It interferes with the navigation of airplanes like certain
electronic devices. It leaves a bruise in the shape of a rose.
It kisses the dreamless foreheads of stones.
Sometimes the light is wounded by my dark cliffs.
Around me even the moon must be kept on a leash.
Whenever I turn you will turn like a flower following
the day's light. Sometimes I feel like Ovid's Jove,
hiding behind the clouds and hills, waiting for you
to happen along some pastoral dell thinking
what I might turn you into next. Then I remember
the way he turned himself into a drooling bull to scour
the pastures of Arcadia for Europa. Forget myth, then.
Forget Ovid. According to Parcelus, God left the world
unfinished from a lack of professional interest
and only my love can complete or destroy it.
Sometimes I come home, open a bottle of Chalone
Pinot Blanc and listen to the Spin Doctors'
"How Could You Want Him (When You Could have Me)?"
My love is so deadly because it holds a gun to every despair.
But this is not the case everywhere. In some places
the heart's shrapnel shreds our only dreams. Even
the trees refuse to believe in one another. Sometimes
it seems we've put a sheet over Love and tagged its toe.
Someone thinks it lives in the mother of the Azeri soldier,
Elkhan Husseinar, because she puts, in a jar on his grave,
the pickled heart of an enemy Armenian soldier.
This is love, she says, *this is devotion*.
Someone else assigns Love a curfew. There's the 25-year-
old sniper who targets women in Sarajevo to see
what he calls "their fantastic faces of love"
as they glance towards their scrambling children.

Most Recent Book: *Heartwall* (University of Massachusetts Press, 2000)

This is when the seeds desert their furrows for rock.
This is when Despair pulls a Saturday Night Special
from its pocket and points it at the cashier in the 7-11 store.
This is when it seems each star is just a chink in our dungeon.
It is at this hour that I think entirely about you.
My love is so deadly because it wants to handcuff
the Death that has put all our lives on parole.
I myself escaped long ago from Love's orphanage.
I invented a world where the moon tips its hat at me.
I have this way of inventing our love by letting
my words rest like a hand on your thigh.
I have this way of gently biting your nipples
just to feel your body curl like the petal of a rose.
Even when I sleep you can detect my love
with the same instruments scientists use to see
the microwave afterglow of the Big Bang that created
the universe. My love is so deadly
the whole world is reinvented just as Parcelus said.
I love even the 90% of the universe that is dark matter
no light will ever embrace. Rilke died from the thorn
of a rose because he thought his love was not so deadly.
My love is so deadly it picks the blossoming fruit tree
of the entire night sky. I can feel, in the deepest part
of you, the soft petals stir and fold with the dusk.
So deadly is my love
the call of the owl is thankful
to find a home in my ear. The smoke
from my cigarette thanks me for releasing it.
The tree changes into a flock of birds.
So deadly is my love other loves fall asleep in its throat.
It is a window not attached to any wall.
It is a boat whose sails are made of days and hours.
It rises like Botticelli's Venus from the sea.
This is not some idle myth.
In fact, it has been discovered that all life
probably began on the surface of deep sea bubbles
which came together in Nature's little cocktail party
carrying most of the weird little elements we are made of,
the kind of molecular sex that excites chemists.
My love is so deadly it starts spontaneous combustions.
The whole universe grows frightened for what comes next.
The sky undresses into dawn then shyly covers its stars.
Sometimes I think your love is a compass pointing away.

Sometimes I discover my love like the little chunks of moon
they dig from under the antarctic ice. My love is
so deadly it will outlast Thomas Edison's last breath
which has been kept alive in a test tube
in Henry Ford's village, Dearborn, Michigan. Even the skeptic,
David Hume, 1711-1776, begins to believe in my love.
My own steps have long since abandoned their tracks.
My own love is not a key that can be duplicated.
It knocks at the door of the speakeasy in Sarajevo
and whispers the right word to a girl named Tatayana.
This, of course, was from before the war,
before everybody's hearts had been amputated from their lives.
Now my love abandons all my theories for it.
This is why my love seems so deadly.
It is scraping its feet on your doormat, about to enter.
Sometimes you have to cut your life down
out of the tree it has been hanging in. My love is
so deadly because it knows the snake that curls inside
each star like one of Van Gogh's brush strokes.
My love is so deadly because it knows the desire of the rain
for the earth, how the astronomer feels watching
the sleeping galaxies drift away from us each night.
I am listening to your own rainy voice.
I am watching the heart's barometer rise and fall.
I am watching like the spider from your easel.
My love is so deadlly, birds abandon the sluggish air.
Their hearts fall from trees like last year's nests.
The smoke awakens in the fire. The rose abandons the trellis.
My love is so deadly it picks the locks of your words.
And even tonight, while someone else's love tries
to scavenge a few feelings from a dumpster, while someone
lies across the exhaust grating like a spent lover,
my own love steps out from my favorite bar under
a sky full of thorns, weaving
a little down the sidewalk, daring the cabs
and after-hours kamikazees like someone stumbling
back into a world redeemed by
the heart's pawn tickets, holding a pair of shoes
in one hand, a hope that breathes in the other.

CXXXII: The Quandary

after Petrarch

If this isn't love, then her heart's dealing from the bottom of the deck.
If this isn't love, then I've been given the wrong role in the wrong play.
If it is good, why does the sky seem to crack above me today?
If it is evil, why is my heart on the gallows, my soul on the rack?
If I burn by my own will, what heresy cast me into the fires?
If it wasn't my will, what good can any prayer accomplish?
Fate, choice, heart, soul, game, role or fanciful wish,
how does she have this power over me if I don't consent or conspire?
If I do consent — shut up, that's what I should do. I'm tumbling
through some
emotional space like a new meteor, aimless, the proverbial
ship on a storm-tossed sea, smarter than some, dumber than others,
so I can't really tally the ledger on what's best for me or her
except to know I am poor without her, rich in memory, and begin to feel
death come each dawn, and most alive when my heart turns stone.

Terzanelle of Kosovo Fields

The soldier thinks he can beat the moon with a stick.
His is a country where roads do not meet, nor words touch.
The walls around him crumble: his heart is a pile of bricks.

We sit with the sky draped across our knees and trust
that the shadows of planes, whispering like children in the fields,
follow roads we will not meet, speak words we will not touch.

The soldier lights a fuse that makes some tragic story real:
that's when our words start scavenging like packs of dogs, derelict,
abandoned, hunted by the shadows of planes that cross the fields.

It's true that the blackbirds fill the air with their terrible music.
How could we think our lives wouldn't turn, like our stars, to rust?
Now our words scavenge the countryside, and our loves are derelict.

I wanted to love you beyond the soldier's aim, beyond the war's clutch.
Now bombs hatch in our hearts. Even the smoke abandons us for the sky.
How could we think our loves wouldn't turn, like our stars, to dust?

We live in a world where the earth refuses to meet the sky.
Our homes are on the march, their smoke abandons us for that sky.
Our soldiers thought they could beat the moon with their sticks.
Now every heart is crumbling, every love is a pile of bricks.

No Turn on Red

It's enough to make the moon turn its face
the way these poets take a kind of bubble bath
in other people's pain. I mean, sure, the dumpsters
of our lives are filling with more mistakes
than we could ever measure. Whenever we reach into
the pockets of hope we pull out the lint of despair.
I mean, all I have to do is lift the eyelids
of the stars to see how distant you could become.
But that doesn't mean my idea of form is a kind of
twelve step approach to vision. I mean, I don't want
to contribute to the body count which, in our major journals,
averages 13.7 deaths/poem, counting major catastrophes and wars.
I'm not going to blame those bodies floating down some
river in Rwanda or Bosnia on Love's failures. But really,
it's not the deaths in those poems, it's the way Death arrives in a tux
and driving a Lamborghini, then says a few rhymed words
over his martini. It's a question of taste, really,
which means, a question for truth. I mean, if someone
says some beastly person enters her room the way Hitler
entered Poland I'd say she's shut her eyes like a Kurdish
tent collapsing under a gas attack, it makes about as
much sense. Truth is too often a last line of defense,
like the way every hospital in America keeps a bag
of maggots on ice to eat away infection when the usual
antibiotics fail. The maggots do a better job
but aren't as elegant. Truth is just bad taste, then?
Not really. Listen to this: "Legless Boy Somersaults
Two Miles To Save Dad," reads the headline from Italy
in *Weekly World News*, a story that includes pictures
of the heroic but bloody torso of the boy. "Twisted
like a pretzel," the story goes on. Bad taste or
world class gymnastics? Which reminds me. One afternoon
I was sitting in a bar watching the Olympics — the singles
of synchronized swimming — how can that be true?
If that's so, why not full contact javelin? Uneven
table tennis? The 1500-meter dive? Even the relay dive?
Someone's going to say I digress? Look, this is a satire
which means, if you look up the original Latin, "mixed dish," —
you have to take a bite of everything. True, some would
argue it's the word we get Satyr from, but I don't like
to think of myself as some cloven-hoofed, horny little
creature sniffing around trees. Well, it's taste, remember.
Besides my satire is set while waiting at Love's traffic

light, which makes it unique. So, I was saying you have
to follow truth's little detours — no, no, it was taste,
the heroic kid twisted like a pretzel. Pretzels are
metaphysical. Did you know a medieval Italian monk
invented them in the year 610 in the shape of crossed,
praying, arms to reward his parish children?
"I like children," said W. C. Fields — "if they're properly
cooked." Taste, and its fellow inmate, truth — how do we
measure anything anymore? Everyone wants me to stick
to a few simple points, or maybe no point at all,
like the tepid broth those new formalists ladle into their
demitasse. How can we write about anything — truth,
love, hope, taste, when someone says the moment, the basis
of all lyric poetry, of all measure and meter, is just
the equivalent of 10 billion atomic vibrations of the cesium
atom when its been excited by microwaves. Twilight chills
in the puddles left by evening's rain. The tiny spider
curled on the bulb begins to cast a huge shadow. No wonder
time is against us. In 1953, Dirty Harry, a "nuclear device,"
as the phrase goes, blossomed in Nevada's desert leaving
more than twice the fallout anyone predicted.
After thirty years no one admits the measurements.
Truth becomes a matter of "duck and cover." Even Love
refuses to come out of its shelter. In Sarajevo,
Dedran Smailovic plays Albinoni's *Adagio* outside
the bakery for 22 days where mortars killed 22,
and the papers are counting the days till the sniper
aims. You can already see the poets lined up on
poetry's dragstrip revving up their 22-line elegies
in time for the *New Yorker*'s deadline, so to speak.
Vision means, I guess, how far down the road of your
career you can see. And numbers not what Pope meant
by rhythm, but $5 per line. Pythagoras (b. 570 B.C.)
thought the world was made entirely of numbers. Truth,
he said, is the formula, and we are just the variables.
But this is from a guy who thought Homer's soul was
reborn in his. Later, that he had the soul of a peacock.
Who could trust him? How do we measure anything?
Each time they clean the standard kilogram bar in Sevres,
France, it loses a few atoms making everything else appear
a little heavier. That's why everything is suddenly
more somber. Love is sitting alone in a rented room
with its hangman's rope waiting for an answer
that's not going to come. All right, so I exaggerate, and
in bad taste. Let's say love has put away its balance,

tape measure and nails and is poking around in its tin
lunch pail. So how can I measure how much I love you?
Except the way the willow measures the universe.
Except the way your hair is tangled among the stars.
The way the turtle's shell reflects the night's sky.
I'm not counting on anything anymore. Even the foot —
originally defined as the shoe length of whatever king
held your life, which made the poets scramble around
to define their own poetic feet. And truth is all this?
That's why it's good to have all these details as
a kind of yardstick to rap across the fingers
of bad taste. "I always keep a supply of stimulants
handy," said Fields, "in case I see a snake;
which I also keep handy." In the end, you still need
something to measure, and maybe that's the problem
that makes living without love or truth so much pain.
I'd have to be crazy. Truth leaves its fingerprints
on everything we do. It's nearly 10 P.M. Crazy.
Here comes another poet embroidering his tragic
childhood with a few loosely lined mirrors.
I'm afraid for what comes next. The birds' warning
song runs up and down the spine of the storm. Who says
any love makes sense? The only thing left is
this little satire and its faceless clock for a soul.
You can't measure anything you want. The basis of all
cleverness is paranoia. 61% of readers never finish
the poem they start. 31% of Americans are afraid to speak
while making love. 57% of Americans have dreamt
of dying in a plane crash. One out of four
Americans is crazy. Look around at your three
best friends. If they're okay, you're in trouble.

Mark Jarman

Dialect

I can't remember the air, the light, the voices
Of what I used to think of as my home.
I truly can't recall how people sounded.
So now, when I hear someone on the news,

Most Recent Book: *Unholy Sonnets* (Story Line Press, 2000)

That guileless Western accent tinged with Spanish
Or vice versa, musical and flat,
Makes me ask, "What *is* that?" Then, I know.
And natives here will ask me when I speak,
"Where you from?" I tell them Greater Los Angeles.
A seedy, little beachtown, I say proudly,
That now, I add, has been yuppified.
I say it was a middle-class, working-class town
Of Anglos, Mexicans, Asians, a Black family,
Draftsmen and riveters for McDonnell-Douglas,
Hughes Aircraft, Northrop, Garrett Air Research.
Sea fog watered the morning rush hour traffic.
Kids snorkled after school and drowned at parties.
A Nike missile base protected us.
Their finned white noses sniffed the onshore breeze
And one day they were trucked off into nowhere.
From their abandoned hill we could look deep
Into the graft on graft of inland cities
And watch the riot smoke, when it erupted,
Blend with the stinging gauze of urban haze.
My parents bought their house for 20 grand.
Today, somebody else's house, it's worth
Half a million dollars — a yellow stucco
Among blue, pink, and white ones, just like it.
The colors made the sameness all seem better.
And just to cut the idyll short, the boys
Of different colors I played football with
Could turn from running plays to drawing knives
And smash each other's windshields and exchange
Curses in each other's mother tongues.
The late-night surf-crash made us all sleep soundly.
I couldn't wait to leave. But thought I'd be back.
Today rain followed snow and hammered nailholes
In the breadlike whiteness covering the heart
Of the continent's heart. All the gutters are singing.
I can't remember the air, the light, the voices.
But that's a lie. I can. Together they
Answer the reporter's questions like experts,
Surveying burning blocks by helicopter.

Goya's Saint Peter Repentant

A little hilltop stepped on by a glacier — that's how he looks, his bald head nearly flat,
And the upward turning dog's eyes humble as heather, and the tufts of eyebrow and beard sheepish.
He's draped with orange clay and a curving seam of granite — his clothes.
I've never seen thicker hands in a painting of a saint. I've seen hands like them
On men who showed me how to do work that would wilt me by lunch hour, making me understand,
Later, why roofers spend half their lunch hour lying in shade, if there is any, one arm flung over their eyes.
He looks sorry. He already has the keys, and yet he's sorry. Asking forgiveness is hard work.

Compare El Greco's Peter doing the same thing. Everything lengthens heavenward.
Beautiful, yes, and saintly, yes, but not Peter. Of all the apostles — the earthiest, the most creaturely.
He said one thing that pleased Jesus, though it pleased him mightily, and others that disappointed them both.
In Goya's painting, the keys to heaven lie on a stone like a mattress corner, their loops lapped by a fold of Peter's robe,
As if Peter, not yet a saint, didn't see them, or had put them aside until he finished his work.

You Lucky People

Lucky? That's everybody else but us.
Except that woman with her screaming children,
Staggering like a bomb victim through K-Mart.
She makes us feel lucky. But that's not it.
Right at this moment, they are with their kind,
Planning a wild success for somebody,
Some beautiful initiate who knows
That she is worthy, just as, in our hearts,
Our TV-dead, remote-control, drunk hearts,
We know we're not. When the magic wand sweeps heaven,
Releasing falling stars, like sticky sequins
That sparkle in our perms and dry look haircuts,
The lucky have already left the planet.

We always knew the Rapture was for them.
And just as well. Good riddance! We can live,
Now, with ourselves, expecting nothing,
And trying not to covet when our neighbors
Find just a little extra in their stockings.
We're born with luck like dimples, bedroom eyes,
And the tendency to keep all of our hair.
The lucky know it. His fatal heart attack
At 36 was lucky. The autopsy
Revealed his father's pancreatic cancer
At work in him already. Lucky people!
You could be lost in K-Mart with bad children.
But I'm going to say that only clouds are lucky.
Only the clouds and what we say they look like.

Unholy Sonnet

The gift for all our waking in this life,
For every time a bad night spoiled the day
With back pain or a sour frame of mind;
The sure reward for staying wide awake
Through buzzing monologues of hours and minutes,
The self-obsession of our span of years;
The grace that is a distant field of vision,
Not like exhaust haze warped by traffic heat,
But spindrift rising from the edge of earth;
The prize for suffering our names, for knowing
More than we thought we knew and knowing less;
The promise of an end like our beginning,
Oblivious to boredom, pain, and hope,
Is, said the man, a dreamless, mindless sleep.

Richard Jones

The Storm

I called my father long distance last night
to let him know how we're doing –
Andrew feeling better, the baby kicking,
me taking a turn with the flu, feeling like
I'm inside a glass bubble. My father patiently
waited for me to finish what I was saying,
then eagerly told me about the terrible
thunderstorm, asking if I could hear
the rain beating down. Suddenly
neither of us was talking.
I stood with the phone to my ear,
listening to drumming on the skylight
in my father's kitchen, picturing an old man
holding the receiver up to the thunder and darkness.

The Fear

I have a secret:
my little boy scares me.
He seems fragile
but barrels through the house
like a Sherman tank toppling lamps,
gleefully shrieking.
He loves the stove's blue flame,
tries to crawl inside the fridge,
dives headfirst into the tub.
He's learning to climb –
would fall out the window
if we didn't pull him back.

Last week, he got into some pills.
His mother and I rushed him to the hospital.
Prying a syringe into his mouth,
a doctor injected black chalk to save him.
That's what I see now:

Most Recent Book: *The Blessing* (Copper Canyon Press, 2000)

my son in the emergency room
helpless on the table,
crying, screaming,
Laura holding him down,
the doctor shooting into his mouth
black stuff that looked like death.

He's okay; nothing happened.
All day in a quiet room divided by blue curtains
we tried to keep him still in the stark white bed.
From a tangle of wires adhering to his chest
a telemetry machine monitored his heart —
glowing lines of steady, rhythmic beats,
like iambs running unstopped across the black screen,
a stubborn poem beating inside him
that cares not one bit for my fear.

The Freight

Winter mornings I see the ghost of my breath
when I get in my cold blue car, turn the engine,
and slowly back out of the garage, looking
over my shoulder to see where I'm going.
My commute takes me down Western
past car lots with white plastic banners
flapping like the wings of wind-blown gulls,
then down Peterson past the cemetery.
At Broadway there's always a traffic jam —
I sit awhile in the shadows of tall buildings.
But when I reach Lake Shore Drive, I race
along the ice-encrusted lake, rushing
through the middle years of life,
always anxious about being late.
Back and forth, every day: my sweet rut.

This morning — before work —
I drove through falling snow
to the thrift store in Wilmette
and bought Andrew one of those beds
shaped like a race car — a blue car
with big, black wheels. I like thinking
of him sleeping in a race car, the engine
of his dreams and visions carrying
the freight of the soul. Reconciled

to being late, I drove home carefully,
going slow, his blue car
tied on top of my blue car,
one hand out the window, holding fast the ropes.

Father's Day

A few days after the storm
spared the beach house,
I spent the morning removing
the plywood that protected the windows,
balancing heavy, unwieldy sheets,
climbing up and down,
my eighty-year-old father steadying the ladder,
insisting he take a turn.

After lunch, when Andrew wanted to go
to the beach, my father stayed
in the cool, dark house,
content to spend the afternoon in solitude,
forsaking the sun for the silence of chores —
small tasks he could accomplish alone.

Carrying our son,
I followed my wife down
a long weathered boardwalk that cut
through white waves of radiant dunes.
On the beach, by sparkling water,
I bent down, one arm around my boy's waist,
and carefully rubbed lotion on his face
as he twisted and squirmed, trying
to break free, eager to build
a castle with his shovel and bucket.

All around there was nothing
but beautiful day, an immense ocean.
I left Andrew with his mother digging in the sand,
walked toward the water
and pushed through the shorebreak's rushing froth,
diving through churning waves
to surface — breathless — beyond the swells,
turning once to site the tiny beach house
between the beleaguered world and open sea.

NEY JONES

ment for My Penis

How do I approach it, bald as it is, dangling
Over the urinal to some golden expression
Of lemony bitterness, an old Trappist,
Blind in one eye, kneeling to his paternosters?
Is it mine? It never seemed to be mine.

It was old when I first saw it. A joke
Chaucer might have told but didn't.
A frumpish soldier slumped in a jeep
Above the caption: *Dejected Nazi Colonel*
Waits to be transported to POW Camp.

Yet even now, in the spatulate dark,
Where it lies all day, secret as escape,
Sometimes it will leap of its own volition.
A young terrorist, sprung from prison
And bound for home, bent on sedition.

No, not that — here was my religion — look
Here, blue in the distances of skin — God
Flowers in this nerve. May it remain
Sovereign, inviolable, and unconfessed.
Honor most delicately this feverish guest.

Elegy for a Bad Example

(Everette Maddox, 1944–1989)

If there is no heaven and you are in it,
What does that make me? An idiot?
Your paradise was never the afterlife,
Only the usual after hours party,
The one with beer and marijuana,

Where the priest, after explaining the rigors
Of extreme unction, happily relieves
Himself on the hostess's potted plant,
Where the engineering student roars
Off naked on the sociologist's Harley,

Most Recent Book: *Elegy for a Southern Drawl* (Houghton Mifflin, 1999)

Where the farm boy turns Buddhist,
And the new marriage makes a fist.
Oh but you are not there to quote Berryman,
To enjoin all stupid dreamers to wake up
By the profound example of passing out.

No, in the real heaven that doesn't exist,
You are only the aging of a premonition.
You have no business here. You only occur
To me on a day of many absences
When I give the lecture on attendance.

Nihilist Time

How stark that life of slouchy avoidance,
Thinking all day and all night of nothing,
Alone in my room with Nietzsche and Sartre.
Nothing is what I'd come from, nowhere
Is where I'd been, and I was nothing's man.

Nothing was the matter, I'd not answer
If no one asked, for nothing was the point,
And nothing the view I'd take on faith.
When I died, I'd not be as I had not been
Before I was born, with nothing for a name.

Meanwhile I'd cuddle in a vacuum with my abyss,
Whispering endearing stuff: "My darling
Emptiness, my almost electron, my blank pet."
Later with no one, I'd not celebrate
No event, for nothing was what I loved.

What I hated were people doing things:
Bouncing balls, counting, squirming into jeans
When oblivion waited in every ditch.
I could hear black motors not starting up,
And zeros going nowhere, nothing's gang.

Raccoon Time

Perhaps in searching for a den, it had squeezed through
The terra-cotta pipe atop the chimney and dropped
In a skittering tumble through the rusted damper
To lie for a while in the soot by the andirons,

Stunned and licking its injuries, and in that instant,
Probably did not know itself raccoon, but went on
Out of a habitual raccoon fastidiousness,
Sniffing the ghosts of the chopping block,
Rearing on the piano bench to touch the dry
Black noses of the keys. What did it glean
Of our sealed wilderness and hidden springs?
The faucet dripped. The soap sang in its dish.
We live in a dim inkling or a rapt afterness,
But something was here and one of us for at least
An hour when Gloria shook me from sleep,
Saying, "Quick, the dog has a live
Animal in Samuel's room," and I went naked
And fearless as I was imagining rabbit or bird.
When it wheeled from the shadow of the bed,
At first it seemed huge as a bear or Bengal tiger,
Making me holler something like huge and rabid,
As it went past me in a fierce downgearing waddle,
Spun, and clawed on down the stairs, with first
The dog and then Gloria, beating a plastic
Laundry tub on the rug, and going *eee-iii*, *eee-iii*,
For she is an impetuous woman descended from generals
While I am a person to stand back in emergencies,
Weighing escape routes. I do not ever cross
A bridge but that whole histories of options
Crop up like bubbles from the river's bottom;
As I pulled on my jeans while hearing
The thumps, *eee-iii*s, masked snarls, and shattering
Of pots, the thought of my wife's resolve
So quickly shamed me to the thick of things,
That there I was, like a lock on the stairs
When it found the open door and trickled out,
No Grendel perhaps, though I put it here shining
As if at the center of a heraldic shield
With her going at it, and me standing back
To tell the story. If that is the place of men,
It will be no less glory for me, and she
Will have that image to balance those more
Cautious nights when she defers to my wisdom.

Richard Katrovas

On the Day After Allen Ginsberg's Death a Woman Thinks of Me

A woman phones whom I've not seen
in eighteen years, and didn't know
that well; she seems put off a bit
I do not recognize her name,
but speaks of Charlottesville and folks
we knew in common, for an awkward
minute, until my memory
unclogs and spills forth images.
She called, she says, just to tell me
she remembers a party where
I punched some guy who, drunk and full
of lip-curled swagger, had loudly cursed
my quoting Ginsberg's poems of love
to an arc of puzzled co-eds.
Of course, I didn't just turn around
and clock him. I tried to reason first,
persuade him to my point of view
that Ginsberg wrote great poems and pounds
of trash, but that the trash cannot
diminish all the sweetness, all
the charged and crazy posturing
and fresh iconoclastic yelping
and magnificent confounding of
the public and the private realms,
and then I wacked him. Of course I was
a fool, and that dyspeptic guy
did not deserve a fool's reproach.
I'd forgotten all about that night
until the woman phoned to mark
from half a continent away
that she recalls a night I fought,
on the porch of a house I would
not recognize these days, about
a man who set his life against
such pettiness and boyish pride.

Most Recent Book: *The Boxer's Embrace* (Carnegie Mellon University Press, 2001)

It was an ugly little fight
that others wisely stopped before
we really hurt our drunken selves,
and which of us was judged by all
who'd witnessed our brief dance the bigger
ass I can't know and don't much care.
The fool I am forgives the fool
I was, and hopes the guy I punched
can say the same. Though both of us
may feel small consolation in
the fact that our grotesque display
is now odd theater in the mind
of one recalling how a man
had married art and life, in art,
as no one ever will again.

Love Poem for an Enemy

I, as sinned against as sinning,
take small pleasure from the winning
of our decades-long guerrilla war.
For from my job I've wanted more
than victory over one who'd tried
to punish me before he died,
and now, neither of us dead,
we haunt these halls in constant dread
of drifting past the other's life
while long-term memory is rife
with slights that sting like paper cuts.
We've occupied our separate ruts
yet simmered in a single rage.
We've grown absurd in middle age
together, and should seek wisdom now
together, by ending this row.
I therefore decommission you
as constant flag ship of my rue.
Below the threshold of my hate
you now my good regard may rate.
For I have let my anger pass.
But, while you're down there, kiss my ass.

The Turn

The gray Mercedes surged to lunge ahead
of our little red Fiesta, even though
the bottleneck of traffic halted all.
He imperiled us, almost caused a crash,
simply to gain a length's advantage
in the stalled and stinky summer queue of cars.
Dominika slammed her palm into the horn,
showed her teeth, and I was delighted by
her anger, so scooted out the door and flipped
the bastard off with both my middle fingers.
He leaped out scowling and ready for a fight.
He tried to kick me but I blocked it, boxed
his ear and plucked his forehead, pointed at
his car as if he were a little boy
and I his daddy pointing to his room.
A swarthy fellow wearing pricey clothes,
he seemed a low-rent Casanova who'd
inherited enough to keep him slick.
But when he popped his trunk and pulled out black
and shiny rags he peeled from metal, then
plucked a cartridge and jammed it in and turned
I saw his fully automatic thing
for killing, his Uzi or whatever god
damned thing it was, an automatic weapon,
the kind that sprays its bullets so that aiming's
not an issue, and suddenly I thought
that here at last I'd done it, I'd finally pissed
off someone with a weapon and the will
to use it, after years of mouthing off
in biker bars and leaning on my horn
in New Orleans — where once good men got lynched
for less — after a youth of not caring whom
I angered and well into middle life
unscarred, unbowed, in Prague, in summer, I
would die of road rage, but thought the noble thing
to do would be to run aslant, drawing fire
away from Dominika, and in that tick
it took to turn I saw her raising Ema
alone, and Ema living fatherless,
and Ema's face, and I heard Ema's voice
and clearly the greasy pimp didn't shoot

or I'd not be writing this, but that tick,
that tiny jagged piece of time, got packed
with self-recrimination, boundless love
for a woman and a child, for every friend
and minor enemy my life had vexed,
and even a little humor, for as
I turned I thought oh shit I'm wearing drawers
with three small holes around the baggy crotch,
and every mother's admonition honked
inside my head, as then I tripped and fell.

Brigit Pegeen Kelly

Black Swan

I told the boy I found him under a bush.
What was the harm? I told him he was sleeping
And that a black swan slept beside him,
The swan's feathers hot, the scent of the hot feathers
And of the bush's hot white flowers
As rank and sweet as the stewed milk of a goat.
The bush was in a strange garden, a place
So old it seemed to exist outside of time.
In one spot, great stone steps leading nowhere.
In another, statues of horsemen posting giant stone horses
Along a high wall. And here were triangular beds
Of flowers flush with red flowers. And there,
Circular beds flush with white. And in every bush
And bed flew small birds and the cries of small birds.
I told the boy I looked for him a long time
And when I found him I watched him sleeping,
His arm around the swan's moist neck,
The swan's head tucked fast behind the boy's back,
The feathered breast and the bare breast breathing as one.
And then very swiftly and without making a sound,
So that I would not wake the sleeping bird,
I picked the boy up and slipped him into my belly,
The way one might slip something stolen

Most Recent Book: *Song* (BOA Editions, 1995)

Into a purse. And brought him here...
And so it was. And so it was. A child with skin
So white it was not like the skin of a boy at all,
But like the skin of a newborn rabbit or like the skin
Of a lily, pulseless and thin. And a giant bird
With burning feathers. And beyond them both
A pond of incredible blackness, overarched
With ancient trees and patterned with shifting shades,
The small wind in the branches making a sound
Like the knocking of a thousand wooden bells....
Things of such beauty. But still I might
Have forgotten, had not the boy, who stands now
To my waist, his hair is a cap of shining feathers,
Come to me today weeping because some older boys
Had taunted him and torn his new coat,
Had he not, when I bent my head to his head,
Said softly, but with great anger, "I wish I had never
Been born. I wish I were back under the bush,"
Which made the old garden rise up again,
Shadowed and more strange. Small birds
Running fast and the grapple of chill coming on.
There was the pond, half-circled with trees. And there
The flowerless bush. But there was no swan.
There was no black swan. And beneath
The sound of the wind, I could hear, dark and low,
The giant stone hooves of the horses
Striking and striking the hardening ground.

Elegy

Wind buffs the waterstained stone cupids and shakes
Old rain from the pine's low branches, small change
Spilling over the graves the years have smashed
With a hammer — *forget this, forget that, leave no*
Stone unturned. The grass grows high, sweet-smelling,
Many-footed, ever-running. No one tends it. No
One comes ... *And where am I now?* ... Is this a beginning,
A middle, or an end? ... Before I knew you I stood
In this place. Now I forsake the past as I knew it
To feed you into it. But that is not right. You *step*
Into it. I *find* you here, in the sifting grass,

In the late light, as if you had always been here.
Behind you two torn black cedars flame white
Against the darkening fields. . . . If you turn to me,
Quiet man? If you turn? If I speak softly?
If I say, *Take off, take off your glasses. . . . Let me see*
Your sightless eyes?. . . . I will be beautiful then. . .
Look, the heart moves as the moths do, scuttering
Like a child's thoughts above this broken stone
And that. And I lie down. I lie down in the long grass,
Something I am not given to doing, and I feel
The weight of your hand on my belly, and the wind
Parts the grasses, and the distance spills through —
The glassy fields, the black black earth, the pale air
Streaming headlong toward the abbey's far stones
And streaming back again . . . The drowned scent of lilacs
By the abbey, it is a drug. It drives one senseless.
It drives one blind. You can cup the enormous lilac cones
In your hands — ripened, weightless, and taut —
And it is like holding someone's heart in your hands,
Or holding a cloud of moths. I lift them up, my hands.
Grave man, bend toward me. Lay your face . . . *here*.
Rest. . . . I took the stalks of dead wisteria
From the glass jar propped against the open grave
And put in the shell-shaped yellow wildflowers
I picked along the road. I cannot name them.
Bread and butter, perhaps. I am not good
With names. But nameless you walked toward me
And I knew you, a swelling in the heart,
A silence in the heart, the wild wind-blown grass
Burning — as the sun falls below the earth —
Brighter than a bed of lilies struck by snow.

Two Boys

The boy drowned in the bog. Not a pretty sight.
Not a pretty end. And it no accident. And him
A stranger in town. Rank the berries in the bushes.
And mute the birds. Not like birds at all.
And the afternoon come too soon and then
Come no longer. *What is the life of a man?*
Or of one not even a man? Is it the shape of a bird?

Or a dog? Or an insect dressed in robes of milk
Or robes of green? And if a life takes its own life?
If a man takes from himself a man? Or a bird
From a bird? Or a dog from a dog *What is*
That like? Birds may fall faster than thought,
But a dog is no lamb, it will not easily strangle —
Greenness like fire will not swiftly stamp out. . . .
The boy drowned in the bog. He came from
A long way off to lie down in such sickly water.
Not like water at all. Poor and brown. Not one
Fish in it. Not one blind fish. There would
Have been a better time. Or place. Better.
But fate, what is it? Who met the boy by
Daylight? And how did he know him? By what
Seal on the boy's forehead? Talon or tail?
Who said, *Thus far shall you come and no*
Farther? This circle of beaten trees. This ring
Of dark water. Who raised the curtain?
Who prompted the action? Who conceived of it
In the first place — what prophet in what
Dark room? Did he weep when he wrote
Down the words? Did he watch till the end
Or did he leave that to others? And what
Did the flesh smell like when the prophecy
Was sealed? A burned flower? Or ripened fruit?
Oh, what sang in the trees before the boy
Lay down or after? A child? Or the light?
Or nothing. Just a bird. Nothing. And then
Night coming on. And morning following after. . . .
And so we have a story. But still the story
Does not end. Green the cress by the water.
Green the insect's wing. Now the living boy
Finds the dead one. A gift for early rising.
A worm for the bird. The boy did not know
What he was seeing. He thought the dead boy
Must be something other. Flesh of a lily.
Or a fallen hat. He thought what he thought.
And then he thought no longer. The wind
Suddenly loud in the trees. The birds loud.
The boy had wanted a brother. But this
Was not what he meant. Had he said
The wrong words? *Did words have such power?*
And then — through veils of white and veils

Of green — he saw what he saw: That from
This day forward, for better or worse, for
Worse or better, he would carry this shadow
Of no certain shape, now a lamb, now a bird,
Now a wolf dressed in the robes of a woman,
From here to there and from there like a load
Of wood with no fire to lay it on back to this
Bog or another. This wood or another. Berries
Bright or rank. Water foul or pure. The birds
Loud in the trees. Or still. And softer than
Fleece, softer than grass, it already raining.

YUSEF KOMUNYAKAA

Outside The Blue Nile

"Can you spare seven cents?"
        I drop two quarters into
                his McDonald's cup,

& he runs after me, saying,
        "Man, I can't take this.
                I don't want to get rich."

I notice the 1st Cav. patch
    on his fatigue jacket. He smells
                like he slept in a field of mint.

He says that he's Benedict
        the Moor. Of course, I've
                never heard of the fellow.

Two days later, I spot him
        outside Cody's Bookstore
                & reach into my pocket,

fingering the pennies. He says,
    "I'm not begging today, brother.
                I'm just paying penance."

He goes back to scrubbing
    the sidewalk with a wirebrush.
                His black & white mutt

Most Recent Book: *Pleasure Dome: New and Collected* (Wesleyan University Press, 2001)

stands there; she guards him
at night while he sleeps
under a crown of stars.

I find what I'm looking for
at the Berkeley Library.
He was born in Sicily

on the estate of Chevalier de
Lanza of San Fratello,
the son of African slaves.

He sold the lumbering oxen
he'd labored years to buy,
gave the money to the poor,

& followed Father Lanza, pledging
a Lenten vow. After the caves
in the mountains near Palermo,

he went to live in a rocky cell
on Mount Pellegrino where
the Duke of Medina-Coeli

visited & built him a chapel.
All the titles at his feet,
Benedict the Moor

rejected. He couldn't
read or write, but recited
biblical passages for days.

Wearing just a few leaves,
he predicted the death
of Princess Bianca,

made the sign of the cross
to give the blind sight. Here
was a man who hid in a thicket

from a crowd's joy.
The Duchess of Montalvo
bowed often before him,

but she never saw his eyes.
"Into thy hands, O Lord,
I commend my spirit,"

were his last words. Three months
later, I sit in The Blue Nile
eating with my hands, folding

pieces of spicy chicken
into spongy white bread
thin as forgiveness,

knowing that one hand
is sacred & the other used
to clean oneself with leaves

or clutch a dagger. No one
touched Benedict the Moor's
hands. Not even the Duchess.

They kissed the hem of his habit.
In Palermo, the senate burned
fourteen torches of white wax

in his honor. When I step out
under Berkeley's cool stars,
I see the face I thought

lost in the Oakland hills
when eucalyptus created
an inferno. I walk up

to him, fingering a nickel
& two pennies. He says,
"Can you spare three cents?"

Queen Marie-Theresa & Nabo

When Daquesne presented
the Queen with a dwarf
from Dahomey named Nabo,

another scandal strolled
into the palace. At first
he was there to show off

her white skin
& carry her train.
She would dress him

in silk robes, bejeweled
bracelets & armbands,
a turban which sparkled

with an aigrette
of rubies & pearls
given by Madame de Maintenon.

He was the only one
who entered her boudoir
before she was out of bed,

& his wit sent plumes
of laughter into the cold
morning air. As she dined

on chocolates, the fat
shook on her royal bones,
her skin like rice paper.

Maybe moonlight
ravaged the room
when she invited him

into her bed, as she
spoke about eating
green fruit & live birds

in her dreams; mystery —
when the Queen birthed
a daughter, Nabo

was already days dead.
The doctors kept
telling the King,

"the color of the child
was caused by a black man
looking at the Queen."

The horse hooves
struck sparks from stone
as the royal carriage

rounded a hairpin curve
in the road, hurrying
a secret to the convent

of Moret. Years later,
Voltaire said the Black Nun
was the King's daughter,

but Le Notre says,
"Would the Queen, Marie-
Theresa, the Dauphin,

the Duke & the Duchess
of Bourgoyne, have shown
the same attachment

to her?" If you stand
before her portrait
at the Library of St. Genevieve

for fifteen minutes,
gazing down to the bottom
of chance & requital,

the vigil of her father's
eyes, you'd see everything
known about love & death.

Forgive & Live

Ralph Ellison didn't
have his right hand
on her left breast

& they weren't kissing
in the doorway of Blackmur's
kitchen. But Delmore

Schwartz tried to slap
his wife, Elizabeth,
at the Christmas party

Anyway. When he pulled
her into a side bedroom
the house swelled into a big

white amp for Caliban's
blues. Maybe their fight
began one evening about sex

years earlier, not enough
money for food & gasoline.
But she'd only been leaning

against Ellison's shoulder
to let him light her cigarette,
just a lull in a conversation

about Duke Ellington's
"Creole Love Call"
& the New Critics.

That night, the falling
snow through the windows
was a white spotlight

on his dark face,
a perfect backdrop
for Delmore's rehearsal

for the women
who would pass
through his life

like stunned llamas,
for the drunken stars
exploding in his head,

for the taxicabs
taken from Cambridge
to Greenwich Village, the fear

of death, the Dexedrine
clouds & poison-pen letters
floating back to earth,

for the notes in margins
of Rilke's *Duino*
Elegies & his love-hate

of T. S. Eliot,
for Chumley's Bar,
those days of grey

boxcars flickering past
as he paced Washington
Square Park, impulsive

bouquets stolen from gardens
& given to lovers with dirt
clinging to the roots,

for his fascination
with Marilyn Monroe,
the Dreyfus case, Kafka

quoting Flaubert, the day
after JFK's assassination
spent wandering the streets

in unbuckled galoshes,
for Cavanaugh's Irish Bar
in Chelsea & the Egyptian

Gardens on West Twenty-ninth,
Dixie's Plantation Lounge,
for his last night on earth,

stumbling from a forest
of crumpled girlie magazines,
as he takes the garbage

down to the lobby,
singing about lovers
in the Duchess's red shoes.

Sydney Lea

Inviting the Moose: a Vision

Sumac thickets by the roadbed, either side,
spangled by snow and the big moon's light.
Deeper in, evergreens, taller, darker,
but still undark in that light, this weather.
And deeper yet, hardwoods that scatter and climb
up Signal Mountain, which I climb down in a car, toward home.
A saxophone keens on the tape machine — slow, sweet
balladry, which seems just right.
I whisper, "What a night."

Twenty minutes east, my twelve-year-old son
composes a story in his upstairs room.
His two younger sisters are breathing, way down in slumber.
Downstairs, my wife eases split remnant lumber
into the stove for kindling,

Most Recent Book: *Pursuit of a Wound* (University of Illinois Press, 2000)

and then — nothing grave — she goes on thinking.
In mind and fact, the world appears
intact, to me at least, who am torn between here
and there, to me who fear

one set of pleasures may cancel another.
It's like the dilemma of any lover,
craving anticipation and, equally, consummation.
But who'd complain at such benign frustration?
Everything glows. The wayside drifts, for all their sand and salt.
are gorgeous as they descend, like the fault-
less bassward glissando of the horn
as I glide by Kettle Pond.
Whenever the season is warm,

its open water invites the moose of our region.
And I? I summon a vision.
My knowledge, for all my years, remains slight
Why, I wonder, tonight of all nights'
should I invite the moose as well?
Antlerless in late winter, the bull
precipitously vaults the righthand guardrail
and comes to a standstill
before my automobile.

One of the daughters shifts in dream. Rolls over. Smiles.
My son's narrative, meanwhile,
proposes at its climax that goodness is a sword.
The saxophone and the sidemen find their resolving chord.
All might end right now, right here.
My wife muses by her warming fire.
There's no moose, of course, just hallucination.
On no particular occasion,
on a flank of Signal Mountain.

No moose at all. Just strange desire.

Conspiracy Theory

Through that Taft Hotel window, the local radio station's neonized call letters
over the New Haven Green
now had the alien look of shimmery desert, deep space, one's oddest dream.

First National's carillon was tolling again,
no longer timely, bullets long since cold in the famous cadaver. Those bells

sounded ugly, more so than ever. Elitists all, we'd come to Yale but inhaled
this murdered Harvardian's meritocratic notions: you could get smart
but have a decent conscience, we thought, could study Locke, Bach,
Chaucer
— and later be a Freedom Rider.
Everything, we tried to believe in our hearts, would work itself out in
the end.

I didn't recognize it then, but this person had been my only
female friend who *was* pure friend, and nothing besides.
We'd hug and weep and sigh, talk out our own inadequacies, hopes.
And that was that. We were, I suppose, merely lonely.
She must have been no wiser than I, must have known no better what
we had.

How but in such ignorance could we two have made our way to bed?
It was an old nexus, sex and death. And faced with this *thing* in Texas,
this sundering of our faith, however callow,
why shouldn't we be irrational too? But now I wonder why we couldn't
value
our never having done what then we did — so pitiable, feckless. Don't
ask me.

It was the last place for us, bed. We would never return to where we'd
been,
not entirely. We just couldn't do that, before she did herself in.
Not suicide, exactly, but not exactly not: she starved herself to death.
By which I don't suggest, or imagine, she did so because of what we'd
done,
just before Thanksgiving vacation: crudely, badly done.

A labor it was, of hours, which stopped at last for no reason, except our lust
to stop at last. After which those radio letters, the mumbling walkers
below,
the looming Sterling Library towers: each had an offputting radium
glow.
The world felt new, strange, worse, even our conversation
leaping off the point completely,

whatever the point may have been. Our talk turned terse, uncustomary.
For all our so-called education, we didn't have a clue.
Advisors were working in Indochina now, but that wasn't in any course.
A group of Englishmen — across the sea, in some German cellar,
their hair absurd (by the times' standards) —

were ripping off black American rhythms and playing their same three
chords
again and again, behind banal words "I Wanna Hold Your Hand." "Love
Me Do."
There lived a sadsack fellow, James Earl Ray, whom nobody knew.
And I might have noticed, but somehow didn't, the yellow
cast to my womanfriend's cheeks, or her ribs, which if not yet quite
Biafran –

another name we didn't yet speak – were on their way. She ate only
aspirin.
Against the smogged night, her profile showed translucent as the drapes.
Her end, I guess, was also on its way: like Watergate, Sirhan, Cambodia,
AIDS,
Ali uncrowned by cretins. *Conspiracy* became a watchword, and is so
today,
though it means a breathing together, as if women and men

could draw a common air, which was precisely what it seemed back there
no two of them would ever – ever – really do again.

November

Mack's insides still ached from the test
at the fancy new clinic. The pain bothered less, though,
than how he'd had to lie there like that – Lord! – rear up,
and even the nurses watching. Almost to home now,

he saw Riddle's herd, the lot of them lying, down on the ground.
Everything pretty and sad: the Holsteins'
black and white that bold and true, and after a rain-day or two,
the grass – more than in summer – that green.

The mountainsides showed their trees shaved clean,
except for the dark of the oak and the beech leaves, over the river,
fog on the bald ridges awful, the white of ice. Already.
Not cancer.

He ought to be relieved, said the doctors.
They only found some little thumbs – a five-dollar word he forgot
the minute they named it – on the bowel wall.
Not uncommon, they called it. Like death, Mack thought.

He passed the school. Everyone up on the swings or on foot:
Tag. Football. Capture the flag. The kids

still looked like October in all their bright clothes.
They raced as if windchased, fast as he drove. So this wasn't it.

Not the six dragged-out months that his young wife got,
and not a shock, either, like their one child Thelma's accident.
He was all right, but he'd die.
You know that the whole while, but then one day it's different,

like going by Fifth Mile Meadow and now there's a house built in it,
or a restaurant you dress up for where Joey Binder's mill was.
Mack determined not to get going on that. Not again.
He'd turn up his hill, check his mailbox,

maybe come back and *fix* the foolish mailbox,
about to lie down on its side. He'd check in on his tiny string
of heifers. Instead he held steady, north.
Watson claimed he'd got out of dairy for good, just barbering

full-time in his little shop in the yellow frame building
across from the feed store: it hadn't changed much, if at all.
"Say that for the rest," Mack whispered. "Say that."
And their talk hadn't changed. Animals, crops. But before Watson could pull

the paper ring from around his neck, Mack spoke: "Well,
I'll have a shave." How did it happen? It felt like dreaming.
"Yes, I guess I'll have a shave," he decided.
And then, the cloth on his face steaming

while his friend gripped the ivory handle in his big fingers, stropping
the blade on dirt-dark leather, Mack said
through the fog, "I haven't had this done in years. Years."
But it felt good. Lord, it did feel good!

Timothy Liu

Western Wars Mitigated by the Confucian Analects

Illegal fund-raising and espionage attempting to ignite
new suspicions: "In a war with China, which side would you
take?" a neighbor asks, each of us rounded up into
camps, *august heaven having no affections*, prestige

Most Recent Book: *Hard Evidence* (Talisman House, 2001)

and technological edge the way we get things done around here
from the trenches of war-torn Europe to the smart bombs
of the Gulf fueling the massive engine of American success —
when the root is established, the law will grow, history
as it really happened — rifle toting hunters storming onto
bleachers at the gym where last night's game was won —
as a thing is cut and filed, as a thing is carved and polished,
machine-gun fire of the underline key on a student's
Smith-Corona but *a correspondence of words and action,
of name and actuality* while voices keep directing airstrikes
on Iraqi positions drowned by strong revanchist passions —
one thread from birth to death if only we could somehow find it,
Rosie Riveter sent back home to assist in our nation's
baby-boom from anti-business animus to economic
renaissance where we were in for "a nice little shoot-'em up,"
hey, hey, LBJ, how many kids did you kill today? —
*to fish with a line but not a net, nor shoot a bird
at rest*, Matthew Shepard the latest hate-crime poster child —
to go too far is the same as not going far enough,
the carcass of James Byrd but an act of "animal
cruelty" posted on that web site "for Whites only" — a Klan
cartoon of newlyweds driving off from church to bedlam
with two blacks tied to their bumper — *in the morning go
and gather grass, in the evening twist your ropes* as China's
Most-Favored-Nation Status undergoes House review, stalled
peace talks ushering restless ground troops in — *the best course
is to establish virtue, the next best is to establish
achievement, and the next best after that to establish words*.

Many Mansions

Lacking gravitas, disillusioned yuppies congregate
in a faux-Etruscan theater, acting out our appetite
for concatenating tactics intended to shock
a brazenly chic high-styled public hardly fungible
for such epiphanic free falls lodged inside
a fissure where nothingness steadily blooms,
halcyon sophisticates parading secondhand hauteur
amid all that ambient razzmatazz abuzz inside
a media-mogul hell nudging us into recklessness —
hortatory slogans fit for anorexic teens passing
entire winter months in bed to keep caloric
expenditures down till spring's explosive riot

of floralia takes root, preening eyes afire
with a weakness for amassing iconographic
bric-a-brac and excess schlock — acrolithic masks
unearthed at sites by *tombaroli* declared
persona non grata plundering troves so Victorian
in their clutter — *objets d 'art* beautiful but mute —
the Euphronios krater cooling off in a Swiss vault.

Georgia O'Keefe: American Icon

Announced to her playmate, "I'm going to be an artist."
Enrolled at Sacred Heart to receive instruction first.
Viewed an exhibition of controversial works on paper.
Discarded old materials and mannerisms to start anew.
Vacationed summers in the Sangre de Cristo Mountains.
Traded in Penitente crosses for animal pelvic bones.
Abstracted nature but still relied on financial support.
Moved into an apartment overlooking Lexington Avenue.
Rejected Freudian notions focussed on her gender.
Invited by Dole Pineapple to produce a corporate ad.
Acquired three acres in Abiquiu an adobe house of course.
Suffered a partial loss, left only with peripheral sight.
Awarded a Presidential medal, the highest civilian honor.
Scattered on the desert floor at the age of ninety-eight.
Commemorated a decade later on a U. S. postage stamp.

Emptying the Mind

Assuming the lotus, his ears and nostrils
sealed with wax, the rime glottidis
blocked by his tongue, Haridasa was slowly raised
like an ancient Buddha hewn from stone
then set inside a wooden box they buried
for forty days. His breath ceased. His pulse

undetectable at the wrists when they
finally dug him out, his bronzed skin
clean-shaven as pupils brought him back to life –

Robert Long

Little Black Dino

When I was a kid I was crazy for cars,
Drew them in art class, in my biology notes,
Wrote away for color brochures.
I'd sit in my parents' powder blue Olds,

Staring at the few gauges, toying
With the slender chrome blinker.
Everything fresh lay in the future.
For seven years – from 1967, when I was 13,

Until 1974, the year I turned 20 –
Enzo Ferrari produced an automobile
He called Dino, after his son,
Dead of leukemia. It didn't wear

The Ferrari badge, a prancing horse.
It just said "Dino," in understated script,
Near the simple round tail lights.
It had a six-cylinder engine mounted mid-chassis,

Behind the hand-stitched seats; it was light –
Less than a ton – and it was fast.
It was the most beautiful car
Enzo ever let out of Modena.

More beautiful than most painting,
Most poetry. But Enzo Ferrari's long dead,
And Fiat runs Ferrari, and no one
Knows good from bad anymore. All I know

Is that there's plenty to keep me happy:
The Dino, for example, which
Is both physical and spiritual fact,
Like the symphony Shostakovich wrote at 19,

Most Recent Book: *Blue* (Canio's Editions, 1999)

Anything by Tiepolo, or just remembering how I knew you.
I'm happy writing to you now: I like the feeling
Of this black pen rolling, liquid, nearly literate
Across the yellow page.

Last summer I saw three Dinos.
One was Italian racing red, one was silver,
And one chrome yellow. The yellow copy
Lived in a driveway just down the road;

Whoever owned it parked it
Behind a grove of baby pines,
To discourage vandals, or the merely curious,
I suppose, though it's hard to hide a yellow Ferrari

In greenery. I've always wanted a black Dino,
Though I doubt they made any. But why am I writing you
About my old obsession when we both know
That no matter what I babble on about.

It's just prelude
To another attempt to tell you
How much I miss you and why I will have to go on
Missing you. The other night I could hear

An ordinary car gliding past my house
And your regular breathing all those miles away,
In your room, on the other end of the phone,
Lying on your bed. speechless, receiver

To your ear. both of us not wanting
To hang up. And when we finally did.
You said "Seeya,"
Though you won't, ever again.

I guess I'm telling you all this, my friend,
My brother, because, loving you,
I want you to know all the things
That make me up, the way I know your secret nickname,

All the little odd things that make you irreplaceable:
It's those I think of now. To my very short list
Of what's far too beautiful ever to lose I add you.

Jack Benny

In five days it will be Arthur Rimbaud's
139th birthday, is what I'm thinking
As I drive home from work

In fog like dry ice,
Home with leftover birthday cake
In the passenger seat

And Van Morrison on the retro FM station.
I'm Jack Benny's age today, and consider
The parallels. There aren't any.

Ten years ago is a blur:
A snootful of coke, half in the bag?
Out to dinner? Writing a poem, like I am now?

Maybe all of these. I'm 39,
Acceptably healthy and solvent. Half of my friends
Are dead. Where was Rimbaud at 39?

And who could have wanted a life like that,
Anyway? Me, at 15. I'm astonished
To be sitting in a bourgeois armchair,

With a car, a cat, credit cards, not only
Alive, but making sounds out of letters, like I did
When I was six, back in that enchanted time

Before meaning took over.

Nowhere to Mosh

I can imagine the scene
As you step from the vaporetto:

Campos, campaniles, muddy smell.
From my crepuscular apartment

I watch birds leave the trees,
The dog curl into sleep. I thought

I saw you walking, today,
But it was someone else. Then

I saw a car like yours: no, again.
What are you doing in that far-off place,

And how happy can you be, speaking
Only midwestern American, wearing

A baseball cap, and nowhere to mosh?

Love Potion No. 9

This is the most beautiful day
Of all time: 80 clear degrees,
Summer sunlight jazzing a slope of trees
Like broccoli against the so-blue sea, boats,

Tiny jewels adrift, silent on the horizon.
From my car parked in front of a church
I can watch the most beautiful boy
I have ever seen mow the lawn: he's blond, maybe 16,

Very tan, skinny, just wearing baggy black shorts,
And all the long young muscles move
Under his warm brown skin
As he shoves the big mower around,

His kid's angel face placid and purposeful. . . .
All the way back along the fast hilly highway
Stands of evergreens and oaks soak up the sun,
The radio blares, I am happy

Thinking of the boy and the sea. Racing
The twist of roads home, the beautiful gargle
Of twin camshafts at 4000 rpm tells me
That this is all I need: 5 P.M. melon-colored sunlight

Slanting over the silver hood. What greens
In the trees, what a rich cerulean sky, what joy
Kicking it down into third
And screaming around the curve,

Soundgarden on the radio, and the retinal image
Of the grass-mowing kid even better than Tiepolo,
Better than Brahms, reachable, ecstatic, true.
O this is the world I want without end.

Adrian Louis

One of the Grim Reaper's Disguises

Death does not speak
to me with meaty breath
although ancient hamburgers
dance through my veins and
the leering buffalo skull
on the wall above my couch
dribbles drool onto my heart.

At fifty, I have learned to see
the Grim Reaper in all his disguises.
I can see him in a can of Budweiser.
I can see him in a shaker of salt.
Tonight, death speaks through spuds.
On my kitchen counter a ten-pound
bag of potatoes is rabid with tendrils.
They smell like a coven of wings.
I'm afraid to go near them. They've
already strangled one of my cats.
Hey, these spuds are not vegetarians.
These are bad-ass rez potatoes.
They'll sucker-punch you
and kick you in the nuts
when you're not looking.
If they're not death
I don't know what is.

Indian Sign Language

Most of our communication
can be done by quirky
movements of the body.
When you're angry because of
some malfunctioning synapse,
I simply nod my head and frown
and you know I'm copiloting
your cerebral space ship.

Most Recent Book: *Ancient Acid Flashes Back* (University of Nevada Press, 2000)

Today when we drove through
the flatlands to Chadron,
I turned on Public Radio and waved
my hands in the air, pretending
I was directing some orchestra.
You chortled gleefully when I passed
cars and then far beyond them,
flipped them the bird like
I was some macho lowrider.

When I beeped the horn
at grazing cows, we both laughed.
Darling, I just looked at you
and twitched my head for no reason
and you laughed so freely.
I pushed my lips out and nodded
when a state trooper passed
and you giggled.

Today you were secure
with my sign language
but at the Safeway store
you screamed at some strange
fat woman for no reason.
The stunned woman's face

was crimson and her two chins
we're quivering with fear.
I put my index finger
to my forehead and circled
it until the woman understood.
I'm sorry, I told her. *I'm sorry*.

Later, as we neared the folly of
Cowturdville, a goofy antelope
got on the road and stopped
directly in front of our car.
I screeched to a halt, but I could
hear its nervous, clattering
feet above the drone
of the air-conditioner.

Its eyes were dark, fluttering hearts
that jumped out and kissed our eyes.
An ancient song of blood rang out
and snapped our human minds.
In an instant of lucidity, you

whispered: *Spirit, it's a spirit*,
and neither one of us laughed.

Dead Skoonk

Driving to the neurologist
in Rapid City, I cannot
draw you into dialogue.
It's been over five years
since the diminutive Chinese
MD told us your brain cells
were tangling forever.
You're silent for thirty minutes
until I take my lower dentures
and wedge them on my nose
and sing: *Dashing through the*
snow, in a one-horse open sleigh . . .

You laugh and say: *You have*
a kitten on your nose!
I repeat what you say. We
toss the phrase back and
forth for ten minutes until
we pass a dead skunk
in the middle of the road
near the Oblaya store.
You ask what it is and I
say it's a *Skooonk!*
Skooonk I say until you
trust the glint in my eyes.
Skooonk you say and
smile, contented with
your mad chauffeur, your
daft cataloguer of beasts.

Old Friend in the Dark

I've never been in a bad car crash,
but I've been on this same hospital
floor for a month and a half so I
know you can and can't hear me.
You are a shadow in a shadow land.

Yes, I've been to the country you're in.
Huge black birds float by and whisper.
When you squeak out fear, they shrug
and coo softness. Do not fear them.
Do not fear the green-faced men
who sit on the edge of your bed.
They are only green with envy.
Stand with me, let's look at you.
What glassy eyes, your brown skin is
stretched over the pale heart of fear.
Let's sing of hot Dakota summer nights.
Let's sing of frybread smell and ice-cold
beer, the sexy eyes of sweet, dark women,
and the dust of cars and kids and ghosts.
Let's sing of everyone, young and strong.
Let's dance backwards
to the strength of summer.
Wake up now friend
and come back home.

VICTOR MARTINEZ

I'm Still Alive

The city is just a cluster of concrete tumors
inside of which we feed, but it's best
not to think about it. Better to let your misery
grope wildly on the sweetness of someone else's bed,
than admit your only true, wise and honest master
is a worm.

In this corporate cubicle of boredom and terror
it's easy to be a weak. For instance, there's a guy
two doors down from here, who masters his girlfriend
with a belt buckle, deliciously tweeks
her pubic hair and plays the bronking cowboy
on the saddle of her tits,
and this evening, coming home, I saw a cop on the corner

Most Recent Book: *Parrot in the Oven: Mi Vida* (Harper Collins, 1998)

perform the magic act of a wound, opening,
and Behold!, a wound opened.

Of course, they're just playing their game of poor-me,
poor-you, and so I pretend
it's all a big spectacle. The truth is, I'm relieved . . . really,
that it's not me being knocked around by that guy's penis, not me
blessed by that cop's magical wand, but two poor jerks
the great stone wheel of misery just
happened to roll over.

Whoever comes to my door selling a lotion of flattery
to butter up my boss's crotch,
or the ultimate razor for shaving my face
to that perfect butt-licking smoothness
the girls all prefer, I'll probably let in.
Because that's the way life is. And tomorrow, I'll strap on
the sutures of my smile, clasp my computer keyboard
and dream the team, kiss the family shrine, or whatever
finger stuck up one's ass buzzword is in fashion.

At the corner newsstand, the glamour magazines are thick
with glossies of starving megastars grinning so tight
it must hurt them down to their groins.
In big corporate powwows they're grinning, too,
grinning and lying, lying and grinning,
it being easy enough to clash two negatives together
and spark a positive.
Empty suits on lunatic life rafts
drift down the center of Wall Street.
My eyes are veined from soaking in advertisements,
my lungs blackened by traffic exhaust,
and my soul is rotted back a thousand generations deep.
Does anyone care then
that I scorch my liver with the thistles of alcohol?

Who turned the warm breath of milk sour
in the mouth of the woman I love? Who,
when I freed every last granule of dream for avalanche,
hauled away my leaking aboriginal boat, and left me
a verb, ready to die: a spirochete
wiggling toward an absent source?
It was you, my love, my tender chance abrasion,
my scab of pain that I peel back again and again

from the horizon's skin,
because it is the window through which I see,
that I am still alive.

Failed Teachers

The guy who taught Himmler how to count wooden pegs,
and Napoleon to read maps, sits with me in my kitchen,
drinking coffee, the years of chalk
erased from his blackboard now tracing his hair.

The woman who studied the alphabets
trampled under the lightning hooves of Genghis Khan,
gave sex therapy lessons to Caligula,
flirts with me at the bar, saying, "My, what a
fine, neatly pressed shirt of grammer
you have on."
                              Both have denounced their times
and vow to end their days burrowing inside a proton.

Over a sugar-glazed donut, the old teacher says, "Why
study, when history will only take you up
like a cat in its paws
and devour you from the head down."
Over a gin gimlet, extra on the sour, the spinster claims
that reality is just corny crayon designs
splashed with puny exhorts of light.

They should marry, these two, grow old together,
wizened by the children they will never have.
Because . . . of this . . . they both agree,
there isn't a child alive not whipped red
with the ink marks of tortured books.

Sisters

My sisters hate me for the shrine my mother
built around my laziness, the kneeling-altar
they were forced to care for
and embellish with flowers.

Now they're tired of my whining embrace,
and want nothing more than to fix my head
between the tumblers of their breasts
and squeeze me like a chocolate-ripened pimple.

My sisters mouth a zero
for the faith they have in me.
One scolds me, and with a deadly look
of milk, says, "You deserve the earth to bury you
inside the same grave
you've tried to reduce me to."
Another says there's never been any truth
to my kingly words
other than what a crown of shit attracts.

Don't mess with us, brother, say my loving . . . loving
sisters. We will fly into you on the wings
of our knitting needles,
unstitch you in every seam.
Lift one finger to have us attend you
and we will scorch you back to the dampened bed
of our mother's small spittoon.

A Tiny Man of Print

I'm examining with a microscope the certificate
that gives me the right to be a tiny man of print.
Whatever it says, the letters are too small
for this lens, but
this much I know: everything
that isn't already rubble
will be plundered from my eyes.

I should be grimacing over this little bite
of wisdom, but I'm pretty much rotted through
with the rust of books, which means I
don't care. I've quit caring for some time. See
those boys, playing marbles?
One will grow up to be a man who read novels
yet whose smile means business
when he levels a gun toward your belly.

You may say, "What better gift than to sit back
at a desk, and pound into ink
the honorable sweat of a man." But I say to you, that
above that desk, there is a clock
gnawing on the minutes, a calendar sticking fast
like a fishhook in everlasting air.

You have to understand, after it's all been said
and done, these schooled tints of tremulous alphabet
will go on faking me better than I fake myself.

Whoever you are, ask why I choose to have every corpuscle
scorched and cindered into these clasping compounds of ash?
Is it to scold those who only want
more generous portions at the feast? Or shoo away
the evil that crowds in on the world like
a host of flies, multiplying, shoulder to shoulder,
on a page? No,
it was because I was once in a forest.
No one around, only trees, a creek that didn't babble,
and a universe above me
wheeling in its soundless hub. And yet I heard
a little boy, talking, as if afraid of the dark. And
for no reason, other than the cold, or maybe
loneliness, I reached for my throat and found
it was my own voice, talking.

Campbell McGrath

Capitalist Poem #38

Consider the human capacity for suffering,
our insatiable appetite for woe.
I do not say this lightly
but the sandwiches at Subway
suck. Foaming lettuce,
mayo like rancid bear grease,
meat the color of a dead dog's tongue.
Yet they are consumed
by the millions
and by the tens of millions.

Most Recent Book: *Road Atlas* (Ecco Press, 1999)

So much for the food. The rest
I must pass over in silence.

Capitalist Poem #36

We've got this cheese down here to give away,
tens of thousands of pounds of cheese.

We're trying to establish procedures and specifications,
rules to discourage speculation and hoarding,

guidelines to foster the proper use of this
extraordinary resource. What we need is a system.

I mean it. Not one damn piece of cheese
leaves here until we get this thing figured out.

The Manatee

Deep sunk in the dream-time of his terminal coma,
the manatee persists like a vegetative outpatient,
victim of the whirling propellers of impatience
and a buoyantly bovine quiescence gone nova.

Dream deep, brother. Dream long and deep, sister sea-cow.
May millennia of soft tides and seagrass sustain thy sleep
across the dark ages of extinction. May your memory keep
heavy the hearts and hulls of your inheritors. Us, for now.

The Miami Beach Holocaust Memorial

A great green hand reaches up to the Florida sky.
Circled in palms, ringed by bowers of white bougainvillea,
its flesh is wrought of mellifluous iron, color
of olive leaves, from which emerge a human multitude
transfigured to forms of tortured supplication,
blind wraiths ascending to grace amid the graven
numerals of the death camps and the lily pond
reflecting clouds like faces cast down in silent vigil.
From his grandmother Sam has learned that these
are people "climbing away from their troubles,"

a formula that quiets without satisfying his curiosity,
piqued daily, en route to the grocery store,
by this incongruous vision across from the golf course,
and I'm glad he isn't with me today, stuck behind tour buses
unleashing lines of mourners come to honor
some black anniversary, elders grim
with the rectitude of their homborgs, a coterie
of teenagers from the high school waving placards
proclaiming *Never Forget* and *Never Again*,
slogans predicated upon an immemorial desire
to believe in the perfectibility of humankind
even in the face of such witness to our monstrosity
as the testimonial obelisk of horrors that is
history. Brick upon brick, blueprint after blueprint,
so the Grand Edifice of Civilization takes shape,
Xanadu abandoned in favor of prison ramparts,
blind walls to guard us from that most savage enemy,
he that abideth within, and you are welcome
to whatever degree of optimism you feel justified
in the efficacy of such constructs to protect us
from ourselves, as witness the wooden horse at Troy,
Joshua's horn at Jericho. When Hadrian's Wall
went up the Scots came down from the hills
to attack the Roman legions naked,
smeared with tallow, keening wildly in the snow.
Even the Great Wall of China could not keep
the Mongols at bay forever. So have we advanced,
horde upon horde, so surmounted wall after
wall after wall. Flood upon fresh flood,
the tide of blood deepens and renews itself,
generation unto generation, the will to remember
overthrown by the flesh's obligation to forget,
to erect its temple on the scorched foundation of the old,
to clean the slate and chalk a new testament
to become a ghostly palimpsest for future ages.
Thus we recall the Provencal only for their troubadours,
the Olmecs for astronomy and the fanged god of tropical rain.
We remember Lucy because the australopithecines
walked upright and killed efficiently,
and we have survived them in like manner,
killing and being killed, strong in a world of strength,
and even when they have outlived their usefulness
we cannot disregard the deep structures

of our inheritance, the genetic press recycling its type,
guanine, adenine, thymine, cytosine,
enzymes comprising a map of the species,
instructions for assembly in a language of universal simplicity
as with the diagrams that accompany architect's lamps
or Scandinavian furniture, G A T C, four irrelevant letters
we share with chimps and whales and lilies
and phytoplankton, all living matter descended
from the original lucky molecule. Which is to say:
evolution. Which is not to say: progress.
This is what I'd like to say to Sam, to tell him
without having to tell him, though I would never
indulge the false bravery to spill this bitter cup
into a child's ear. Someday Sam's children,
the children of my children's children, however many times
removed, will remember us, dimly and inaccurately,
for the mythic splendor of our golden arches,
as they peer forth from places of hiding in the ghettos
or scrublands of whatever bogs or deserts remain,
as they are hunted down, one by one, whether
for the red hair of the Celts still clinging to their forearms
or the life-force of the Jews bequeathed them by Elizabeth
or the vestigial memory of some as yet undreamed
category of violent distinction and hatred.
Up from the swamplands and avenues of Florida,
and the edenic faiths and faces of Florida,
and the towers that spring from the fertile sands of Florida,
and the flowers that predate the golden cities of Florida,
a great green hand ascends toward the heavens.
People have assembled around it in the sunshine.
They are singing or they are weeping. They are
fingering its wrist, crowding its tower of stairs to a standstill.
They are climbing away from their troubles,
crying out. They are green and floral. They are metal.
They are ash. They are flesh. They are us.

Heather McHugh

Ghazal of the Better-Unbegun

A book is a suicide postponed.
— Cioran

Too volatile, am I? too voluble? too much a word-person?
I blame the soup: I'm a primordially
stirred person.

Two pronouns and a vehicle was Icarus with wings.
The apparatus of his selves made an ab-
surd person.

The sound I make is sympathy's: sad dogs are tied afar.
But howling I become an ever more un-
heard person.

I need a hundred more of you to make a likelihood.
The mirror's not convincing — that at-best in-
ferred person.

As time's revealing gets revolting, I start looking out.
Look in and what you see is one unholy
blurred person.

The only cure for birth one doesn't love to contemplate.
Better to be an unsung song, an unoc-
curred person.

McHugh, you'll be the death of me — each self and second studied!
Addressing you like this, I'm halfway to the
third person.

Most Recent Book: *The Father of the Predicaments*
(Wesleyan/University Press of New England, 1999)

Past All Understanding

The langouste's longfeelers may be the result of a single gush of thought.
— Ezra Pound
For it is the opinion of choice virtuosi that the brain is only a crowd of little animals, but with teeth and claws extremely sharp. . . .
— Jonathan Swift

A woman there was balancing her baby
back-to-back. They held each other's hands,
did tilts and bends and teeter-totters on
each other's inclinations, making
casual covalency into
a human idiogram,
spontaneous Pilobolus —
a spectacle at which
the estimable Kooch
(half Border and half Lab)

began to bark. He wouldn't stop. The child slid off
the woman's back — now they were two again (and so
he quieted a bit). But they were two who
scowled and stared (now it was I who grew
disquieted). You looked,
I started to explain, like one

big oddity to him. (They weren't appeased.) He barks at
crippled people too. (Now they were horrified.) Meanwhile a wind

rose at the kiosk, stapled with yard jobs, sub-clubs, bands somebody named
for animals. The whole park fluttered up and flailed, and Kooch, unquenchable,
perceived the higher truth. The upshot was a bout of barking wild enough
to make the bicyclists bypassing (bent beneath their packs),
an assortment of teaching assistants (harried, earnest, hardly earning) —
and even the white-haired full professorships
all come to a halt, in the wake
of the wave of their tracks.
What brouhahas! What flaps!
To Kooch's mind, if you
could call it that,
the worst was
yet to come —

for looming overhead, a host of red and yellow kites appeared
intent on swooping even to the cowlicks of the humans — Were
these people blind? — that woman in pink, that man in blue, who
paused there in his purview, stupidly, to shake their heads? He thinks

we're in danger, I tried again
to reason with my fellow man. But now the dog

was past all understanding, he was uncontainable. He burst
into a pure fur paroxysm, blaming the sky for all that we
were worth: he held his ground with four feet braced

against the overturning earth...

The Gulf Between the Given and the Gift

Between the driven and the drift, you're moved —
whether air, or a cattle prod, does it.
Art, said the naturalist, in heaven. Said the blind:
Long time no touch. The hooker interjected:
Come again. But I, I once more was unable

even to converse. (I could not get the lion
out of mind, intending to tear a gazelle
from the love of the leap of her life.) There was much
we would catch. There was much we would miss.
There was some we would have to do twice.

Qua Qua *Qua*

Philosophical duck, it takes
some fine conjunctive paste to put
this nothing back together, gluing glue to glue —

a fine conjunction, and a weakness too
inside the nature of the noun. O duck, it doesn't
bother you. You live in a dive, you daub the lawn,

you dabble bodily aloft: more wakes
awake, where sheerness shares
its force. The hot air moves

you up, and then
the cool removes. There's no
such thing as things, and as for as:

it's just an alias, a form of time,
a self of other, something between thinking
and a thought (one minds his mom,

one brains his brother). You seem
so calm, o Cain of the corpus callosum,
o fondler of pondlife's fallopian gore,

knowing nowheres the way we don't
dare to, your web-message
subjectless (nothing a person could

pray or pry predicates from). From a log
to a logos and back, you go flinging
the thing that you are — and you sing

as you dare — on a current of
nerve. On a wing
and a wing.

LYNNE MCMAHON

We Take Our Children to Ireland

What will they remember best? The barbed wire
still looped around the Belfast airport,
the building-high Ulster murals —
but those were fleeting, car window sights,
more likely the turf fires lit each night,
the cups of tea their father brought
and the buttered soda farls, the sea wall
where they leaped shrieking into the Irish Sea
and emerged, purpling, to applause;
perhaps the green castle at Carrickfergus,
but more likely the candy store
with its alien crisps — vinegar? they ask,
prawn cocktail? Worcestershire leek?
More certainly still the sleekly syllabled
odd new words, gleet and shite,
and grand responses to everyday events:
How was your breakfast? Brilliant.
How's your crust? Gorgeous.

Most Recent Book: *The House of Entertaining Science* (David R. Godine, 2000)

Everything after that was gorgeous,
brilliant. How's your gleeted shite?
And the polite indictment from parents
everywhere, the nicely dressed matrons
pushing prams, brushing away their older kids
with a Fuck off, will ye? Which stopped
our children cold. Is the water cold,
they asked Damian, before they dared it.
No, he said, it's not cold, it's
fooking cold, ye idjits.
And the mundane hyperbole of rebuke —
you little puke, I'll tear your arm off
and beat you with it, I'll row you out to sea
and drop you, I'll bury you in sand
and top you off with rocks —
to which the toddler would contentedly nod
and continue to drill his shovel
into the sill. All this will play on
long past the fisherman's cottage and farmer's
slurry, the tall hedgerows lining the narrow
drive up the coast, the most beautiful
of Irish landscapes indelibly fixed
in the smeared face of two-year-old Jack —
Would you look at that, his father said
to Ben and Zach, shite everywhere, brilliant.
Gorgeous, they replied. And meant it.

Marriage Dissolving in the Upstairs Room

Mites in their cypress kingdom
prepare the feast they're unaware they'll be
for flycatchers and chisel beaks. Squirrels in their brown
on nut brown barber pole
race around and down

as if all rounds were spirals
set to hypnotize the man inside, dissolving
marriage in the upstairs room, while the vacuum cleaner
and broom suck up and lift away evidence
of each day's brief decay.

Too brief, the poets say,
though art may be long, to keep the nuptial
song and its attendant sentiment. Sediment, he'd say,

for what grows stale impales
the mind as well as heart,

keeps the whole brain revolving
through the puncture wound to the outer edge
and back again, a carousel of pain.
But wait, that metaphor is mixed,
though fixable,

perhaps, if that were all
that needed fixing, a recasting of the vehicle
to make the tenor clear, but he's wearier than he's ever been
of making that third thing
resemblances become.

Third things break
the ground of being, and though it may be true
the triangle is the stablest geometric form, the Edenic form
was two, at least it was till doubt
made marriage food for thought.

These Same, These Many Birds

that daily skim the railings of the deck
and wait their turn at the shallow bath,
or wait dispersal at the grackles' crack
of black command and then come back,
won't break their pledge to keep me fixed
on degrees of home and distances.
The parabola their tree to house to feeder makes
— though sketched on air — remains crosshatched
by each day's partial looping back,
a record I log each evening at the sink
in sinking geometries of my own.
These same, these many birds
drag the ragged hem of light to earth
then fold their hollow bones. Are there birds
there, where you are, in the dark? Heart,
this skein of thought flings out
to net and bring you near. Husband
your wife, the nightjars call, before
the fall the fall the fall.

Christopher Merrill

Because

variation on a theme by Yannis Ritsos

Because the Dead Sea released its hostages — the taste for salt, a rudder
and a sail;
Because a band of Roman slaves, disguised in their master's robes, fled
across the Continent;
Because one manuscript, one waxen shoal of words, burned a monastery
down;
Because the sun spurned the Black Forest, and windmills ground the
peasants into the earth, into the air, into the voice of the boy who
cried wolf;
Because the crowd hissed at the empty stage, and the prompter drank
himself to sleep, and the diva hid in the pit;
Because we let barbed wire replace our wooden faces and fences;
Because a scream left a trail through the ruined air;
Because I followed that trail into the woods, where my hands dissolved
in smoke and rain;
Because I wandered for days, weeks, until I found himself outside a
walled city, a city abandoned hundreds of years ago;
Because I couldn't scale the walls nor find a way to return to my home-
land, and so I settled along a river in the desert;
Because the river changed course, and its banks crumbled into the dry
bed, where I was on my knees, speechless and afraid;
Because whenever I hike into the desert, I talk and talk and talk;
Because I have never been to the desert;
Because I refuse to follow any trail whose markings are not completely
clear;
Because I distrust signs, guideposts, land- and seamarks;
Because on my single visit to the ancient city I rifled the ruins for pot-
sherds and stone tools — and was warned never to return;
Because I heed all warnings, all directives from the crowd;
Because I won't listen to anyone but myself;
Because I love to cry wolf;
Because everything I read smells of smoke;
Because sometimes I wake at night to find my hands covered with salt,
my sheet wrapped around me like a sail;
Because I can't tell if this is the desert or the sea;

Most Recent Book: *Only the Nails Remain* (Rowman & Littlefield, 1999)

Because I never learned to read the stars and don't know where we're
heading;
Because of this and more, much more, I hid your name in the well . . .
and here it is again, filling my cup.

Three Weeds

I. Horsetail

Swishing the flat backs of boxwood and stone,
The stems of dusty miller, and a spread
Of daffodil leaves drying in the sun,
The horsetail rears, unbridled, wild as seed.

It gallops through the garden, leaving its shoots
And markings everywhere. It drags the hired man,
Who twisted a rope of roots around his wrists
And waist, down to his knees. And when the twine

Breaks, the rushes bolt, trampling flower
Borders and beds, strewing their litter through
The compost pile, until one stalk, one augur
Of empire, clears the wall and lopes away.

II. Purple Loosestrife

Another interloper staking out its claim —
These spires of purple loosestrife moving through the ranks
Of roadside swamps and ditches, these slick managers
Of a vast seed system, of bees and wind and water,
Weed out reeds, and rushes with the diligence
Of an auditor denying ordinary deductions.
Yet here it is dissolving differences again:
To calm a team of oxen driven mad by mosquitoes,
The plowman cuts a switch of willow-herb and whips
The backs of the broad animals, clearing the air.

III. Fireweed

For towhees, mice, and mule deer, fireweed blazes
A trail into the underbrush, a violet

Smoldering overtaking ruts the road
Crew, like a flash flood, left — a path no one

Will follow home tonight . . . This is the fire
An orphan fans, hitchhiking toward the pass,

Cursing the ones who walked away from him
The fever raging in the rearview mirror

Of a woman in a pickup, pulling over
To let him in. The burning. The flowering.

Words

Paint blistering on the ceiling of the den:
Excuses gathered speed, helping no one.
So I walked up the same mountain as before.

Passed the same barbed wire, broken glass, tire tracks.
Then vetch, and penstemon, and the rusted water
Pipe coursing down through stands of scrub oak, aspen.

In the dry creek: a rattlesnake, coiling,
Guarding the rocks and ripped oak roots, head swaying,
Shaking its only bead, like a fanatic.

I know the little ones can kill: their venom's
Pure as the fury of the lovers' first
Attempts at cruelty, before they learn

What words or gestures will end an argument
Without destroying everything again —
And yet I stood there for a while, listening

To a woodpecker addling an aspen,
A mule deer thrashing in the underbrush,
And near the city thunder rumbling. . .

Some rattlesnakes can grow as long as humans.
This one I sidestepped in the end, then headed
Up the steep part of the trail, holding my tongue.

Doppelgänger

The man who called and wanted my wife's measurements;
Who sent me to the closet, the bureau, and the trunk,
Gathering clothes like a stockboy; who took away
Her favorite colors, her pants' length, the cut of her bra —

For a surprise; who claimed he had a photograph;
Who said she was carrying his child; who needed her,
Like me; who promised not to hurt her, like me; whose lines
Of speech blurred in the wake of passing cars and sirens;
Whose name kept changing, like the weather and the leaves;
Who said we'd talk again; who refused to say goodbye;
Who's hidden now among these words; who tilts my pencil
Toward the ocean and the sky, still writing, *Are you there?*

Susan Mitchell

Pussy Willow (An Apology)

Why delay? Today I stopped
to rub the fur, like the tender
ear of a cat, stopped

to stroke the lush grey
plush (and oh, the pink!) as if
the cat had rasped

itself to frenzy, to an
ecstasy of itch
all raw

this steak tartare, this
chafe of meat, and
because of this

I was late (the willows in
their bins outside
the florist almost as tall as I)

and once again, have traded
friendship for
dillydally.

I had to take off
my gloves, and I would have
taken off my skin

(for why should I put
a barrier between
myself and anything?)

Most Recent Book: *Erotikon* (HarperCollins, 2000)

to pluck, to blow back
each separate tuft
of foam (in down, sink down)

because I cannot keep my hands
off the world and the world
out of my breath. What

does the world want (anyway)
of me with its pussy willows, with
its tears and angers

its greeds and splendors, its
petitions of
skyscrapers and waterfalls?

And what do I want with
its famous and forgotten? And is
this the purpose of my life,

to figure this out? Or is it
to touch and be touched? And if
I love the world more than

any one person, or if I love
one person more
than the world, what

does this say of me?
And what do I say to friends
when they keep me waiting,

Oh dally, friend, delight
so that I may rub
it from your body

its furs and gewgaws, its
horrors and sweetnesses, so you may
deliver it to me, you

the messenger, the unwinged
the prosaic in all
its scratch and bliss?

Girl Tearing Up Her Face

Where it's rubbed out, start there, where it's torn
where something like a burn in cloth the hot
metal pressed too long, forgotten

                                        in paper the worm-
hole, the eaten up, the petal frayed browning
at the edges the flower's
flesh like cigarette paper

consumed by the breath sucked back into
the body: yes, body, that's what
that is what — no, I'm not stalling   body

is what I mean to talk about, what I have
on my mind   in my mind   my mind
in the body   of the body

and what's disturbing, yes, that above all: the joy
right there in her face, the girl's, as if she
had been smacked with it, the big fish joy

a cold hard wet smack by something flailing out, this
joy thing throwing itself around

or as if someone had thrown a pudding, a thick batter
and now her face was trying to work its way
through that mess — yes, joy, the mess

the ugliness of it because it has not yet
been practiced, the mouth trying out
positions before the mirror   the mouth

performing little sounds up and down the scale
of pleasure   the joy not yet prepared
for anyone else to look at   the shock like

a flashbulb going off, a camera
pouncing before one is ready   before
one has run the tongue over   taken a bite

out of the smile   hands arranging the hair
the girl looks all doors open, the sheer
weight of her coming starting

to come and her body sucking it back
inhaling each tooth of bliss
running her fingers up and down the comb:

it's that ugly I want to rub my face in, that
blossoming, as if a tree had suddenly —
the stamen pushing up out of

the petals, the throat of the apple, its
woods and the dark seeds
bursting the blossom, so I push

her back, I open her mouth right there
where she sits on the swing
a rage of delight shivering the tree's —

can I say flesh, can I say skin? — and
I can't bear to look at her
doing that, it seems too private, as if she

had been caught having a dream she
didn't know she was having,
all her wings run over by pleasure, joy

having a tantrum all over her, this
limp rag of beaten down, and the photographer
thinking, Yeah, this is it, the moment

he wants to last and last — the forever: now with
the girl falling asleep on the swing,
her sleep in full view, its lids

pulled open so the deep anaesthesia
of her pleasure is suddenly visible, sucked
inside out so he can hear every sound

a face can make and it's those sounds
he wants to shudder down on, those
cries with the flesh still

attached to them and what they have
been pulled from gaping and
ragged and this is what will be handed

to the girl in black and white, this face
which in two seconds would have
changed and gone on changing, this face

she never suspected and of course, she'll have to
rip it into pieces and keep ripping
because even now I can't bear

to look at her suddenly awake, I want
her asleep again, unbegun, unstarted, the shades
drawn so I can float every which possible, all

manner of across her face accommodating
as a lap, and I don't think
For God's sake, she's only eleven, what does she

know or understand of anything? I'm — I'm flooding
even as she rips herself in two, even as
she vows never to be this person

I'm putting my head down in her lap, pushing
her back on the swing with so much force —
What could split open? What could eat her up?

David Mura

First-Generation Angels

They lived behind the fire house and Little Saigon Auto.
In spring he sat on the porch while his mother,
the manicurist at Khan's salon, clipped his hair.
Smells of lilac, exhaust. A siren sucking up the distance.
A black corona drops to his shoulders. An impatient sigh.

How soon he vanished from her. Like his father staring
from the couch at the color TV, his black Veteran's cap
from the surplus store sliding a mask over his eyes.
Five sisters, three brothers. Smells of pho and coriander.
While he's gone to fry stacks of tortillas at Little Tijuana's.

With lean bad-ass cheeks. Hair pomaded back. A thin mustache.
You know then he's written poems descrying *Miss Saigon*.
His life as Nuprin, a little yellow pill for your pains.
His uncle dead years ago in a paddy. VC bullet in his brow.
He and his poems will read next week at Patrick's Cabaret.

But if you look up from your salsa and he's not in the kitchen?
You fear he' s sitting in a room with the social worker,
the clock above ticking, the lawyer not yet arrived, and he

Most Recent Book: *After We Lost Our Way*
(Carnegie Mellon University Press, 1998)

recording his story, muttering I've outlived all your stories,
man. Eyes like a panther. A caged bird. A jaded small boy.

Back in the apartment his mother conjures with the shaman,
rocks to and fro for the spirits, so far from Laos hills,
herbal hallucinogens that once brought them forth.
Hot blood wrung from a rooster's neck. Ancestral prayers.
Her head wrapped in a black cloth, her eyes dry weeping.

Then you know he's not Vietnamese. That Mai was with him.
That she was the one shouting, *Shoot him, shoot the motherfucker*.
And the other girl screaming. He staring at the dark pool.
Man, I didn't know you could bleed that much. . . . How'd they find us?
Came right up to our apartment. My mom was crying. . . .

The words won't translate. Like years ago, winter at the window —
He's looking down University, his head echoing with
his father's nightmares, his mother's weeping. He counts
the tire tracks, a police car sluicing past. Then it's nothing
but snow and snow and snow, and each flake a small angel

sprouting wings in the dark, spiraling down upon us all.

from "Dahmer"

To anatomize and preserve as a boy
their small-boned bodies

I splayed them out on a cutting board, wings,
claws, fur and feathers, whiskers

and teeth, beaks
for crying out

as babies
in the nest, asking their sufferance

of worms, of caterpillars and beetles, ladybugs
on which

they lived as infants, and lived on as adults:
I pickled them

in a magical
brine, echoed a process ancient

as Egypt, cradle
of civilizations. There is a secret

I believed, a secret elixir of life over death
like the medieval relics of clerics

in dank cloisters, fostering a cult
of bodies and their parts, hair, teeth, nails

clipped from eternity, for eternity.
Last week

the priest asked me if I thought I possessed
a soul. I

stared at him for several seconds.
Did not answer. Who

is he to talk of the soul? What has
he eaten

except a wafer
which he takes for a body

even a child
knows is not a body

but flour and egg and water
baked in an oven

like bread, like common bread?

*

Who has not, in nightmare,

suddenly seized

an image so despicable, so horrifying, so sick, almost
always it vanishes

the moment
you wake, scarcely

a glint remaining —
                    a fist or knife.
a sexual tongue penetrating
parent or child or other holy figure —

and the ditch foaming
with blood or shit or sperm

suddenly vanishes,

and you're whole, alive and moral once more,
and not

the depraved being whose imagination fostered those images
ancient and barbaric and beyond

recall. And yet

there are some, like me, who see those images —
it was no dream, I lay broad waking —

even after the nightmare
ends. . . . Yes. I saw someone's heart

in a dish; it sat steaming before me,
I sliced it open

and there lay all the ventricles
of my life, the meal

I so desired — Who placed that vision

inside me? Could I
have chosen it?

And if I had,
                    would that make me
                                                  more
or less
                    insane?

The Young Asian Women

The young Asian women are shaving their heads,
piercing eyelids and ears. They stare holes
in curators, shop clerks and geisha chasers,
bubble gum popping like caps in their jaws.
Their names? Juliana, Vong, Lee and Lily.
Could be Mina from the outskirts of Tokyo
but more likely she's Nkauj'lis of the famous
or infamous Lyfongs (depending on your clan
and your anti-Communist persuasions).
Check out that siren named Sonia too in love
with her looks, a nasty curl of Seoul
in her smile. Or if her name is Hoa,
she's tough as her mother, bad girl, bitch,
it doesn't matter, she'll survive like nettles,
flower in what ditch she finds herself, with

or without a man, or her lesbian lover who left
for Alaska, the smell of bearshit on the trail.
With her Taiwanese aunt, digs tales of Toisan
ladies, dragons and the water marsh where bandit
ghosts steal years with a kiss, talking tongues
down your throat to your belly, slipping
a demon seed inside you to grow. Oh, they
are like that, these young women, their art alive
like pepper on your tongue, hurtling hurt
with a half pint gleaming on the night stand.
They know how mysteriously the body is written,
how thundering colors of Benetton befit
statistics on garment workers in the Third
and First Worlds. They know Woman Warrior,
bell hooks, how the moon waxes red like
the sheets where they write out scripts, stories
and poems, unwrapping their dreams before
you, a palm of paint, pearls, I-Ching stones.
Their boots are black and buckled, their jeans frayed,
their lips bruised purple or incandescent red;
on the dance floor their bodies catch hip-hop
as a sail seizes breeze, turbulent, taut and driven.
Their voices are hoarse after nights on the floor,
their faces smeared with sweat. Their cheeks glow.
They scare the pants off the young men they know.

Immigration Angel

(Among the women named in a suit against U. S. Customs was an African American minister)

The room is blinding, pale with fluorescence.
Her skin seethes, ashy and full of flesh;
sweat a sea of sheen pouring off her,

sweat of Miami, palm trees and Caribbean
(oh it's oil of Tropicana for those who require it,
interrogation for those who do not).

And she recalls for some reason this passage
in Micah, *to pass on your way, inhabitants of Shaphir,*
in nakedness and shame, the wailing of Bethezel

to *tell it not in Gath, weep not at all*, and she is
weeping, yet still anxiously *waits for good*,
chariots for the chosen of Samaria, Jerusalem.

But all this face before her asks, excepting
her passport, stems from Negril, and not the white
sand beaches nor the international resorts,

but inhabitants of Gomorrah, the ganja hills,
light planes from Columbia via
St. Lucia, the Bahamas, the high seas. Chilled,

she recalls, *I will go stripped and naked*,
and moments later, in another room, is ordered
by the agent in her Picone suit, cuffs at her belt,

who sees the mule's butt bare and blubbering,
and thinks, *nerves*, another sure sign
this harlot's been hired, some crevice or crack,

or emboweled in a condom, undigested
in her belly: All for a many figured sum,
like any new immigrant so eager to hit

the streets of America, pavements of gold,
that brawling Chicago where her church
opens Sunday, her congregation flows in,

hears her Hallelujahs and gospel shouting
Jesus, thank Jesus, she's home now, scouring
the deserts and precincts of her city for

the boys and girls who nod off at her sermons
and do not see her naked like this, a thief
before Pilate, oh angel seized for the Lord.

Jack Myers

Narcissus

I am still hypnotized by perfection,
still hostage to a glimpse:

Most Recent Book: *OneOneOne* (Autumn House Press, 1999)

the curve of that woman's leg,
some distant musical laughter,
fierce micro-bursts of intimacy

that desolate the evening,
leave tomorrow stuck on flashback
and all the sweat and songs of years
stunned and obliterated
by a dazzling cameo appearance.

I should write tiny poems
on the wind about wine and love
like the great minimal poet Rumi
who invented the Whirling Dervishes
and spiraled into climax
and got stuck inside the glimpse.

I want to know who I was as a child,
how I came to be left paralyzed
and fevered like a tree by its greenery,
dreaming and swaying and futilely reaching out
while mad birds hop and screech inside it.

What comfort to be plain and blind
and smug inside the given,
to be swallowed whole and live
in a house of dead wood
and delivered from desire.

What terror to be beautiful and immobile,
kissed against a taut blue skin of water
while something out of nowhere,
something broken off within me,
outside memory or purpose,
plummets murderously down.

Taking the Children Away

They will pack the sky blue car
with blankets and pillows
and puzzles and snacks
enough to end a life,
and the last thing I will see
will be the stuffed animals

pressed against the window,
like a happy ending in a Muppet movie,
tiny hands like wings
waving goodbye, little voices
trailing out the sides like streamers.

I will stand there
in the suicidal, accelerating, horizontal draft
of the car longer than is natural,
feeling liberated,
like a bombed-out town,
as the sad blue car dwindles and darkens
and inhales itself,
and I enter the house,
turn off the lights,
sit in foreclosure,
watching the twinkling half-life
of fallout begin floating down the years,
scattered toys appearing one by one
the way the first evening stars
look left behind.

This must be the missing that begins
inside the waiting for something larger
to take over, the being over to be over
that feels like the cobalt hand of air
I think my soul must be. I am afraid
that it will take a breath and then another
and another, like steps, until I begin to glow
like the small dull bulb inside a doorbell
as the evening sun slowly, simply disappears.

On Sitting

On the first day, the Master said to his students,
"After you have considered the chair you will sit in
as you have considered your life in relations to others —
who has more knowledge than you, who has less,
whose life is better, whose is worse;
in other words, whether it would better to be
the nail, the wood, the glue, or the varnish —
you may be seated."

Bread, Meat, Greens, and Soap

It feels like deja vu *all over again.*
— Yogi Berra

I feel like I'm about to be fired,
or my doctor will say I have
the obstruction he suspected,
or my 2nd-story-divorce-efficiency apartment
will be rubbed out by a clear blue sky
when I get back.

For instance, right now I'm walking around
this brand new cost-saver supermarket
conscious of this weird impingement
of loss, the way amputees feel the ache
of a phantom limb only I'm talking about all of me,
when I stop and ask an illegal alien stockboy
what street is this, and he croons to me
"Larmanda, Larmanda," which means Larmanda,
some nameless City Father's long lost wife,
and I realize, Holy Mackerel, right where I'm standing,
between the fresh fish and the meatcase
is my old bedroom where me and Willa,
which means Willa, made love every day
after laps and breaststrokes in the pool
of our lovely torn-down walk-up.

And not fifty feet away, years ago,
behind the pharmacy, I slipped a disc
but kept on crawling forward, thinking
who on earth has stabbed me in the back?

Right here in the hyped-up screaming
of the cereal aisle, the kids used to fly around
the kitchen like cartoon characters.
I wanted to grab the old lady
blocking my bedroom with her cart
and argue about this, let her know
how it was with us, but then I figured
what's the use, what are you going to do
about a past that is now
hundreds of thousands of tons of processed food,
a seven-billion-pound carrot to keep me going?

See how crazy with excitement I can get,
as if my life were living proof
of the Unified Field Theory,
which, in fact, to anyone who's hungry
is business as usual, a big so what?
Like taking pride in a miserable grocery list.
I mean, if you can feel it
about to rain in your bones,
and goddamn monkeys and geese
can sense a disaster
a priori,
if someone with some cash
can raze the past
and plunk a Safeway down on top of it,
then what else needs to happen before
the future will have me convinced?

I consult my list, the instructions I wrote
that amount to a soap opera on how to keep going,
written with such a magnificent sense of ease,
such amputated detachment, that right here in the store
I'm firing myself, divorcing the past from the present,
saying, Get your things,
just get what you came to get
and get out.

NAOMI SHIHAB NYE

Mona's Taco

Dear Mona, do you know
how your old building's smooth stucco lines
mark the spot of Something True?
The hand-lettered sign rises up,
a flag on Highway 90 West.
Surely familiar conjunctions
reign inside,
bean & cheese, potato & egg,
perhaps a specialty of your own making —
avocado twist or smoky salsa.
Where are you, Mona, when the moon rises

Most Recent Book: *Fuel* (BOA Editions, 1998)

over Castroville? Your sign says CLOSED.
The singularity of your *nombre* touches me.
One taco might be enough.
Here come the ranchers who just lived through
the worst drought and flood back-to-back
and the truckers on the Del Rio route.
Hats with an oily brim.
Don't we all need someone to greet us
to make us feel like we're here?
West of town, soft fields
ease our city-cluttered eyes.
There's a rim of hills to hope for up ahead.
Mona mysterious Mona
I don't have to eat with you to love you.
Every morning I think *Mona's up*.

Bill's Beans

for William Stafford

Under the leaves, they're long and curling.
I pull a perfect question mark and two lean twins,
feeling the magnetic snap of stem, the ripened weight.
At the end of a day, the earth smells thirsty.
He left his brown hat, his shovel, and his pen.
I don't know how deep bean roots go.
We could experiment.
He left the sky over Oregon and the fluent trees.
He gave us our lives that were hiding under our feet,
saying, You know what to do.
So we'll take these beans
back into the house and steam them.
We'll eat them one by one with our fingers,
the clean click and freshness.
We'll thank him forever for our breath,
and the brevity of bean.

Knitting, Crocheting, Sewing...

Small striped sleeve in her lap, navy and white,
needles whipping in yarn from two sides.
She reminds me of the wide-angled women

filled with calm
I pretended to be related to
in crowds.

In the next seat
a burst of yellow wool
grows into a hat with a tassel.
This woman looks young to crochet.
At least history isn't totally lost.
Her silver hook dips in and out.

And when's the last time you saw
anyone sew a pocket onto a gray linen shirt
in public? Then buttons, and cuffs.
Her stitches must be invisible.
A bevelled thimble glitters in the light.

On Mother's Day
three women who aren't together
conduct delicate operations
in adjoining seats
between La Guardia and Dallas.
Miraculously, they never speak.
Three different kinds of needles,
three snippy scissors,
everyone else on the plane
snoozing with the *Times*.

When the flight attendant
offers free wine to celebrate mothers,
you'd think they'd sit back,
chat a minute,
tell who they're making it for,
or trade patterns
yes?

Has a grave separateness
invaded the world?
They sip with eyes shut
and never say
Amazing
or
Look at us
or
May your thread
never break.

Ongoing

The shape of talk would sag
but the birds be brighter than ever

O I needed the birds worse & worse as I got older
as if some crack had opened in the human scheme of things
& only birds with their sharp morning notes
had the sense for any new day

The people went round & round
in the old arenas
dragging their sacks
of troubles & stones & jaggedy love
I could not help them
I was one of them
the people pitched advice
in its flat hat back & forth
across the table

But the birds so far above us
hardly complete sentences
just fragments & dashes
the birds who had seen the towns
grow up & topple
who caught the changing wind
before anyone on the ground did
who left for Mexico when we were not
paying attention
what could they tell us
about lives in heavy bodies

what could they tell us
about being
caught?

William Olsen

Deer Traffic

Tonight's a night the frantic signatures
slip off the suicide notes,

Most Recent Book: *Vision of a Storm Cloud* (TriQuarterly Books, 1996)

it is a night that
rips up the standing warrants
for our arrests
till I imagine I can almost see my happiness
as clearly as I sorrow
for the others.
Like the guy who talks
to a gingko tree —
that living stick without one ruthless
entrepreneurial leaf
to scowl back at him —
advising it not to join the army.
Or the woman whose beggarly hands
rev up like cars as she directs
the movie of an alien poverty
she never planned to star in;
or the suited buffoon in the phone booth
with a fat wallet to vomit
all the money in the world
and still no quarter,
kicking at the plexiglass constructions
of the republic's privacies and weeping
into the polygamous wives
of his two coat sleeves.
Bankrupt departures
and sad validated fares,
in our midwestern Amtrak stop of
group seizures, I want to cry
like a baby at my good station,
watching this orchard of a boulevard —
its ripe white streetlights don't fall —
till I can caterwaul my happiness,
I can see the traffic almost shine through it
bearing a harvest of deer, their tongues
unfurled almost upon
the salt-spray of the stars
and the salt-lick of the moon
and into our Holy Mission
of charities that don't exist for them —
carcasses strapped to pickup trucks,
with such strange distances for faces
that even dead don't seem to want to die.

Electric Church

I either play very very soft or very very loud.
— Jimi Hendrix

Peace and love are shit but I believe
no napalm fell out of the American heavens,
no cities burned
when Johnie Allen
Hendricks
burned his Strat at Monterrey.
No demons
were in the neighborhood —
when that fey spring of the Summer of Love
went up in lighter-fluid smoke
and the final buzz-saw grace-note
fed the sweet
leaping flames,
something other
than Armageddon happened,
than mere hallucinogens.
It was as if the roar of those killed dead
would never stop

and that last subway rush of feedback
was not apocalypse
but animal memory,
a full sustain of consciousness
freaked
to keening,
smoke that never burns
making its way in time —
it lasts. It exceeds
the strictest ember.
It wastes its little heat
while the heart, breaking on
and on,
merely is,
and loss is everything else
and what this means,
already over,
is just beginning.
Someone said that somewhere into the murderous
suspended bridge of "Wild Thing"

he bore his Strat
above his head
and the damned thing
played without him
and gasped like someone crying
as this someone's country dies
and dies.
Years of idolatrous viewings and I believe
that he was not a Voodoo Child
but some motherless family's
little man,
to whom the feedback sounded
as a big plane had
lumbering through Georgia skies
to an enlistee parachutist,
a Screaming Eagle,
throwing open
the cabin door —
falling away from the sound
of a howling machine
down towards a quiet airforce base,
its thousand quonset huts
a regiment of endless mailboxes,
its airfield
of silenced moths. . .
and the surrounding farms,
red roads and everyday casualties —
the one, unbroken,
rising
deafening world.

Fear in Style

A box of barbed hooks looks like a printer's box
of Russian letters unstrung from their epic sentences.
You write our names out with them,
then back away then —
if someone's life can never be my own,
if the soul is the distance between the two of us,
and doesn't read or talk and won't take us in
for the evening or for the rest of our lives,

then its elegances decline into the daily awkwardnesses,
who stand evoking each other at each other,
lurking above some hooks like two time-dial shark fins,
our steely names spelled out by hooks.
The names say the hook evolved from a lost tooth,
the styles from the hook, style from the style.
We're two blunt oars in this nautical museum
of all the years the animal got stylishly flensed,
the fog horn barely plowing its way through fog,
Nova Scotia, and the clarified aperture opens,
our fury and pity and psychology and fire
and the open moment pour through this porthole
with all the aspects of the woman you are
posed there in the nave of two whale ribs.
The rest of the whale has fallen out of the ocean,
out of the earth for that matter, out of matter,
and the cathedral whale is now invisible — your hand
doing its stylish little wave.
Your mouth clenches against its given name.
Your mouth is closed but eyes and face stay open,
I think they have no choice that they are,
your human eyes upon the human ocean,
your human smile lowered to a slow blue pilot light burn,
our premonitions have not yet invented regret,
nothing goes wrong yet,
so what is it I wish to throw a rope to,
whose eye is it in the hook I wish to thread —
the boats are rocking with their names,
the names rock, too, the names shall grasp to a straw.

St. Ives, Winter Night

Nights this long of only you and me the universe seems one brief lucky cry. We live in it darkly, brightly. They say that for the dead to fly, man or woman, wings would have to stretch all the way from birth to the very instant of death. All the distances on all the trade routes are going to have to be covered at that moment when time rushes upon itself incestuously. The whole family will be there but few allies may call out. People disappear all at once when you die or when you tell a bad joke. What a cloud could sing if it had an audience. All day schoolyard voices cried till crying couldn't think up one last child. It's winter, I write, the tourists have vanished, the sober lights of the shops have been turned off, the publights go next, the sun comes back, how can my friend have stood her last moment. The sound of the guy wires smacking metal masts is the sound of Charon turning up a new upturned shoe, its eyelets rusted, its tongue sticking out, a shipwreck of a shoe. The poor ones on the shore still feel the urge to warm their hands over the shadows of tyrants. All rivers lead to the sea but the sea doesn't have the heart to say: stop. I have one less friend to admire about myself. The schoolchildren call the pony we feed carrots to Fat Boy. Scorn, like education, is without end, without a final point. Why can't their shadows blow away when it's this windy? Shipwrecks only sink so far, while working ships pass over these like wooden clouds. In the Italian bureaucracy called the imagination it takes eternity for anyone to get off the dole. It turns out pubs are waiting rooms for other pubs, and the same can be said about funerals. At least she was not there at hers even if her hands were, the ones that said everything in a hurry because the mouth can't say it all in a lifetime of talking.

STEVE ORLEN

Monkey Mind

When I was a child I had what is called an *inner life*.
For example, I looked at that girl over there
In the second aisle of seats and wondered what it was like
To have buck teeth pushing out your upper lip
And how it felt to have those little florets the breasts
Swelling her pajama top before she went to sleep.
Walking home, I asked her both questions
And instead of answering she told her mother
Who told the teacher who told my father.
After all these years, I can almost feel his hand
Rising in the room, the moment in the air of his decision,
Then coming down so hard it took my breath away,
And up again in that small arc
To smack his open palm against my butt.
I'm a slow learner
And still sometimes I'm sitting here wondering what my father
Is thinking, blind and frail and eighty-five,
Plunged down into his easy chair half the night
Listening to Bach cantatas. I know he knows

Most Recent Book: *Kisses* (Miami University Press, 1998)

At every minute of every hour that he's going to die
Because he told my mother and my mother told me.
I didn't cry or cry out or say I'm sorry.
I lay across his lap and wondered what
He could be thinking to hit a kid like that.

Happy As I Am

Trailer parks, projects, Circle K parking lots,
And trash-ridden vacant places,
And coldly illuminated side streets with front porches
Peeling their rented paint. He's sullen. She's screaming. Two fat babies
Sit dazed on a couch. There's maybe a knife or a gun, and blood,
A few drops already scabbing on her face or pooled dry
On the sidewalk, mapping a wound, and it's always afterwards,
Ten minutes later, a half hour.
                                        Every night I watch the show *Cops*
After dinner. I'm by myself because it upsets my wife, the voyeurism
Of it, the high-pitched, tension emergency sounds,
And my son, a good boy who by now has fallen far from the tree,
Hates the unpredictability, the chaos, and blood, *especially the blood,*
He says, but he loves the verbal violence of *rap* music, so who knows
How far he's fallen,
                              and I love the opening *rap* song, *Bad Boys*,
Because that's what I thought I always was, what my father called me
As a boy, the neighbors, too, the relatives, the principal of the junior high
Who told my father on the phone, *You don't have to worry*
About your son going to college, he's going to jail, and hung up.

Why do you watch that stuff? my wife asks from the kitchen.
Because I feel I sort of *know* these people, from childhood —
The perps, the cops, the victims —
Especially when they show the smaller cities,
Like the one I grew up in, Holyoke, Massachusetts, which is not
This TV city in fact, so the show is both real and not real
And I can believe whatever I want. I'm waiting to see
Someone I used to know, one of the screw-offs, the junior high
Falling down drunks, the burglars, window smashers, car stealers,
Famous street fighters, the greater and the lesser clowns, those in groups
And those mysterious maniacs who worked alone.
                                                                  Those people gathered
On the television porch, still arguing, the very sullen, bare-chested man
In close-up with SUGAR tattooed over one nipple and CREAM

Over the other, and the very frightened, dispossessed-looking
Plump woman biting her nails, and through the screen door
Three children asleep on a couch, crumpled like pieces of dropped paper
Nobody notices, and the cops — I think if I look closer
I'll recognize one of them.
                                        I know
I know that woman smothered in light on the front porch
Because I went out with her once.
Actually, I sat next to her *doppelgänger*
In the *Victory Theatre* on one of those Friday nights
When all the kids went to the movies in summer.
Her name was always *Bunny*
Or *Beverly*, one sitting on my right and one on my left,
Shadows only, in profile, and after the opening credits
I put my arm around Bunny's shoulder and we started kissing,
And then I felt her up. I didn't know her. I couldn't even
Quite see her face, but I liked the slight glow of her, and the girl-smell
Of her rose petal soap, and the way her girlfriend nibbled
At her cuticles and watched us instead of the movie,
Until I turned to her and we went at it, too, back and forth like that.

And now she — Beverly, Bunny, I can't tell — is on TV,
Famous for several minutes in a humiliating scene, almost live
And pretty much unedited, with a long slash on her right cheek
And a smudged bump on her pale forehead, and she seems —
Not happy, of course — but *in* it, in her life,
While one cop is taking notes on a pad and another
Is frisking the squirming man, asking
Do you have any needles in your pockets, sir?

Someone you can't see is filming the whole slow chaos
With an unsteady hand, panning to
The small crowd gathered like a chorus in their nightclothes,
And the red lights twirling, surveilling The cops are being nice to
    everyone.
They're used to this. They know they're on TV. They've taken courses
In courtesy. With a bit of bad luck or a wrong turn taken
It could have been them being frisked and cuffed on some Hillside
    Avenue.

Sometimes, proudly, I tell my son stories
About burglaries at "midnight lumber," then one siren coming in,
Then the voices exploding at us like those inchers on the Fourth of July,
The running, scrambling over back fences, hiding, the whispered laughing,

While the cops looked for us desultorily, though if caught
We would get a smack or two.
                                        The woman is mumbling something
We can't hear in our living rooms. I *know*
She is either Beverly or Bunny, though whatever was glowing about her,
Whatever innocence comprised her being,
Has dimmed to a cold illumination
On a front porch. Somebody in me is hearing her say,
Hey, Turk — they used to call me Turk — *Why don't you*
Come out and join us, or *Why are you out there*
And I'm in here on your television set? Or *Are you happy in your life?*
Actually, she's laughing, mildly, inaudibly, at her situation of this night.
It's just life. *Everybody's life is just life, right?* she seems to be saying.
And *Some nights you're in the chorus and some nights*
You're in the middle of the mess, right?
                                                  My wife
Has put the cookies out to cool. To some *rap*
My son is break-dancing for me, interrupting my favorite show,
Irritating me on purpose. *How do you like that move?* he asks.
It's a good one, pal, I tell him, very happy with how he's turning out,
But wondering, stupidly, why he's not like me, out in the street
Getting into trouble, and wondering why I'm watching strangers on TV,
Peeping through a keyhole into the alternate universe.

Happy as I am, happy as anyone is, I still have this normal, natural,
Nostalgic and irrational urge to be with Beverly tonight, with Bunny, too.
Not on that front porch, though. Not anymore.
I want to be in the chorus, watching. It's what happens
When you get older, right?
You want to move from center stage to stage left, where
Nobody can quite see your face.
                                          There was something
Special, singular, threatening, free. Not a word spoken.
Not thinking much. Only the body's chemical fuming.
Only a movie theater where half the kids are necking
Furiously and the other half watching, and Bunny and Beverly and I
Are touching each other in a twisted, anonymous passion
Within the smells of Beverly's soap, the cigarette smoke in Bunny's
Endlessly long brown hair, their urgent sweat, their lips, their lipstick,
The overly-sweet candy everyone around us is sucking on.

Frankie Paino

The Old Religion

That was the world before the world,
        where we drifted,

weightless, in each other's arms.
        Or before there were arms,

when we were only quiet together,
        wrapped in countless

swizzles of DNA, magenta nets
        of veins weaving themselves

upon that astonishing loom. And
        there was the swift music of our

hummingbird hearts, the steady
        boom of a distant drum,

unimportant and ignorable.
        We could not grasp the notion

of anything other than us,
        did not even know which colour

the dark had chosen for our eyes. Or
        even that we had eyes. That

was the world without desire.
        We had all we could ever want, the

urgent arithmetic of cell upon cell
        like the golden honeycombs

our tongues would plunder
        years later, the liquid sweet

and warm on our lips. How we would
        play each translucent scale of

fragile ribs like wind chimes, the
        twenty bones of each hand intertwined

the way wild roses will trellis
        a tangle of dead branches and give

Most Recent Book: *Out of Eden* (Cleveland State University Press, 1997)

them life again. What more could we
have asked for than to be timeless,

sexual as horses whose feathered manes
float above rippling throats, the deep

thunder of hooves as they break free
from their muddy half-acre.

The old religion. The world before
the artifice of guilt. Desire is

what came after, borne with us in the
relentless tug of that crimson undertow

when the dome of our world fell
around us like the final pocket of breath

in a dying man's lungs and we became
children of air, the blade tearing through,

baptizing us with the room's sterile
light, the sour scent of steel,

our eyes unsealed by cold hands which
broke our long embrace, our music

trampled like a bird which, on the way
to some better world, tumbles unseen

out of an autumn sky when a heedless
boy's bullet passes through

its violent heart so that it
shudders, then chokes on its own song.

The Martyrdom of St. Sebastian

Someone had put a scythe to the sweet grass —
its torn blades, like fistfuls of emerald
fire, bled into summer dusk the scent of something
half-remembered, while crows drifted
in wide arcs as if to mimic the farmer
who paused in his work to watch them thrust
toward sun, their hollow feathers
like those which kept the sleek Mauretanian arrows

true as soldiers kissed each silver tip
pulled from quiver, to bow, to level

with their squinting eyes on the Palatine
Hill, each shaft singing against the small
breeze, going deep as love into the young man's flesh,
slim thighs, chest oiled with sweat, one
blade ringing against the bones of his left ankle
like a grim toast, though his executioners were less

cruel than drunk on sour wine which spilled,
almost black in the half-light, from earthen jugs,
Sebastian's hands drawn tight above his head
with three straps of fine leather, one arrow
driving hard into the pit of his arm, though even
then he refused to break, would not look away
from that final, beautiful light which sent copper
spears into the feathered clouds; and when the moon

began to rise the soldiers left him for dead or
for the faces of exotic women veiled
in showers of perfumed hair so that the faithful
crept out of the sheltering black and cut him
from the wounded tree, brought him back from the light
he wished to fly into, though he was intent
on death's certain fame and appeared, weeks after,
before the emperor, opening his robes to flaunt

a scar on his groin which resembled a crow, until
he was beaten with clubs, cast into a common
sewer where he was later found, though this time he
could not come back. Finally, in death, he was
broken, not by unbelief, but by young men
with names like swift rivers who fingered the dark
silk of his hair, then severed him
from himself. Head to the west. Heart to the south.

Alchemy

(John William Polidori, M.D. 1795–1821)

Such precision in your death.
You'd found the colour
of forgiveness, or, at least,
forgetting –
Mottled purple. Blue-black

like the bruise which wove
around your ankle when you leapt,
on Byron's advice, from Diodati's
balcony. For weeks after,
foot propped on a tattered pillow,
you dreamed you were his
crippled twin —
though he grew sullen
when you said as much
and sailed with Shelley to Chillon.

Long days of summer rain.
Snowy drams of laudanum.
Even the sky seemed in sympathy,
clouds shirred like the gauzy veils
of opium smoke with which you tried
to blunt the absence of his weight
rising above you, his savage grace
so perfect you and your desire
became one, wrists shredded,
bloody from pounding out the rhythm
of his lust upon your crucifix.

And when he would have nothing more
from *Dear Polly*, you returned
to London's filthy streets
with your leeches, potions, madness,
your dark horse
all slather and sheened sweat,
careening over cobblestones,
leaving you amnesic,
stuttering at the base of a tree.
And the days after, your sentences
a child's babble,
your book ghosting *his* plot.
Everything which brought you to this
silver cup, brimming,
Promethean. To swallow this fire
as if it were fine wine, a good
year, or the warmth of his tongue
gliding along your throat.

Honey.
For his hands — softer than he'd like

to think;
plump flesh of his thighs.
        For his siren's voice.

Oil of amber.
Arsenic.
        Adding light to light.
Morning and evening star.

Powdered charcoal.
        To eclipse this liquid sun.
For his silhouette scything candleflame.

Prussic acid.
        The colour of his eyes,
blue shadows.
Almost the colour of regret.

Robert Pinsky

Samurai Song

When I had no roof I made
Audacity my roof. When I had
No supper my eyes dined.

When I had no eyes I listened.
When I had no ears I thought.
When I had no thought I waited.

When I had no father I made
Care my father. When I had
No mother I embraced order.

When I had no friend I made
Quiet my friend. When I had no
Enemy I opposed my body.

When I had no temple I made
My voice my temple. I have
No priest, my tongue is my choir.

Most Recent Book: *Jersey Rain* (Farrar Strauss & Giroux, 2000)

When I have no means fortune
Is my means. When I have
Nothing, death will be my fortune.

Need is my tactic, detachment
Is my strategy. When I had
No lover I courted my sleep.

The Green Piano

Aeolian. Gratis. Great thunderer, half-ton infant of miracles
Torn free of charge from the universe by my mother's will.
You must have amazed that half-respectable street

Of triple-decker families and rooming-house housepainters
The day that the bole-ankled oversized hams of your legs
Bobbed in procession up the crazy-paved front walk

Embraced by the arms of Mr. Poppik the seltzer man
And Corydon his black-skinned helper, tendering your thighs
Thick as a man up our steps. We are not reptiles:

Even the male body bears nipples, as if to remind us
We are designed for dependence and nutriment, past
Into future. O Europe, they budged your case, its ponderous

Guts of iron and brass, ten kinds of hardwood and felt
Up those heel-pocked risers and treads splintering tinder.
Angelic nurse of clamor, yearner, tinkler, dominator —

O Elephant, you were for me! When the tuner Mr. Otto Van Brunt
Pronounced you excellent despite the cracked sounding board, we
Obeyed him and swabbed your ivories with hydrogen peroxide.

You blocked a doorway and filled most of the living room.
The sofa and chairs dwindled to a ram and ewes, cowering: now,
The colored neighbors could be positive we were crazy and rich,

As we thought the people were who gave you away for the moving
Out of their carriage house — they had painted you the color of pea soup.
The drunk man my mother hired never finished antiquing you

Ivory and umber, so you stood half-done, a throbbing mistreated noble,
Genuine — my mother's swollen livestock of love: lost one, unmastered:
You were the beast she led to the shrine of my genius, mistaken.

Endlessly I bonged according to my own chord system *Humoresque*,
The Talk of the Town, What'd I Say. Then one day they painted you pink.
Pink is how my sister remembers you the Saturday afternoon

When our mother fell on her head, dusty pink as I turn on the bench
In my sister's memory to see them carrying our mother up the last
Steps and into the living room, inaugurating the reign of our confusion.

They sued the builder of the house she fell in, with the settlement
They bought a house at last and one day when I came home from college
You were gone, mahogany breast, who nursed me through those

Years of the Concussion, and there was a crappy little Baldwin Acrosonic
In your place, gleaming, walnut shell. You were gone, despoiled one —
Pink one, forever-green one, white and gold one, comforter, a living soul.

The Haunted Ruin

Even your computer is a haunted ruin, as your
Blood leaves something of itself, warming
The tool in your hand.

From far off, down the billion corridors
Of the semiconductor, military
Pipes grieve at the junctures.

This too smells of the body, its heated
Polymers smell of breast milk
And worry-sweat.

Hum of so many cycles in current, voltage
Of the past. Sing, wires. Feel, hand. Eyes,
Watch and form

Legs and bellies of characters:
Beak and eye of A. Serpentine hiss
S of the foregoers, claw-tines

Of E and of the claw hammer
You bought yesterday, its head
Tasting of light oil, the juice

Of dead striving — the heft
Of ash, for all its urethane varnish, is
Polished by body salts.

Pull, clawhead. Hold, shaft. Steelface,
Strike and relieve me. Voice
Of the maker locked in the baritone

Whine of the handsaw working.
Lost, lingerer like the dead souls of
Vilna, revenant. Machine-soul.

To Television

Not a "window on the world"
But as we call you,
A box a tube

Terrarium of dreams and wonders.
Coffer of shades, ordained
Cotillion of phosphors
Or liquid crystal

Homey miracle, tub
Of acquiescence, vein of defiance.
Your patron in the pantheon would be Hermes

Raster dance,
Quick one, little thief, escort
Of the dying and comfort of the sick,

In a blue glow my father and little sister sat
Snuggled in one chair watching you
Their wife and mother was sick in the head
I scorned you and them as I scorned so much

Now I like you best in a hotel room,
Maybe minutes
Before I have to face an audience: behind
The doors of the armoire, box
Within a box — Tom & Jerry, or also brilliant
And reassuring, Oprah Winfrey.

Thank you, for I watched, I watched
Sid Caesar speaking French and Japanese not
Through knowledge but imagination,
His quickness, and Thank you, I watched live
Jackie Robinson stealing

Home, the image — O strung shell — enduring
Fleeter than light like these words we
Remember in: they too are winged
At the helmet and ankles.

Gas. Gossamer. My poker friends
Question your presence
In a poem by me, passing the magazine
One to another.

Not the stone and not the words, you
Like a veil over Arthur's headstone,
The passage from Proverbs he chose
While he was too ill to teach
And still well enough to read, *I was*
Beside the master craftsman
Delighting him day after day, ever
At play in his presence — you

A soothing veil of distraction playing over
Dying Arthur playing in the hospital,
Thumbing the Bible, fuzzy from medication,
Ever courting your presence.
And you the prognosis,
You in the cough.

Gesturer, when is your spur, your cloud?
You in the airport rituals of greeting and parting.
Indicter, who is your claimant?
Bell at the gate. Spiderweb iron bridge.
Cloak, video, aroma, rue, what is your
Elected silence, where was your seed?

What is Imagination
But your lost child born to give birth to you?

Dire one. Desired one.
Savior, sentencer —

Absence,
Or presence ever at play:
Let those scorn you who never
Starved in your dearth. If I
Dare to disparage
Your harp of shadows I taste
Wormwood and motor oil, I pour
Ashes on my head. You are the wound. You
Be the medicine.

Keith Ratzlaff

Group Portrait With Ukuleles

Once I was a boy
in a classroom
of boys learning to play

the ukulele. In the end, even
the stumpfingered
learned three chords:

G, C, D7. Our big felt picks,
our whiny
little strings. We were a part

of the American Folksong
Revival
in spite of ourselves,

in spite of our penises
and voices
rising and falling like elevators.

Imagine us, our 25 faces
still forming,
heads slightly out of round,

singing "I Gave My Love
A Cherry,"
or "Big Rock Candy Mountain."

There was the recital
we never gave
because, to tell the truth,

we weren't very good.
One boy is dead
now, three are welders,

two joined the navy, one
sells used cars,
half a dozen are farmers,

one has been convicted
of exporting
Nazi literature to Germany.

Most Recent Book: *Man Under a Pear Tree* (Anhinga Press, 1997)

I don't remember any of us
as mortal
or talented or cruel.

All we ever learned was that
chord progression,
knowable and sequential —

beautiful as gears shifting —
something useful
and at the bottom of all

the music we imagined we
could care about.
We knew who Mozart was

but there wasn't any Mozart
for the ukulele.
That would have been wrong

and we knew it — some of us.
Or none
of us. Either way.

Fitful Angel

after Paul Klee

Here my dreams are shifted slightly; my arms are always in the air when I wake up. I dream of singing, but of course my throat has other business. Mostly my body is completely on its own. Somewhere, in a hollow I used to have, is a little scar of pines and unstable grass. I miss the crisis of sparrows and the slump of water in useless pools. Oh God, who once was behind the door, this is a terrible room to wake in as if it were everywhere.

I used to have dreams I was a peasant with a monkey I could sing to. The songs were impromptu, the kind you find stupidly in the air. "Oh don't tell the monkey," I sang once, "oh don't tell the monkey, oh don't tell the monkey, that you are going away." Paul McCartney sorts of things. These were the ways my dreams really worked.

Usually it wasn't clear just who I was or where. But once I was a painter with a monkey. We would load a big canvas onto a wheelbarrow and wobble down the lane to the marsh where I painted the yellow grass and purplish water. The monkey handed me brushes I didn't need. I dreamed this, night after night, until the painting was finished, but by then it was of pines and the monkey had a blue shirt on and stole from me.

Table Prayer

My grandmother has a canary
blind in one eye
that sings as if the world

had just one blue window
framing a garden,
and one bad picture — this one

hanging above his cage
in the dining room —
of Christ, ghostly and plasmic

helping a sailor steer
his ship
through a gale.

The weather's rough, buckets
plunging overboard,
halyards running away

on the wind. Soon, Christ or no,
this one's going down.
The canary doesn't know this;

it's not his job. But
I'm a sinner
when I sit at her table

and I play the drama out
during the drone
of grace: *Kommt Herr Jesu. . . .*

I'm a sailor on that ship,
a bit player
flung heavily overboard

into the scud and dark
obsidian water.
Then the wreck's petals

scattering on the shore.
Then sharks,
so my lost soul

is both eaten and drowned.
But *amen* and
I am in the eternal now

of family dinners: saved
by white bread
and beef and canned beans.

The canary's song is muffled
under the towel
we've put over the cage

to shut him up. Grandma's old.
God is real to her
if not perfect. She loves

the metaphor of sailing,
the rocking
and spray. The continuous moment

of never going down
is what
being saved means to her.

Oh Lord come be our guest.
Bless us,
keep us from your harm.

Keep the bird quiet.
Give us
your grace, which is like

these pickles, which are like
last year's,
God-awful and abundant

world without end. Amen.

Victoria Redel

The Bounty

for Gerald Stern

Dear Gerry, While you and your Pittsburgh buddy, the great Jack Gilbert,
were reading to poets gathered in that same city,
I was walking the aisles of COSTCO with Jonah and Gabriel. Have you ever
been there, or in one of these warehouse food chains, stores of the Alice "eat me"
variety, everything enlarged, larger than life, at least my life with its city cupboards,
but, also, stores where my all-American – albeit first generation – appetite
for purchase is born and born again in the next aisle where a forklift pulls out
a crate of Dunkaroos? The boys scream for everything big.
You, with grown children, what do you know from Dunkaroos?
And my God, the austere Jack Gilbert, what would Gilbert think of the double-sized
cart overfilled with thirty-six rolls of Charmin and bulk-wrapped Bounty,
twelve for eight dollars and seventy-nine cents, and cases of Juicy-Juice
juice boxes? Food chains with not a thing in my cart from the food chain.
But you understand, Gerry, the deals, Gerry, the deals.
Gilbert, with his mountain and his poem "Hunger" that I read to students
to take them to that line, "going beyond the seeds," what would Gilbert think
of Jonah and me filling to overflowing the oversized cart, and Gabriel piled high
in the cart, holding a two and one-half pound box of cheddar goldfish.
Did he read that poem "Hunger"? Did you read your song of the green willow?
Or was it all new poems and in your hometown, too.
I would have liked that, too, to be childless in Pittsburgh,
among poets, even with my shyness of poets.
Instead, there was enough French's Mustard to squirt the boys through childhood.
But the deals, Gerry, and I have the receipt to prove it.
That's thirty-six rolls of toilet paper at twenty-four cents a roll and the

---

Most Recent Book: *Loverboy* (Graywolf Press, 2001)

twelve for
eight dollars and seventy-nine cents comes to seventy-three cents a roll
of paper
towel and so on and on up to two hundred eighty-eight dollars and
fifty-seven
cents. With not a vegetable or fruit in the cart.
I remember my first time, not in COSTCO but in BJ'S,
which is the same but with a different name.
Jonah, maybe just two months, woke with a raucous hunger.
I nursed sitting on stacked crates below the stocked warehouse shelves.
The shoppers gave me terrible looks. I tried to write that BJ's poem but
got stuck
with a fake Whitman love of the things and a true highbrow hatred of glut
without even a mention of Jonah's delicious suck.
This time there was also a frenzy of sucking, the kids wanting to eat and
drink
everything in the car and both boys screaming,
"There's nothing at all here to eat." What's left?
I got lost on ninety-five, brought Jonah late to his violin lesson,
waited out front with Gabe asleep in back.
That's when I had the chance to think of Pittsburgh, of poems,
of you and your friend. Imagine Jonah with his quarter size violin.
Imagine Dunkaroos. His small fingers, his wrist held just right to bow.
The bounty of your music. Gilbert's strict beauty. Gabe sleeping
through it.
And, this, my happiness, Gerry, the whole heartbreaking deal.

Tilted Man, Tilted Woman

or Singing to Tony Bennett's Cock

Does it really matter, really, if it's true or not,
but just, really, to think of it, Tony Bennett's cock
in his hotel room at the San Juan Americana
while Rosario knelt over it, her mouth brushing over it,
her crooning, "Ladies and Gentleman,
here tonight, straight from six-sold-out weeks
at the fabulous, the world famous Atlantic City's Taj Mahal
is the one, the only, Mister Tony Bennett."
And with that she'd sing, tilting and leaning into
the purpled head, all the old Tony Bennett classics
and for an encore some new songs

she'd make up for him on the spot.
What if it is true, really? What if I told you Rosario is a twin —
would that stretch your belief?
That they dance flamenco in separate cities?
That they are over fifty? That the sister's name means hope?
Are you with me still? Are you really ready to know
that all Tony Bennett wanted was to go down on her,
that she claims that after coming
her mouth goes cold as marble? She has lost me
with this intrusion of limestone, and I refuse to lose you.
It's just her claim, after all. I have heard a woman claim
that she didn't like it, a man's mouth on her,
or women who will not take a man in their mouths,
let alone to sing the cock, sing the cock,
and other women, still, exhausted by claims.
I want none of it, I want it all, your castanet heart,
your secrets walking around naked, a rash of honesty,
your raucous coming, not stilled. Does the twin's mouth
marble too? The San Juan Americana, that sounds
good enough to me. And for you, can we say love?
Can we say he went there thirsting her ocherous menses
and came up smeary and beyond any backyard God.
Tell me, really, Tony, is it true — ochred or purpled
or San Juan ? How are the new classics?
In the next suite there is always a man on a phone
claiming, "I'm just the same in real life."
In the next to the next room, room service knocks twice.
The hotel charges fifty cents a call. *Can we say love?*
"Is that what you wanted?" he said. Plates and forks,
eggs and meat ransacked on the tray outside the door.
"Not till you went there," she said. "Now it's all I want."

Damsels, I

Not for pleasure alone do I pleasure
standing in a dark corner of our home
leaning into your hand fuck
while in their room the children toss in sleep.

If not for paradise than for what
do I rut, incorrigible in the palm of your hand?

Damsels I have been, in waiting, larcenous
all my olden days ago, the one of me righted
to never love, the other of me clasped entirely in attendance.
Now is she whole parceled in me.

Now brilliant pleasure, in truthe, in soule, in hearte, verily.
What is true manifests truly against my ancient thieving topology.

Intact Woman

Because she finds it once in his closet, she begins looking for it all the time and comes to find that each month, just before the month ends, just like magic, there, in the closet on top of the neat stack, is the new one. But she knows it is not magic, it is him, his doing, his handiwork. She wants to understand what is in it for him and because she feels she knows him, she feels she knows what in it particularly interests him, which pages do the trick — which is exactly what, this trick? — that is what she is trying to find out. She looks at the pages that she is certain get to him, and she tries to let them get to her, which she finds is easy enough, though she is not sure if that is because she is thinking that they — she and he — are both being gotten by the same thing or because she has now her own secret which is bigger than his secret because it includes his secret. She is surprised a little by how easy it is, an abracadabra, a one two three, and she is surprised, too, by how often she goes to his closet to be with him, though she understands her not being there is part of what is in it for him. But what if she is wrong? What if it is not the pages she thinks, but different ones, and when she thinks this she feels stupid and wrong and embarrassed and tricked by him. She is angry and feels he has forced her to go there. Then she is angry because she feels he has deserted her in their secret place. And then she remembers he does not know where she is, but she keeps it open just to what she thought was right for him because she is right in the middle of things, and she needs, all on her own, to finish up the dirty work.

Alberto Ríos

From the Life of Don Margarito

He was a serious man
But for one afternoon
Late in his life
With serious friends.
They adjourned to a bar
Away from the office
And its endless matters.
Something before dinner,
Something for the appetite
One of them had said,
And the three of them walked
In long sleeves
Into the *Molino Rojo*.
The cafe's twenty tables
Were pushed together
Almost entirely
Or pulled apart barely,
Giving not the tables
But the space between them
A dark and ragged shine
Amidst the white tablecloths.
The tables
And the spaces they made
Looked like pieces of a child's puzzle
Almost done,
A continent breaking, something
From the beginning of time.
To get by them
Don Margarito had to walk
Sideways, and then sideways
Again, with arms outstretched
And up.
It was a good trick of the place
Conspiring with the music
To make the science
In this man's movement
Look like dance.

Most Recent Book: *The Curtain of Trees* (University of New Mexico Press, 1999)

Writing from Memory

My father got up and put on his dress.
It's the Fifties and there are stockings,

The kind with lines that go up like a part
In the thick hair of his calf.

He adjusts his bra like anyone
And we don't think much of it this morning

When he misses the catch and asks for help.
He bends over and looks through the closet

Picking out a right-colored pair of shoes,
Something he knows will be, even in that dimness,

Pale enough to match his purse.
My mother doesn't get up, not right away, not easy

Making some noise as she lies there
Rubbing her hand across the thick stubble of her face.

She asks if her brown trousers are clean,
But nobody answers, and she shakes her head.

As she gets up she puts a hand inside her underwear
Rubbing a buttock hard.

She puts on a sleeveless T-shirt
Then a shoulder holster, but no gun,

Not before breakfast. We've all agreed on that one.
And for God's sake, we say, Mom, brush your teeth.

My sister puts on her jeans and after zipping up
She moves her thing around as if anyone cares

Until she gets it just right, just to the side of the seam.
She keeps leaving the toilet seat up

And walking around the house without a shirt on
To show her pecs off. She flexes one for me

That little bounce looking like a wink.
Then there's me. The golden boy, the good

Reader. Oh yeah, I was perfect
Is what I remember.

I would pull on a cotton blouse
Blue, with a neat, pleated skirt,

Then a sweater. I held my books up to my chest.
It made my parents feel better.

The day started. We were off, to our jobs,
To Coronado Elementary School, to whatever was next.

Finally, we just got in the family car
And drove it straight out of the Fifties.

By the end of the century we'd be different people.
We'd be fond of saying *Those days don't seem real anymore*.

And it's true.
We've forgotten all of this about each other.

Now when we talk about who we were
We tell some other family's story.

Some Extensions on the Sovereignty of Science

for my father

1.

When the thought came to him it was so simple he shook his head.
People are always looking for kidneys when their kidneys go bad.

But why wait? Why not look when you're healthy?
If two good kidneys Do the trick, wouldn't three do the job even better?

Three kidneys. Maybe two livers. You know. Two hearts of course.
Instead of repairing damage, why not think ahead?

Why not soup up the car? Why not be a touring eight-cylinder classic,
Or one of those old, sixteen-cylinder, half-mile long Duesenbergs?

2.

The hardest work of the last quarter of the 20th century is to find
An edge in the middle. When something explodes, for example,

Nobody is confused about what to do — you look toward it.
Loud is a magnet. But the laws of magnetism are more complex.

One might just as well try this: when something explodes,
Turn exactly opposite from it and see what there is to see.

The loud will take care of itself, and everyone will be able to say
What happened in that direction. But who is looking

The other way? Nature, that magician and author of loud sounds,
Zookeeper and cook, electrician and provocateur —

Maybe these events are Nature's sleight of hand, and the real
Thing that's happening is in the other hand,

Or behind or above or below or inside us.

3.

On a recent trip to Bloomington, Indiana, I was being driven there
From Indianapolis, and my friend along the way pointed out some hills,

Saying that these hills were made as a result of the farthest reach of
The Ice Age glacier. I had been waiting for this moment

Ever since fifth grade. I could hardly contain myself,
Though I'm sure I just said *uh-huh* in the conversation.

I took a small and delicious breath. "So," I said, slowly,
"That's the terminal moraine, huh?" There, I'd said it,

The phrase I had saved up since the moment I found it
In that fifth grade reader: "terminal moraine."

I had never said it aloud. What's a little scary, of course,
Is that I was more excited about remembering

Than about the hills themselves. But if it was scary it was sweet
In the mouth too. In a larger picture, one way or another,

The Ice Age glacier was still a force to be reckoned with.

4.

The reason you can't lose weight later on in life is simple enough.
It's because of how so many people you know have died,

And that you carry a little of each of them with you.

5.

The smallest muscle in the human body is in the ear.
It is also the only muscle that does not have blood vessels;

It has fluid instead. The reason for this is clear:
The ear is so sensitive that the body, if it heard its own pulse,

Would be devastated by the amplification of its own sound.
In this knowledge I sense a great metaphor,

But I do not want to be hasty in trying to capture or describe it.
Words are our weakest hold on the world.

David Rivard

Versace

Perfume off the pages of a magazine   inexplicable
vendettas   pollen   of beach grass   from beachtowns
the constant talk of weapons   American   American
sins   & ads for antihistamines   & all this

was the wind's news, especially

poor Versace: neither plug ugly
nor a looker, himself,

of all the day's dead guys   the tastiest   & most
tasteless,
who'd gone out
fishing for his morning
newspaper;

whatever new fashion he has taken up

(now that the old is abandoned,

that style the spiders call
running-back & forth-inside-ourselves,
as they themselves run,
inside silk wisps
spun from their bellies)

whatever new fashion has taken him up —

fine, fine!

Question for the Magic Hour

Out of pocket & just before dark
the wind simpers into town — tired,
and a little annoyed,
after having stewed for such
a long longtime
in its own bittersweet schemes
and choices.

Most Recent Book: *Bewitched Playground* (Graywolf Press, 2000)

A wind that's
distracted, & vague,
sniffly —
like a rabbit, or professor.

It should come instead
like a helpful devil or deadly god
this wind.

This wind should carry the horny
summer smell of pine needles,
such as those
a boatload of nippled sleepers might breathe
if anchored not
too far from shore.

Or else it should wander out of
that alley
back of the crossroad tavern
my witchy sister-in-law once owned,
the alley paved with pissed-on brick
and crud
spilled from dumpsters,
a breeze fed by the dreamless constant
roar of fryolator vents.

Like a deadly god, or a helpful devil —
let the wind come like
either of these, & fit
to be
tied, all right?

I plan to hug it & hide it from my neighbors.

Jung

Sitting down at age eighty-one to record his life
Jung made no mention of the fin-de-siecle
Swiss bath or the fifteen-year-old boy he had been
long ago standing there in a mirror & watching
as he stepped carefully into the underpants of a girl.
Slipping them over his thighs — nervous, but
not rushing, attentive. The girl his blond cousin.
Jung wrote nothing of this, he told no one.

Though about the evening a long carving knife
snapped itself into four more or less equal pieces
he managed ten pages describing & interpreting
how as it lay untouched in an oaken sideboard
the scratched steel blade shattered with a loud bang.
Whatever force broke it caused him also to abandon
his medical studies & start to survey the psyche.
He believed this & could report it straightfaced,
fervent, but told no one of the other earlier
scene — his ears bee-stung, his chest a riptide
of the silk of his cousin's pants rubbing against
his penis, his balls, touching the tightening coarse
sparse hairs alert to the cloth. In his book
he gives away almost all his secrets. That he had to
toward the end of his life give away nearly all
this was one source of his power, his healing
of the untuned unstrung souls who came freely
or by reference & authority were ferried to him —
the murderess, the catatonic rug-maker, paranoids,
an impotent wine merchant, the city planner,
a fearful Jesuit, scribbler of puns — those
filled with silence or willing to say anything,
like *I am Socrates, the unjustly accused,*
I am the double polytechnic irreplaceable,
Naples & I must supply the world with noodles.
He healed because he was filled by secrets
he understood he must eventually give up,
all but one. That was the bargain, a covenant.
But between being empty or being full
what difference is there & what gondola
shuttles us from one shore to the other?
What if no difference exists, though Jung lived
as if it did? His mother walked into the bathroom
unexpectedly, they looked at each other & she
removed herself shutting the door quietly. About
the incident neither said a word to the other.
Jung carried the pieces of the shattered knife
the rest of his life & each time he moved carefully
put the four pieces of blade in the top drawer
of his desk, in the corners, the four directions wind
blows from, the names of which are only names.

Pattiann Rogers

Murder in the Good Land

Murder among the creek narrows
and shafts of rice grass, among lacy
coverlets and field sacks, among basement
apple barrels and cellar staples
of onion and beet;
                                        beneath piled stones,
razed, broken and scattered stones,
beneath cow bridges, drawbridges, T girders
crossed, and cables, beneath brome, spadefoot,
beneath roots of three-awn
                                                    and heaven; murder
in the sky between stalks of spikesedge,
between harrier and wolf willow, between
the bedroom walls of formidable sluts
and saints, in the sad blindnesses
of moon and mole, in light as curt
and clearcut as blades of frost
magnified;
                        through blanks of winter wind
through summer soapweed, through welcoming
gates and bolted gates, throughout the blood-rushing
grief of the swarmy sea;
                                                murder beside gods
down heathen colonnades, down corridors of scholars
and beggars, down the cathedral colonnades
of orchards in harvest;
                                            murder with the clench
of white clover, with the slip of the wandering
tattler, with the slow splash of window
curtains flowing inward
                                                with morning air; murder
in the winsome, murder in the wayward,
murder in canyon wrens, in the low beating bell
in the womb, in bone rafters,
                                                      in mushroom
rings and rosy rings; murder, murder,

Most Recent Book: *Song of the World Becoming* (Milkweed Editions, 2001)

murder immortal, pervasive, supreme
everywhere in the good land.

Reiteration

This contract is not singular.
It is present in each shaft
of the chickadee's chestnut feathers
holding to flesh. Part them
on the wing or on the belly down
to hot skin and touch the document.
The bonds of this contract are plural
and solitary, present in coon paw
and river print, in swallow and scat,
in rain falling on dry leaves,
like time in meter, chord
to arpeggio to chord.

Its terms are forest ashes and crystal,
scarlet persimmon and blood, the cave
and sunlit chamber of winter, wind
across corn tassel and granite.

One might believe this contract
to be invisible, invisible where
the disappearing points of the urchin's
spines appear as the motion
of the sea, where the shifting
reflection of the water willow
and the wavering shadow of the water
willow merge and part, where truth
and lie first draw together and link
from pre-death to presence.

Like anise-pleasure contained
in the seed-size dry fruits
of the fennel, so the binding
signature is contained in the agitation
of poplars taken by wind, in the sucker-
tipped tube feet of the slender purple
starfish, in the release of midnight's
cry by root cricket, by poaching owl.

Again and again, inside the purity
of tone in the ear of the mind
of the bell caster at his fire,
this signal tolling will continue
to repeat itself. Like the pause
of the winged ant stopped, extinct
and unbroken in rock amber, this contract
remains its own reiterated event,
from coming to coming.

Here is my hand on it.

Opus from Space

Almost everything I know is glad
to be born — not only the desert orangetip,
on the twist flower or tansy, shaking
birth moisture from its wings, but also the naked
warbler nestling, head wavering toward sky,
and the honey possum, the pygmy possum,
blind, hairless thimbles of forward,
press and part.

Almost everything I've seen pushes
toward the place of that state as if there were
no knowing any other — the violent crack
and seed-propelling shot of the witch hazel pod,
the philosophy implicit in the inside out
seed-thrust of the wood sorrel. All hairy
saltcedar seeds are single-minded
in their grasping of wind and spinning
for luck toward birth by water.

And I'm fairly shocked to consider
all the bludgeonings and batterings going on
continually, the head-rammings, wing-furors,
and beak-crackings fighting for release
inside gelatinous shells, leather shells,
calcium shells or rough, horny shells. Legs
and shoulders, knees and elbows flail likewise
against their womb walls everywhere, in pine
forest niches, seepage banks and boggy
prairies, among savannah grasses, on woven
mats and perfumed linen sheets.

Mad zealots, every one, even before
beginning they are dark dust-congealings
of pure frenzy to come into light.

Almost everything I know rages to be born,
the obsession founding itself explicitly
in the coming bone harps and ladders,
the heart-thrusts, vessels and voices
of all those speeding with clear and total
fury toward this singular honor.

Come, Drink Here

Drink from this circle of night right here,
blind and sudden with currents and waves
like the wellside of the moon.

Put your mouth here where I'm showing you,
against this darkness as full of the taste
of sky as snow water caught early
in clean cave rock.

Easy between your lips again and again,
roll this slight berry possessing
the texture of violet at the root,
having the nature of a solid grain
of clear, flowing river.

Swallow at this narrow crevassing
shadow of faint salt whose ending can never
be savored or known. Tongue this tight,
gathered petal and that other small winding
of rose too, with its glassy sap.

Lick here, round and round this warm
nub, a taste a little like butter and sea,
a little like liquid sun left
on dense green mosses after dusk.

Close your eyes, and where I'm placing
your finger, here at this single flume,
like a funnel of iris leaf lithe
and rolled at the stem, suck
morning.

At this swelling, from this soft
cistern, from this heated damp like wet
day on summer grasses, drink first.

Then answer me.

Lee Ann Roripaugh

Transplanting

for my mother, Yoshiko Horikoshi Roripaugh.

I. X-Ray

My mother carried the chest x-ray
in her lap on the plane, inside
a manila envelope that read
Do Not Bend, and garnished
with leis at the Honolulu Airport
waited in line — this strange image
of ribcage, chain-link vertebrae,
pearled milk of lung and the murky
enigmatic chambers of her heart
in hand. Until it was her turn
and the immigration officer held
the black and white film up
to sun, light pierced clean through
her, and she was ushered from one
life through the gate of another,
wreathed in the dubious and illusory
perfume of plucked orchids.

II. Ceramic Pig

Newly arrived in New Mexico,
stiff and crisp in new dungarees,
her honeymoon, they drove
into the mountains in a borrowed car,
spiraling up and up toward the rumor
of deer, into the green tangy turpentine

Most Recent Book: *Beyond Heart Mountain* (Penguin Books, 1999)

scent of pine, where air crackled
with the sizzling collision of bees,
furred legs grappling velvet bodies
as they mated mid-air, and where
they came upon the disconsolate gaze
of a Madonna alcoved against
the side of the road, her feet wreathed
in candles, fruit, flowers and other
offerings. Nearby, a vendor
with a wooden plank balanced between
two folding chairs and the glossy
row of ceramic pigs lined up across,
brilliant glaze shimmering the heat.
My mother fell in love with the red
and blue splash of flowers tattooed
into fat flanks and bellies, the green
arabesques of stem and leaf circling
hoof, snout and ear. So *exotic*.
Years later she still describes the pig
with a sigh — *heartbroken*, the word
she chooses with careful consideration.
She'd filled the pig with Kennedy dollars
from the grocery budget, each dollar
a small luxury denied at the local
Piggly Wiggly until one day, jingling
the shift and clink of the pig's
growing silver weight, she shook
too hard, and as if the hoarded wealth
of her future were too much to contain,
the pig broke open — spilling coins
like water, a cold shiny music, into her lap —
fragments of bright pottery shards
scattering delicate as Easter eggshell.

III. Sneeze

My mother sneezes in Japanese. Ke-sho!
An exclamation of surprise — two sharp
crisp syllables before pulling out
the neatly folded and quartered tissue
she keeps tucked inside the wrist
of her sweater sleeve. Sometimes,
when ragweed blooms, I wonder why

her sneeze isn't mine, why something
so involuntary, so deeply rooted
in the seed of speech, breaks free from
my mouth like thistle in a stiff breeze,
in a language other than my mother's
tongue. How do you chart the diaspora
of a sneeze? I don't know how
you turned out this way, she always
tells me, and I think that we are each
her own moon — one face in shadow,
undisclosed seas and surprising mountains,
rotating in the circular music
of separate spheres, but held in orbit
by the gravitational muscle
of the same mercurial spinning heart.

iv. Dalmatian

There is an art to this. To shish
kebab the varnished pit of avocado
on three toothpicks above a pickle jar
of cool water, tease down the pale
thirsty hairs of root until one sinewy
arm punches up and unclenches its green
fisted hand, palm open, to the sun.
To discern the oniony starstruck
subterfuge of bulbs, their perverse
desires, deathlike sleeps, and conspire
behind the scenes to embroider
the Elizabethan ruffles and festoons
of their flamboyant resurrections.
To trick the tomatoes into letting down
their swelling, tumescent orbs
in the cottony baked heat of the attic
until their sunburnt faces glow
like round orange lanterns under
the crepuscular twilight of the eaves.
Unwrapping the cuttings of succulents
from their moist, paper towel bandages,
and snugging them down into firm
dimples of dirt and peat, coaxing up
the apple-green serpentine coils of sweet
pea with a snake charmer's song to wind

around the trellis and flicker their quick
pink petaled tongues. The tender slips
of mint, sueded upturned bells of petunia,
and slim fingers of pine that pluck
the metal window screen like a tin harp
by the breakfast nook where my father
stirs his morning coffee and waits
for the neighbors' dalmatian to hurl
itself over the back fence and hang,
limply twisting and gasping on the end
of its chain and collar like a polka-dotted
petticoat, until my father goes outside
and takes its baleful kicking weight
in his arms and gently tosses it back
over the fence into the neighbors' yard.
Year after year, the dandelions
and clover are weeded out, summers
come and go, and roots stubbornly inch
down around the foundation of the house —
labyrinthine, powerful and deep.

V. Japanese Apple

She was given an apple on the plane,
round and fragrant with the scent
of her grandfather's fruit orchards
during autumn, when chestnuts
dropped from their trees and struck
the metal rooftop like the small heavy
tongues of bells, and black dragon-
flies like quick shiny needles darted
in and out of the spin and turn
of leaves fluttering down like soft
bright scraps of silk. She wrapped
the apple in a napkin to save
for later, and it was confiscated
at customs before she had the chance
for even a taste. Over the years it
seemed to grow larger, yellower, juicier
and more delicious, and even though
there were burnished rows of apples
stacked in gleaming pyramids
at the supermarket with quaint

names like Macintosh, Winesap,
and Granny Smith, and even though
there were sunlit apple orchards
at my American grandfather's ranch,
where rattlesnakes slumbered
in the heat and redolence of fruit
flesh, frightening the horses,
she sampled one after another
but they never tasted as sweet
or as bright as the apple taken from her,
the one she had to leave behind.

Jill Allyn Rosser

Lover Release Agreement

Against his lip, whose service has been tendered
lavishly to me, I hold no lien.
Here's his heart, which finally has blundered
from my custody. Here's his spleen.
Hereafter let your hair and eyes and breasts
be venue for his daydreams and his nights.
Here are smart things I've said, and all the rest
you'll hear about. Here are all our fights.
Now, whereas I waive rights to his kiss,
the bed you've shared with him has rendered null
his privilege in mine. Know that, and this:
undying love was paid to me in full.
No matter how your pleasures with him shine,
you'll always be comparing them to mine.

Resurfaced

At the end of a long paycheck an archaeologist came up.
Did digs, had spelunked. Land's End eyes.
I was standing starving beside the cheese cubes

Most Recent Book: *Misery Prefigured* (Southern Illinois University Press, 2001)

because it was my job to be dithered at
fanatically all day by well-fed people
who didn't know how hungry I was.
I listened, not reaching for a single cube.
I am only that polite when I don't want to be.
You just have to accept that about me,
I told my first husband, then my second.
Eventually he quit dithering and
(probably rehearsing the day's lecture)
started describing this nomadic tribe who dwelt
in cliffy regions of I think Albania, and the persons
among this people who would laboriously
hew footholds into the loftiest cliffs,
there being no other access to the top;
they'd chisel and hack and chop rock
just to get up there, then solitarily carve
their large meaning — abstract or mammalian —
and then just as painstakingly shave off
every last foothold on their way down.
I stood there striding my spike heels
on the starprinted ballroom carpet,
recalling the look on my first's face when I left,
stony and pale, as though someone had
not only deepened his pained expression
but erased some features too, and thinking that still
was not enough. Let me tell you,
it hadn't been easy getting under his skin
and it was no picnic getting back out.
He mentioned the tribe's name twice
but my things were in another wing
of the hotel, twenty flights up,
so I didn't record it, I'm not one of those
types who carries a pen, you just have
to accept that about me, but I do carry
that look everywhere, and the way
it inspired me to refuse all the money
I had coming — on top of everything
I'd said and refrained from saying
I knew that would cut him good
and prevent anyone from ever
getting up there as high with him
as I had. It's true I'm only generous
when I'm hungry for something,

but I'm honest. And I can assure you
that he left the reverse of a mark on me;
some men just don't know when to quit,
they wind up resurfacing women like marble
when they most want to rough them up.
The archaeologist went off to give his talk
and I piled one of those little plates so high
with toothpicked cubes, carefully
impaling them pick over pick,
that the servant behind the immaculate cloth
raised both eyebrows, which I could have
had him fired for, but I didn't. What I want
is for you to see how unmarked I am.
By the time the archaeologist came back
looking for me, I had eaten every inch of that cheese
and wiped the plate until it gleamed.

Quest of the Prell

We were functioning as one because it was a flying dream.
I was holding his hand, he mine.
I hadn't yet glimpsed his face,
but when you're flying you don't care.
Sand-hued gazelles sipped at a green lagoon.
No question but that we both needed
to get closer;
                    descending, found instead a playground
beside a green pond — no,
                                        massive bottle of Prell Shampoo,
like the one in the commercial where a man's hand drops
a pearl, which slowly sinks through the green murk
to show how thick the murk must be to slow the pearl.
And he sighed with a look I knew from somewhere,
as if he'd said *What's wrong?* and I'd said *Nothing*
unconvincingly — a tired, determined look,
suggesting this was yet another test of love.
His quest: to swim the Prell.
What's worse, I seemed to want him to;
and woke up in horror, not sure whose.
Is this what the male psyche thinks it's up against
in a relationship (the very word ungainly)

with a woman? Manning the unbalanced
swingset of romance,
trying to swing as she swings,
at the same velocity and height
so as to keep everything even
between them; then off to navigate
her jungle gym without getting to the top
first, trying not to put his foot down
on hers, her career, her herness,
or lose his tender grip on her notion
of what their life should be like?

Oh, must he seesaw with her endlessly
on that creaking, warped emery board
laid across the moat of her past,
swirling with such desires as she herself
can hardly see, with prehistorically
huge appetites and indiscriminate teeth?

Not to say it isn't terrifying on the woman's end
of things, like going down the slide backwards
sans underwear, and which will it be this time
at bottom: the burning sands of his indifference;
the asphalt of disdain; or will he laughing catch her up?

This all sounds so fifties, I know, the Prell,
the desire to be caught, but it was his look
that left me shaking. I've seen it on every lover
and husband of every last one of my women friends,
and now on you — though it wasn't your face
really, let's not forget this was a dream —
inheriting that look from every man regarding
every woman, that awful look of resignation
to face the rich green goo of her being;
the hero hardily willing to hold his breath
grimaceless, refrain from muttering *Oh, swell*,
and blindly dive to retrieve that cultured pearl,
dropped long ago by an unknown man's
unthinking hand (just to prove a point)
into the opaque murk of her self, her very *elle*;
into the thick, slick, deep, man-handled,
bottled-up, unreal green of her Prell.

As she heroically must stand there
helpless, watching him.

Clare Rossini

Brief History of a Sentence

Let's start with the big picture:

The universe, i.e., great outward rush
Of fires and nights, and at its edge, among thickets of matter
Fraying, a star
Devolving into helium
And its sidekick, shine.

Which light
(Wave or particle? Music or poetry?) dashes
Through eons of miles until it impales our own
Blue-green wonder
Of continental drift, brokenhearted kin of the Hominidae.
You know the place.

Whereon stands (say it's a woman) a woman
On her porch, cold clear night in autumn, another summer
Trashed, let's pause
To mark our seasonal acquiescence to the powers
Of wind, the planet's dogged whirl. . . .

She draws her sweater close. The star punches its pinhole beam
Through the city's
Steady nerveless glow, arriving
Just as the woman — let's make her me —

Just as I look up,
A scintillating pebble sinking
Into my eye,
The retinal rods and cones
Honing the star to a hot
Potato of light tossed neuron to neuron.

And I, for a moment, a filament burning.

Under the power lines, among the sagging porches of my
Broken city, I am
Emerson on the Common, stoked
By the beyond, stowing for the universe
Its own erupted face.

Most Recent Book: *Winter Morning with Crow* (University of Akron Press, 1997)

Whereupon I make my sentence
For nothing and no one
But the rosebush my landlady tied
Sebastian-like to a stick
And cajoled into bloom, I say to that now defunct,
Thorned, stem-of-a-thing,

Hey, that's a star I haven't seen before.

And the bush listens.

Rice County Soliloquy

I come from Minnesota.
What do I know of the flamingo?

Its long and s-curved neck, its awkward flight?
If fly it does.

In my town, foreign food is pizza.
In winter and in spring, it snows.

The thought of something pink with wings
Wounds all of us, we natives

Of this land of grays and whites,
Where the template of winter was struck.

I've stood in arctic winds and felt them
Grind against my human frame.

I've looked out bleakly and borne up.
That's our way here.

Coral reefs, cabanas striped and scattered
Across beaches, blue-colored drinks:

What god made them and this place, too?
I guess he had a range,

A taste for the superfluous
Exhausted by the time he shook out north.

When the going gets tough!
If the shoe fits!

Sometimes, we're surprised to find our bodies
Beneath the multiple layers,

Radiant with mammal warmth.
Dear,

If the trees would not stand leafless
As long as they do, each rivulet of bark

Caked with frost, each forked twig scratching
A sky so blue and deep it hurts —

Busy hands! Light work!
After all, we have our crocuses,

And the balm of our May dusks will thaw
The most Protestant among us.

But the days grow short.
The light grows small.

Then come those Januarial hours
When I turn the TV chitchat off

And stand on my porch, in the rigid air,
The backyard stiff with snow.

Comes something pink and winged. Goes.
Call it a crave.

"Why Talk When You Can Paint?"

— Milton Avery

The guy is right.

How could a bunch of syllables compete
With the lifting of a brush
To canvas, brash move that has brought us
The likes of Hals's burgomasters, up to their ruffs
In whole milk and lard?

Not to mention Bonnard's
Fluorescent gardens, Basquiat's
Wordy acrylics of rage.

That hush
In which paint is daubed,
Stroked, scumbled, scouraging
The canvas's blank — why trade that
Hush for chat, tit for tat,

If you can trash another void
With the shapely ways of color, the seasonless
Amours of light?

Don't talk if you can paint.

But if you can't paint, talk.

Better, get those words on paper. It's another
Kind of horseplay,
Version of worship, way
To get through a day, a life.

Words are cheap.

A painter's in need
Of turpentines, brushes and glues,
Gessoes, stretchers, staplers, scrapers,
Whatnot. And believe it, a tube of cadmium yellow
Could put you in the red.

This, in a world where wizards of software
Find Nirvana-dot-com to the tune
Of a million bucks a week.

Why compute
When you can paint or write? Nail some boards together,
Sew a button on?

Our computations bred machines
That drove the songbirds off.

Now we're calculating
Rather precisely
The number of *leider* lost, the day on which the planet —
Dear old earth! —
Might be hobbled once and for all.

Why do anything at all
When you can sleep? Dream,
As if an image could still
Save you —

Keats's blissed-out nightingale, nursing wounds
In drowsy iambic,
True to its singing whatever dark
At last happens to fall.

Eve to Adam, in Retrospect

For awhile, we were riled up,
And all of it inspired by the body, incubate of appetite,
On which the senses hang like fruit.

And didn't we pluck them? Wasn't that
What night was about? Stellar cave of moan and cloud.

I would chart the hours
To and from you; you beckoned and I came.

And weren't there trails of clothes toward the bed?
We rode roughshod
Over that plain, oblivious to the sheeted verge.

And didn't we know what inoperable condition
We had assumed? Desire
Without love, smolder-house without a furnace.
And didn't we burn?

And the moon raked us like coals and brought back the blaze.

The leaves hang in yellow tatters now.
The fields are busy with crows. Still, old darling,
As I walk through this ruined world we built,
Heat for you
Clings to me, dogged as bramble.

Mary Ruefle

Seven Postcards from Dover

I

The teacher said *inner truth*
and the chalk said *like a fresco inside the earth*
that no one has ever seen
and one day decides to be discovered
and begins to breathe —
do you know what that means?

Most Recent Book: *Post Meridian* (Carnegie Mellon University Press, 2000)

II

The child broke the chalk.
The mother said *be strong*.
The child said *when I die I want to be a dwarf*.

III

A detective has just drawn a circle
with a piece of chalk, a private circle
from which the victim will eventually look
up, not at random, not at will,
but when it calls to her,
the chalk, the crushed bones
of sea creatures who ringed the earth
when it was under water.

IV

A man sits in the bath house
in a deep tub of fizzling yellow water
that surrounds every hair on his body
and makes it stand upright.
When the attendant comes, she will
clean the tub by moving her hand
slowly around the ring, like a snail.

V

An atoll is a ring of coral
protecting a tureen of plankton.
It is easy and Japanese to be sad
knowing something is going to pass.
He put the ring on her chalky finger.

VI

Long after chalk had passed out of use,
carpenters still felt for it in their pockets
and looked aimlessly at the sky.

VII

The cathedral was roofless.
It began to snow inside.
A half-broken pillar in the nave
grew taller.

No Comparison

In the dream your face was rippling everywhere
like banners of Mao.
How unlucky you are not to be loved
by a million people, but only by one,
one who likes the word Mao
out of a million words.
The cat knows.
The sun sometimes
finds it way through a river of garbage
spilling down an alley
and lights on a litter.
And anyone who chances by stops to marvel.
The hairs of your head are all numbered.
You are of more value than many sparrows.
Mao thought we could make a difference.
Many of his countrymen thoughtfully concluded
that would be true — if we existed.
So he rippled there for awhile.
Those that ate manna are dead.
So it is not your face I remember
but the wind —
it lifted the hairs of your head
and I was able to count them
it dispersed the sparrows in the square
and sent them in different directions
it ran through the banners
like a hand on the back of a cat
and it woke me suddenly
like a vivid face.
May it live ten thousand years.

10 April

The young cherry tree is naked and alone
trying to hide from the cold night.
Which is impossible so the man has come
and put his arms around the tree.
He is wearing the clothes of his dead mother,
a white slip, a thin buff-colored kimono,

a heavier black one on top.
He begins to tremble with all the anxiety
a young tree feels in the spring,
his face white with rice powder,
the wind blowing hair across it
without breaking a strand.
He isn't a man pretending to be a tree,
he's a man honoring a woman
who is trying to become a tree.
Only once does he open his mouth:
there is rouge on his tongue
as if he's been eating cherries off the ground
and is deeply ashamed, but purified
like a well.

Among the Musk Ox People

They were aesthetes, which means
I was forced to eat a hard peach,
commissioned to paint a twelve-foot abstraction
based on watching host cells collaborate
in bacterial infection, and at night
chewed the soles of their mukluks
till they were soft again.
If I ventured outside the igloo
and saw a celebrity,
I felt so inferior
I wanted to die.
To conceal my envy
I was given dark glasses.
If, on the other hand, I encountered
someone to whom I was vastly superior,
one of those ill-clad, raving, wandering hags,
I felt ashamed and wanted to die.
To appease my guilt
they were given by the Elders a little of my grub.
If I met with an Ordinary,
someone not dissimilar to myself,
with dissatisfactions roughly the same,
I felt the world was senseless
supporting so many look-alikes

and again I asked to die:
life reached a maddening peak
out there on the ice when
we were hunting and could move only our eyes.
Still, like a seal reaching his blowhole
in the dark, every seventy-two hours
I came to my senses for thirteen minutes
and continued to live with the knowledge
that deep in the oyster bed of my blood
layered spheres continued to build round
my name, cold, calciferous, and forgotten.
When the Giant Orphan At The Bottom Of The Sea
appeared in my dreams,
demanding I write the story
of three generations of Ox women
resulting in the birth of a performance artist,
I knew I would need a knife, gun, needles,
kettle, scissors and soap,
and gave up, at last, my finest skins.
I made my escape across the shrouded inlet
away from those who believe that outside
our thoughts there is only mist,
and with my skills at flensing
never feared for the future.

Michael Ryan

My Other Self

for Greg and Trish Orr

He could have smacked you
for running out of gas, at midnight,
in December, at a middle-of-nowhere place,
coasting a few sorry yards toward home on the shoulder
as a passing eighteen-wheeler's Hawaiian-sized wave of air
whomped the side of the car like a two-story pillow.
As we sat there immobile — the four of us (including him),
as if waiting for the movie to start at a surreal drive-in —

Most Recent Book: *A Difficult Grace* (University of Georgia Press, 2000)

he wanted to reach into the front seat
and bonk your heads together
the way the leader of the Three Stooges did
when the other two did something stupid.
What had been *road* was now a cold place
without a house light in sight in the rural South.
What had been a passionate highway talk
about the culture's indifference to the artist's work
would have been silence except for him
giggling at us, at how danger dissolves discontent
and flashes before us a life lost to pettiness,
which we soon start to lose again.
"What's that adage about wartime curing neurotics?"
he planned to mock us with my voice, but when I got out
to see where we were, he didn't. He brooded in the car.
He didn't feel the pleasure of a skyful of stars
so cold and clear when you look up
its light illuminates your breath.
Nor was he worried about anyone but himself,
being the only one with nothing to worry about,
not made of flesh. He was crying
I wanna go home inside the car
like a child trapped in a junkyard refrigerator.

This was one time I felt exactly like him,
as we three stood pondering our dilemma calmly, maturely.
And I did again when he yelled *I'm scared*
as the clunker with wide headlights and bad muffler
("Hell Wagon" or "Devil's Dream" no doubt inscribed on the fender —
voted Car Of The Year by escaped convicts and serial killers)
glided like a crocodile toward our throbbing, imported taillights
and idled there. When I approached the monster
alone — my other self was having none of this action —
what I found when the window inched down
was reality: a couple with a baby
asleep between them: country people
who still stop for anyone in trouble,
although they were wary. So was I,
squinting into the warm darkness in which they stirred
as if at the bottom of a moonlit pool,
as if what should surface nonetheless was a gun in my face.
They got back with a can of gas so fast
the whole event took about the time of a Howard Johnson hamburger,

and probably less time than a Howard Johnson hamburger off a life
in which it's nearly impossible
not to feel blessed. How lucky we are,
we said on the smooth way home again,
trying to etch it into our brains.
And he probably would have chimed in
if we hadn't ditched him back there
where he still is, thumb out and grinning
into the high beams of every approaching car
since the next one's always the starlet in the Jaguar
wrapped in a mink with nothing underneath.

Against Self-Torment

Grant nothing to the one
who monitors your life
with insult and complaint
like an ambitious wife

Provoked by your insouciance
to flambé your underpants
in Gran Marnier-soaked-
chocolate-covered ants

her mother sent from Paris
on the fling with Giggolo Rex
that did in the trust fund
but not the hatred of sex

she took out on her daughter
as each damned day shrieked through
and now and forever her daughter
is taking out on you.

Complete Semen Study

morphology: "pinheads": two per cent

Laborious, stumpy, droopy, askew,
blundering into the microscopic equivalent of paths of busses
as the healthiest sperm zips by like the varsity water polo team
on their way to a party with the best-looking cheerleaders —

unbeautiful losers, unfittest and unmourned,
o my five-hundred-thousand-or-so pinheads
floundering in this plastic cup's murky bottom,
what would *you* do to be half of someone?
Wank it sitting on the toilet in a fluorescent
pea-green hospital bathroom while learning to juggle one-handed
one cup and three brown-bagged *Penthouses*
offered by the deadpan female lab attendant?
You'd wank it anyplace, I think.
They'd tie your wrists if you had wrists
to stop your rubbing off on fireplugs and brick buildings,
much less on a hand's elastic flesh
you're too dim to recognize is your own.
You're the ones who can't be taken to church
because you hump the scarlet pew cushions
while the rest of us are praying,
and try to straddle the priest's leg like a puppy
while he exchanges an inspirational personal word or two
with each of his congregation as they file from the service.
I, on the other hand, am too mature for this.
The Pet-of-the-Month could almost be my granddaughter.
My metabolism has decelerated
to that of an elderly Galapagos Tortoise.
I could do very well all day sunning myself
under a thick, warm shell, and could easily take the next century
to burn the calories in a slice of pizza.
In the world for which my body was designed
I would have checked out long ago,
immolated at the ritual bonfire by my two hundred great-grandchildren
roasting a whole mammoth in my honor,
dancing for days stoned on sacred leaf-juice,
and intermarrying like howler monkeys in the bushes.
It's no doubt due to nights like this
that you weakened and malformed
and chase your own watery tails until you decompose
into what the complete semen study classifies as "debris."
The doctors say it's age or car exhaust or groundwater toxins
or they-don't-know-what, but there must have been a boy
waiting for the dopey old patriarch to die
so he could do his sister when she was stoned out of her cheesewhiz,
sweaty and writhing in the firelight. If their child, slow-witted
and guileless, showed the endearing but useless gift
to greet everyone's spirit no matter their status,

they might have thrown him the bones the dogs had finished with,
which is how they fed the shunned and the shamed,
unbeautiful losers, unfittest and unmourned,
o my five-hundred-thousand-or-so pinheads
floundering in this plastic cup's murky bottom
I hereby hand over for removal and disposal
to the now-surgically-gloved
deadpan female lab attendant.

In the Sink

(Paul H. Ryan, 1909-1964)

Tiny red spider, in your weird world
of instructive vibrations and spikes of heat,
you're spread like a nerve-end naively unfurled
as if my touch would be a treat.

You're safe for now, at least from me —
although your utter otherness
jolts my not being what I don't want to be,
which, in your case, would be obvious

except you're stuck in a porcelain bowl
where any drunk who wants a drink
can send you swirling down a hole
never noticing you in the sink.

Influence is too pale a word
for how a father lives in his son.
Rejoice you're not his drop of blood.
I'd flick this faucet and be done.

IRA SADOFF

On the Day of Nixon's Funeral

It's time to put the aside the old resentments; lies,
machinations, the paranoia, bugs in telephones,
the body bags, secret bombings, his sweaty upper lip,
my cousin Arnie, too dumb to go to school,

Most Recent Book: *Grazing* (University of Illinois Press, 1998)

too virtuous to confess he'd give blow jobs
for nothing at the Paramount, so he lost a leg
in Da Nang. Now it's time for amnesiacs to play
Beethoven's Eroica by Nixon's casket.

To applaud his loyalty, to grant a few mistakes,
to honor his diplomacy, him and his pal Kissinger
who bombed the lush green paddies of Cambodia.
And now for a few lyric moments as I wait patiently

for my fiftieth birthday. Wood ducks decorate the pond
near this farmhouse, and in the marsh I've spied
a meadow lark, a fox, a white-tailed hawk who soars
above the Western Mountain peaks. Oh, I'm in love

with the country all right. So I can forget my friend
Sweeney, who shot Congressman Lowenstein
because the radio in his tooth insisted on it.
I remember the march on the Pentagon in purple,

a proud member of the Vegetarian Brigade. I was drugged,
as many of us were drugged, as my parents
were drugged by a few major networks, by a ranch house
and an Oldsmobile. I once spit on Hubert Humphrey,

threw a brick through Dow Chemical's plate-glass door.
I wrote insane letters to Senators, burying them
in moral rectitude: I got a response from one:
Senator Kennedy — the dead one — whose office wrongly

argued for slow withdrawal instead of Instant Victory.
I remember Tricky Dick in Nineteen Fifty-three:
I'm eight years old, frightened and ignorant,
lying down before my parents' first TV: my aunts

and uncles sitting in a circle, biting their nails,
whispering names of relatives awaiting trial, who,
thanks to Nixon, lost their sorry jobs. You can see why
I'd want to bury this man whose blood would not circulate,

whose face was paralyzed, who should have died
in shame and solitude, without benefit of eulogy or twenty-one
gun salutes. I want to bury him in Southern California
with the Birchers and the Libertarians. I want to look out

my window and cheer the remaining cedars
that require swampy habitats to survive. To be done
with shame and rage this April afternoon, where embryonic
fiddleheads, fuzzy and curled and pale as wings,

have risen to meet me. After all, they say he was a scrappy man,
wily and sage, who served as Lucifer, scapegoat, scoundrel,
a receptacle for acrimony and rage — one human being
whose life I have no reverence for, which is why I'm singing now.

My Mother's Funeral

The rabbi doesn't say she was sly and peevish,
fragile and voracious, disheveled, voiceless and useless,
at the end of her very long rope. He never sat beside her
like a statue while radio voices called to her from God.
He doesn't say how she mamboed with her broom,
staggered, swayed, and sighed afternoons,
till we came from school to feed her. She never frightened *him*,
or bent to kiss him, sponged him with a fever, never held his hand,
bone-white, bolted doors and shut the blinds. She never sent
roaches in a letter, he never saw her fall down stairs, dead sober.
He never watched her sweep and murmur, he never saw
spider webs she read as signs her life was over, long before
her frightened husband left, long before
they dropped her in a box, before her children turned
shyly from each other, since they never learned to pray.
If I must think of her, if I can spare her moment on the earth,
I'll say she was one of God's small sculptures,
polished to a glaze, one the wind blew off a shelf.

Izzy

The prettiest shadows were impalpable, so I stored them
in this sentence, where nothing's more than a sequence of words,
thereby degrading them, the scale of gray they cast on the wall,
say, of his parents' bedroom, reduced to a silhouette,
the kind they sold on the Lower East Side to old Jewish families
who could not afford family portraits. Do you feel the pity of it, the boy
making animal shapes on the wall with his fingers, because they had
        nothing,
making the figures dreamy and incandescent, ancient and mythological,
half-man and half-horse, neighing and bucking, mimicking
the boarders' voices in the kitchen? They were building a subway
and wore their mining hats to breakfast, and like him, lived in a tunnel,

inside their own field of vision, meaning all nuances of pain and pleasure,
— unless you felt them like a steam iron on your forearm — were
 abstractions,
so as he told me the story, extracting bits of cloth from a moment in
 1909,
one from the year preceding, a few after he began working at the cinema,
projecting shadows: Chaplin outwitting a bully,
Keaton escaping a speeding train as his house collapses at his feet —
Izzy's broom shadow to the celluloid swept up and startled into
 nothing —
I tried to hold everything in place, to draw a picture, since he was half-
 blind by then,
and he had nothing but a string of words to raise us up from — should
 I say
the tenement? — no, from his wing chair where I felt like the horse
"shaded" from peripheral view, one who carted him all over the park
so he could sharpen knives, but that was another story, and his face
was no longer draped in lamplight, his face had never been
"draped" in lamplight, but his mouth was shadow, and the tunnel of his
 voice,
as he brought the veil of his hand down over his eyes, gave no sign
the curtain was closing, no sign of how I'd carry on.

Delirious

It's all savagery and appropriation,
all butt-fucking and scarring faces with broken bottles,
buying a new Toyota to ape the neighbors,

it's all coughing in the cities, feces in the rivers,
a few old gossips in the Laundromat,
a wrinkled magazine where a neighbor's suddenly famous,

it's all a welt on the baby's forehead, a mirror
for the greasy corned beef sandwich on East Thirty-Fourth,
and then it's not. Then it's Linda and me

trailing through the country, a noisy Casey
and Julie behind us, then it's the snowbells seeping
through the muddy riverbank, and the stream finding its way

to the sewer, and then its being attached to the sea
at dusk, the murky afflatus of water,
violet and copper, the picture window framing the harbor,

before we're floating downriver, a little serenade
from the terns and the pines
smudged charcoal in reflection. You don't want to hear

about my happiness. It amounts to one person for a minute
walking through a park, the same park,
whose momentary blooms — the shrub rose with saw-tooth leaves,

its green thorns spiking the dew, the flimsy petals,
palmlike, somewhere between violet
and pink, like skin scraped raw — could make him cringe.

It's dark by now, so we can close the doors
whose hinges seem to be crying
to infuse a little emotion in the privacy of our apartments,

where we're sacred individuals, gorging our urgent body parts.
in blood and screams, no longer willing
to shave the hair off chimpanzees, to attach them to wires

to see how we behave, and yet, and yet, and yet...

Natasha Saje

Why I Won't Pierce My Ears

Even though

I've dropped the gold
you've given me

into the wide world of asphalt
and of forest,

caught gems in the collars of coats
and trod them into the carpets of movie theaters,

I won't do it.

I could say I don't like the idea
of my body being marred

even in the tiniest way,

but that's only half of it,

Most Recent Book: *Red Under the Skin* (University of Pittsburgh Press, 1994)

I know,
that when I lose the next earring,

you will console me:

take my lobe between your lips
and apply

love

like a compress of ether and sea.

And the pearl I'll have lost is nothing
compared to that morsel of me

wholly yours,
no ornament except your own

sweet tongue.

I am peeling four pink grapefruit

to make sorbet with Campari, for a party,
removing the bitter white pith,
but I am also eating so many sweet globules
that the I who is doing the work
is clearly not the I swallowing the fruit.
Soon there's no hope of sorbet for six,
only enough for two; one of us
boils the rind and sugar into syrup,
freezes the small mound into dessert.

The self who hops to conclusions
like popcorn, who falls in love on the basis
of a bare arm, the self always
drunk with the pleasure at hand, shares a body
with the woman who has been true to one man,
who even at midnight when the other I wants
only to roll into bed, is reaching for chocolate and eggs,
melting and separating, envisioning the faces
of her guests at the first mouthful of mousse,

dark as the heart of a faithless wife.

Wonders of the Invisible World

Muses are no better than harlots.
— Cotton Mather, 1726

Strange that he mentions the muses.
Demons, yes. God, of course.
But harlots? Perhaps

in his last year, nearly
destitute, having out-lived
thirteen of his children,

the doctor of divinity — this man
who once wrote in his diary
about the wife who nearly killed

him with her madness, *Misera*
mea conjux in Paroxysmos
illos vere Satanicos — felt

another sorceress nuzzling
his ears about the price of flesh
before spinning it into words,

and he knew that she too would leave
and he would be bereft
of a sweet and wicked thing

that gave him sustenance. Or
perhaps he remembered thirty years
before, the *Time of the Devils*

coming down in great Wrath,
too many Tongues and Hearts
set on fire of Hell,

and imagined a world pervaded
by the biting wind of harmattan
with wraithlike women moving

soul to soul, streaming like water
off a roof, flooding the mouth of every man
who had ever meant to hang them.

Story of a Marriage

A purple grey sky resembles ashes of roses.

Inside the house ceilings sag.

She is one farmer who talks to dairy cows inventively.

He wears earmuffs even when he feeds the pigs.

The *other woman* vomits regularly.

When the sap evaporates, grit seeps under their eyelids.

Her imagination is a hair shirt, his has holes.

Texas clay sinks around their foundation.

The heel of his shoe, the barometer of her face — are not rubber.

Near the end her skin blooms with violet rugosa.

Like a hemlock he loses his needles.

They keep the one key that doesn't work.

Sherod Santos

Romeo & Juliet

"O true apothecary"

With that same unsettling instinct for how human love
can fall by chance to the borrowed grave of a coldwater flat,
the broadcast snows heaped up since dawn against our two small
street-level windows, walling out the staticky, offstage noise
of the early morning traffic, the stink of trash and exhaust pipe fumes.

But when setting aside our breakfast trays, and drawing the goose-
down coverlet off, you climbed up over me, late for work,
and filled my mouth with a nut-brown, poppied aureole,
I couldn't believe that either of us would ever die, or that,
given the choice, we wouldn't choose this and be buried alive.

Most Recent Book: *The Pilot Star Elegies* (W. W. Norton & Company, 2000)

The Book of Blessings

The reserved and slightly weary-eyed doctor in the ER who,
having awakened him late, curled up in a blanket
on the waiting room floor, said two times softly, 'She'll
be fine now,' that doctor was writ in his Book of Blessings.

As were the windfall apples the horses ate (the trailing slobber's
acrid stain like the wrack of nature across his hand)
at the Shaker village in Kentucky, where his mother had gone
to recover. And the tears of his mother, muffled, exhausted,

utterly undone by her night-long struggles in the room next door,
while the boy sat watching on a television screen
the man a following crowd called 'King,' though the crowd
surrounding did not bow down in the Selma of 1958.

And yet the King's high seeing still gazed beyond the fear
in everyone's eyes to a place made quiet by him
in them, so that the crowd as it passed made a papery sound,
like the scrape of leaves (or, as the boy now saw it, like the theme

of leaves) across the threshold that opened within him there.
That too was writ in his Book of Blessings.
As were the songs he'd committed to memory, the one about
a fast-falling eventide, the one about stardust and a garden wall;

and before that there was learning to read, the alphabet,
syllable, word and phrase, the vanishing point
of the period, the tripled period's placid sea . . . and suspended
roundly above that sea, the fluent figure of a risen moon,

and the loosed imagining *moon* adds to speech,
the sea change its four letters form in the mind of a boy
sitting up in bed, until the bed's no longer a bed at all,
but a boat whose filling spinnaker has hauled it out

from a foreign shore overgrown with shadow-shapes
and rustlings. And his penis erect in a dream that boat now
carries him toward, a dream in which the towering secret
of his begetting is at last spelled out in the bright pearl-

droplets of a falling rain, as though the moon were weeping
on the open sea, and the sea were a body it yearned for.
All that was writ in his book as well, all that
and more than he is able to recall tonight, for after

forty-eight years he has come to find so many erasures
appear there now, so many passages torn out whole,
while in the Book of Death the pages are already filling up,
and in the Book of Silence, and in the Book of Forgetting.

Illuminated Manuscript

Like motes embedded in the vitreous humor, those odd, unsorted
cryptographs of memory and blood underwrite our lives in texts,
it seems, we've somehow lost the sense to read; and yet, setting aside
my book last night, I thought for a moment I could just make out,
beneath the fluent features of your sleeping face, the mute particulars
of a dream begin, its self-reflecting secrets start to ramify and clear.

Your eyelids quickened, and your brow assumed the worried look of
someone
reading on a garden bench (October sunlight fretting the page) a story
that might've been her own, a story enciphered with those same bright
photons
and free-floating threads which, when the lamp's turned off, or the eyelid
closes on a sun-touched page, resolve into our field of vision as a lost
cuneiform
of burnished signs whose meanings we've somehow unknowingly
become.

The Talking Cure

No sadness
Is greater than in misery to rehearse
Memories of joy.
— Inferno

Eyes shut. Lapsed time. The 2 A.M. aquarium light.
The background noise of my parents' party
winding down upstairs. A suspended moment
between two worlds while the mind's uprooted
from a sleep that won't quite blink away,
and a woman from one or the other of those worlds
who has found her way beside my bed saying,
Shhh, shhh, it's only me, though I can't imagine
who *me* might be. And before I'm able to ask her,

she has passed a finger across my lips, unfastened
the topmost pearl-snap button on her ecru blouse
(the sound a flame makes touched to glass, the glass
then touched to water), and guided my hand
held trembling beneath the rustle of that enfolded cloth.
And in that still assembling hour, assembling now

through the same stirred waterlight that it did then,
I have felt for the first time in my life, have felt
as something inside of me, as another body within
my own, her breathing deepen, and its guttering.
Things aren't always what they seem to be,
and neither, I suppose, are the things we feel.
But the truth is I was scared to think that dream
might actually *be* a dream, or that, in turn,
it might prove not to be a dream at all, for it seemed
blood-bidden what happens then, when she eases
my hand to a place I can only conceive of as
a vacancy, a chill alongside that pillowed hillock
she'd closed it on. She moves it, you see, along
the raised abrasion of a surgical scar that cut
in a transverse angle from her rib cage to her shoulder.

And that, she whispers, is the reason she's come.
The reason she's left the party upstairs. The reason
she simply wants me now to look at her, wants me
just to look and see the body her husband refuses
to see. But could that really have happened?
I wondered about it even then. And what
could it have to do with tears? The tears that all
too readily come when she finally steps back
from my side, lets fall her blouse and underthings,
and stands there backlit by an aquarium glow
her body inflected with a sorrow that lay
well beyond the reach of my thirteen years.
And this is where I ask myself if all of this
was only a fantasy, just another freak,
enciphered scene unspooled from the bobbin

of an adolescent's dreams. Believing that,
my parents both earnestly stood their ground
the following fall, when her husband found her
four months pregnant, sprawled out naked
on the bathroom floor beside an emptied bottle

of Nembutal. I talked to people about it when
things came to light. One caseworker in particular
took the better part of an afternoon to explain
why it was the letters this woman and I exchanged
had nothing to do with love at all, not with
'real' love anyway, but with something more
how did he put it? — 'unnatural,' I think, though
clearly he meant to say 'perverse.' I accepted that.
I saw the sense. But what I recall (and, admittedly,
it took me years to sort what's fact from fiction),

what I recall is that, as she stands there figured in
the pale aquarelles her ever-receding memory
paints, I swim out toward her to be taken up by
the current of her inclining arms, to be folded back
into another world where my own tears start,
though what I wept for I can't say — *that* is what
I remember. That and the more unlikely fact
that all of this happened even as she was somehow
muffling the sounds I could not keep down,
easing me under and taking me in, taking me into
the mind's all suddenly silvered light, and inside that
to a welling in the blood, a fullness in the heart,
the secret, solitary, nowhere of a place where in
one brief fluorescing stroke a shudder of grief
and arousal struck a lifelong, inwrought, echoing chord.

I can tell by the way you peer up over your glasses
that you're probably wondering why, in thirty-five years
of marriage, I never told my wife about any of this.
But let me ask you something, now that our hour
has come to an end, now that I've chattered on and on
while you, as usual, say nothing. Let me ask
if you and the others in your profession
don't sometimes feel like the ones to whom
it has devolved — from God, no less — to serve
as the guardians for our souls? The ones who keep
from raveling into oblivion that elaborate tapestry
of self-delusions upon which our community
now depends for moral and spiritual guidance?
No, I didn't think you'd answer that. You're right
not to, of course. Where were we then? Ah, yes,

the reason I haven't told my wife. It's simple really.
I just didn't want to hurt her. I know you'll say
my *not* telling her has hurt her more, but
it seems to me, despite the conventional wisdom,
some truths can do more harm than good. Or maybe
I've only come to feel, as time has passed,
that we understand less than we pretend about how
to love, or why we should, or when it's right,
or what we ought to expect from it. And who's to say,
given the passionless affections, the pent-up malice
and forbearance with which most couples tend to treat
each other for the better part of their married lives,
who's to say that what I had with that poor woman
years ago wasn't actually love of a finer kind
than I've known since, or am ever likely to know again?

Philip Schultz

The Displaced

Grandma hated the Russians who attacked the Ukrainians
who tormented the Romanians who pissed on everyone's roses
and played around with everyone's wives. This was Rochester, N.Y.,
in the fifties, when all the Displaced Persons moved in and suddenly
even the oaks looked defeated. Grandma believed they came here
so we all could suffer, that soon we'd all dress like undertakers
and march around whispering to the dead. Mr. Schwartzman hired me
to write letters nobody answered. He wrote about Mrs. Tillem's
boarding house, where everyone stank of sardines and spat in the sink;
about his job at the A & P providing for everyone else's appetite.
He never wrote about what'd happened to his music or family.
Saturday mornings for two years he spoke Yiddish as I wrote
my twelve-year-old English until I found him hanging in his closet
with a note pinned to his tie: 'Live outwardly, objectify!' Yes, Goethe,
famous for beating hexameters on his mistress's back while lovemaking
because art was long, life was short and the dead also didn't belong
anyplace.

Most Recent Book: *The Holy Worm of Praise* (Harcourt, 2002)

The Extra

We recognized his dark Slavic eyes
under horned helmets and sombreros,

his fervid lips behind fuming beards and putty noses.
Short, bald and bouncy, he played lunatic gangsters

with hysterical left eyes and angry pagans in biblical epics,
but we liked him best as the hiccuping bandit in *Viva Zapata!*

and the paranoid deputy in *The Phoenix City Story*.
Doors slammed in his face without provocation

and he was never listed in the credits. Hey you, is what everyone
called him.
Perhaps it was the contumacious gleam in his eye

or the congratulatory angle of his fedora,
but so many bad things happened, finally,

he just disappeared. Or retired.
Then he started showing up in our old photos,

eating oysters at Uncle Hy's first retirement party
and fixing his tie at Aunt Becky's second wedding.

Decorously ambiguous, he always kept his distance,
like a shadow. But being an extra isn't something

one just stops doing. It isn't like playing the cello.
Last week he followed me up 7th Avenue disguised as a policeman

and this morning he stepped out of the Empire State Building
smiling like a tourist after an audience with God

and then faded into the background. Perhaps
he understands anonymity is the supreme vanity

and is trying to tell us something about forgiveness,
or begging for recognition in spectacles which end badly,

or waking into the surprising present of someone else's story.

In Medias Res

All this is by way of saying
we found seven minutes of movie film
of a wedding, my mother's second
cousin, Henrietta's, we think,
which was taken forty years ago,
judging by my mother's age,
but imagine our surprise
rummaging in a closet
and suddenly so many familiar
faces grimacing as things
are getting started but as yet
haven't erupted into memorable,
if curious, behavior, when a quick kiss
on the back stairs is permission
to unwind toward self-invention,
or a window suddenly offers
a denatured view of the future,
which no one ever noticed before.
Yes, it's 1956 again & father is back-
slapping and ordering everyone around
and dear Aunt Rosemarie looks so elegant
smiling at the camera years before
anyone imagined they weren't thriving,
everyone so busy performing the geometry
of haphazard gestures, every upper lip
and fermenting brow frozen between
expectation and disappointment,
between wanting a little less
insulation and not feeling quite
so cheated, yes, all these names
and faces listening to their own
footsteps approaching everything
they meant to accomplish
but paused in the middle...
seven minutes in a January evening
in the midst of a century still
too young to owe anyone even
one small moment of forgiveness.

The Holy Worm of Praise

to my friends on my 50th birthday

Let's raise our glasses and give thanks
to our great excitement and hunger
for the hereafter the joyful sleep
of expectation the pentecostal suffering
that seizes entire winter afternoons in amber
our best days that shake us with fear and envy
our nights of provocative kissing
behind hotel rhododendrons
the secret lives we cannot remember
the deathbeds we visit like locusts
like holy scripture the fragile facade
of our psyche and its ricocheting runways
our appetite for remorse and belly-laughter and Kafka
our Knights of Infinite Resignation
our merciless opinions and monotonous disappointments
which fill our mouths with ash and feathers
our successes which beat us unconscious
demanding homage and impeccable manners
the white noise of self-loathing
and boomerang of self-pity
our kowtowing and bootlicking and toad-eating
the propitious future of our unforgiving past
our quoting Descartes without thinking
our pockets filled with blasphemy and fluster
our enemies who find us original and therefore hateful
our stuttering like Moses whom God entrusted
with so many important messages
the mistakes we mistook for privilege
the allegiance pledged to satisfaction
the delusion framed and hung over mantles
the illegitimate ideas abandoned on roadsides
our gargling garlic and hot ginger while drifting
down the Lethe of rainy Sundays
our eulogizing memories of tranquility
and hoarding apples of discord
our ontological orgies and losing
of couth in games of quoit our prophecies
scribbled on napkins in differential equations
our Nijinsky leaping off the tongue's springboard

our talmudic rapture and musical pajamas
our brass candlesticks gleaming like Statues of Liberty
our circular journey to singular moments
the organ crescendos of our lies and promises
our crawling dubitably along godless lifelines
our daily umbrage and masticating jaws and death row memoirs
our Euclidean fornication and obsessive sucking
our forgiving no one anything
our hands trembling like trophies of prophetic plunder
our hair breasts and genitals adorned with salutations
our rhythmic breathing and sphinxlike smiling
our being yanked headfirst out of kindness
our immigrant embarking our forty years
of wandering in the present moment
our fifty years of looking for it
our indomitable gardens
our craving constant illumination
the haloes of our eyes mouths nipples and anuses
the holy worm of our tongues singing praise
our faces shining like cities our being one among many
our climbing Jacob's ladder to rock in the arms of angels
our walking here and there on the earth and looking around

Maureen Seaton

The Zen of Crime

I advise her to shoplift something minor,
panties, perhaps, wad of silky skin in her hip pocket.

Or stroll away with coral earlobes, hands
full of jellies or pistachios in harmless white shells.

A side-by-side refrigerator, she says,
and I'll drag it off singing — so you better be there

to bail me out. I tell her my friend
stripped naked and climbed the bars of her cell

making chimp sounds to entertain the other women.
She tells me *her* friend ran from police

Most Recent Book: *Little Ice Age* (Invisible Cities Press, 2001)

into a quarry where she ditched her Mustang
and swam beneath the yellow water to Wisconsin.

Now we begin to admit things: I applied at a topless bar.
I spoke to a madam in Chicago. I stole sirloins

from Dominick's. Like Thelma and Louise. I
was Dillinger in a former life. *I* worked

on Wall Street. Seriously, I say,
what can you steal today to make yourself happy?

Raybans, she says, for the eyes of blind Justice.
All the tea in America.

Whining Prairie

I don't want to die in this wild onion smelly belly mire of the Midwest
        stinking marsh this
drenchy swaly swamp but I might and who would note the fragrant
        corruption of my poor

élan this moorish bog this poachy fen who come from sea with salt and
        myrrh to burn my
rotting flesh? I don't want to fail in grass that stabs my neck this turkey
        foot as tall as life

no roses for my ghostly face my face face-down in chicory and culver's
        root get these
nettles off of me that milkweed from my mouth your thistles catnip
        purple phlox your

funeral mint you've never seen a mermaid in your livelong buckwheat
        life? I'd rather not
allow it lie on land that's locked near fetid ponds this glacial run-off
        promised conch and

bass I'm innocent at pool side foreign standing stagnant pocket plash
        and laky sump you'll
find me in your placid blue I'll gnaw a hole my teeth as long as lurid
        lurking coasts.

Don't want to twist to Oz in funnel rage of shopping mall and trailer
        park your horizontal
lightning hailstone shelters dug beneath the earth your warnings and
        your watches trees

uptorn your vessels lost in scolding felon wind. I'd rather die in outer space unlucky
astrogirl balloonish letting go to float and float or cyberspace Big Brother nailed my

cursing on a message board in front of kids *there are no prisons bad enough* I'd sooner die
on Mars in bars or cars at camp of cramps in June beneath the King of Beers the Eagle on

the Jersey Pike beside the boy who pinched my tit and kissed me young as I was I'd rather
die where the ocean drowned me thirteen times then spit me back to life.

Miss Molly Rockin' in the House of Blue Light

Now you trade your wings for incarnation, commit a quick sin and leap into technicolor,
you're visible as sweat, your feet leave prints. Is the desert dead as they say?

The hummingbird sharpens her beak then disappears, unsolved caper, arrow of possibility.
There is no best time to move, I think, only that moment when you can, when the plate tilts

and the peas fall off, when the window opens and the wind sucks you through. Here's
the posture of free will, the wind pulling you with your feet firm on either side. I'm

gone in a day, sleeping bag, arrow pointing *Go*, that sly permissive. I set off in a white Mazda,
low to the ground with sleek lines screaming "Ticket me!" Eighty miles per hour, ninety.

In St. Louis, I switch to something indigo with the lines of a shadow and slip South and West.
Yukka, rabbits, bubonic plague. I need the same heat on me as in me, dry and crisp, to be

the only water for miles around. Bugs hover like disciples, bright revelation on exposed flesh.
The humans are pruney and caught in a grin. Everything looms at night as if listening to see

if I'll break, if my prayer will lift me to the tops of rocks then throw me
to the canyon floor
crying *Whoa*. Ghosts walk the canyon talking about nothing much. The
one who drew me

in a game of straws approaches my tent, leans on my bladder and
attaches electrodes to my
heart. Still, I pee on red earth, hear death stroll away, silent as ants on an
inchworm.

When the rain comes I dream of sex, the kind you wake up to, glowing.

Woman Circling Lake

Oh transcendent, this aqua blue and all these health nuts
running back and forth hold nothing — no sea gnome,
no salt to scour your bones clean — only placidity
and motionlessness, no dark fugues or phosphorescence.
It's your turn to stir the waters. Don't
back away from brittle plains and dry wheat saying
you're too far above us for encumbrances. This
is your place, your time: Chicago, gate of a millennium.
Your fainthearted sallies fall deep into space, closer
to no one who knows you. See, cloudling, how the collie pup
chases the gray squirrel up bare sleeping trees. How
old snow banks the blue-green line of Michigan.
The collie is so happy and powerful. The squirrel
steals from ash to oak as if possessed by abandon,
rising higher into sky than any jubilant unchained creature.
You are the end of winter, sea light. Little star eater,
come back, it's not your turn to die.

Lateral Time

I'd never held the ashes of a dead man but I'd always wanted to know a famous artist, so I reached out my left hand and she spilled him into my palm. He was flame-white, his flesh dust, he was tiny bones you could play with — they could be doll parts — peaceful in my hand like light. I kept my hand open in case he needed air and I knew it was not the essence of him but nevertheless I whispered: Don't worry, you're safe with me. I whispered: I love your paintings. This happened on the Upper West Side in '89 as the light changed over the Hudson, and that light was in the apartment sliding on floor and walls as we passed a dead man's bones between us, weeping.

Once I spent the winter in Manhattan with a woman whose desires were so unlike mine the air in the kitchen was sweetly skewed. She told me: *Pleasure*, and I bent at the refrigerator choosing the precise onion. I told her: *Juice*, and she stood at the stove removing lemon seeds from basmati. We were perfect as thumbs, we were starved and greedy as shorebirds, dipping down, grabbing our food, devouring it.

Now I've begun to write "NO!" on my body parts, small cross-stitched reminders to throw me back and hook another. Tattoo on my right breast, sticker on my colon, scribble of bright blue between my ovaries, hollowed now of eggs but still handy to balance me out. The day I decide to go I'll erase the words from my body then disintegrate quickly like any dying fool, you'll see me rising from the shore — equal time lateral time — don't hurry into anything but love.

The man who lives in 4D sleeps above me every night in the same rectangle of space, one floor up, beside the door, our double beds appearing to the gods like open face sandwiches with two chubby figures shifting and rolling in dreams or trooping to the bathroom. Sometimes I watch Tai Chi on cable at 6 A.M. because the man upstairs has jumped so hard from his bed, and sometimes I sleep right through til 9 or 10, his footfalls barely piercing dawn.

The Freezing Point of the Universe

I used to speak in anagrams during sex no wonder
you often left me for girls uninterested in the shift

between "Fawlty Towers" and *flowery twats*. Scold me.
Whenever I think in four-dimensional hypercubic

numerals (1, 16, 81, 256, and so on) you have the right
to demand a simple lunch (pot roast, corn) and tip

me on my head for equilibrium. You're off again I know it,
eyes glazed with dull numbers (although the set

of dull numbers is a null set, go figure). Randomness
steeps in the eye of the beholder; willfulness percolates.

Asked to choose a random number between 10 and 20
you confidently choose 17 like everyone else, a maximally

unremarkable number and here is the catch:
You wish I were one of the Nine Virtuous Women don't you,

the middle pretty sister of the Seven Sisters of Sorrow
and who can blame you. All this talk of radios and "10-codes."

In Shippensburg, Pennsylvania, a 10-45 means "automobile
collision." Elsewhere in the same commonwealth

it stands for "carcass of an unlucky beast." In Maine,
"domestic disturbance." 10-4, Good Buddy. The difference

between the number of pebbles in Newton's calculus
and this four-room house which exhausts the potential

for expansion in the dimensions of width and depth
seems a churlish substitute for the flinty accolades you've been

dealing me lately. And why shouldn't you. Absolute Zero
is where it all begins, the clean slate. Walk out now, you're freezing.

Betsy Sholl

Half the Music

What's that noise? my stepfather asks,
hearing all the way from Florida the falling racks
of cassette tapes the plumber knocks off the wall.
What's that racket? he repeats, quick relief
from his sad story of how many times
my mother has fallen this week, how little she eats.

It's just the new hot water heater
getting wrestled from kitchen to cellar,
and half the music of my life crashing
to the floor, cases split, lids snapped off,
skittering across the tile, sax, blues harp,
piano unraveled, tossed and turned —

like my stepfather last night, waking

Most Recent Book: *Don't Explain* (University of Wisconsin Press, 1997)

to phone-fright and a sweltering apartment,
air-conditioner shot. Fear soaked, he reached
for the receiver, expecting the night nurse,
but it was just some drunk dialing random,
from God knows where, *Hey, man, howya doing?* –

which almost could be God, if the words
weren't slurred, if the voice gave a shit
how scary it was, that shrill in the night
making an old man think whatever he's
tethered to just broke. He's got grief
clogged in his throat, talking these blues,

and others too – how his legs ache,
all shaky, betraying the brain's commands.
We're on the fritz, he says, meaning my frail
mother with her panic and tears, her broken
words like birds on a wire that scatter
and rebunch, one note hopping to the end

of the line, so the song's frayed, always
changing, and my mother weeps that she can't
keep it straight, weeps like someone with no tongue,
who can't say what she knows, though we strain
to grasp, like woodsmen chasing
some mythic birdsong into thick forests,

seduced by its tenuous trill, haunting
and almost clear, till we're lost in a craze
of branches, no path, no light overhead –
except my stepfather's ever ready
yellow pad, his new list: three end-of-life
scenarios he clears his throat and reads now,

though I try not to hear how the tree
I've lived in all my life could crash,
ripping out a big patch of ground; or, *two*,
could remain standing but turn stark
and barren from lightning's quick stroke; or, *three* –
but I have to say stop, it's too sad, sad,

this sparrow, her music spilled, the tissues
and cups on her bedside stand she fumbles for
and knocks on the floor, then falls trying to reach.
Nothing to do but wail out this sorrow.
Though now a crow does what crows do best:
harass, croak as people pass, as if checking

our names on a list: Today we live, today
we get to sing or sweep up what's fallen —
the little bird, sparrowlike, but with a bright
yellow belly, I picked up this morning
and held, its death in my hands, and my heart
flying full speed as if straight at plate glass.

Queen of the Night

for Ruth Welting

They're not gone yet, those notes my friend lifts
from deep inside, like a quarterback
she says, lofting up and out, not knowing
if they'll be caught or spin down off orbit
and slip from the receiver's hands. Last week
they soared across the opera's stadium

so everyone received the pass. *Brava! Brava!* —
five full minutes before they let her go.
Next day, she walked up to the gate, got bumped
flight after flight, as if from elation, she says —
as if it's a law: one day the Met, the next
you can't get out of bed. There's the time

she rose from the basement on a platform —
no rails, a stagehand stuffed her skirts —
but something snagged on the wobbly ascent
into smoke and lights, so just as her aria
climbed to its heights her skirts came undone.
Comic version, same rule: whatever rises, falls.

Sometimes, though, it seems to go another way:
that voice arriving uninvited to both her sister
and herself, lifting them out of such a lowdown
childhood, for years those bad times still bubbled
and steamed underneath any stage they were on,
like the opera's cave of death, its dry ice

and writhing souls backlit on a gauzy veil.
Once she blew that voice off in smoke rings and slurs,
didn't ask for it back, though it came, deepened
into parts she'd been too high for: the Queen's
daughter, who pleads to her lover's back —
pure *sehnsucht*, "longing beyond longing,"

the part her sister sang, whose own stupendous voice
was choked off in a husband's seething rage —
no one there to hear the last cries crushed
in her throat. *Sehnsucht*. Over tea, my friend
closes her eyes, and that aria wells up
again, then trails off to such thin decibels,

such quiet notes they could sift through loam
and stir the dead, if longing didn't dissolve
before it got to bone, if motion didn't
involve both rise and fall, sack and hail mary,
the Met's bright cheers, then next morning's lone soul
at the gate, ordinary voice seeking flight.

Late Psalm

I am hating myself for the last time.
I'm rolling up angst like a slice of bread,
squish it into a glob that will rot
  into blue medicine — another joke,
delivered by God, who when you finally
elbow and nudge to the front of the line,
says, *Oh, but the first shall be last*. . .
  I'm considering the roadside grass,
all dressed up and headed straight for the fire.
        "Who isn't?" say the flames,
though it's easy to pretend not to hear
in this mountain resort with its windows
all finely dressed for the busiest season,
filled with glass fish, turquoise earrings,
infusers that turn weeds into tea.
"Who isn't poor already?" sing the stalks
of dried milkweed, though it's hard to
imagine these shoppers in bright ski jackets
coated with road grit, dust from the chunks
of bituminous coal left outside mines
for the poor to glean. The poor —
   just driving by those bent figures,
filling their plastic bags, here in the 1990s,
took my breath, made me stop nodding
yeah yeah to the music and pull off the road,
stunned by the way the years press hard

to fossilize plants, and the poor too,
  who seem to age a month for every
middle-class day. How could they
possibly hear a blade of grass sigh, "Poor?
There is no such thing." Did I say
  I'm hating myself for the last time?
It's not easy, but I'm loving instead —
brown teeth, Kool-Aid mustaches, swollen
knuckles, nature's answer to all questions —
  prodigality, those countless insects
and missionary weeds spending themselves
  freely and as far as I can tell, never
rescinding a thing. I'm loving a man
with his pockets full of pen caps, receipts,
crumpled dollars to put in a beggar's
dented cup, briefcase bulging with papers,
leftover crusts for the ducks,
 and out of his eyes little fish of light,
glimmering minnows and fingerlings
      leaping between us, flashing
like the tiny carp we watched last night
in the restaurant tank, appearing through
weeds, miniature castles, a bubbly
  tube resuscitating their atmosphere.
Do they ever conceive of worlds outside
the only world they've known? Because *he* is,
my man says they're serene, swimming in
      a seamless rippling universe,
not quaking at the sight of monstrous eyes
    leering into the tank, not aching
with the lure of light, lethal burn of air,
declaring their world a glass prison house.
Rich or poor — who decides? Who wrote
  the stories in which women cry out
all the more when folks tell them to hush,
  and beggars asking for money, get
wild rapture instead?

Jane Shore

The Yawner

for Gail Mazur

No one ever talked to her, or knew her name –
the woman who came to poetry readings
every Monday night at The Blacksmith House
the twenty years I lived in Cambridge, Mass. –

but we called her "The Yawner" behind her back.
As far as I know, she never missed a reading.
She'd slip through the door while Gail was busy
putting out the donation basket and electric

coffee pot, checking the podium and the mic.
The Yawner took her usual seat – first row
aisle on the left side of the auditorium,
placing her raincoat on a folding chair

under her Filene's shopping bag and purse,
putting space between herself and the locals
who filed in, greeting noisily, extravagantly,
the famous, newly published, and the wannabes.

Bag-lady long before the crop of homeless
invaded Harvard Square, in winter
she'd come inside the building to get warm,
wearing her dowdy tan cardigan and London Fog

and brown chunky shoes and not-bad haircut.
In the spring, when it started warming up,
she'd still be dressed in the same outfit.
She could have been forty-five, or sixty,

someone's dotty aunt or cousin; crazy, but
not sick enough to cart off and lock away.
There were rumors that she lived in a fancy
duplex apartment on the Charles, rumors

she slept in the locked Ladies Room at night
in the Red Line Station under Harvard Square.
But, as Gail used to say, she wasn't harming
anyone; why she'd probably attended

Most Recent Book: *Happy Family* (Picador USA, 1999)

more readings at the Blacksmith than any
other person in the room, except for Gail.
At her usual eight-fifteen, Gail stepped up
to the podium and welcomed tonight's poet

who sat humbly in his chair, as once again
he heard that he'd graduated from Dartmouth,
heard the year he'd published his first prize-
winning volume, congratulating himself

as Gail unscrolled his honors, grants he'd won,
the famous story about his conversation with X.
The audience clapped politely, the poet mounted
the stage, blew Gail a kiss, then got down

to business. About halfway through his program,
as the poet was reading his most-requested poem,
his eyes awash with tears, his manly voice
about to rise and break on the pungent iambs

of his father's dying words — as if on cue,
but purely randomly, you understand,
the Yawner took a big deep breath
and yawned out loud a half-yawn half-groan,

then vented three very long very audible sighs
loud enough to be heard in the last row
thirty rows back — a sound not to be mistaken
for a gasp of someone moved profoundly, no,

not to be confused with anything but a yawn
and all that a yawn like that implied.
No stranger to interruptions — rude whispers,
sneezes, coughing fits, the emergency trip

to the john, or people just plain walking out —
the poet pretended he didn't hear what he'd
so clearly heard, and we, in turn, pretended
to ignore it, too, because we knew she yawned

only one yawn per reading. The poet blinked,
picking up where he'd left off, but you could see
it took him down a peg or two, it *irked* him,
that someone had *yawned* at him, *in public*.

Chastened, he resumed reading his poems, but
never quite recovering his former equilibrium.
Week after week, we regulars knew what to expect,
but I remember a few occasions when I glanced

at Gail, in her front row seat, at the moment
she suddenly remembered that she'd forgotten
to warn that evening's poet about the yawn,
and as he'd already started reading,

Gail couldn't stop him once he'd started,
(like stifling a yawn), so she had to sit there
panicking, counting the minutes until the yawn,
hoping it would happen quick and soon.

The Yawner yawned at Joseph Brodsky.
She yawned at Phil Levine.
She yawned at Robert Lowell and Derek Walcott.
She yawned at Seamus Heaney, Ai, Tom Clark,

she yawned at fledglings, she yawned at pros,
she yawned when the sobbing Lady-poet read
her entire book of sonnets in one sitting,
she yawned at East and West Coast poets,

at nature poets, urban poets, traditional, surreal,
she yawned and yawned at L=A=N=G=U=A=G=E Poets,
she yawned at poets in sequined jeans clutching
the microphone like rock stars, she yawned

at their marital tragedies, a big ho hum,
she yawned at their funny Southern accents,
silly Boston accents, their Eastern-European-
tinged-English though they'd grown up in Philly,

she yawned while they couldn't stop themselves
from reading, when only the poet's wife and Gail
and the Yawner and I were left sitting
in the empty room after two-and-a-quarter hours,

she yawned at their haikus, tankas, sestinas,
their clumsy terza rimas, she yawned at their
breasts, their buttocks, their prostate glands,
she yawned while they tossed their wild hair,

she yawned while their throats got dry and raspy
and they stopped reading and slowly poured
a glass of ice water from the sweating pitcher
without spilling a drop and gulped it down,

she yawned at all the American poetry written
in the nineteen-seventies and -eighties,

and at all poetry written in translation, too,
she yawned her yawn, oblivious to the shock waves

spreading concentric rings around the epicenter
of her yawn, her epic yawn, her fabulous yawn,
and she'll yawn until the last word of the last poem
is written, and applause breaks out and wakes us all.

I Dream About My Dead

> *The soul remains attached to the physical body after death for the first seven days, when it flits from its home to the cemetery and back. For twelve months after death the soul ascends and descends, until the body disintegrates and the soul is freed.* — Jewish Encyclopedia

I

My husband steps on the gas.
Flipping down the sun visor, I check the mirror
for the baby, slumped and dozing in her car seat
buckled to safest place in our station wagon,
when by chance I glimpse my father behind me,
sitting where he always sits, crammed between
her car seat and the window glass
on which autumnal Vermont reels by.

My husband hasn't yet noticed my father
who seems happy just gazing at the scenery.
I feel vaguely uncomfortable, peculiar —
as if I'm about to sneeze — the dusty car
like the inside of a snow globe, huge tufts
of pollen drifting though the liquid air.

This must be a dream. Otherwise,
I'd be feeling something more than mild surprise.
My father's got that same
apologetic look he had the last time I saw him
nursing the cold he couldn't shake,
spoon poised over the bowl of chicken soup
I'd cooked and made him eat,
just as my mother would have done.

Bundled up in his musty winter coat,
seatbelt strapped across his chest and lap,

what could possibly hurt him now?
Will he be sad if we don't recognize him?
Like Ulysses' dog, I'm sniffing the scent,
but I won't tip anybody off.

He's trusting us to take him somewhere, anywhere,
just being in our company again is enough.
If we keep driving, if I don't
turn around, look at him, or talk to him —
he'll stay with us.
But if I blink, he'll disappear.

2

Wearing her old blue nylon nightgown,
and not the muslin shroud we buried her in,
my mother stands puzzled before my closet.
Is she trying to decide what to wear,
or wondering what *her* clothes are doing there?
Clothes I haven't the heart to give to charity
even nine years after her death.

For once, my mother doesn't talk.
She bears no message from Jewish Heaven,
where the dead have nothing to do all day
but sit around and advise the living.
My whole life, my mother gave plenty:
never wear white in winter or velvet in summer,
buy life insurance, file a will.

Why is she here? Does she want me
to throw together an outfit for her —
something that never happened in real life, ever.
Maybe when you die, the first thing to go
is your fashion sense, because in Paradise
everyone's dressed the same.

She's counting on me. This is a first.
Naturally, I used to dress my daughter,
choosing from among the miniature T-shirts
and turtleneck sweaters,
pushing the huge head through the stretched
collar like a dilated cervix,
forcing the flailing arms into sleeves.

I remember, in our dress store,
my mother would stand before the racks,
and, running her eyes over the merchandise,

she'd know exactly which dress
her favorite customers should try on
if they had a fund-raiser, a christening, a cocktail party...
and had to look especially nice.

Where could she be going? To a wedding? A funeral?
Now that she's lost all that weight,
her old clothes will hang off her.
She might as well be naked.
Her eyes implore me to help her, please
help her find something to wear.
But her soul wants the final undressing.
Her soul wants to be freed, at last, from clothes.

Tom Sleigh

Newsreel

It was like being in the crosshairs of a magnifying glass
Or in the beams of the planets concentrating in a death ray
Passing right through me, boring a hole between

My shoes through the concrete floor all the way
To the far side of the earth. Yet it was only not knowing
Where I was and how to get where I was going,

I'd gotten lost in the parking lot on the way
To the cinder block bunker where my mother
Worked the snack bar, my father the projector.

The drive-in movie screen stretched horizon
To horizon, the whole of Texas sprawled around,
The cathedral-like De Sotos and great-finned Pontiacs

Flickering and sinister in torrents of light flooding
From the screen. Frozen in that light, I
Might have been the ancient disconsolate

Ageless stone-eyed child ornamenting a pillar
In a dead Roman city high up on a desert plateau.
I wasn't even as tall as the speakers mumbling

Most Recent Book: *The Dreamhouse* (University of Chicago, 1999)

On and on the way now in my dream of extreme
Old age I hear voices mumbling interminably...
Where was it, my refuge, grotto of my swimming pool

Lapping in the infinite leisure of the newsreel?
At last my mother appeared from among the cars
And led me back to the snack bar but I was still

Out there, turned loose among the shadows'
Disembodied passions striving for mastery
Above the tensed windshields. There was

Marilyn Monroe movie star enjoying her fame
In the voluptuous, eternal, present tense
Of celebrity being worked over by hands

Of her masseur. Bougainvillaea was overgrowing
Her beach bungalow retreat of peace and pleasure,
The screen nothing now but layer on layer

Of flesh the fingers kneaded in a delirious ballet
Pushing, pulling, palms slippery and quick,
Ambiguous instruments of comfort or of pain.

The rush of blood to her face began to cloud
Into white light as the film stock jerked across
A void half coma blackout, half nightmare aura:

The film jammed, raw light pulsing like a bandage
On a face wrapped round and round in surgical gauze.
Wherever I was, I wasn't there among the candy bars

And gum wrappers blazing under glass. The movie poster
Death ray stopped the earth revolving, time had stopped,
My mother's black slacks and my father's not yet grown goatee,

My own hands shaking nervously about were silently dissolving
In that ray bombarding from beyond the galaxy
Being invaded by the screeching, beseeching noises

Of alien beings searching for a planetary home.
Then up there on the screen, frenetic in the light
Was a hair trembling between two cloven lobes

Of shadow that were part of the projector's
Overheating brain, its brilliantly babbling, delusional,
Possessed by shadows, dispossessed brain.

The Grid

Faces swell, then flatten into the million-celled grid
of windows replicating day and night
until no part of the sky remains unlit.

Words spoken between chasms of the avenues
are sucked up into stillness after rain:
Is my strength the strength of stones? Is my flesh of brass?

Lying on the sidewalk, tendons bulging in his wrists,
he stares straight into the armada of rush hour shoes,
his head lolling backward at a hard right angle to his neck

as the police hoist him by his armpits and sockless ankles.
Under the purple blackness of his face
a jaundiced pallor shadows the whites, unblinking, of his eyes.

The waters wear the stones. My face is foul with weeping
and on my eyelids is the shadow of death.
Sunlight steams up from humid pavement,

the subway air shafts warmly breathe,
the parapets of the bridge towers gleam
through mist swirling off the water's satin-sheen.

Smoking, joking, he used to recline on one elbow
in front of the storefront's steel-grated doors,
his boutique laid out on the sidewalk: A child's overalls,

soggy magazines, jewelry nicked and scratched. . .
Downriver, huddled on thin ledges of granite
the fledging sparrows reach toward their mothers' beaks,

the traffic blare funnelling up past the office windows
to expand and mingle with the brine-tinged air,
the tugboats lifting and falling in the swell

that rolls beneath the heaving pier. Now another vendor
spreads out his wares in the same square of sidewalk his hands
gently laying out each cast-off garment.

The other's goods still lie on the cement-damp
canvas laundry sack that each day he carefully unpacked.
By midnight his sack will be scavenged clean,

the aura of his hands on the canvas
already fading beneath the warmth of another's palms,
his square of the city washing back into the grid

that arranges and rearranges into the lights and darks
of numbered faces pressed into the coroner's files. . .
Hast thou entered into the springs of the sea?

Have the gates of death been opened unto thee?
When I looked for good, then evil came unto me.
The river's mouth widens, pouring out past

the harbor to open ocean, black swells
running off the freighters' hulls. Drifting in the mist
looms the island where they hung the mutineer,

upriver lies the entrance to the tunnel
that runs beneath the waters,
those cuttings mark the tracks that radiate outward

toward the cities spread out across the plain,
and there under the mountain through lightless caverns
the sun at night makes its smouldering way.

William Loran Smith

Speaking Louder

Not that I blame in you in the least, boy,
but I can hardly get you on the phone anymore.
I know you're thinking that gang of little reapers
you hang with, hoods up, Celtic-tattooed arms
drawn inside your sleeves, the whole bearing-
against-bearing whir of skateboards is a spike
in the heart of this cold unmovable world.
And yeah, when you guys fly past we flinch.
We shake our disgusted heads and remember
what we wanted from our romance with youth.
Like my father raising his silver whiskey flask
the night Dorsey's clarinet called them off to war.
The Chinese lanterns above Air Devil's beer garden
swaying to the first sip he nailed in his coffin.
And me, well you know I have a problem with hope.
But that's not why I called, not at all, son.
What I really want to say is how much I miss you.

Most Recent Book: *Night Train* (Plinth Books, 1997)

That I have loved you since the first night
your mother's bitch cat wailed in the bushes
as the midwife chanted to the buttery moon
and pulled your wailing self into the candlelight.
And for weeks I slurred your name in all
the neighborhood bars while my two o'clock girlfriends
sulked in their booths, dangerously close to sober.

I loved you, boy, through all those bright Sundays
you had to wait by the garret window as the happy
families drove home from church. But above all,
I hope you remember the night we went camping
along the bank of Otter Creek, how those pine needles
felt like velvet under our sleeping bags. How the moon
broke through the fast clouds and the Coleman lantern
hung out shadows up into the very tops of the trees.
That's the whole deal, I think, one or two moments like that.
The whole ball wax, like your grandpa used to say.
his delicate scarred hands arched around an idea.
Our lonely little planet spinning out of control,
you leaning into me, smelling like cedar and Dinty Moore.
Falling fast asleep in my arms while I tried vainly
to name all the constellations, like my whole life.
All the easy ones first, the Big Dipper, and the little one.
and the faint moving light of two or three satellites.

Hairspray

It had to be about the hottest day of this bad year,
when Shanda Lee killed her little babies.
You could see it all at six o'clock, the cutter steaming
out in slow motion, the grappling hooks splashing
in the muddy water, and Shanda, she's sitting on the bank,
telling the reporters about her so-called life.
Said she wiped their asses to stop the screaming,
wrapped the stink and ooze in a plastic bag,
Just like Momma had always taught her.

And though she's wet, her big fast food belly clinging
to her shirt, and though she keeps pressing
this plastic, purple-maned pony to her breast,
like it's every girl's best and loving friend,
what we really want to see is some regret,
why she made them hold each other's hands,

pictures from her wallet, a hazel twinkle in their eyes,
some clover hair blowing in the wind. But we don't.
We just see this worn-out girl, a yellow shadow underneath
her eyes where Jimmy came to visit last Sunday,
and got so drunk, he thought her cow-eyed face
was the world he couldn't even begin to beat,
thought her throat was another dead-end job.

They hook one baby now, and next week the jokes
will fly around the fax machine, "What's red and blue,
and pops like a big balloon?" And then by the next week
we'll forget the whole thing, a mental inquest and the usual delays.
"Not that bitch again, they play it for all its worth,"
until some other Shanda Lee, or Amber Sue,
holes up in a cheap hotel, and while the kids eat Cheerios
off the floor, she'll call every street punk she knows.
Like they're gonna give her a piece of the rock,
like blow jobs are hard to come by in this day and time.

And all those dreamy little babies with their tight curls,
they never learn you can't cry for wanting here.
So suck on your thumb? or beat your sister,
twist the arms off that robot hero, cause nobody's watching.
Blame on the hairspray, and for God's sake learn how
to unlatch the seat restraint. It's press in and pull out.
In and out. I hope you get it, 'cause it's getting old, these
dreamy little bloated children, and all their petty woes.
And Shanda Lee is rocking ever so slightly now.
They found them both, and the sun is going down,
and the waves are lapping gently over the dog food cans.

The Family Man

There are men so crazy from not having something,
that they build temples to it, and walk under the groins
and spires, chanting to the emptiness of it, and when night
unrolls its mattress for their pallet, they put a picture
of it on the table, and lie down pretending it has come
to keep them warm into its green sparkling dress,
with the mink head on the shoulder curling back its vicious lip.

There are men so crazy from not having something,
that they dress their daughters in blue skirts and white tights,

and take them to the circus where the children squeal
at the clowns bumping and tumbling in their eyes.
So crazy, they promise their daughter white plumed horses,
and cotton candy, and pinwheels of happiness forever.
And then these crazy men go home, and while the house
is four ticks of their antique clocks, and two winter breaths,
they close the garage door, lie down on the front seats
of their Chevys and let the engine sing its sweet song.

There are men so crazy from not having something,
they drive to a bar in Albuquerque, and laugh
at the lewd cartoon napkins of big chested women
leaning over just so, and they sit there for years
until she sidles up and claiming to have it, bends
her legs back, and lets him taste the juicy red eye of it.
There are men so crazy that George Jones is their hero,
and while, "He stopped loving her today" plays on the radio.
they wash down the pills from the silver, turquoise locket,
and see god's blue face, blank and pure above the buttes.

There are men so crazy from not having something,
they marry prom queens at the Love Forever chapel,
and then for twenty years slap their silly faces for looking
at them while they eat, and the kids listen through
the ears of the honey yellow walls to their father's voice
making their mother a tiny, dried up flower, all light
and shed of skin when she comes to kiss them in the dark.

There are men so crazy from not having something,
that they become women and stick their fingers into
the wet, dark, cave of themselves to feel the ribs
of where they were pulled out by the stainless steel tongs,
and wrapped in cotton receiving blankets, and taught
by the nurse to take the rubber nipple without choking.
So crazy like this, that they smell the kinky black hair
under a woman's arms, and become insane with a memory
like a hand thrusting up and up again through the icy water.

There are men so crazy from not having something,
that in one day, nothing and everything is it.
The wafer of moon burning in their foreheads is it,
and the Uncle Sam in his red and white rags waving
a novelty flag at all the cars on fourth street,
and wives who give it away they have so much of it,
even the slobbering smile of their black dogs are it.

There are men so crazy from not having something,
that their bones are it, and the muscles of their hearts,
and the eyes, and the night, all of the night and the path.
The light and Christ are it. The cells flying off their fat
bodies are it. The gallery of suits are it, the needle's last rites,
the governor playing golf and the phone not ringing are it.
The crow engulfing its own huge shadow,
the grass, the insects, the wars, the missile biting
into the children's ward. Everything is crazy with it.
Wanting it, dreaming it, sucking it, needing it,
until all the tunnels and the ends of the earth are it.

Gary Soto

Raisin Factory

The sound of nightfall was the chain
Looping around a pole and the click of a giant lock.
The security guard held up a girlie magazine
And slapped it against his knee,
His punishment for kicking his teacher in the head,
Thirty years before. Expelled, he drifted.
Now, duncelike, he sat on a stool,
A twenty-watt bulb shining on his face.
He was watching the raisin factory. Steam rose
From vents, and a single machine churned the raisins
For the night shift. A forklift groaned,
A wrench for two men clanged against the cement.
His yawns could have raised a blimp.
O, Jesus, this man thought. If only a mule
Could appear and kick him in the head, hard for twenty years,
But now soft from inhaling the stink of washed raisins.
He looked at his magazine,
And the breasts were the color of raisins,
The eyes and hair, and down below
Raisins, too. A car passed and his eyes followed it,
The driver with the head of a raisin,

Most Recent Book: *Baseball in April and Other Stories* (Harcourt Brace, 2000)

With little raisin children in the back.
One on his knees.

The security guard shaded his eyes
From the light in his booth. But he couldn't keep
His hand up like that. The shame of it,
He saluting the first trucks
As they left the dock, loaded with raisins,
Lucky little bastards going somewhere sweet.

Devising Your Own Time

I can set the clock five minutes ahead,
Just enough to give me a head start,
A fair chance on my legs that are water and bone.
I could set the clock back, too,
Say seven minutes to nine — I miss a flight
And the plane goes down among black Angus cows.
In my house, none of the clocks is right,
Each with its own metallic breathing,
Its own oily click of sprockets and spools,
Springs with the leap of a feisty frog.
I keep six watches in our *tansu*,
Occasionally holding them like lizards,
All with their spiderlike hands up in surrender.

I tell my wife, I'll cook for you,
And shake my sleeve to examine my Timex.
I throw a pumpkin into a pot,
A pumpkin that I measured with a smile,
Three teeth, a wedge-shaped nose.
I boil this fatboy fruit and lose track,
My mind collapsing like a pumpkin in boiling water.
I pace the house, another measure of time,
My steps like a sick man in a robe.
I watch shade move across the lawn
And a single leaf swing from the poor-postured elm.
These, too, are time, and my cat's meowing at the door
To tell you the truth, I'm losing confidence.
In my heart, I know it's ten to ten,
That I'm somewhere in my 40s,
That the calendar has gutted most of January,

That my watch is panting on my wrist.
Maybe I'll make my flight
And over Iowa grip my armrest, tears
Pulled from my eyes by the gravity of falling.
In the field, a cow chews its chud,
Indifferent to the idleness of the dead.

Teaching English from an Old Composition Book

My chalk is no longer than a chip of fingernail,
Chip by which I must explain this Monday
Night the verbs "to get," "to wear, "to cut."
I'm not given much, these tired students,
Knuckle-wrapped from work as roofers,
Sour from scrubbing toilets and pedestal sinks.
I'm given this room with five windows,
A coffee machine, a piano with busted strings,
The music of how we feel as the sun falls,
Exhausted from keeping up.

I stand at
The blackboard. The chalk is worn to a hangnail,
Nearly gone, the dust of some educational bone.
By and by I'm Cantiflas, the comic
Busybody in front. I say, "I get the coffee."
I pick up a coffee cup and sip.
I click my heels and say, "I wear my shoes."
I bring an invisible fork to my mouth
And say, "I eat the chicken."
Suddenly the class is alive —
Each one putting on hats and shoes,
Drinking sodas and beers, cutting flowers
And steaks — a pantomine of sumptuous living.

At break I pass out cookies.
Augustine, the Guatemalan, asks in Spanish,
"Teacher, what is 'tally-ho'?"
I look at the word in the composition book.
I raise my face to the bare bulb for a blind answer.
I stutter, then say, "*Es como adelante*."
Augustine smiles, then nudges a friend
In the next desk, now smarter by one word.

After the cookies are eaten,
We move ahead to prepositions —
"Under," "over," and "between,"
Useful words when *la migra* opens the doors
Of their idling vans.
At ten to nine, I'm tired of acting,
And they're tired of their roles.
When class ends, I clap my hands of chalk dust,
And two students applaud, thinking it's a new verb.
I tell them *adelante*,
And they pick up their old books.
They smile and, in return, cry, "Tally-ho."
As they head for the door.

Late Confession

Monsignor, I believed Jesus followed me
With his eyes, and when I slept,
An angel peeled an orange
And waited for me to wake up.
This was 1962. I was ten, small as the flame
Of a struck match, my lungs fiery
From hard, wintery play. When I returned home,
Legs hurting, I placed my hands on the windowsill
And looked out — clouds dirty as towels
And geese I have yet to see again
Darkening the western sky.

Monsignor, a machine
Had painted on the eyes of my toy soldier,
Little dots off center,
Almost on his cheeks. Such a cheap toy,
I drowned him over and over in my bath,
Drowned him until the painted-on eyes flaked off.
Then a leg fell off — surge of dirty water
Sunk him to the bottom.

Now, in my late 40s, I place hands on the windowsill
My eyes nearly on my cheeks,
My belly with its rising tide.
There is no angel with an orange at the edge
Of my bed. There is no soldier

Of God. Only a pane between the inside
And the outside, between this living
And this dying. Monsignor,
Saintly man of this child's wonderment,
When will I see the geese again?

Maura Stanton

Practicing T'ai Chi Ch'uan

From where I waver in the tall mirror
shaping my arms and legs into the postures
of the photographs, I see I've got them wrong.
I'll never learn *Deflect, Parry and Punch,*
Strike With Palm and Descend, or *Kick With Right Heel.*
But then I come across *White Crane Spreads Wings*
and imagine gliding high above my town,
headed south out over the reservoir
casting a shadow. Suddenly I see
how other movements may be hidden inside
my body like paper ready to be unfolded.
Grasp the Bird's Tail. Wave Hands Like Clouds.
I sweep my arms first this way, and then that,
watching a sleek crow dive past my window
as I shift left and right. Here's *Work at Shuttles.*
That's how I shop the grocery store each week,
gliding dreamily behind my wire cart,
my fingers mechanically gathering stuff
though what they long to do is *Strum the Lute*
and fill the bright aisles with heavenly music.
The White Snake Flicks Out Tongue. I know
that quick hello from living in this town
for years, but where inside me is the skill
to *Part the Wild Horse's Mane?* I lift
my arms above my head, trying to remember
backwards through centuries to a seacoast,
where a shadowy person with my DNA
saw the first hoofprints across the wet sand.

Most Recent Book: *Life Among the Trolls* (David R. Godine, 1988)

But it must have been æons ago when something
slimy and quick, that evolved to be me,
learned to *Insert Needle to Sea Bottom*.
I close my eyes, trying to conjure the warm
watery planet, sizzling with lightning bolts,
where I darted and turned my somersaults
and then, diving through transparent depths,
inserted myself through the waving seaweed
and came back up, my eye filled with joy.

Posthuman

. . . the trope of the posthuman is usually associated with changing representations of embodiment and especially the idea that we are entering a "post-body age."

I used to peer inside
your windows while you slept,
and give you jolts of dreams.
Sometimes you glimpsed my eye
pressed against the pane
just as you woke, and screamed,
horrified by my lashes
blinking over the sun,
so I had to turn invisible.
But I kept my files on you,
recording your baby prattle,
and your first tottering steps,
proud of what I'd made,
amazed by how the linear
brain I'd invented
kept surprising me. You sang
as you fashioned slingshots,
amphoras, grand pianos,
even tiny telescopes. You began
counting the stars I'd sprinkled
across your night sky,
experiencing emotions
under the trees in fall,
naming the colors of the leaves
visionary shades of red —
crimson, plum, claret. . .
I admired you, hoping

that in a few more centuries
you'd learn to resemble
what I most desired,
a reflection of myself
conjured out of the slime
of my immense matter,
unlike my angels, failures
shaped from my thoughts,
who waste heavenly time
crowding together,
dancing on the heads of pins.

Why did I start to think
you were eternal like me?
I got excited, daydreaming,
of all you'd achieve
when you perfected yourselves.
But you've begun to wear out.
Tear ducts plugged, hearts
exercised on a treadmill,
some of you insist
your familiar human faces
are only romantic delusions,
that you're just fleshy
versions of your own Stiquito,
the android mosquito,
you invented by yourselves
to fetch ping pong balls
all day in a laboratory,
triggered by radio waves
it obeys but cannot feel.
Here in my void, far above
the universe I made
by rubbing together some stars
off my enormous robe
until they exploded in a bang,
I'm frowning and pacing,
deciding what I should do.
Shall I wipe you all out
or just leave you alone?
It's hard to think up here,
surrounded by noisy angels
standing inside one another,
debating the size of nothing.

Outside St.-Remy-de-Provence

Where are the grand olives with gnarled bark
That Van Gogh painted a hundred years ago?
These little trees rustle as if in talk,
Newly planted along the ancient rows.
Beyond, I see the clinique of St. Paul
Where Van Gogh wrestled madness into art
And broke this landscape into molecules
That make us dizzy. He took it all apart.

Today it's only pretty, tame and small.
In the garden I look for his portrait bust
Sculpted after his death, but nothing's there.
A sign says vandals have destroyed it. Appalled
I gaze at the pedestal covered with dust –
And nothing stares at me with his mad stare.

Searches

Once again TV detectives are searching the suspects' rooms in some old rambling house in England. The Chief Inspector opens the bureau drawers in tiers, pulling out striped ties and folded white shirts; he sniffs every cut-glass bottle; he ruffles through papers on the desk, unclasps a small leather book and turns unerringly to the suspicious entry. In another room his tweed-coated assistant pushes back filmy dresses, and holds up a black high heel checking for traces of a red garden clay. "Why is there a dead wasp on the nightstand," he wonders aloud, while his superior calls him across the hall. "Why has someone thrown a glass of brandy into the fireplace?" Red herrings, these questions will never be answered, but the two men exchange knowing looks as the musical score, something in imitation of Elgar, swells in excitement. Downstairs in a library of mullioned windows and walls of gilt-stamped books, the impatient suspects drink sherry and smoke cigarettes, their faces twitching, their eyes shifty or worried or insouciant. Later, alone here in my own room, I wonder if I have any secrets from myself, and I open my top drawer briskly to see who this person is who calls herself by my name. What's this? All these curious hair ornaments, barrettes, tortoiseshell combs, silvery elastic bands. Here's a snood; here are chiffon ribbons and satin ribbons; a box full of black bobby pins with blunt plastic tips and another containing thin sharp spidery hairpins; here's an ancient torn hairnet for blonds; here's an unopened package containing a nylon flexible comb tossed on top of jeweled pony-tail holders, a lime-plastic device for creating a French roll, a spongy nylon doughnut for a bun, and more barrettes, some cloisonne, others burnished metal. Oh how unerringly a detective's hands sort through this distracting clutter! The camera zooms in on a small box of "Bronchial-Pastillen" from the Hertenstein Drogerie in Luzern, Switzerland. Throat lozenges or cyanide tablets? I'm as surprised as the audience when I pry open the tin lid to discover a catch of fifty yellowed slips saved from the centers of crisp fortune cookies devoured years ago in forgotten Chinese restaurants. What can it mean? The camera moves in on my expression. Another red herring? Or the real clue to her existence?

David St. John

Merlin

Italo Calvino (1923–1985)

It was like a cave of snow, no...
More like that temple of frosted, milk-veined marble
I came upon one evening in Selinunte,
Athena's white owl flying suddenly out of its open eaves.
I saw the walls lined with slender black-spined
Texts, rolled codices, heavy leather-bound volumes
Of the mysteries. Ancient masks of beaten copper and tin,
All ornamented with rare feathers, scattered jewels.
His table was filled with meditative beakers, bubbling
Here and there like clocks; the soldierly
Rows of slim vials were labeled in several foreign hands.
Stacks of parchments, cosmological recipes, nature's
Wild equivalencies. A globe's golden armature of the earth,
Its movable bones ringing a core of empty
Space. High above the chair, a hanging Oriental scroll,
Like the origami of a crane unfolded, the Universe inked
So blue it seemed almost ebony in daylight,
The stars and their courses plotted along its shallow folds
In a luminous silver paint. On an ivory pole,
His chameleon robe, draped casually, hieroglyphics
Passing over it as across a movie screen, odd formulas
Projected endlessly — its elaborate layers of

Most Recent Book: *The Red Leaves of Night* (Harper Flamingo, 1999)

Embroidery depicting impossible mathematical equations;
Stitched along the hem, the lyrics
Of every song one hears the nightingale sing, as dusk falls
On summer evenings. All of our stories so much
Of the world they must be spoken by
A voice that rests beyond it . . . his voice, its ideal melody,
Its fragile elegance guiding our paper boats,
Our so slowly burning wings,
Towards any immanent imagination, our horizon's carved sunset,
The last wisdoms of Avalon.

Los Angeles, 1954

It was in the old days,
When she used to hang out at a place
Called *Club Zombie*,
A black cabaret that the police liked
To raid now and then. As she
Stepped through the door, the light
Would hit her platinum hair,
And believe me, heads would turn. Maestro
Loved it; he'd have her by
The arm as he led us through the packed crowd
To a private corner
Where her secluded oak table always waited.
She'd say, *Jordan . . .*
And I'd order her usual,
A champagne cocktail with a tall shot of bourbon
On the side. She'd let her eyes
Trail the length of the sleek neck
Of the old stand-up bass, as
The bass player knocked out the bottom line,
His forehead glowing, glossy
With sweat in the blue lights;
Her own face, smooth and shining, as
The liquor slowly blanketed the pills
She'd slipped beneath her tongue.
Maestro'd kick the shit out of anybody
Who tried to sneak up for an autograph;
He'd say, *Jordan, just let me know if*
Somebody gets too close . . .

Then he'd turn to her and whisper, *Here's*
Where you get to be Miss Nobody . . .
And she'd smile as she let him
Kiss her hand. For a while, there was a singer
At the club, a guy named Louis —
But Maestro'd changed his name to "Michael Champion";
Well, when this guy leaned forward,
Cradling the microphone in his huge hands,
All the legs went weak
Underneath the ladies.
He'd look over at her, letting his eyelids
Droop real low, singing, *Oh Baby I . . .*
Oh Baby I Love . . . I Love You . . .
And she'd be gone, those little mermaid tears
Running down her cheeks. Maestro
Was always cool. He'd let them use his room upstairs,
Sometimes, because they couldn't go out —
Black and white couldn't mix like that then.
I mean, think about it —
This kid star and a cool beauty who made King Cole
Sound raw? No, they had to keep it
To the club; though sometimes,
Near the end, he'd come out to her place
At the beach, always taking the iced whiskey
I brought to him with a sly, sweet smile.
Once, sweeping his arm out in a slow
Half-circle, the way at the club he'd
Show the audience how far his endless love
Had grown, he marked
The circumference of the glare whitening the patio
Where her friends all sat, sunglasses
Masking their eyes . . .
And he said to me, *Jordan, why do*
White people love the sun so? —
God's spotlight, my man?
Leaning back, he looked over to where she
Stood at one end of the patio, watching
The breakers flatten along the beach below,
Her body reflected and mirrored
Perfectly in the bedroom's sliding black glass
Door. He stared at her
Reflection for a while, then looked up at me
And said, *Jordan, I think that I must be*
Like a pool of water in a cave that sometimes
She steps into . . .

Later, as I drove him back into the city,
He hummed a Bessie Smith tune he'd sing
For her, but he didn't say a word until
We stopped at last back at the club. He stepped
Slowly out of the back
Of the Cadillac, and reaching to shake my hand
Through the open driver's window, said,
My man, Jordan . . . Goodbye.

I Know

The definition of beauty is easy;
it is what leads to desperation.
— Valéry

I know the moon is troubling;

Its pale eloquence is always such a meddling,
Intrusive lie. I know the pearl sheen of the sheets
Remains the screen I'll draw back against the night;

I know all of those silences invented for me approximate
Those real silences I cannot lose to daylight. . .
I know the orchid smell of your skin

The way I know the blackened path to the marina,
When gathering clouds obscure the summer moon —
Just as I know the chambered heart where I begin.

I know too the lacquered jewel box, its obsidian patina;
The sexual trumpeting of the diving, sweeping loons. . .
I know the slow combinations of the night, & the glow

Of fireflies, deepening the shadows of all I do not know.

KEVIN STEIN

Beanstalk

How mundane those things that change us,
the line from crashed finch to sliced finger

Most Recent Book: *Chance Ransom* (University of Illinois Press, 2000)

to my daughter's loathing for homemade bread —
twelve tinny notes linking one story to another
as on "All Things Considered," where D.C.
cherry blossoms segue to Kabul's bone trade,
family plots unearthed because Pakistanis
will pay to grind the bones for cooking oil,
soap, chicken feed: the dead unplanted
to feed the starving and their starving poultry.
What's a body worth? Chickenfeed.
Yet, meaning *yes, but*, ask the dozen finches
who risk dusk for one last seed among
the husks brusquely tossed aside. Husk — a word
for those finch bodies as well as ours, though

what prize each enwraps is only speculation.
Chickenfeed? Being, Heidegger says, resides
in being-in-the-world not out of it. Yet.
How are we to know till we've left it,
smashed headlong into the glass we saw too late,
happy to be meeting the sister Other
eye to eye? Oh sure. I don't buy that.
Ask the crashed finch, flushed by the neighbor's
flabby tabby — tuft of feather on windowpane,
wing dust as serrated as our bread knife.
Worth what, a couple good rhymes.
Ask Jack in the Beanstalk, whose English bones
a giant threatened to grind for bread.
Ask Man Ray, fresh from Nazi Paris,
hitching NY to LA with a tie salesman

who pitched cheap wares at truck stop
and tourist trap. Paisley and polka dots,
collegiate hues, a blood red bold enough
to enliven even the stiffest pin stripe.
Capitalism's knot, the noose about our neck,
two for ten dollars. What can't be sold?
Safe in LA, Ray exchanged every tie he owned
for the shoe string he looped beneath his collar.
A price for everything, I'm thinking, as my daughter
slices her loaf of silence: "So hungry, they dig up
their dead?" At ten, she's learned the names
of bone, muscle, organ, and the other names
for those other parts, too, in classroom
and all-night slumber party confession.
What's a body worth? *Fe, fi, fo, fum.*

Showering, she runs the well dry, pondering
the angle of water on belly and thigh.
The pump coughs air and still she stares,
unrecognizable, in the frantic antiseptic
bathroom light, mirror so fogged one body
meets the other along a path toward the river
she knows is there but can't see. Yet,
meaning *still to come*. The answer?
It turns out 98 cents, that old joke,
if hauled across the mountains to Pakistan.
Just 50 cents, 7,000 Afghanis, in Kabul.
Then what's a shovel for? To plant the dead
and dig them up. Meaning you shouldn't listen
to the radio if you've enough bread and few do.
What price guilt? Sliced finger and Band-Aid.

Fact is, each breath becomes bone
becomes dust. *Yes, but* what's a shovel for?
To plant the living who bloom right here.
Meaning if I had a hammer, if I had a hammer...
I'd still choose a shovel to plant the carload
of untagged, close-out perennials I bought
not knowing what, pledged to the double edge
of faith and desolation any life rides.
Any life, any ride. Who knows what you get?
Beans. I'd waited fall through summer to find out.
Ask Jack. I'd dusted bone meal so their roots
knuckled down. What can't be bought?
Go ask my daughter. It's time, time. *Yes, but*.
Oh shut up! I love this slew of blue lupine
and immaculate black-eyed Susan, a plenum of delphinium

blowing its gold-throated trumpet now. This now.

Because I Wanted to Write a Happy Poem, I Thought of Harry Caray's Dying

No, not the actual instant, days delayed,
the cord unplugged, all the possible perils
of the possible soul — not that I've in mind
his boozeless Valentine's dinner with Dutchie
the long-suffering, imperturbable wife.
His turning away the wine list with wrist flick
and head shake, lemon tottering his water

among ice. I've in mind beads his hand
stitched free raising that glass against
the stroke-addled tongue he'd wrap
around *Andres Gala-Rala-Allah-Angora*,
or *Hector Villa-Who-New-Wave-Ahh*.
Look, I'm no Cubs fan. I don't even have cable.
But Harry's "good friend" Pete Vonachen
my wife treats for diabetes, and I've driven
past Wainwright Welding in Moline whose picnic
Harry pronounced around Spike & Daisy's
50th announcement. All the malted hop
bar hopping I'll not get into, or his feud
with Augie Busch the Teutonic Turtleneck.
Neither Bill Veeck nor Steve Stone's helmet head
Consort hair spray, nor the time Harry...
No, not that. Honestly, Harry's already
half out the door as I fondly remember him.
When he practiced death eleven years before
perfecting it, when he stroked and recouped
all spring, Harry beseeched Bill Murray to guest
play-by-play April 17, 1987, Good Friday.
And it was. My wife lay in labor, our first,
she undaunted but as shorn of good cheer
as the Easter lamb we'd planned the family dinner
over. She laughed and so contracted, afflicted
by a husband hyperventilating Lamaze
in her good ear until she hollered, sweetly,
how she couldn't hear a damn thing.
The ball game, Bill Murray. Then our daughter's
post postgame squall. When I think of Harry
it's of his masterful absence and my daughter's
entrance. He'd a lifetime of practiced exits —
closed-down bars, bottomless bottles. None as deft
as the toppled nod of acknowledgment he lent
that restaurant crowd, last he heard on earth: Applause.

Confessional

I loved the ritual of spiritual spot removal.
I loved forgiveness, O cosmic delete key,
your dewy screw-ups zapped to ether

by fingering *Sorry* in a little holy water.
I loved the retrospective summary Father B
taught me: my sins spinning the twin Ferris wheel
venial and *mortal*, the latter reserved
for ax murder or presidential adultery.
I loved nods of mumbled prayer, their ransom.
None of that alone-in-your-room stuff for Rome.
Side by side you entered those booths,
the priest center-throned, wine-flushed.
Waiting on knee, you hoped for the daft one
who exacted small penance – say, three Hail Mary's,
the Our Father, a couple Glory Be's –
at least the young priest so you'll not shout
your mistakes like a carnie barking crowds
to this week's geek of earthly perdition.
Once I confessed the swoon of petting Julie,
who, kneeling in the next booth, burst out,
"You swore you'd never tell!" It was a sin
not to. Later, jaded by age, at the rat end
of my braided rope, I'd leave out things I'd done
or ladle in some I'd not, just to fluster Father B,
and then confess *that* lie – expurgation's high
sublime as sin. Such rush attends forgiveness,
as the priest knows of our bent-knee plea.
Thus my liturgical study, the Bishop's workshops –
a way to wear black robes and still kiss girls.
I played dress up to hear confession, morosely
curious as any rubbernecked accident gawker
slowing traffic in quest of mournful cry,
blood-spangled forehead. When finally I heard
what I'd thought I wanted, saw it full face and long
before the cops waved everyone move along,
we'd swapped places: I lay on the alluring gurney,
gory from the wreck of good intentions,
while victims motored away their lives. Wait.
That's what art would twist of it, dear gullible reader.
Nah, the usual dopey kid, I confess to dropping out
and stumbling home to punish the insolent green
of my parents' lawn. For this too I was forgiven.

Arthur Sze

The String Diamond

1

An apricot blossom opens to five petals.
You step on a nail, and, even as you wince,
a man closes a mailbox, a cook sears
shredded pork in a wok, a surgeon sews
a woman up but forgets to remove a sponge.
In the waiting room, you stare at a diagram
and sense compression of a nerve where
it passes through the wrist and into the hand.
You are staring at black and white counters
on a crisscrossed board and have no idea
where to begin. A gardener trims chamisa
in a driveway; a roofer mops hot tar;
a plumber asphyxiates in a room with
a faulty gas heater; a mechanic becomes
an irrational number and spirals into himself.
And you wonder what inchoate griefs
are beginning to form? A daykeeper sets
A random handful of seeds and crystals into lots.

2

Pin a mourning cloak to a board and observe
brown in the wings spreading out to a series

of blue circles along a cream-yellow outer band.
A retired oceanographer remembers his father

acted as a double agent during the Japanese occupation,
but the Kuomintang general who promised a pardon

was assassinated; his father was later sentenced
as a collaborator to life in prison, where he died.

Drinking snake blood and eating deer antler
is no guarantee the mind will deepen and glow.

You notice three of the four corners of an intersection
are marked by ginkgo, horse chestnut, cluster

Most Recent Book: *The Redshifting* (Web Copper Canyon Press, 1998)

of pear trees, and wonder what the significance is.
Is the motion of a red-dye droplet descending

in clear water the ineluctable motion of a life?
The melting point of ice is a point of transparency,

as is a kiss, or a leaf beginning to redden,
or below a thunderhead lines of rain vanishing in air.

3

Deltoid spurge,
red wolf,
ocelot,
green-blossom pearly mussel,
razorback sucker,
wireweed,
blunt-nosed leopard lizard,
mat-forming quillwort,
longspurred mint,
kern mallow,
Schaus swallowtail,
pygmy madtom,
relict trillium,
tan riffleshell,
humpback chub,
large-flowered skullcap,
black lace cactus,
tidewater goby,
slender-horned spineflower,
sentry milk-vetch,
tulotoma snail,
rice rat,
blowout penstemon,
rough pigtoe,
marsh sandwort,
snakeroot,
scrub plum,
bluemask darter,
crested honeycreeper,
rough-leaved loosestrife.

4

In the mind, an emotion dissolves into a hue;
there's the violet haze when a teen drinks
a pint of paint thinner, the incarnadined

when, by accident, you draw a piece of
Xerox paper across your palm and slit
open your skin, the yellow when you hear
they have dug up a four-thousand-year-old
corpse in the Taklamakan Desert,
the scarlet when you struggle to decipher
a series of glyphs which appear to
represent sunlight dropping to earth
at equinoctial noon, there's the azure
when the acupuncturist son of a rabbi
extols the virtues of lentils, the brown
when you hear a man iced in the Alps
for four thousand years carried dried
polypores on a string, the green when
ravens cry from the tops of swaying spruces.

5

The first leaves on an apricot, a new moon,
a woman in a wheelchair smoking in a patio,
a CAT scan of a brain: these are the beginnings
of strings. The pattern of black and white
stones never repeats. Each loss is particular:
a gold ginkgo leaf lying on the sidewalk,
the room where a girl sobs. A man returns
to China, invites an old friend to dinner,
and later hears his friend felt he missed
the moment he was asked a favor and was
humiliated; he tells others never to see
this person from America, "He's cunning, ruthless."
The struggle to sense a nuance of emotion
resembles a chrysalis hanging from a twig.
The upstairs bedroom filling with the aroma
of lilies becomes a breathing diamond.
Can a chrysalis pump milkweed toxins into wings?
In the mind, what never repeats? Or repeats endlessly?

6

Dropping circles of gold paper,
before he dies,
onto Piazza San Marco;

        pulling a U-turn
        and throwing the finger;

a giant puffball
filling the car
with the smell of almonds;

> a daykeeper pronounces the day,
> "Net";

slits a wrist,
writes the characters "revolt"
in blood on a white T-shirt;

> a dead bumblebee
> in the greenhouse;

the flaring tail of a comet,
dessicated vineyard,
tsunami;

> a ten-dimensional
> form of go;

slicing abalone on the counter —
sea urchins
piled in a Styrofoam box;

> honeydew seeds
> germinating in darkness.

7

A hummingbird alights on a lilac branch
and stills the mind. A million monarchs
may die in a frost? I follow the wave
of blooming in the yard: from iris to
wild rose to dianthus to poppy to lobelia
to hollyhock. You may find a wave in
a black-headed grosbeak singing from a cottonwood
or in listening to a cricket at dusk.
I inhale the smell of your hair and see
the cloud of ink a cuttlefish releases in water.
You may find a wave in a smoked and
flattened pig's head at a Chengdu market,
or in the diamond pulse of a butterfly.
I may find it pulling yarn out of an indigo vat
for the twentieth time, watching the yarn
turn dark, darker in air. I find it
with my hand along the curve of your waist,
sensing in slow seconds the tilt of the Milky Way.

James Tate

A Knock on the Door

They ask me if I've ever thought
about the end of the world,
and I say, "Come in, come in,
let me give you some lunch, for God's sake.
After a few bites it's the afterlife
they want to talk about. "Ouch," I say,
"did you see that grape leaf skeletonizer?"
Then they're talking about redemption
and the chosen few sitting right by His side.
"Doing what?" I ask. "Just sitting?"
I am surrounded by burned-up zombies.
"Let's have some lemon chiffon pie
I bought yesterday at the 3 Dog Bakery."
But they want to talk about my soul.
I'm getting drowsy and see butterflies
everywhere. "Would you gentlemen
like to take a nap, I know I would."
They stand and back away from me,
out the door, walking toward my neighbors,
a black cloud over their heads
and they see nothing without end.

Never Again the Same

Speaking of sunsets,
last night's was shocking.
I mean, sunsets aren't supposed to frighten you, are they?
Well, this one was terrifying.
People were screaming in the streets.
Sure, it was beautiful, but far too beautiful.
It wasn't natural.
One climax followed another and then another
until your knees went weak
and you couldn't breathe.

Most Recent Book: *Six Mile Mountain* (Story Line Press, 2001)

The colors were definitely not of this world,
peaches dripping opium,
pandemonium of tangerines,
inferno of irises,
Plutonian emeralds,
all swirling and churning, swabbing,
like it was playing with us,
like we were nothing,
as if our whole lives were a preparation for this,
this for which nothing could have prepared us
and for which we could not have been less prepared.
The mockery of it all stung us bitterly.
And when it was finally over
we whimpered and cried and howled.
And then the streetlights came on as always
and we looked into one another's eyes —
ancient caves with still pools
and those little transparent fish
who have never seen even one ray of light.
And the calm that returned to us
was not even our own.

The New Ergonomics

The new ergonomics were delivered
just before lunchtime
so we ignored them.
Without revealing the particulars
let me just say that
lunch was most satisfying.
Jack and Roberta went with
the corned beef for a change.
Jack believes in alien abduction
and Roberta does not,
although she has had
several lost weekends lately
and one or two unexplained scars
on her buttocks. I thought
I recognized someone
from my childhood
at a table across the room,

the same teeth, the same hair,
but when he stood up,
I wasn't sure, Squid with a red tie?
Impossible. I finished
my quiche lorraine
and returned my thoughts
to Jack's new jag:
"Well, I guess anything's
possible. People disappear
all the time, and most of them
have no explanation
when and if they return.
Look at Tony's daughter
and she's never been the same."
Jack was looking as if
he'd bet on the right horse now.
"And these new ergonomics,
who really designed them?
Does anybody know?
Do they tell us anything?
A name, an address? Hell no."
Squid was paying his bill
in a standard-issue blue blazer.
He looked across the room at me
several times. He looked tired,
like he wanted to sleep for a long time
in a barn somewhere, in Kansas.
I wanted to sleep there, too.

How the Pope Is Chosen

Any poodle under ten inches high is a toy.
Almost always a toy is an imitation
of something grown-ups use.
Popes with unclipped hair are called *corded popes*.
If a Pope's hair is allowed to grow unchecked,
it becomes extremely long and twists
into long strands that look like ropes.
When it is shorter it is tightly curled.
Popes are very intelligent.
There are three different sizes.

The largest are called standard Popes.
The medium-sized ones are called miniature Popes.
I could go on like this, I could say:
"He is a squarely built Pope, neat,
well-proportioned, with an alert stance
and an expression of bright curiosity,"
but I won't. After a poodle dies
all the cardinals flock to the nearest 7-Eleven.
They drink Slurpies until one of them throws up
and then he's the new Pope.
He is then fully armed and rides through the wilderness alone,
day and night in all kinds of weather.
The new Pope chooses the name he will use as Pope,
like "Wild Bill" or "Buffalo Bill."
He wears red shoes with a cross embroidered on the front.
Most Popes are called "Babe" because
growing up to become a Pope is a lot of fun.
All the time their bodies are becoming bigger and stranger,
but sometimes things happen to make them unhappy.
They have to go to the bathroom by themselves,
and they spend almost all of their time sleeping.
Parents seem to be incapable of helping their little popes grow up.
Fathers tell them over and over again not to lean out of windows,
but the sky is full of them.
It looks as if they are just taking it easy,
But they are learning something else.
What, we don't know, because we are not like them.
We can't even dress like them.
We are like red bugs or mites compared to them.
We think we are having a good time cutting cartoons out of the paper,
but really we are eating crumbs out of their hands.
We are tiny germs that cannot be seen under microscopes.
When a Pope is ready to come into the world,
we try to sing a song, but the words do not fit the music too well.
Some of the full-bodied popes are a million times bigger than us.
They open their mouths at regular intervals.
They are continually grinding up pieces of the cross
and spitting them out. Black flies cling to their lips.
Once they are elected they are given a bowl of cream
and a puppy clip. Eyebrows are a protection
when the Pope must plunge through dense underbrush

in search of a sheep.

Richard Tillinghast

Exilium

The imperial city toward which all roads tend,
Which codifies the laws and dispatches them
By runner or fax to expectant provinces
This is not. It's an improvised mélange
Mushrooming along the banks of a tidal river,
Suffering the moods of its irrational weather
And a population with much to complain about.

Though you could dignify what draws you here
By calling it exile, your solitude is your choice,
Even when it racks you, even when
Your tendons stretch with what you have to carry.
Out you go tonight making the rounds, mapping
A route through the city's drizzly melancholia,
Down streets of broad colonial emptiness.

Step inside a stained-glass door or two
Where shag and porter cloud the conversation.
Sip a slow pint in the company of strangers
While outside the rain slurs through globed lamp-glow.
The evening ages. A notebook fills with your
Idiosyncratic alphabet. Then the pubs close.

The pubs close, the streets rain-slick and desultory.
A cafeteria then — everybody's
Hangout, where plain lives put in appearances
Over tea and a bun. The cash register whirrs,
The steamy rush of the coffee machine backgrounds
A clink of ironstone plates and stainless steel.
No sigh of leisure here — every life
In the room carries the imprint of having worked
The livelong day — not to boast or prove
A point, but simply because what else is there?

The way an old sufferer, grey hair wispy and thin,
Handles her knife, addressing a plate of fish,
Reaches you, touches some common chord.
Despite what they say about you — beyond your remoteness,
Your severe judgments on your fellow creatures —
You've some connection still to the human race.

Most Recent Book: *Six Mile Mountain* (Story Line Press, 2000)

Hypercritical, incommunicado,
It's good to know deep down you're one of us.

Incident

I slept, dead to the world, then awoke.
My daughter stood at the foot of the bed
calling me to dinner, her corn-stubble hair
dyed red in the sunset. The honest wells
of her eyes brimmed toward me. I was grateful.
My sleep had been summery and boatlike.

Nothing had stopped. My sheets were not marble,
the earthy savor of death did not surround me.
All it was, was a June afternoon and time
for dinner. I lay in bed a moment longer
and studied the lifeline on my palm,
how it cut passionately into the flesh,
then jagged abruptly to one side
like a slantwise heartbeat.

I was dead no longer, I had come back
from that slow place, that backward-flowing river,
that acre of reticence. Now I had eyes
once more to see and perceive in this world.
It was "Hi, honey," "Hi, Dad" and "How was your nap?" —
corn on the cob and salad from the garden
and coffee in my favorite cup.

Southbound Pullman, 1945

Discharge papers in duffle bags,
Their train thumps half-speed out of Boston.
Sunset kindles the cokey haze
Over Back Bay Station.

Bricky courtyards, windswept corners and
Clotheslines, a view of someone's kitchen.
A Victory garden with fists of cabbage.
Then the lights switch on.

A boy and his father burning leaves,
Obscured by dusk on a patch of green,

Wave up at faces starred in the southbound's
Passing constellation.

Stewards uncork bottles, ice clinks
In the club car. A new deck
Crackles. Atlantic sea-salt blows in,
And a whiff of coalsmoke.

Steam builds. The whistle finds its pitch
And sounds an airy, unstopped note
Over darkling marshes and shore towns
Shutting down for the night.

Dinner is gonged through aisles of opened
Collars and bourbon. The galley
Vents coffee-scald and steak-sizzle
Down the Connecticut valley.

Penn Station at midnight. Bustle of redcaps,
Morning editions, hot java, trainmen
Tuning the wheels with big wrenches.
Then distances again.

Porterly hands tuck ironed cotton
And turn drowsy blankets back.
Darkness cradles the swaying coaches
Over strumming track.

Snoring. Then a nightmare scream
Jangles to its feet the whole sleeper.
Home voices murmur "You're okay, son."
"The war's over, soldier."

All night the breathing of ploughed fields.
The continent opens like a hand.
Tomorrow, bands and a convertible.
Then fresh mistakes begin.

The Alley Behind Ocean Drive

On beach sand two thousand footprints
Cross and overlay
And form or seem to form a pattern.
Girls speaking Italian
Take off their tops
And breathe the sun in through their pores.

The sun sets gorgeously
And then the *jeunesse dorée*, or
Eurotrash as they are called locally,
Drift back to their suites to change.
Then they emanate out onto Ocean Drive,
Sherbet-colored, to please the night air.

Behind Ocean Drive and the Colony Hotel
Runs an alley, unnamed,
Where Cuba comes to work.
When someone in the grill orders in English
The dishes get shouted
Out through the kitchen in Spanish.

People come here from far away
To spend money. Behind the Imperial,
In the alley, someone chops ice, fish are gutted,
Dirt gets washed off roots.
The ditch that runs down the
Middle of it runs red.

Out on Ocean the guy with the parrot angles for tips,
Madame Amnesia deals out a Tarot hand,
Iguana-on-a-bicycle lady wobbles
Amongst the Eurotrash. I write
My page, my way is paid.
All of us ride the swell of a tide.

The offal, the scales, the T-bones from steaks,
The hearts and lemon rinds, are put in bags
That the city comes by and collects.
Two towels hang on a balcony overlooking the alley.
A man in a white apron
Stands outside alone and smokes.

Chase Twichell

Road Tar

A kid said you could chew road tar
if you got it before it cooled,
black globule with a just-forming skin.

Most Recent Book: *The Snow Watcher* (Ontario Review Press, 1998)

He said it was better than cigarettes.
He said he *had a taste for it*.

On the same road, a squirrel
was doing the Watusi to free itself
from its crushed hindquarters.
A man on a bicycle stomped on its head,
then wiped his shoe on the grass.

It was *autumn*, the adult word for fall.
In school we saw a film called *Reproduction*.
The little snake-father poked his head
into the slippery future,
and a girl with a burned tongue was conceived.

Erotic Energy

Don't tell me we're not like plants,
sending out a shoot when we need to,
or spikes, poisonous oils, or flowers.

Come to me but only when I say,
that's how plants announce

the rules of propagation.
Even children know this. You can
see them imitating all the moves

with their bright plastic toys.
So that, years later, at the moment

the girl's body finally says yes
to the end of childhood,
a green pail with an orange shovel

will appear in her mind like a tropical
blossom she has never seen before.

A Last Look Back

Things change behind my back.
The starting snow I was just watching
has escaped into the past.

Well, not the past, but the part of the world
that surrounds the moment at hand.

That's why, whenever I see
animal tracks in a light snow like this,
I think of footnotes.

So strange, to inhabit a space
and then leave it vacant, standing open.

Each change in me is a stone step
beneath the blur of snow.
In spring the sharp edges cut through.

When I look back, I see my former selves,
numerous as the trees.

To the Reader: If You Asked Me

I want you with me, and yet you are the end
of my privacy. Do you see how these rooms
have become public? How we glance to see if –
who? Who did you imagine?
Surely we're not here alone, you and I.

I've been wandering
where the cold tracks of language
collapse into cinders, unburnable trash.
Beyond that, all I can see is the remote cold
of meteors before their avalanches of farewell.

If you asked me what words
a voice like this one says in parting,
I'd say, *I'm sweeping an empty factory*
toward which I feel neither hostility nor nostalgia.
I'm just a broom, sweeping.

To the Reader: Polaroids

Who are you, austere little cloud
drawn to this page, this sky in the dream
I'm having of meeting you here?

There should be a word that means "tiny sky."
Probably there is, in Japanese.
A verbal Polaroid of a Polaroid.

But you're the sky, not a cloud.
I'm the cloud. I gather and dissipate,
but you are always here.

Leave a message for me if you can.
Break a twig on the lilac, or toss
a few dried petals on the hood of my car.

May neither of us forsake the other.
The cloud persists in the darkness,
but the darkness does not persist.

Decade

I had only one prayer, but it spread
like lilies, a single flower duplicating
itself over and over until it was rampant,

uncountable. At ten I lay dreaming
in its crushed green blades.

How did I come by it, strange notion
that the hard stems of rage could be broken,
that the lilies were made of words,

my words? Each one I picked
laid a wish to rest. I mean killed it.

The difference between prayer
and a wish is that a wish knows it will be
a failure even as it sets out,

whereas a prayer is still innocent.
Wishing wants prayer to find that out.

Leslie Ullman

Calypso, Twilight

The blind stallion, having learned
my braille of leg and hand,
carries me without flinching
at the wind. His back has softened,
an extinct volcano, and my hips
hold me there, settled
by something I no longer
try to name. I am past the years

for bearing. My skin
turns to the work of wind
and salt, as the sun shortens
its arc above my diminished gardens.
I have little use for the silver-
wreathed mirror brought by a lover
who kept finding his way back.

If a wanderer should drift
ashore now and then, spent
and nameless, he will still find
in my eyes a trace of green.
Or blue. Depths in which to rest.
He will still find in my flesh
a firm *yes*, not padding
or pillow, but sinew like his —
from gathering wood for the long nights,
from sending men back to the sea
at first light (they swim strongest then),

from rising alone most mornings
to light that never lies
and the continuous waves.

But this poet who tries to slip
into my skin — she bathes me
in stage light, too bright
yet too soft, scribbling in
her journal. She would have me say,

Most Recent Book: *Slow Work Through Sand* (University of Iowa Press, 1998)

This is the dance my mothers
and grandmothers might have learned
had they slipped away from
children and set themselves loose
beneath the moon.

I give her back her words, a wish
blown like a kiss as the bloom
leaves her face, and love
leaves a jagged wake behind her.
It would do her little good

to know that lately I slip
like the breeze between the island's
tall rocks. I travel without
green or blue lining my eyes,
without rare flowers
from my garden, and disappear
into rooms filled with smoke, jazz,
the braid and flow of tongues.

I walk through the teeming streets
without desire or dread, the way
the old stallion accepts
the bit and lets himself be guided
among the last of the wild iris,
the shrinking berries —

and sometimes my weakened eyes
feel immense, turning me
inside out, as a young man or woman
appears beside me
speaking slowly at first, as though
cracking the door to a vault
and is surprised at the words,
the rush of words,
the voice full of great birds lifting.

Neap Tide

> *At half-moon the sun and moon are at right angles to the earth, tugging in opposite directions. . . . Then the tides are at their lowest: neap tide. Their apparent docility is the result of an impasse.*
>
> — Lynne Sharon Schwartz, The Fatigue Artist

For four nights I have slept
near the sea, that slow animal
licking the rim of a vast bowl.
For four nights, after meetings,
smalltalk and wine, my dreams
have turned up tears like letters
I haven't read for years —
something is stolen, I can't
remember what, only myself turned
inside-out with betrayal, or my heart
clenched in dismay as my legs
turn to stone on a busy street. . . .
Or I've wakened to a thrill I once craved
and then taught myself to put
aside — the memory of a man's
touch light as breath over my neck
and shoulders, his hand an eye
seeing my body gladly, and leaving
in me something sunlit, blue,
startling as morning glories
that find their way each autumn into
rows of cotton where I live.

When I was five, a grief
enduring and raw first surfaced
like ruins among the pastels
and mahoganies of my grandparents'
spare room, where I was banished
while adults gathered at the oval table.
I could hear ice in golden drinks,
bracelets making a sound like stars,
and talk circling the room in a current
of perfume. *I want a hollyhock,*
I want a hollyhock! I screamed
full-tilt into tantrum, not knowing
what a hollyhock was but daring them to
guess, to work a miracle, to open the door
and bow to my huge and famished loneliness.

These days I barely nod to old demons
on my way to work. To dinner. To planes.
I answer questions. I answer phonecalls.
I get the oil changed. I stand at the podium.
My man eases beside me at night
with a book, like a weary foot into
its slipper, and lately I feel like the essence
of slipper, a durable comfort
creased with tiny lines. My body
bleeds off-schedule now, my skin
loosens its hold over muscle and bone
but I can run three miles without effort
and seem to be leaning full-tilt into
outliving nature's use for me.

Today I sit on Gulf sand white and cool
as sugar, amazed that the sea allows me
to come so close to its green edge
and stay. Far from light, a labyrinth
of currents must send up
these little waves, these twitchings
of the huge animal in its sleep;
they leave bits of shell at my feet
and retreat, their rhythms
seeping in to bring forgotten parts of me,
once omnivorous, tamed
to the reef of my wakings

and to ease the grip of muscle
over vein, of vein over blood as my thoughts
subside to a cruising speed. . . .
Those hollyhocks? Maybe
they were the essence of
morning glories not reduced
to simile. Constructs of indigo and air
weaving through green and stealing
nothing, greeting the sun and holding it
pooled during the night's evolution,
maybe visiting other fields — or even
planets — before floating
back to their places. I see them
when I jog, their blue so clear
it seems a form of insight.

Estrogen

One day I too will be
found, a lightning root
in a sky underground,

marked by whatever the years
will have done — the fur
my hands have stroked, the greens

that pushed through soil
and passed my lips,
the darkness my bones carried

and yes, something
glittering in the champagne
those nights I thought I would live

forever, petal that I was.
The wind wrapped me in a skein of cries.
I aged closer to the ground

and fell in with the weather as she
changed and changed her mind.
My breasts ached.

Then shrank. My bones
thinned to lace. Was this
a departure? Some

would have it so — some
who walk the world with one
blind eye and one empty socket.

Martha Modena Vertreace

Iron Brigade Highway

Old folks say snow days are for making love
so I turn my palms toward a new moon

Most Recent Book: *Dragon Lady — Tsukimi* (Riverstone 1999)

wet and fertile in the morning sky
draining into the lake and tell you

my veins are maps, blue rivers in black flesh,
a painting with mistakes

left haunting the surface — Picasso's dark lines
beneath the old guitarist, the shadow

of wings strumming frozen ground.
When you believe me, I regret I said it,

knowing limits to gravity's work-a-day pull
to Earth's core whirling opposite from the crust,

as if we spin against each other. Make a list,
you tell me, of the places we've not found:

Amish Acres — Indiana
Clock Tower — Illinois

We rent a car, drive east for hours
as if we could still see my mother's house —

its cracked cellar windows, paint flaking
under gutters clogged with redgum balls,

prickly stars with no home galaxy — the way
she left it. The car, uncertain cradle, rocks us

on hawk's wings. Beneath my soft chin,
the folds a woman even less my age has worn

a long time making peace with skin,
I wear my mother's gold chain, her black cameo

warm between my breasts. Over a slate of snow,
contrails rune clouds and sky, the jet veiled

in the sun's first rays which miss
the woods we drive through, crowns of trees

which glower like a night gone bad.
On the radio, orchestral strings drone

as if catgut binds us to the open road:
yes, if I had to, yes I would
yes I could choose you again.

Night of the Moon

after Saira Malik

The window, shaped like a minaret, frames a woman
leaning toward three others, faces hidden
in butter-rich moonlight where a wisteria vine
climbs the violet wall, a rejected suitor who offers
his hopeless case to us, lost in this painting. What jewels
can we bring, ask violet petals, pointed leaves,

of the onion dome where saris flutter like silk leaves
when a thousand stories bloom, a womanly
urge when the tabla pulses a jeweled
raga, the flute croons half-hidden
in the topaz courtyard, the sitar offers
ribbons of melodies which vine

coiling tendrils in jasmine words. Vines
are the point, the teller says. Ivy leaves
are emerald hearts which offer
themselves without guile to a woman
whose heart breaks when Earth moves, hiding
in gossamer veils, lapis lazuli, mango yellow, her jewels

of hope mixed in crystalline stone, cayenne red jewels
of betrayal. So spin us a tale, says the vine
as it weaves your impatience. Her song — l love a man who hides
among day stars, who does not love me, whose heart leaves
me for a woman
who cannot love him as I do, who offers

to firelight his hair with a phosphorous torch, offering
to teach him the meaning of star-smeared sky. Jewels
brighten the canvas when you know the woman's
tune, each brushstroke, all too well, proving vines
cling, then sometimes kill their host. A man must leave
behind what blessed fate denies him, then hide

his grief in the arms of another who hides
her joy in his sorrow, offering
to etch his name on valentine leaves
which saints read. I am a rare jewel,
your darkest angel, my hand, a vine
of striped bindweed which no ex-woman's

twining memory hides when you finally leave
her wooden frame; find a real woman's offering
of jewels when you shelter in my vine.

Conjuries in Amber

Bewleys apologizes for any inconvenience during our alterations.
— table placard
for Karen Kuehne

Near Charlotte Square off Princes Street, Edinburgh,
not paradise, but Bewleys Oriental Café: white coffee

I drank in Dublin, scones of stone-ground wheat,
full breakfast with white and black pudding;

mulberry wallpaper with geishas trapped in stamens
of bamboo cages above red velvet booths, plush chairs.

I down a second mug of white, a bowl of soup — potato
and leeks, a dash of Tabasco — just to hear the steamer

froth milk into a proper lid. Karen, when I send you here
to relax, to get you out of your own way, I could

come with you, tell you what to eat, what not — have
a persimmon tart, avoid boiled hakes freighted in

on a Boston whaler. You can believe anyone
whose open face hides the lie it tells about a chime

of stacked plates in the kitchen corridor.
In white aprons, black skirts an inch below the knee,

lace collars, svelte servers angle for the pound
left on the tray. More like Klimt nudes

shedding silk tapestry, nipples plump under black blouses,
a kindness to seedy men with raspy voices

stammering *please* and *thank you*,
hovering in praise of blond braids under white hats.

So watch yourself. In spite of Bewley's simpering
apology, there are always reasons for a disturbance

of sandalwood. Do you agree that men read
your ragg wool sweatshirt? The one with *Bakersfield*

across your pointy bits? When it rains,
licorice on your breath, you ask, who killed a spider? —

guessing that there are ancestral intensities that matter
in the long run, ideas which skate on stilts

of Coltrane jazz, early morning Radio Four.
Shortcutting to the café through the Woodland —

past a king's territory for hunting, hawking, and games —
I pass a woman petting a calico cat. Three more, she tells me,

on High Street near North Bridge. Cats
with yellow hair, hyacinth eyes. This one

circles her legs; eats moist from a tin can, then dry
from a plastic dish; circles again. He ignores woodpigeons

preening within a paw's easy reach — too big — but takes
a finch or wagtail if rain makes her late with his kibbles.

Fingering a paper clip bracelet — rainbow worry beads —
she says the cat is Louis; she is Cat-Annie, not Catherine.

Now is that clear? So when you say I am a docile hawk,
blunt claws, nibbling meat scraps from your hand,

I know there is no such thing.

Charles Harper Webb

"Did That Really Happen?"

— Asked after readings

Do I ask you, reader, if that's your own hair?
If those are your real breasts? If that fat is natural,
or you had it pumped in to fend off what otherwise
would be unbearable celebrity? What if,

like the President, I "don't recall"? Memory's
a wisp of thread, a broken hair about to fall,
a dandelion-seed in a breeze, a blob of oil in water,
changing constantly. Did my Cub Scout den mother

Most Recent Book: *Tulip Farms and Leper Colonies* (BOA Editions, 2002)

pull her panties down, and make me "kiss the kitty"?
Yes, if wishing counts. (Haven't you dreamed
someone loved you, and wakened, certain it was true?)
We know embarrassment erases memory;

look what it did after Mom found you modeling
her bra, whispering "Boo, bees!" I admit
I birddogged my best friend's girl in seventh grade.
But I didn't get her pregnant, as I've said in print.

She didn't give birth to a hairball with seven eyes.
(Though could I really make that up out of blue sky?)
Maybe that day care worker did kill elephants,
and make kids foo-woo on one anothers' heads.

Maybe Satan did rear out of the sandbox to gulp babies.
Maybe Manassas and Agincourt were tulip farms,
or leper colonies, or old ladies who repaired lederhosen,
and made the world's lightest bean soufflé.

Ten years ago the *Times* blistered my book.
I doctored the review, then used revised "quotes"
in my resumé. A week ago, a reporter
read the resumé; today, the *Times* quotes me.

Cornflowers sway outside my window, pink
and blue. Orange milkworts pogo in the breeze.
Or did I see them in a coffee table book?
What's the difference? Now they belong to you.

To Prove That We Existed Before You Were Born

we'll tell you how your mom worked at the hospital,
"treating" people like the tattered, gray-faced man
who shoves his shopping cart down Verdugo,
muttering to the Tsar. How, between bouts
at my desk, I'd bumble barefoot through the house,
feeding our fish, or patting Marvin, the cat.

Mom will tell how, at her first job, age 16,
she found a dead mouse in Baskin-Robbins's hot fudge,
called the manager at home, and when he didn't
believe her, dropped the chocolate-covered Mickey
on his big desk-blotter, and never returned.
I'll tell about playing The Catacombs, and resurrect

my sunburst Stratocaster from its coffin-case.
I might even tell how I clubbed a Bandido with a mike-
stand when he rushed the stage, and how I'd pull away
from girlfriends in Portland, Billings, Coeur d'Alene,
my red pickup sagging with band gear, and barely see
the road for tears until, in a few miles, the clouds lifted,

a surge of freedom picked me up, and surfing
on its crest, I'd start to sing. You'll hear the way
you heard "Jack the Giant-Killer," and "Snow White,"
as if our lives are fairy tales from "olden days."
Your world will be about your friends, your baseball,
your Tickle Me Elmo, or whatever the fad is.

You won't know for many years that the musk
of narcissus on a March day made us feel sexy,
just as it will you. You'd never guess
that, when you were a neural tube, an ember
trying to make a flame, your mom felt sick,
so we went walking on the street we were leaving

to find a better place for you. A north wind
gnawed our lips, but as we walked, holding hands
inside my parka pocket, your mom's nausea lifted,
and my grief to feel you stealing her from me.
Inventing songs about our turtles — Mr. Cow,
Peg Webb, Trout-Boy, and Tammy Faye —

we started laughing, and stopped on the sidewalk
(cracked by the last earthquake), and kissed
as long and desperately as if we were saying goodbye —
kissed the way our parents may have
(since we're both eldest children) — kissed as if
we didn't need you, one last time.

Tone of Voice

It pinks the cheeks of speech, or flushes the forehead.
It's a spring breeze in which words play, a scorching sun
that burns them red, slate clouds that cover them in ice.
Mastering tone, the child outgrows his sticks and stones.

"*Okay*," he sneers, twisting the word in Mommie's eye.
Elipses, dashes, all capitals, underlines —
these are tuna nets through which tone's minnows slide.
"I love you" may arrive spiked like a mace, or snickering.

"State your name" from lawyers' lips can mean "You lie!"
Tone leaks the truth despite our best efforts to hide.
It's verbal garlic; mistress on a husband's hands.
Consider, dear, when you ask, "Where are my French fries?"

how you may stand in a silk teddy holding grapes,
a suit of mail holding a lance, a hangman's hood holding
a rope. As useless to protest, "I didn't mean that,"
as to tell a corpse, "Stand up. You misinterpreted my car."

Funktionslust

It's German for "the pleasure in what one does best."
Don't fret the accent; savor the sense
of gibbons swinging tree to tree, cats creeping

through high weeds, dogs chasing frisbees
into seaside froth. I always knew "fun"
just began describing what I felt; "lust"

was the ignoble hind-end. I loved to watch
a scissortail flycatcher pluck gnats from thin air
while its long tail kicked and fluttered,

treading sky. I loved to see box turtles bull
through dewberry tangles, their red, orange,
and yellow heads stained deep maroon.

Football and basketball were fine, but the first time
I slipped a leather fielder's mitt on my left hand,
and stretched my five-year-old fingers around

a slick white Spalding ball, the first time my varnished
Louisville Slugger split the air, I knew there had
to be some word to celebrate my certainty

that on the Dad's Club All Stars, August, 1965,
I'd leap to catch a line drive, scramble on my knees
to second base to make an unassisted double play,

then go four-for-five, and triple in the winning run.
Microphone in hand, singing "Knights in White Satin"
at the Houston Colosseum, or kissing Linda

in the room I'd dared to rent after the prom,
I knew some caveman must have uttered sounds
that have survived — syllables to describe

that feeling that makes us bear our fardels, pay
our taxes, undergo our chemotherapy — a word
for what a sailboat knows, running before the wind —

a rattler knows, as it sinks fangs into a mouse —
a baby who'll never speak a word of German knows,
tasting the nipple, the sweet milk flooding in.

Biblical Also-Rans

Hanoch, Pallu, Hezron, Carmi,
Jemuel, Ohad, Zohar, Shuni:
one *Genesis* mention's all you got.

Ziphion, Muppim, Arodi: lost
in a list even the most devout skip over
like small towns on the road to L.A.

How tall were you, Shillim?
What was your favorite color, Ard?
Did you love your wife, Iob?

Not even her name survives.
Adam, Eve, Abel, Cain —
these are the stars crowds surge to see.

Each hour thousands of Josephs,
Jacobs, Benjamins are born.
How many Oholibamahs? How many

Mizzahs draw first breath today?
Gatam, Kenaz, Reuel? Sidemen
in the band. Waiters who bring

the Perignon and disappear.
Yet they loved dawn's garnet light
as much as Moses did. They drank

wine with as much delight.
I thought my life would line me up
with Samuel, Isaac, Joshua.

Instead I stand with Basemath, Hoglah,
Ammihud. Theirs are the names
I honor; theirs, the deaths I feel,

their children's tears loud as any
on the corpse of Abraham, their smiles
as missed, the earth as desolate

without them: Pebbles on a hill.
Crumbs carried off by ants.
Jeush. Dishan. Nahath. Shammah.

Bruce Weigl

One of the Wives of God

I know what distant
        sirens mean;
see,
        already they have

come and passed
        for another. I know
dismantlement. Up
        until the moment

they come for you,
        it is always
another. Sister
        Mary Catherine

taught me that
        in catechism
Father held on Saturdays
        for kids

who couldn't pay
        for Catholic school
so learned the rites
        and the beautiful

suffering from a missal,
        and from sister,
sweet
        who was my

Most Recent Book: *After the Others* (Northwestern University Press, 1999)

light of spirit
        and my holy ghost
and who,
        in my unholy imaginings,

lifted me
        above the ordinary
into condemnation.
        In the pew I sat upright

but didn't hear the Father's
        words except their drone
beyond the
        indeterminate

boundaries of my
        stupor for Sister Mary,
not yet twenty,
        her eyes

the still blue pond
        of all of my longing;
the way she
        smiled

down on me
        a warmth
that must have been
        the soul. So

I found ways
        to see her when I could,
pretending
        there was something

that I did not understand,
        and once
in my swoon
        for Sister's

body that I could
        somehow feel,
even through the habit's shroud,
        I wandered, drowsy,

into the house
        where the wives of Jesus

slept
        and lived their secret lives,

and I saw her,
        lit by a small light,
through a crack
        in the wooden door.

Elegy for Matthews

The best long flight
I saw you sleek through,
late summer,
late evening in Penn Station,
the white
Casablanca suit
I'd seen you wear
that same morning,
splattered now with your blood.
I watched you too long
for the sake of goodness,
or for the sake of
even the most simple
kind of grace
we may manage.
I watched you
across the station
move your hips
to the funky music
from a box
some kid rested
on his shoulder,
your formerly
impeccable suit
covered with your dried
and your drying blood.
What hasn't been lost to me,
even now,
is the way that you
walked through that hubbub
after our eyes had met
across the distance between us,

stride of the fox maybe, or maybe
stride of the clever dog,
until you were right there,
before me,
where I felt the generous
light of you again.
I asked your bloody suit
what had happened
with my eyes,
and without a moment's
hesitation
you said you'd just auditioned
for a part
in a Brian DePalma movie,
and then you
smiled that way you did
inside the place that exists
between the kiss
and the last breath
where you had loved
to dwell.
When you told me
the story of your bleeding,
I did not want to take you
up in my arms
and make it stop.
I wanted to run away.

The Super

I met the super
on the battleship-
gray painted stoop
of the five-floor walk-up,
Macdougal street, back
when it was neighborhood
and I'd
hooked up with a woman
who had money
from her folks and a job
that paid good

and who told me
Come stay with me, honey, that
nearly forgotten summer
in the post-war
black grief and loss and
all I had to do was
sleep up there
on the fifth floor with her and
love her some nights.
We ate dinner
together in restaurants.
But that first morning
I got there ahead of her
and met the super
on the battleship-
gray painted stoop
on Macdougal Street. I
was twenty. I
had already seen
inside the storm of shit,
but this woman
said with a nasal screech
that she was the super and
that I couldn't get in
no how, as it wasn't my place, and
she called some Puerto Rican
young men to her aid
when I barely resisted
in defense of my
stupid rights
and the rights
of the not yet arrived
woman who expected me, she
expected things of me if
I were to get this walk-up
room to write in or
no, I never wrote, I couldn't
write when I heard her
breathe at night so close,
although there was some
loveliness there too I recall.
The tough guys said
they'd cut my fucking

heart out if I didn't
leave the super alone and
get the hell back
to where I was supposed to be,
a question, I believe,
they had no idea
how to answer. I know
that I didn't. Later
when the would-be
keeper of me
finally showed up,
the super relented, and
later still,
once summer
had become something
we could both bear,
we got to talking
one evening on the stoop,
August night time traffic and
lovers I watched, unworthy,
and in the middle
of the super's
winter story about
how the heat went off
one night in the place
so she nearly froze and
so dragged her chair
to the gas stove's
open door, propped
her tired feet there and
fell hard to sleep, she
lifted her dress
to show me. Like you
I could hardly believe the
scars on her legs from
where they'd caught fire,
open sores still oozing
that human acid and this
eight months after the fact.
Give us back our lives, I say.

Roger Weingarten

Into the Mouth of the Rat

My Father's Skin

Into the hotel shower to scald
the plane ride and the terror
of seeing him and Stepmother
out of my pores, out of the years
of pretending he possessed even a penny's
worth of love for me. Into the no-man's-land
behind the flimsy curtain of my
resolve not to let them
get to me, I remember my uncle, once my
old man's business partner and confidante,
describing him over blintzes and stewed
prunes: Roger, your dad never
made a bad deal and never loved a soul outside
his own skin. I drive under the jackknifed
security gate, under orange trumpets
of hibiscus hedge, under sun-bleached
tile roofs and palm fronds like twirling skirts
over green coconuts that remind me of his
custom-made silver and jade cock
and ball key ring: rabbinical
seminarian, self-made
cuckold, survivor of a twelve-year
string of surgeries, proud owner of a powder
blue Rolls and a diamond pinkie, you can bet
that I'm his firstborn passing a convoy of golf cart
drivers and great birds corkscrewing
their necks to take a gander at this interloper
turning a rented red Mustang
into the Guest space. A chameleon
scurries over stucco. The doorman's stare
starts at my shoes and works its way like a patient
lover to my buckle embossed with the word
plumber amidst a bouquet of tools. I step out
of the mirrored world of the service
elevator snapping shut like a guillotine

Most Recent Book: *Ghost Wrestling* (David R. Godine, 1997)

turned sideways. My old man propped on pillows
stares out of his chemical tan at the miniature
Republican ex-governor on TV pretending
to be president. The nurse
shakes my hand and her head when Stepmother,
at the top of her voice, says, Mike, it's Roger.
When I lean to kiss his forehead, he uses
my cover to slide his right hand over his left
to pick at a scab over a raised dark blue vein.
I take the slender hand in both of mine,
and massaging the transparent
skin around it with my thumbs,
stare into the demilitarized
zone of his eyes and wonder — after having
his secretary fire my brother
over the phone, all to meet the requirements
of the second wife and his need to strike
back at the first — how he could live
with himself. Dad, I ask out loud, surprising
myself, do you understand? Squeezing
my finger curled under his palms he looks — curious,
loving, who can tell — into my version
of his brown eyes. The nurse
wants to know, has he always
been this passive. Stepmother charges
the bedroom in a flurry of arms
and sobs, shrieking
my Mikey, my Mikey and pulls the black and blue,
scabbed, scarred and cratered
rag doll to her sleepless kisser,
kissing him like a wounded child,
while he struggles to purse
his lips to get a kiss in, then his eyes
close and he falls
out of the moment
into a defensive
sleep.

Shaving My Father

The nurse wheeling him into the master bath a la mode
the hall of mirrors at Versailles, confides she can feel
her ulcer when she lifts him. Together, we prop

his upper torso on knife-thin legs she tells me
will never again support what's left
of his life, and, gripping his puppet arms,
we strip the urine-soaked diaper,
shimmy him through another door
onto a plastic potty with raised sides strapped
over the porcelain throne in his private stall,
where he relieves himself
and falls asleep. How long
can he survive like this? He'll be in a coma
in a week, so if you want to see him again,
don't leave. In slow motion, brushing
his own teeth, he spits into the brass hole
in the green marble sink, takes the razor
out of my hand just as the phone rings,
brings it to his ear, and in the torn,
paper-thin rasp I can't get used to, asks
the razor, Who's calling? I take it back,
push the button, lift the skin on his neck,
and recall my uncle, decades ago, shaving
his father, a retired carpenter, with a brush
and lather, a scene more beautiful
than any Mary washing the body of Christ.
I scrape the hidden blades across
his delicate skin.

In Their Apartment

Stepmother easing father into the recliner
next to the easy chair, where I'm deep
into John Irving's *A Widow for One Year*, says Roger
everyone still blames you for his heart attack,
but — she bends to kiss the top
of his pale sleeping skull — we can still be pals
when this is finished. At least you'll have
half a family. Brewing my own
mixture of outrage and guilt, I blurt,
Thanks. I'm sorry if I ever
hurt either one of you, wondering
how the other half died on the battlefield
of her imagination, this aging warrior/stepmother,
her vodka-and-cake-bloated gut, breastless, flesh
of her arms dangling like melted armor, always,

even in her shark-like sleep, devising
ways to divide her enemies. I'll never
forget my ex — in bed with her semi-
secret lover — calling me after midnight
at the Midwest Writers Conference for the deaf,
dumb and blind to tell me my father,
who I hadn't spoken to for a year of blame-
filled silence, had been driven
on his back to the hospital. My last words:
Don't stuff your wife
down my throat, counterpunching
his battering ram of accusations, hanging up
on him and Stepmother breathing
through her mouth on the other phone
in their apartment.

        I can fly back at a moment's notice.
What are you talking about, she replies.
        You know what I mean — why make it hard?
You father's brother's in charge of all
arrangements.
        Are you saying my uncle, who doesn't
        even speak to his children, will decide
        whether I'm allowed to attend
        my father's funeral?
You'll have to get an even
shorter haircut, unwrinkle your clothes,
make sure your brother doesn't
show his face — and don't talk crazy
to my friends. (Which reminds me
of her monologue while driving my father,
his nurse — who told me Stepmother
didn't have a friend — and me to the promised land
of the beach.) They removed polyps
from his rectum in January, '98 . . . He underwent
a quadruple bypass in the summer, followed
by a double hernia and a softball-
sized growth cut out of his abdomen
after Labor Day. This
is where I buy your father's
monogrammed hankies — where Whatshername
owns the top three floors — no one
shops here anymore — you can get

AIDS from a baked potato
in that restaurant because illegal
aliens handle them — and both his knees
replaced in winter turned
into an endless rehab — he would have died
without me — then that tumor
attacked his brain — I discovered it, telling
the doctors they were all
full of it, chemo, the first
pneumonia, electric stimulation for
his vocal chords torn by tubes
snaked down his throat so what little
food he could eat wouldn't fall
into a lung. Now that the tumor's
back in business, do you think
they should operate — it's queer to roll
your shirtsleeves more than twice, never
above the elbow. Look at you. You could
have visited once a year — no one believes
your girlfriend's Jewish — don't open
your window for charity workers
working the streets. Even if they're dressed
like Santa, they're all
drug addicts.

I've got to leave.
But your plane's not for hours. You can't
say goodbye, he's asleep on the balcony.

I signal the nurse next to him
reading a romance novel
to give us a minute. Remembering
my stepsister explaining the first night
I arrived how my father had been
almost deaf since forever, which
is why, she said, they shout at him, I lifted
his chin up, buried in his chest, asked
in a whisper if he could hear me. He
squeezed my hand
lightly.
I put everything — fifty years of needing
this mysteriously
disappearing hero of my heart, who
put his arm around me in May of '73 and said

Everything's all right.
I put everything I've got: my only memory
of all of us around the table,
where my father kidding my brother
threatens to take off his belt
to punish him, when my mother, over a forkful
of Spanish tongue and succotash, says
Then your pants will fall down.

I put everything I've got left in me –
how he tried with a tough guy look
On his face to answer my son, who wanted
only to know why his grandfather wouldn't speak
for a lifetime to his own daughter –
everything into a last
I love you, Dad.
His lips move.
His eyelids droop.
I close the screen door behind me.
Awkwardly,
I hug Stepmother leaning
on both elbows into the kitchen
island, but she's
not having any.

I'll walk out on the balcony, she says, and watch
as you drive away.

Dara Wier

One Enchanted Evening

You found me in quicksand
and did not ask me stupid questions.
You peeled a mandarin drake
and did not ask me to watch.
You sent away the doctors
and the doctors of the church.
You photographed an indigo mosquitohawk

Most Recent Book: *Our Master Plan* (Carnegie Mellon University Press, 1999)

and showed me the result.
You crosshatched something in a book
and lowered the brim of your hat.
You touched a long pole to the top of my head
and walked in circles around me.
You kept the measure of the distance between us
inside a secret pocket.
You pried open an oyster
and kept your eyes shut.
You poured yourself a glass of cold vodka
and did not offer me any.
You picked up a dispatch in a bottle
and did not ask me to witness it.
You brought me a lop-eared rabbit
and let me watch it sleep.
You showed me a cicada still in its tuxedo
and let me watch it eat an elder leaf.
Seasons came and seasons went
and in between a boy and girl grew up.
You did not ask me what that was about.
You sang a while to the stars and the wind
and did not let me stop you.

Catholic

You're creeping on your knees down the dark hall
on the lookout at all times for fanged serpents
dripping phosphorous poisons and you bump into something
tangible and neither you nor the tangible move.
Around the corner you two slither together
in a kind of dance macabre like a gruesome tango
celebrating the anniversary of somebody's death.
You're covered with so much paraphernalia it's a wonder
you don't just slump over. You've got your little whips
and big whips and your thorns and your chains
and your hot irons and your pokers and your sores
that smell like roses, you say, and wounds that come
and go as they please. You're pierced in so many places
your insides work like a grater and that hurts
your insides. On the bright side, when light streams
through you you can pass for luminaria.

At the edge of a gray granite cliff
you and the tangible come to an impasse.
There's a struggle.
One of you slips and the other one stomps its bootheel
on your fingertips, actually grinds its heel in your nails.
You're howling. Wolves are gathering.
Everything has gone oily.
Souls and ghosts and angels and saints are hunting you down.
You don't stand a chance in hell.
A little girl dressed in chickenfeed sacks climbs up
beside you and offers you an iceblue snowcone.
You reach for it. You fall.

Prayer That the Rod of the Prede Stined Spouse May Blossom

Broken-down fishing rod leaning across a bookstack,
you can do it.
Fish with two legs, two arms, with crimson claws,
you can do it.
Secret of secrets hiding inside a black mitten,
you hang in there.
Fish with a grappling hook hung on your back,
we wish you luck.
Gills with wings, wings with tails,
you can do it.
Fox with walrus's tusks, with golden-fringed
mourning jacket, with your bow rightly strung,
take your time.
Hindpaws in slippers, forepaws in gloves,
take your time.
Slack of rope looped around a deadman's neck,
stay where you are.
Landslide high up in the mountains,
stay where you are.
Iceflow without destination, without hope,
keep from melting yet.
Deadman coming back to the land of the living,
you don't have to say anything.
Season way off in the other hemisphere,
remember your children.

Apology for and Further Explanation of an Attempt to Divert Accusations of Equivocation

In my hometown it was like January,
like January in Oaxaca, in Fortin

de las Flores, like Fortin
in the mid-forties, like the 40s

in December, like December
on the river, a forest of willows

half in, half out of water,
like the river in the picture,

like the picture above your bureau,
like your bureau filled to over-flowing

with feathers every color of the spectrum
feathers blown through vowels,

through curtains of bougainvillaea, going
on forever, forever as it formerly was,

in the lustre of a loved one's luggage,
baggage to carry lightly or solemnly

toss off into the Bay of Fundy.
Thank you for four golden mice

who never wake me up at night,
for the pocket-size surveillance device,

for books which tell me nothing's unakin.
In January it was like my hometown

in the 1940s in the middle of December,
December a cool glass of water at noon

in the summer, a clinking of cowbells
to signal it's evening. I was seven,

four, eight, eleven, still unborn,
brother to my younger sister,

sister to my mother, father like a twin,
twins like vapor trails on clear nights

in October. You were my shadow
I dared not step into. You stood by

my shoulder, champion, angel, faithful
companion I dared not look in the eye.

What was it like for you?
Were you about to step into your skin,

like water poured from a pitcher,
like an ant into amber, like molten gold?

Was the gold like someone's fortune
or folly, folly a moving picture you'd get

into for a quarter, when a quarter meant
more than a dollar, a dollar a bit

of a future you'd be expected to furnish,
I'd be with you to finish,

of a finish wearing the date of your birth,
polished with everyone's hopes,

polished with everyone's dreams,
lost in a basket of keepsakes.

VALERIE WOHLFELD

Between Zero and Ten

0: Phoenix-nest's ring of ashes. Penelope's
loom unlaced with night and knots set free.
Secret geography: the flower's centered pollen
compass-spun of sun and tongue of honeybees.

1: Tiny stem of indivisibility,
little wand to conduct the galactic symphony;
to what purpose does the Milky Way spiral-dance, while you
stand apart: spinal column severed from head and body?

2: Opened stitches, where are you going?
Beautiful needle, sewing
the hematite-dark night with your flight,
as if all of life were only a twining and unraveling.

Most Recent Book: *Thinking the World Visible* (Yale University Press, 1994)

3: Broken wing, half of a butterfly
violet-veined, chrysalis-cast, in your dye
the world manifests itself
whorled as lustrous lazuli.

4: Crossroads at a boundless
intersection: in chess the queen, prophetess
of white, foretells the king of midnight's flight, jet-lagged,
to lands of rain and ruin, to citadel and wilderness.

5: Dangling half-heart or ear,
to beat the port-wined blood, or hear
a pulse through endless corridors of veins,
where plasmic atmospheres appear and disappear.

6: Doilied sieve, net to enclose
a butterfly for the poisoned jar: repose
suits every corpse; loosen a noose
to gently coax a knot around each end-of-summer rose.

7: Pedestal to hold a firelit, foretold
world, star-drifting in a snowy wall of stars, gold and manifold;
or, cane for the Ancient of Days telling his twice-told tale
of creation's squall, as he sways over his vainglorious threshold.

8: How can the limitless
embrace itself when it cannot possess
itself? Two closed wombs
enclose two unending worlds in caress.

9: Hoop for the unfettered lion
who finds redemption
navigating between the master's whip
and the flame's oblivion.

10: To begin again, finite and infinite in rehearsal,
two players the matchmaker assigns for betrothal:
which contains the other, side by side in their marriage bed,
king and queen gardened in tiles' and pools' star-gemmed Taj Majal?

Yad

I saw the eerie hand:
the rippled drapery of the Ark slid

open and the steely pointer was unfastened.
What had happened to the tempered limb,
the leaden arm, to be brought to earth
in silver form, endlessly transcribing —
compass needle steering the universe,
forever turned to only one direction: Torah.

Whose rhetorical arm? — dove-colored,
color of armor. Did this ashen fingertip unfold
the world, Brailled, in traced pages?
Who would place the nickled hand
over their heart, mercurous arm
which might ride our multitude of hearts?
Chained to the Torah, the manacled hand
secreted itself in tightly-swaddled velvet wrappings.

I wanted to touch my finger to its finger.
What would I feel?
Errant philosopher's stone of bitter
and sweet, flux of shadow and light:
out of aurum might come tin,
out of tin might come gold;
if I touched the pewtery hand,
would I touch forever what glittered and what dimmed?

The Drowning and the Drowned

Caught in his arms — great ruffled
fish rococo-scaled in petals of calico
folds and scrolls of lace — in matching Maypole
dress and hair bow, pressed to his buttonhole,
where a carnation's fringed and mottled
lips pursed to my closed lips — I stood soul
to spectral soul with the drowning and the drowned.

Wax-lit eye to gelid sea, the fish is outward-bound.
The sea wave-seized as my cameo's
onyx: the pale profile, the darker stone below.
Dressed in flawless pleats, a canopy's unwound
dorsal and ventral banners, in camisole
of flounced spines and silk-veiled fins rayed in poison:
the masked scorpionfish's coral-hung deception.

Slow he held me. Slow we danced in the grotto
brindled in calico conflagration.
Fishermen threw the hinged-eyed fish back to requisite
water. On sand I danced with Mother;
Father danced in sonic-sounded deep no echo
could outwit. I opened my patent-leather
purse: all the unclasped ocean poured out of it.

Furnaced in topaz fires among misfits and angels fever-
fed, I could not burn in the massacre of fire;
I could not drown in water's apposite
uncompassed quarters: all was psaltery-sounded golden
statuary with the dead still undead beside Abednego
unlit in flame in Babylon. Sea-bittered brine unbound
a grave to lave the restive dead in each wave's climax.

My carved cameo — snow-bound, white-
isleted, stilled figure riding solo
on her floe, held in her grave of agate —
does the little knife-notched goddess know
once she gloried in Father's arms not Mother's,
moving with him as planets turn in parallax —
obscured in infinite waves and counterfeit fires?

Conundrum

I ate the heart — if eating is an art
when the sweet-sour heart — wine-wreathed, animal-torn,
seasoned with curries pinched from out of battered tins —
grows tender and dumb. Whorled conundrum,
iambic of contract and swell — gory lord on war-torn
throne upholstered in lymph and gases and cabbage roses,
cranks up, lets fall, all the gated moated bridges
blood-soldiering each breath's tedium.

Billets-doux, returned to sender, round and round the eclipsed heart:
all blood is love to you, clandestine valentine, —
plate to palate another's heart greets mine.
Heart, maudlin mummer mute and masked, lent a savory
spiced skin to costume the old — find counterpart
in my heart: turn to tessera glaze-crackled,
cell-by-cell blood-tile my mausoleum:

the enameled-spired heart glass-speckled
in tiny lozenged shining bits that stammer

on the tungsten-tip of anvil, hammer.
Cradled, webbed in arteries, a distended
universe's appetite born of systole and diastole:
anorexic-seized blood-starved starts force-fed.

I ate the heart — if eating is an art —
eating, all of me was as the eaten heart —
cloying and tart, tender and dumb underling
domed in oxygen as in a tomb marble crystals' ancient design —
watered, fire-pressed, fossil-ringed, limestone turned apostasy —
sea-changed into some new-atomed thing.

David Wojahn

Excavation Photo

After making love she'd found it, asking me to touch the place
as well:
her left breast, I remember that precisely, & just below the nipple
I can also still recall,

half-dollar sized, a dusky pink that grew erect so often in
my mouth & hands.
But the year, the details of the room, all blown apart in memory,
broken vessels, potsherds

gleaming in the excavation photo's sepia, sunlight & long shadows;
& if only my hand remains,
circling, pushing, probing, *it's a lump I'm sure of it* & if
I could tell you what would happen

next, which sound from her throat, which sound from mine, the days
& weeks to follow
& the bitter eschatologies of touch, what profit would
such knowledge give you?

Would you hear our bedside clock? Cars outside in the rain? —
& where is she now? Could you tell me
that much? Sand & gravel sifted & the sought thing rises,
stroked & circled with a tiny

horsehair brush. Bead, shard, incised bone, it does not flare
in the toothless worker's

Most Recent Book: *The Falling Hour* (University of Pittsburgh Press, 1997)

whorled palm; & my hand keeps moving even now, the fine
transparent hairs

erect as they waken from gooseflesh-speckled aureole, my circles
tight, concentric. *Do you*
feel it now? The push & probe & spiral & the sudden
yes I can feel it too.

Stalin's Library Card

A recent piece in Pravda *gives the library books checked out by Stalin between April and December, 1926. Much has been made of their oddity...*
— Robert Conquest

i.
The Essence of Hypnosis
(Paris: LeGrande, 1902)

The woman has agreed to swallow pins,
and here, white-robed,
stands great Dr. Charcot,

pointing to the needles in her palm. The photo
makes them gleam. The stovepipe-hatted amphitheatre strains,

heads abob for better looks. She's about
to lap them like sugar, but the Doctor's minion

stays her hand; down her dress they glitter and rain.
And now from the murmuring crowd he procures a hat,

placing it upon her lap.
Your child is crying.
Can you soothe him? Tenderly the hat's caressed.

To and fro she rocks it as she sings — a case
of "simple congestive hysteria." *He is dying,*

woman, your child is dying! The tears cascade,
her shoulders twitch and tremble. *Diagnosis confirmed.*

ii.
Syphilis: Its Detection, History,
and Treatment — Illustrated
(Munich: Insel Verlag, 1922)

"The shoulders twitch and tremble at the tertiary stage,
signaling generally the advent of paresis."

Comrade Stalin tamps his pipe and struts
the carpet to the phone, having marked another passage

with red pen. *Do not put him through, I said.*
I am trying to relax. The receiver's slammed down:

collectivization can wait.
He re-cracks the spine,
relights the meerschaum to Nietzsche gone mad,

to Schumann demented, to sepias of six noseless
Neopolitans, an aged whore whose arms are candlewax,

spirochettes that marinate the blood, *x*-es
and arrows to mark their swim. His pulse

crescendos and his forehead glistens,
x and asterisks —
all night the margins redden.

iii.
The Right to Kill
(Moscow: Bezbozhnik, third ed., 1913)

X and asterisk: shorthand all night flowing
out the stenographer's hand. Agent Shivarov:

Why do you think we've arrested you? He cups
his face in his hands while Mandalstam fidgets, blowing

on his tea to cool it.
Could it be your poems?
(The bulb's faint hum, the stenographer's cough.)

On the desk a bulging file, from which Shivarov
removes a smudged carbon, sliding it toward Mandalstam

along the tabletop. *A recitation, please?*
The hand begins to quiver as the carbon blues

his palm —

"the Kremlin mountaineer . . . the thick worms
of his fingers . . . executions on his tongue like berries."

Do you recognize yourself as guilty of composing tracts
of counter-revolutionary nature? And the blue hand shakes.

iv.
Is Resurrection of the Dead Possible?
(London: Theosophy International, 1921)

Against the table the cadaver thrashes: its blue arms quiver —
a little. More voltage to the genitals

and a kind of erection is achieved, which Dr. Lysenko
duly notes, yet Lazarus does not stir,

exactly.
One week to Comrade Stalin's visit,
and the demonstrations must impress:

too much voltage and the corpses combust,
too little and the limbs remain inert

as noodles. Notes scratched on his clipboard, the doctor
scowls to his humpbacked assistant, who hits

the switch.
And Lazarus sizzles — flames emit
from the electroded temples. The good doctor swears

and flails his arms, as the corpse performs
its own suttee. The corpse has the final word.

v.
Ritual Murder Among the Jews
(St. Petersburg: Grani Vot, 1910)

Do not wait until we force you: we will have the final say.
Begin your confession.
Precise as a slide rule

and always natural as the smell of dill —
interrogation, too, is art. Babel sways

upon his stool, his neck goes limp. The aesthetics
of confession must be formalist:

The Trotskyist Babel will weep and stutter but list
in the end his cohort spies.
Yet first he must wake.

Cold water to the face, a truncheon to the legs
and the writer's block is over. The singing

commences with the truncheon's sting,
the singing and the singing and the singing —

its own dark Kaddish, its own crematorium smoke.
The verdict is final, the case is closed.

vi.
Practical Versification
(Moscow: Nova Mysl, 1908)

Should the couplets be open or should they be closed?
The day requires signatures, decrees.

He longs for verse, but must speak in prose.
All the endless signatures.
                                        A photo shoot: he poses

with pen in hand, the *Pravda* newsman on his knees.
Should the couplets be open or should they be closed?

Signatures of every sort, the pace never slows.
The State revised, rewritten endlessly.

He hungers for verse but lives by prose,
Redrafted, retouched. The coffins set in rows

like Red Square parades, marching to infinity.
Should the couplets be open
                                        or should they be closed?

Late in the Kremlin, his desk lamp glows.
So much to excise, he's up until three.

(O to live by verse instead of prose.)
The drafts soar upward. On his desk the pile grows

skyscraper high, Babel tower and gallows tree.
O sentence in verse, o sentence in prose.

Should the couplets be open or should they be closed?

vii.
Proposal for Revision of the First Soviet Encylopedia
(Moscow: Kommunisticheskoy Partii, 1926)

The people can be made to swallow anything.
For example Comrade Yezhov,
                                        Special Marshal

of the Secret Police, has been shot. He will
now require closure, require editing,

His service to the party, his Trotskyite past,
all must now be excised, even his birth

converted to white space.
                    And first
his face must pentimento down to nothingness.

No longer can he pose with Comrade Stalin
admiring the Moscow-Volga Canal. Now he is water.

No longer at His right in parades at Red Square.
Now he is air, is brickwork on the viewing stand.

And now the past itself is air, is water, and finally fire,
whitening to ash.
                    In his fat fingers its pages flare.

Carolyne Wright

The Room

for Margaret Gibson, R. N.

She stood in the room where Allende died.
It was two months later,
Armistice Day, 1973,
and she was on a package tour
for which all refunds had been canceled.
Below the bombed-out windows
with their twisted grillework,
Pinochet's troops patrolled the streets,
and she wore a scarlet poppy
for that other war — Flanders Field
and the black-edged telegram
that had stopped her father's face
in its frame on the mantelpiece.

For years she would not tell this story:
how she walked through Santiago's
rubble-strewn streets until soldiers
leaped from a van with naked bayonets

Most Recent Book: *Seasons of Mangoes and Brainfire* (Christopher Howell, 2000)

and surrounded her, ripping her camera
from her shoulder. All afternoon in the *cuartel*
she showed them blurry Polaroids
of palm trees and big hotels,
and told them she knew nothing.
She wasn't working for anyone.
As late sun slanted through the one window's
iron bars, the *comandante* suddenly
relented. "We have something special
to show you." His tone said
You'd better not refuse.

A guard led her through cratered beds
and shattered statuary of the garden,
into the high-ceilinged room
already beginning to fill with twilight.

Everything was as they had left it.
She gazed a long time
at the red plush chair,
the heavy desk with bullet marks,
scorched books piled kneedeep
on the floor.
"Communist books,"
the guard said, shifting
the rifle on his shoulder.
There was a battered telephone
on the desktop, and a letter
handwritten in Spanish,
the fountain pen lying across it
where the words trailed off.

She knew no Spanish.
The guard stepped to the window.
She wanted to take the letter
or engrave it in her thoughts
for her friends outside, but the guard
turned back and there was no way
she could go beyond this warning.
She studied the prescription bottle
by the inkwell: nitroglycerin
he took for his congested heart.
On the floor under the sideboard
a whiskey bottle on its side, cracked open,
a spill of dark residue beside it.
"*El Presidente* liked his booze,"

the guard smirked, as if
that justified everything.

Her eyes had been saving the blood
for last. In the failing light
the dark stains stood out black —
his last call to his wife,
his farewell to Chile on the radio
when he knew they were coming for him.
Spatter on the walls still echoing
the burst door, the rifle barrels
raised, automatic fire going on and on.
Vanishing in shadow the pool
of himself into which he fell.

Outside, wail of the curfew sirens,
footsteps of those who could be shot
on sight for delaying. "Don't worry,
we escort you back," the guard said.
"We know how to treat our friends."

For years she would feel the click
of the safety catch, chill of steel
at her temple, the poppy's crimson
deepening on her breast.
She said *No thank you*
and walked out.
If soldiers tried to stop her
she would turn and face them
as she still wanted to believe
he had.

The Conjure Woman

(Salvador, Bahia)

She blows on the crystal ball,
tells me I can have anything.
Hibiscus flowers.
Jacarandá wood charms.
A powder from the Mercado Modelo
that drives men wild.

In the waiting room, the man I want
drums his fingers, makes eyes

at the honey-colored woman
stirring something in the kitchen.
Strands of blue pearls,
passion flower *lenço* on her head.
A little *samba* on the red floor tiles.
Yemanjá, sea goddess,
smiles and waves her fish tail
from the poster on the wall.

The conjure woman turns her wedding rings
around a long story about the sea.
Bahia dialect — the hushed syllables,
palm trees reflecting
on the water, whole sentences
I want to understand.

Samba school drums at the corners,
cachaça bottles passed around.
Women singing the Carnaval tune
Não Se Esqueça De Mim.
Don't leave me, don't forget.
My future — full of missing words,
eavesdropping at the tables
of the deaf, late afternoon
smell of exhaustion.

He's gone. Lady Yemanjá laughs
in the room above the kitchen.
I cross the conjure woman's palm
and go out. The whole town
is in the streets, masked dancers
drumming their true names
from continents that still would fit

together — embracing face to face
like lovers in the salt and sweat
of their sea-displacing passion.
Fishermen drag in their nets
and fall to their knees between
the silver thighs of women.

Note from the Stop-Gap Motor Inn

The man who crosses the street may be already out of reach.
— Bertolt Brecht

Blues librettist, piano vamper,
transposer of the heart's iambics
to the ideographs of anything goes,
I'm a fool to leave you.

I've traded you for this
dead-end town, this South-
by-Midwest zipcode. *What the hell*
for? friends ask. *Don't I know*

a good thing? I tell them
I've led a charmed life.
Whatever I wanted
I got. Whatever I didn't

drove off alone. In a country
where it's dangerous to say *No*
to strangers, I've walked the streets
wearing my Silent Majority look,

my Welcome to America complexion.
I've got no talent for concealment,
and no profile but yours
is missing from the picture.

What would the true believers say
if they knew? The preacher
who crosses the street to avoid me?
Who, if I asked the time of day,

would turn his digital watch dial
off? *Too late to change us, lady.*
Too late to take the next train
or erase the lovers pressed back

to back in the ink blots,
in a town where everyone thinks
memory is enough. Who's laying bets
we get out of this alive?

I'm drawing my own geography
of cowardice, and you're home, not even

whistling Dixie to remind yourself.
You know the old score —

those who live in the dreamstates
of the saved, calling themselves
the Beautiful People: your name cut off,
a broadcast across enemy lines.

C. D. Wright

Floating Lady Retablo

This is the shape of the sound   all the information you need
Comes with the light   which melts away   odd   how
Some of the letters   of a life   get printed backwards   how
One pupil looks   for solace   while the other is sweeping the ground
For trouble   how your skin is sensitive as a snail   easy baby
That's my electric eye   it can open anything from ketchup
To old trousseaus   the Venetian eye I saved for you   easy
Baby   I must disabuse you   of your whiny bugaboos   your
Churlish defenses   from here to yonder baby   it's zero visibility

Floating Lady Retablo

Remember I remember   I lay my young bullocks
On thine altar   bald and cold as the truth   I was your
Personal all purpose all weather fuck machine   before the finger
Of suspicion could fire one bad shot   the door
Closed on us   I am the emancipated white man   in the paddock
Common as dirt   I scare the horses   I can lie
At any speed   Recuerda me   as I dig you from the short stob
Of memory in my path   Love Letter #3   recuerda me
Siempre   go try your luck on the mountain   if it pleases ye

---

Most Recent Book: *Deepstep Come Shining* (Copper Canyon, 1998)

Handfishing Retablo

Followed us to the shaft end of the song Que milagro
At the nock end our flight at the point your breath
The worst man a stone the worst woman
A mill the hair Chupa Rosa the hair always gets caught
Leaf on leaf worm by worm we museum in a box
On the other side of the clearing is another
Forest fraught with unknowns O my flammable
Pajamas O my degenerating fibroids
When they lift the prints off our breast will they be yours
Young epitaph kiss me then count your teeth

Handfishing Retablo

Leftover shoofly pie charred baby bed
Stuffed bear in the raked dirt
Smoke coming out of its butt snake eyes
In the robin nest piano repossessed who decides
Who sits down to pee who stands in the mist if
There is something worth knowing if
There is some one thing important for us
To know we come to build worlds arriba los corazones
Media Naranja pray keep us in contact with our ground

Rosesucker Retablo

Though it be the season of falling men
Presaged by crop circles
And compact moving masses
Long dresses made all the more dolorous by dark umbrellas
From these very fingers emerge pistols of love
Lilies of forgiveness
And as you enter the eye in this palm
Chupa Rosa bind me to your secrecy
Open your munificent purse hoard me

Rosesucker Retablo

And though my birds be torn   to rags of smoke
And I into a nexus   of feather and ash
You must move ahead   unencumbered
By melancholy or defects
Behold the woman   Chupa Rosa
May you never endure a week
Without letters from an inmate
Never the day without apples nor bread
Come in   from distant penetralia   blasted immaculacy

Dean Young

Today's Visibility

I don't know what I was thinking
taking us to the Museum of Surgery
but we left very glad of anesthetic
and the sky entirely not cut open.

Later, it was nearly impossible to see
the haystacks because it turned out
we were in the Museum of Museum Guards.
One woman was eight feet tall, her head

a spectacular aluminum oval that floated
around the gallery. But the exhibit
of Incan place mats turned out to be
an exhibit of descriptions of Incan

place mats because the mats themselves
were too delicate to be looked at.
Certainly the Museum of Shadows
was full of shadows but I got the feeling

people were seeing things I wasn't.
A window made you cry in a good way.
I wanted to go to the Museum of Staircases
because of what happened once in Rome

Most Recent Book: *First Course in Turbulence*
(University of Pittsburgh Press, 1999)

but by the time we found the escalator
to catch the elevator, we realized
the Retrospect of the Future
would soon be closed so we rushed away.

The Museum of Weather was between shows
(again) and you felt tetchy and volumetric
so we went to the Café of One Thousand
Adjectives where they searched for a sandwich.

Afterwards, the driver of our museum-quality
cab was from the Ivory Coast and seemed
to want to take us there. I loved what
was happening to your hair in the Museum

of This Moment we did share. A man ran
between the blocked cars trying to sell
a rose, chunks of ice bobbing in the lake.

Howl Upone Eskaping, I Learne Mey Vehikle Is Not Sea-Worthie & Upone Mey Tragik Recapture & Longe Internmynt During Whyche I Wrighte These Words Thorough a Secret System Infolfing Mey Owne Blood

When I got up from my nap in 1999,
there were fewer of my kind around.
Apparently it had been circulated
that if you cracked our oblongatas
correctly, you could harvest
a fair amount of plutonium 57
although, in my experience, no one
knew the proper technique.
Still, they tried, the shattered
remains of my tribe hauled to the curb
every Monday night when the downstairs people
screamed about their ranunculi until
I called the authorities. Mid 17th-century
Holland, it was tulips but now it's ranunculi.
In the bathroom was a book of poems
by H**** C*** about how sad and exquisite
and made of goopy lace everything was.

I hated those poems. Even a regular burrito,
no guacamole, was more full of life
than those poems yet each time his school
met mine, they won, walking away.
Often our guards would complain of pangs
mysterioso the night before engagement
and their hearts would go trochaic.
It was March, month of human discourse
before the human intercourse
that makes such a mess of April.
So I tried to file my report but
part of what I wanted I knew I'd never get
yet when I didn't, I felt driven to account
for the contrary forces within.
Can you see what I was up against?
I was just like you until I was alone
then I was a cherry blossom.

Lives of the Painters

When I hatched from my black egg,
I ate as many of my brothers and sisters
as I could and got big.
They would have done the same.
But who am I?
Never do I want to see my mother again.
When you want something, that means
you're injured. My father, who I never
want to see again, said he didn't think
I crawled enough so he ripped my gold filter
but then gave me fifteen pairs of suede gloves.
Now I like to fall down hard.
You could be the one for me.
More and more I am saddest in summertime.
Once I planted a peony to surprise someone
I thought cared for me. Now I can't
turn my head suddenly to the left
when pulling erratically into the passing lanes
because erratically is how energy behaves
when you put it in too tight a hive.
There's something wrong with my connective tissue.

My T-cells are very mad.
But there is no end to treatment
because the body too is a kind of paper.
Would you like this frottage?
Funny how the pitchfork just appeared.
Darling, how good it would be to lick you
and catch your expression getting all lofty
with a little crayon. Red leaves growing
all around the wound. Then I'd finally
have something on that son of a bitch
Caravaggio who thinks he's the only one
to look into the face of ecstasy and see
a beggar, a thief, a burning church.
Then to crawl down to the concrete hall
and eat mashed potatoes,
mashed potatoes for every meal!
Then to come back and do it all again
until the volumetric depiction of human form
becomes more and more distorted
as it must when the Renaissance
gives way to the Baroque, as evening
gives way to afternoon: impossible ulnas,
swan sperm, beautiful beautiful bicycles.

Sunflower

When Dean Young vacuums he hears
not just time's winged whatchamacallit
hurrying near but some sort of music
that isn't the motor or the attic
or the sucked-up spider's hosannahs
or his mother pounded into a rectangle
or what's inside him breaking
because the only thing conclusive
all those tests showed is inside him
is some sort of crow so unsure of its
crowness, it thinks it's a stone
just as the stone thinks it's
a dark joke in the withered fields
and has to be so opaque to keep
all its ketchupy light inside because

you never know what sonuvabitch
is hanging around, waiting for a chance
to steal your thunder. When Dean Young
has his thunder, nothing moves. Not
the dust in the hose, not the music,
not even the eye of the crow. It drives him
crazy how little effect he has. He thinks
of his friends at ball parks and feels
miserable. He thinks of women's behinds
and feels radiant. He's afraid how he invented
running by moving his legs very fast
will be forgotten, attributed elsewhere.
He can't resign himself to losing the patent
on masturbation. On the other side
of the back of his head hangs his face
which he puts strawberries into.
He dreads strawberries because their mouth
is bigger than his. He dreads his wife
because he loves her. His strong opinions
re: capital punishment, arts education,
the numen dissolve in water,
the universal solvent that falls from clouds,
clouds that were *his* idea.

Side Effects

Your papillae momentus is shot, these pills
may help but you'll probably lose your right arm.
My right arm! How will I live? So the client
thrashes out of the office like a man learning
to swim by drowning but after a couple weeks,
he can almost float, button his own coat.
So he goes back to the specialist who says,
I bet your Palace of Moranzini's collapsed,
maybe this drug will work, it seems to have
some effect on black widow bites, only thing is
you'll have to lose your lake. My lake!
For days afterward, everyone he sees is carrying
a kayak, nautical analogies overflow
even the financial section. Now would be
a good time for a couple strangelets to shred

the fabric of reality but his experiments
at the cyclotron don't amount to much dark matter
so reality goes on with a sloshing sound,
a pointless flopping in his chest then the doctor
says, It's got to be your heart and the man cries out,
Lord, you've got me in your tweezers now!
Ha, ha, what an opportunity to meet the deductible,
you just fly three inches over yourself
and declare a national disaster. Look
at those miserable robots down there
trying to start their cars, pay their interest,
cook eggplant. Let's see what happens
when we drop this big rock, saith the Lord,
the whole planet wobbling on its loose axle
while the patients come and go, some getting weaker,
buying expensive sunglasses and losing them,
some getting stronger, buying expensive sunglasses
and breaking them, puddled in mud, the bones
ground down and thrown upon the hibiscus
to encourage sturdier blooms.
So the waters freeze and melt, the mountains
rise and shrug, the bolts of the Ferris wheel
loosen and are tightened, snow approaches
the house and turns back, forgetting why it came.
So the dead father says in the dream, I didn't
want you to know but now you know. BAM BAM BAM,
you think you want out but you want in.
You're on the wrong side of the door.
You're on the fifth green when the lightning comes.
You're halfway through your sandwich
and they've already taken your plate.
The food is good here but the service
crazy and you wonder why you came,
why you've been coming for years and still
no one knows you. Because no one knows you?
Silly you to be known anyway
now that the grid is showing,
the chicken wire they affix the flowers to.
It's almost 3 and the rain has stopped.
The sun comes out and it's not an accusation
or a plea. You can sit in it for a minute,
drink your tea before the declensions
of evening into the infinitive of sleep.
First you will wake in disbelief, then
in sadness and grief and when you wake

the last time, the forest you've been
looking for will turn out to be
right in the middle of your chest.

Kevin Young

Warhol Attends Roy Cohn's Final Birthday Party at the Palladium, June 1985

Welcome, won't you sit
down sir, the whole
world's here. Who's she

with? What's he think
he's wearing? Warhol dishes
the guest list, giving

friends dirt the next day.
Cohn in the crowd, center,
feeble but no one

asks. From the walls
monitors lower
the boom — Cohn

back in the day, cheeks
full. Bald. Bow-tied.
Dozen-faced. Speaks

about Red Tide, those pinkos
in the Cabinet. Closet
cases. Names his black

list, where we're all
guests. Domino effect —
Warhol thinks back to the Love

Boat where he played
himself — was the nine hundred
ninety-ninth guest —

his snapshot beside Isaac
the black bar-
tender, the mermaids, the party

Most Recent Book: *Most Way Home* (Zoland Books, 2000)

where they paraded
past guests cursed to appear
in the life preserver

who'd since died — Ethel Merman,
Peter Lawford, Slim Pickens —
then the lucky thousandth

guest announced! Where is
Warhol's name on the roll?
Balloons fall like dirigibles

the cake battleship-big
covered in Old Glory. Singing.
Candles blown out

with some help Cohn rises
to talk, thanks, the years
have been good —

from the rafters God
Bless America & the shredded
plastic flag unfurls —

Cohn soon dead, secreted
like the dark hair, buried
awkward, beneath Warhol's wig.

Negative

Wake to find everything black
what was white, all the vice
versa — white maids on TV, black

sitcoms that star white dwarfs
cute as pearl buttons. Black Presidents,
Black Houses. White horse

candidates. All bleach burns
clothes black. Drive roads
white as you are, white songs

on the radio stolen by black bands
like secret pancake recipes, white back-up
singers, ball-players & boxers all

white as tar. Feathers on chickens
dark as everything, boiling in the pot
that called the kettle honky. Even

whites of the eye turn dark, pupils
clear & changing as a cat's.
Is this what we've wanted

& waited for? to see snow
covering everything black
as Christmas, dark pages written

white upon? All our eclipses bright,
dark stars shooting across pale
sky, glowing like ash in fire, shower

every skin. Only money keeps
green, still grows & burns like grass
under dark daylight.

Campbell's Black Bean Soup

Candid, Warhol
scoffed, coined it
a nigger's loft —

not The Factory,
Basquiat's studio stood
anything but lofty —

skid rows of canvases,
paint peeling like bananas,
scabs. Bartering work

for horse, Basquiat churned
out butter, signing each
SAMO©. Sameold. Sambo's

soup. How to sell out
something bankrupt
already? How to copy

rights? Basquiat stripped
labels, opened & ate
alphabets, chicken

& noodle. Not even brown
broth left beneath, not one
black bean, he smacked

the very bottom, scraping
the uncanny, making
A tin thing sing.

Acknowledgments

Ralph Angel: "Twilight" first appeared in *American Poetry Review* and is used by permission of the author. Copyright © 1995 Ralph Angel. "Twice Removed" first appeared in *Volt* and *The Pushcart Prize XIX* and is used by permission of the author. Copyright © 1995 Ralph Angel. "Months Later" first appeared in *American Voice* and is used by permission of the author. Copyright © 1992 Ralph Angel. "Untitled" first appeared in *American Poetry Review* and *The Anthology of Magazine Verse and Yearbook of American Poetry*. Copyright © 1997 Ralph Angel.

Robin Becker: "Why We Fear the Amish" first appeared in *American Poetry Review* and is used by permission of the author. Copyright © 1999 Robin Becker. "Midnight at the Third Street Sculpture Garden" first appeared in *American Poetry Review* and is used by permission of the author. Copyright © 1999 Robin Becker. "Sisters In Perpetual Motion" first appeared in *American Poetry Review* and is used by permission of the author. Copyright © 1996 Robin Becker. "Rustic Portrait" is reprinted from *After Leaping Upriver* by permission of University of Pittsburgh Press and the author. Copyright © 2000 Robin Becker.

Robin Behn: "Interlude: Still Still" is used by permission of the author. Copyright © 2000 Robin Behn. "Whether or Not There Are Apples" first appeared in *Kenyon Review* and is used by permission of the author. Copyright © 1999 Robin Behn. "Elegy for Lessons" and "Dark Yellow Poem" are used by permission of the author. Copyright © 2000 Robin Behn.

Stephen Berg: "The Chair" is reprinted from *Oblivion* by permission of University of Illinois Press and the author. Copyright © 1995 Stephen Berg. "Nights at the Cedar" is used by permission of the author. Copyright © 1998 Stephen Berg. "All I Can Say" is reprinted from *Shaving* and is used by permission of Four Way Books and the author. Copyright © 1998 Stephen Berg.

Linda Bierds: "Burning the Fields" is reprinted from *The Profile Makers* by permission of Henry Holt & Co. and the author. Copyright © 1997 Henry Holt & Co. "The Lacemaker's Condenser" is used by permission of the author. Copyright © 2000 Linda Bierds. "The Suicide of Clover Adams: 1885" is reprinted from *The Profile Makers* by permission of Henry Holt & Co. and the author. Copyright © 1997 Henry Holt & Co.

Marianne Boruch: "The Vietnam Birthday Lottery, 1970," "X-Ray Vision" and "Smoking" are reprinted from *A Stick That Breaks and Breaks* by permission of Oberlin College and the author. Copyright © 1997 Marianne Boruch. "Piano Tuning" first appeared in *Kenyon Review* and is used by permission of the author. Copyright © 1999 Marianne Boruch.

Marcus Cafagña: "The Cockroaches of Tuol Sleng Museum," "Gloomy Sunday," "Haldol" and "Crack" are reprinted from *Roman Fever* by permission of Invisible Cities Press and the author. Copyright © 2001 Marcus Cafagña.

Billy Collins: "Genius" and "Today" first appeared in *Poetry* and are used by permission of the Modern Poetry Association and the author. Copyright © 2000 Billy Collins. "The Country" first appeared in *Doubletake* and is used by permission of the author. Copyright © 2000 Billy Collins. "Absence" and "Velocity" first appeared in *Field* and are used by permission of the author. Copyright © 2000 Billy Collins.

Peter Cooley: "A Place Made of Starlight" and "Brothers' Keepers" are used by permission of the author. Copyright © 1999 Peter Cooley. "For Jude the Obscure" and "To My Hypocrite Reader" are reprinted from *Sacred Conversations* by permission of Carnegie Mellon University and the author. Copyright © 1998 Peter Cooley.

Robert Cording: "Gratitude" first appeared in *Paris Review* and is used by permission of the author. Copyright © 2000 Robert Cording. "Fashion Shoot, Frijoles Canyon" first appeared in *American Voice* and is used by permission of the author. Copyright © 1998 Robert Cording. "Memorial Day" first appeared in *Press* and is used by permission of the author. Copyright ©

1998 Robert Cording. "Moths" first appeared in *TriQuarterly* and is used by permission of the author. Copyright © 1999 Robert Cording.

Mark Cox: "Red Lead, 1978," "Joyland" and "After the Sea Parts, My Daughter Walks Among Gravestones" are used by permission of the author. Copyright © 1999 Mark Cox. "Like a Simile" is reprinted from *Thirty-Seven Years from the Stone* by permission of Pitt and the author. Copyright © 1999 Mark Cox.

Craig Crist-Evans: "Heat," "Morphine," "First Solo Flight" and "Clown Prince" are used by permission of the author. Copyright © 2000 Craig Crist-Evans.

Jim Daniels: "The Day After," "My Mother's See-Through Blouse" and "Night Light" are reprinted from *Blessing the House* by permission of the University of Pittsburgh Press and the author. Copyright © 1997 Jim Daniels. "Brown's Farm" first appeared in *Quarterly West* and is used by permission of the author. Copyright © 1998 Jim Daniels.

Greg Delanty: "Tagging the Stealer" first appeared in *The Atlantic Monthly* and is used by permission of the author. Copyright © 1997. "The Bindi Mirror" first appeared in *The Atlantic Monthly* and is used by permission of the author. Copyright © 2001 Greg Delanty. "Ululu" first appeared in *The New Republic* and is used by permission of the author. Copyright © 2000 Greg Delanty. "The Stilt Fisherman" is used by permission of the author. Copyright © 2000 Greg Delanty.

Allison Hawthorne Deming: "Biophilia" and "God" are used by permission of the author. Copyright © 1999 Allison Deming.

Toi Derricotte: "Clitoris" and "Dead Baby Speaks" are reprinted from *Tender* by permission of the University of Pittsburgh Press and the author. Copyright © 1997 Toi Derricotte.

Deborah Digges: "Two of the Lost Five Virgins" first appeared in *The Boston Review of Books* and is used by permission of the author. Copyright © 2001 Deborah Digges. "The Rainbow Bridge in the Painting of the Sung Dynasty" first appeared in *The Boston Review of Books* and is used by permission of the author. Copyright © 2000 Deborah Digges. "Guillotine Windows" first appeared in *Kenyon Review* and is reprinted from *The Breadloaf Anthology* by permission of the University Press of New England and the author. Copyright © 2000 Deborah Digges.

Stephen Dobyns: "Unexpected Holidays" first appeared in *American Poetry Review* and is used by permission of the author. Copyright © 1999 Stephen Dobyns. "Often in Dreams, He Moved," "That Day He Spent Hours" and "Mystery, So Long" are used by permission of the author. Copyright © 1999 Stephen Dobyns.

Mark Doty: "At the Gym" first appeared in *Slate* (www.slate.com) and is used by permission of the author. Copyright © 1999 Mark Doty. "Fish-R-Us" first appeared in *The Boston Phoenix* and is used by permission of the author. Copyright © 1999 Mark Doty. "Sea Grape Valentine" and "Watermelon Soda" previously appeared in a limited edition chapbook and are reprinted with permission from Dim Gray Bar Press and the author. Copyright © 1999 Mark Doty.

Norman Dubie: "On the Chinese Abduction of Tibet's Panchen Lama" and "The Caste Wife Speaks to the Enigmatic Parabolas" first appeared in *American Poetry Review* and are used by permission of the author. Copyright © 1999 Norman Dubie. "A Genesis Text for Larry Levis, Who Died Alone" first appeared in *West Virginia Review* and is used by permission of the author. Copyright © 1999 Norman Dubie. "Elegy for My Brother" first appeared in *Southern Review* and is used by permission of the author. Copyright © 1999 Norman Dubie.

Stephen Dunn: "The Death of God" first appeared in *American Poetry Review* and is used by permission of the author. Copyright © 2000 Stephen Dunn. "Nature" and "Different Hours" first appeared in *Prairie Schooner* and are used by permission of the author. Copyright © 2000 Stephen Dunn. "A Postmortem Guide" is used by permission of the author. Copyright © 2000 Stephen Dunn.

Stuart Dybek: "Inspiration" first appeared in *TriQuarterly* and is used by permission of the author. Copyright © 1998 Stuart Dybek. "Vigil" first appeared in *Poetry* and is used by permission of *Poetry* and the author. Copyright © 1998 Stuart Dybek. "Narcissus" first appeared in *Ontario Review* and is used by permission of the author. Copyright © 1998 Stuart Dybek. "Overhead Fan" first appeared in *Poetry* and is used by permission of *The Modern Poetry Association* and the author. Copyright © 1998 Stuart Dybek.

Nancy Eimers: "Exam" and "Outer Space" are reprinted from *No Moon* by permission of Purdue University Press and the author. Copyright © 1997 Nancy Eimers. "Passing Things" is used by permission of the author. Copyright © 2000 Nancy Eimers.

Lynn Emanuel: "The Instruction Manual" first appeared in *Harvard Review* and is used by permission of the author. Copyright © 1996 Lynn Emanuel. "The White Dress" and "She" first appeared in *American Poetry Review* and are used by permission of the author. Copyright © 1998 Lynn Emanuel. "Walt, I Salute You!" first appeared in *Boulevard* and is used by permission of the author. Copyright © 1999 Lynn Emanuel.

Beth Ann Fennelly: "Madame L. Describes the Siege of Paris" first appeared *Michigan Quarterly Review* and is used by permission of the author. Copyright © 2000 Beth Ann Fennelly.

Alice Fulton: "Split the Lark" is reprinted from *Felt* by permission of W. W. Norton and the author. Copyright © 2001 Alice Fulton.

Tess Gallagher: "One Kiss" and "Invaded by Souls" are reprinted from *Portable Kisses* by permission of Bloodaxe Press and the author. Copyright © 1996 Tess Gallagher. "When the Enemy Is Illiterate" and "Laughter and Stars" are reprinted from *My Black Horse* by permission of Bloodaxe Press and the author. Copyright © 1995 Tess Gallagher.

Jody Gladding: "Rooms and Their Airs" first appeared in *Wild Earth* and is used by permission of the author. Copyright © 1996 Jody Gladding. "White Asparagus" is used by permission of the author. Copyright © 2000 Jody Gladding.

Albert Goldbarth: "What We're Used To," "Imps" and "*Ancestored-Back* is the Presiding Spirit of This Poem" are reprinted from *Troubled Lovers in History* by permission of Ohio State University Press and the author. Copyright © 1999 Albert Goldbarth.

Beckian Fritz Goldberg: "Refugees" first appeared in *The Gettysburg Review* and is used by permission of the author. Copyright © 1993 Beckian Fritz Goldberg. "Twentieth-Century Children (5): Blood Kissing" first appeared in *Field* and is used by permission of the author. Copyright © 1988 Beckian Fritz Goldberg. "Torture Boy's Watch, Burn Boy's Boat of Souls" is reprinted from the chapbook *Twentieth-Century Children* by permission of Graphic Design Press and the author. Copyright © 1999 Beckian Fritz Goldberg. "Retro Lullaby" first appeared in *Hayden's Ferry Review* and is used by permission of the author. Copyright © 1996 Beckian Fritz Goldberg.

Barry Goldensohn: "Law and Sensibility" first appeared in *Poetry* and is used by permission of the author. Copyright © 1994 Barry Goldensohn. "The Bat," "The Summer I Spent Screwing in the Back Seats of Station Wagons" and "Rest" first appeared in *Salamagundi* and are used by permission of the author. Copyright © 1999 Barry Goldensohn. "Lao Tzu Rebuked" first appeared in *Yale Review* and is used by permission of the author. Copyright © 1999 Barry Goldensohn.

Eamon Grennan: "Lesson" first appeared in the *Times Literary Supplement* and is used by permission of the author. Copyright © 1997 Eamon Grennan. "Artist at Work" first appeared in *The New Yorker* and is used by permission of the author. Copyright © 1997 Eamon Grennan. "Heart Attack" first appeared in *Poetry Ireland* and is used by permission of the author. Copyright © 1997 Eamon Grennan. "Approximation 7" first appeared in *New Hibernia* and is used by permission of the author. Copyright © 1997 Eamon Grennan.

Mark Halliday: "Wrong Poem" first appeared in *Michigan Quarterly Review* and is used by permission of the author. Copyright © 1998 Mark Halliday. "Frankfort Laundromat" and "Parkersburg" first appeared in *Slate* (www.slate.com) and are used by permission of the author. "Your Visit to Drettinghob" first appeared in *Colorado Review* and is used by permission of the author. Copyright © 1999 Mark Halliday.

Daniel Halpern: "Desperados," "Her Body" and "The Eternal Light of Talk" are reprinted from *Something Shining* by permission of Knopf and the author. Copyright © 2000 Daniel Halpern.

Joy Harjo: "The Path to the Milky Way Leads Through Los Angeles," "Song from the House of Death, Or How to Make It Through the End of a Relationship," "This Is My Heart" and "The End" are reprinted from *A Map to the Next World* by permission of W. W. Norton and the author. Copyright © 2000 Joy Harjo.

Jeffrey Harrison: "Our Other Sister," "Sex and Poetry" and "Rowing" are used by permission of the author. Copyright © 2000 Jeffrey Harrison. "A Shave by the Ganges" and "Swifts at Evening" are reprinted from *Signs of Arrival* by permission of Copper Beach and the author. Copyright © 1996 Jeffrey Harrison. "My Double Non-Conversion" first appeared in *Poetry* and is used by permission of *The Modern Poetry Association* and the author. Copyright © 1999 Jeffrey Harrison.

Bob Hicock: "The Party" first appeared in *Black Warrior Review* and is used by permission of the author. Copyright © 1999 Bob Hicock. "Miscarriage and Echo" is used by permission of the author. Copyright ©2000 Bob Hicock. "Birth of a Saint" first appeared in *Black Warrior Review* and is used by permission of the author. Copyright ©1999 Bob Hicock. "Neither Here nor There" first appeared in *Michigan Quarterly Review* and is used by permission of the author. Copyright © 1999 Bob Hicock.

Richard Higgerson: "The Strong Hollow Life Force of Hot Tub Jesus," "Evel Knievel: The Fountain at Caesar's Palace (151 feet 3 inches) Las Vegas, Nevada, September 4th, 1968," "Blanket on Grass" and "Lullaby Rub" are used by permission of the author. Copyright © 2001 Richard Higgerson.

Brenda Hillman: "A Power," "Empty Spires," "A Window" and "The Thicket" are used by permission of the author. Copyright ©2000 Brenda Hillman.

Edward Hirsch: "Ethics of Twilight" and "Days of 1968" first appeared in *Ploughshares* and are used by permission of the author. "Colette" and "Ocean of Grass" are reprinted from *On Love* by permission of Knopf and the author. Copyright © 1998 Edward Hirsch.

Tony Hoagland: "Windchime," "Lawrence," "Benevolence" and "How It Adds Up" are reprinted from *Donkey Gospel* by permission of Graywolf Press and the author. Copyright © 1998 Tony Hoagland.

Jonathan Holden: "Teaching My Son to Drive," "Integrals" and "The Third Party" are reprinted from *The Sublime* by permission of University of North Texas Press and the author. Copyright © 1996 Jonathan Holden. "Such Beauty" first appeared in *Prairie Schooner* and is used by permission of the author. Copyright © 1996 Jonathan Holden.

David Huddle: "Model Father" and "Ooly Pop a Cow" are reprinted from *Summer Lake: New and Selected Poems* by permission of Louisiana State University Press and the author. Copyright © 1999 David Huddle. "Crossing New River" first appeared in *The Hollins Critic* and is used by permission of the author. Copyright © 2001 David Huddle.

Cynthia Huntington: "Home Fires," "For Love," "For Dora Maar" and "The Rapture" are used by permission of the author. Copyright © 2000 Cynthia Huntington.

Richard Jackson: "Do Not Duplicate This Key" first appeared in *Third Coast* and is reprinted from *Touchstones* by permission of New England University Press and the author. Copyright © 1997 Richard Jackson. "CXXXII: The Quandary" is reprinted from *The Half Life of Dreams* by permission of Black Dirt Press and the author. Copyright © 1998 Richard Jackson. "Terzanelle of Kosovo Fields" is used by permission of the author. Copyright © 2000 Richard Jackson. "No Turn on Red" first appeared in *Marlboro Review* and is reprinted from *Introspections* by permission of New England University Press and the author. Copyright © 1998 Richard Jackson.

Mark Jarman: "Dialect" first appeared in *Doubletake* and is used by permission of the author. Copyright © 1997 Mark Jarman. "Goya's *Saint Peter Repentant*" first appeared in *Crab Orchard Review* and is used by permission of the author. Copyright © 1997 Mark Jarman. "You Lucky People" first appeared in *The Journal* and is used by permission of the author. Copyright © 1998 Mark Jarman. "Unholy Sonnet" first appeared in *The Gettysburg Review* and is reprinted from *Unholy Sonnet* by permission of Story Line Press and the author. Copyright © 2000 Mark Jarman.

Richard Jones: "The Fear" and "Father's Day" are reprinted from *Rough Grace: New and Selected Poems* by permission of Copper Canyon Press and the author. Copyright © 2000 Richard Jones. "The Freight" and "The Storm" are reprinted from *The Blessing* by permission of Copper Canyon and the author. Copyright © 2000 Richard Jones.

Rodney Jones: "Sacrament for My Penis," "Elegy for a Bad Example," "Nihilist Time" and "Raccoon Time" are reprinted from *Elegy for the Southern Drawl* by permission of Houghton Mifflin and the author. Copyright © 1999 Rodney Jones.

Richard Katrovas: "On the Day After Allen Ginsberg's Death a Woman Thinks of Me," "Love Poem for an Enemy" and "The Turn" are reprinted from *The Boxers Embrace* by permission of Carnegie Mellon University Press and the author. Copyright © 2000 Richard Katrovas.

Brigit Pegeen Kelly: "Black Swan" first appeared in *The Carolina Quarterly* and is used by permission of the author. Copyright © 1996 Brigit Pegeen Kelly. "Elegy" first appeared in *TriQuarterly Review* and is used by permission of the author. Copyright © 1997 Brigit Pegeen Kelly. "Two Boys" is used by permission of the author. Copyright © 1999 Brigit Pegeen Kelly.

Yusef Komunyakaa: "Outside The Blue Nile" first appeared in *Boston Review* and is used by permission of the author. Copyright © 1994 Yusef Komunyakaa. "Queen Marie-Therese & Nabo" first appeared in *Black Warrior Review* and is used by permission of the author. Copyright © 1996 Yusef Komunyakaa. "Forgive & Live" first appeared in *American Poetry Review* and is used by permission of the author. Copyright © 1996 Yusef Komunyakaa.

Sydney Lea: "Inviting the Moose: a Vision," "Conspiracy Theory" and "November" are reprinted from *Pursuit of a Wound* by permission of University of Illinois Press and the author. Copyright © 2000 Sydney Lea.

Timothy Liu: "Western Wars Mitigated by the Confucian Analects" first appeared in *The Progressive* and is used by permission of the author. Copyright © 2001 Timothy Liu. "Many Mansions," "Georgia O'Keefe: American Icon" and "Emptying the Mind" are used by permission of the author. Copyright © 2001 Timothy Liu.

Robert Long: "Little Black Dino," "Jack Benny," "Nowhere to Mosh" and "Love Potion No. 9" are reprinted from *Blue* by permission of Canio's Editions and the author. Copyright © 1999 Robert Long.

Adrian Louis: "One of the Grim Reaper's Disguises" first appeared in *Ploughshares* and is used by permission of the author. Copyright © 2000 Adrian Louis. "Indian Sign Language" first appeared in *Waterstone* and is used by permission of the author. Copyright © 1999 Adrian Louis. "Dead Skoonk" is used by permission of the author. Copyright © 2001 Adrian Louis. "Old Friend in the Dark" first appeared in *Rattle* and is used by permission of the author. Copyright © 2000 Adrian Louis.

Victor Martinez: "I'm Still Alive," "Failed Teachers," "Sisters" and "A Tiny Man of Print" are used by permission of the author. Copyright © 2000 Victor Martinez.

Campbell McGrath: "Capitalist Poem #38" and "Capitalist Poem #36" first appeared in *Witness* and are used by permission of the author. Copyright © 1996 Campbell McGrath. "The Manatee" and "The Miami Beach Holocaust Memorial" are reprinted from the chapbook *Mangrovia* by permission of Short Line Editions and the author. Copyright © 1999 Campbell McGrath.

Heather McHugh: "Ghazal of the Better-Unbegun," "Past All Understanding," "The Gulf Between the Given and the Gift" and "Qua *Qua* Qua" are reprinted from *The Father of All Predicaments* by permission of Wesleyan University Press and the author. Copyright © 1999 Heather McHugh.

Lynne McMahon: "We Take Our Children to Ireland" is used by permission of the author. Copyright © 1999 Lynne McMahon. "Marriage Dissolving in the Upstairs Room" first appeared in *The Yale Review* and is used by permission of the author. Copyright © 1999 Lynne McMahon. "These Same, These Many Birds" is reprinted from *The House of Entertaining Science* by permission of David R. Godine and the author. Copyright © 1999 Lynne McMahon.

Christopher Merrill: "Because," "Words" and "Doppelgänger" are reprinted from *Watch Fire* by permission of White Pine Press and the author. Copyright © 1994 Christopher Merrill. "Three Weeds" first appeared in *Salt Hill Journal* and is used by permission of the author. Copyright © 1997 Christopher Merrill.

Susan Mitchell: "Pussy Willow (An Apology)" and "Girl Tearing Up Her Face" are reprinted from *Erotikon* by permission of HarperCollins and the author. Copyright © 2000 Susan Mitchell.

David Mura: "First Generation Angels," "from 'Dahmer'" and "Immigration Angel" are used by permission of the author. Copyright © 2000 David Mura. "The Young Asian Women" first appeared in *The Asian Pacific American Journal* and is used by permission of the author. Copyright © 1995 David Mura.

Jack Myers: "Narcissus," "Taking the Children Away," "On Sitting" and "Bread, Meat, Greens, and Soap" are reprinted from *OneOneOne* by permission of Autumn House Press and the author. Copyright © 1999 Jack Myers.

Naomi Shihab Nye: "Bill's Beans" and "Ongoing" are reprinted from *Fuel* by permission of Boa Editions and the author. Copyright © 1998 Naomi Shihab Nye. "Mona's Taco" first appeared in *The Texas Observer* and is used by permission of the author. Copyright © 1998 Naomi Shihab Nye. "Knitting, Crocheting, Sewing" is used by permission of the author. Copyright © 2000 Naomi Shihab Nye.

William Olsen: "Deer Traffic" first appeared in *Colorado Review* and is used by permission of the author. Copyright © 1996 William Olsen. "Electric Church" first appeared in *Crazyhorse* and is used by permission of the author. Copyright © 1996 William Olsen. "Fear in Style" is used by permission of the author. Copyright © 2000 William Olsen. "St. Ives, Winter Night" first appeared in *Crab Orchard Review* and is used by permission of the author. Copyright © 1998 William Olsen.

Steve Orlen: "Monkey Mind" and "Happy As I Am" are used by permission of the author. Copyright © 2000 Steve Orlen.

Frankie Paino: "The Old Religion" and "Alchemy" first appeared in *The Kenyon Review* and are used by permission of the author. Copyright © 1994 Frankie Paino. "The Martyrdom of St. Sebastian" first appeared in *Iowa Review* and is used by permission of the author. Copyright © 1994 Frankie Paino.

Robert Pinsky: "Samurai Song," "The Green Piano" and "To Television" first appeared in *The New Yorker* and are used by permission of the author. Copyright ©1998, 1999 Robert Pinsky. "The Haunted Ruin" first appeared in *Slate* (www.slate.com) and is used by permission of the author. Copyright © 1999 Robert Pinsky.

Keith Ratzlaff: "Group Portrait with Ukeleles" and "Fitful Angel" are reprinted from *Man Under a Pear Tree* by permission of Anhinga Press and the author. Copyright © 1996 Keith Ratzlaff. "Table Prayer" first appeared in *The Georgia Review* and is used by permission of the author. Copyright © 2000 Keith Ratzlaff.

Victoria Redel: "The Bounty" and "Damsels, I" are used by permission of the author. Copyright © 2001 Victoria Redel. "Tilted Man, Tilted Woman" first appeared as "Singing to Tony Bennett's Cock" and is reprinted from *The KGB Bar Book of Poems* by permission of HarperPerrenial and the author. Copyright © 2000 Victoria Redel. "Intact Woman" first appeared as "Abracadabra" in *Story Quarterly Magazine* and is used by permission of the author. Copyright © 1996 Victoria Redel.

Alberto Ríos: "From the Life of Don Margarito" first appeared in *Glimmer Train* and is used by permission of the author. Copyright © 1998 Alberto Ríos. "Writing From Memory" first appeared in *Meridian* and is used by permission of the author. Copyright © 1998 Alberto Ríos. "Some Extensions on the Sovereignty of Science" first appeared in *Clackamas Literary Review* and is used by permission of the author. Copyright © 1998 Alberto Ríos.

David Rivard: "Versace," "Question for the Magic Hour" and "Jung" are reprinted from *Bewitched Playground* by permission of Graywolf Press and the author. Copyright © 2000 David Rivard.

Pattiann Rogers: "Murder in the Good Land" and "Opus from Space" are reprinted from *Eating Bread and Honey* by permission of Milkweed Editions and the author. Copyright © 1997 Pattiann Rogers. "Reiteration" first appeared in *Poetry* and is used by permission of The Modern Poetry Association and the author. Copyright © 1998 Pattiann Rogers. "Come, Drink Here" first appeared in *The Hudson Review* and is used by permission of the author. Copyright © 1997 Pattiann Rogers.

Lee Ann Roripaugh: "Transplanting" is used by permission of the author. Copyright © 2000 Lee Ann Roripaugh.

Jill Allyn Rosser: "Lover Release Agreement" first appeared in *Poetry* and is used by permission of *The Modern Poetry Association* and the author. Copyright © 1996 Jill Allyn Rosser. "Resurfaced" and "Quest of the Prell" are used by permission of the author. Copyright © 2000 Jill Allyn Rosser.

Clare Rossini: "Brief History of a Sentence," "Rice County Soliloquy" and "'Why Talk When You Can Paint?'" are used by permission of the author. Copyright © 2000 Clare Rossini. "Eve to Adam in Retrospect" first appeared in *The Hungry Mind Review* and is used by permission of the author. Copyright © 2000 Clare Rossini.

Mary Ruefle: "Seven Postcards from Dover," "No Comparison" and "Among the Musk Ox People" all first appeared in *Fence* and are used by permission of the author. Copyright © 1999 Mary Ruefle. "10 April" first appeared in *Shenandoah* and is used by permission of the author. Copyright © 1999 Mary Ruefle.

Michael Ryan: "Against Self-Torment," "Complete Semen Study" and "In the Sink" first appeared in *American Poetry Review* and are used by permission of the author. Copyright © 1999 Michael Ryan. "My Other Self" first appeared in *Slate* (www.slate.com) and is used by permission of the author. Copyright © 1999 Michael Ryan.

Ira Sadoff: "On the Day of Nixon's Funeral," "My Mother's Funeral," "Izzy," and "Delirious" are reprinted from *Grazing* by permission of University of Illinois Press and the author. Copyright © 1999 Ira Sadoff.

Natasha Saje: "Why I Won't Pierce My Ears" first appeared in *Crab Orchard Review* and is used by permission of the author. Copyright © 1999 Natasha Saje. "I am peeling four pink grape fruit" first appeared in *Shenandoah* and is used by permission of the author. Copyright © 1999 Natasha Saje. "Story of a Marriage" first appeared in *Two Rivers Review* and is used by permission of the author. Copyright © 1999 Natasha Saje. "Wonders of the Invisible World" is used by permission of the author. Copyright © 2000 Natasha Saje.

Sherod Santos: "Romeo & Juliet" and "The Book of Blessings" are used by permission of the author. Copyright © 2000 Sherod Santos. "Illuminated Manuscript" first appeared in *Slate* (www.slate.com) and is used by permission of the author. Copyright © 1999 Sherod Santos. "The Talking Cure" first appeared in *The Yale Review* and is used by permission of the author. Copyright ©2000 Sherod Santos.

Philip Schultz: "The Displaced" first appeared in *The New Yorker* and is used by permission of the author. Copyright © 2000 Philip Schultz. "The Extra" first appeared in *The Georgia Review* and is used by permission of the author. Copyright © 1997 Philip Schultz. "In Medias Res" first appeared in *The Yale Review* and is used by permission of the author. Copyright © 1998 Philip Schultz. "The Holy Worm of Praise" first appeared in *Poetry* and is used by permission of the author. Copyright © 1998 Phillip Schultz.

Maureen Seaton: "The Zen of Crime," "Whining Prairie," "Miss Molly Rockin' in the House of Blue Light," "Woman Circling Lake," "Lateral Time" and "The Freezing Point of the Universe" are reprinted from *Little Ice Age* by permission of Invisible Cities Press and the author. Copyright © 2000 Maureen Seaton.

Betsy Sholl: "Half the Music" first appeared in *Massachusetts Review* and is used by permission of the author. Copyright © 1999 Betsy Sholl. "Queen of the Night" first appeared in *Prairie Schooner* and is used by permission of the author. Copyright © 2001 Betsy Sholl. "Late Psalm" first appeared in *Kenyon Review* and is used by permission of the author. Copyright © 2001 Betsy Sholl.

Jane Shore: "The Yawner" and "I Dream About My Dead" are used by permission of the author. Copyright © 2001 Jane Shore.

Tom Sleigh: "Newsreel" is used by permission of the author. Copyright © 2000 Tom Sleigh. "The Grid" is reprinted from *Dreamhouse* by permission of the University of Chicago Press and the author. Copyright © 1999 Tom Sleigh.

William Loran Smith: "Speaking Louder" first appeared in *The Round Table* and is used by permission of the author. Copyright © 1998 William Loran Smith. "Hairspray" is reprinted from *Night Train* by permission of Plinth Books and the author. Copyright © 1997 William Loran Smith. "The Family Man" is reprinted from *Last Call: Poems on Alcoholism, Addiction and Deliverance* by permission of Sarabande Books and the author. Copyright © 1997 William Loran Smith.

Gary Soto: "Raisin Factory" first appeared in *Green Mountain Review* and is used by permission of the author. Copyright © 2001 Gary Soto. "Devising Your Own Time," "Teaching English from an Old Composition Book," and "Late Confession" are reprinted from *A Natural Man* by permission of Chronicle Books and the author. Copyright © 1999 Gary Soto.

Maura Stanton: "Practicing T'ai Chi Ch'uan" first appeared in *Many Mountains Moving* and is used by permission of the author. Copyright © 1997 Maura Stanton. "Posthuman" first appeared in *American Poetry Review* and is used by permission of the author. Copyright © 1997 Maura Stanton. "Outside St.-Remy-de-Provence" first appeared in *The Formalist* and is used by permission of the author. Copyright © 1996 Maura Stanton. "Searches" first appeared in *The Prose Poem: An International Journal* and is used by permission of the author. Copyright © 1996 Maura Stanton.

David St. John: "Merlin," "Los Angeles, 1954" and "I Know" are reprinted from *Study for the World's Body* by permission of HarperPerrenial and the author. Copyright © 1994 David St. John.

Kevin Stein: "Beanstalk," "Because I Wanted to Write a Happy Poem, I Thought of Harry Caray's Dying" and "Confessional" are reprinted from *Chance Ransom* by permission of University of Illinois Press and the author. Copyright © 2000 Kevin Stein.

Arthur Sze: "The String Diamond" is reprinted from *The Redshifting Web: Poems 1970–1998* by permission of Copper Canyon Press and the author. Copyright © 1998 Arthur Sze.

James Tate: "A Knock on the Door," "Never Again the Same" and "The New Ergonomics" are reprinted from *Shroud of the Gnome* by permission of Ecco Press and the author. Copyright © 1997 James Tate. "How the Pope Is Chosen" is reprinted from *Worshipful Company of Fletchers* by permission of Ecco Press and the author. Copyright © 1994 James Tate.

Richard Tillinghast: "Exillium" and "Incident" are reprinted from *Six Mile Mountain* by permission of Story Line Press and the author. Copyright © 2000 Richard Tillinghast. "Southbound Pullman, 1945" is reprinted from *The Stonecutter's Hand* by permission of David R. Godine and the author. Copyright © 1995 Richard Tillinghast. "The Alley Behind Ocean Drive" is used by permission of the author. Copyright © 2000 Richard Tillinghast.

Chase Twichell: "Road Tar," "Erotic Energy," "A Last Look Back," "To the Reader: If You Asked Me," "To the Reader: Polaroids" and "Decade" are reprinted from *The Snow Watcher* by permission of Ontario Review Press and the author. Copyright © 1998 Chase Twichell.

Leslie Ullman: "Calypso, Twilight" and "Estrogen" are reprinted from *Slow Work Through Sand* by permission of University of Iowa Press and the author. Copyright © 1998 Leslie Ullman. "Neap Tide" is used by permission of the author.

Martha Modena Vertreace: "Iron Brigade Highway," "Night of the Moon," and "Conjuries in Amber" are used by permission of the author. Copyright © 2000 Martha Modena Vertreace.

Charles Harper Webb: "'Did That Really Happen?'" first appeared in *Poetry International* and is used by permission of the author. Copyright © 1999 Charles Harper Webb. "To Prove That We Existed Before You Were Born" first appeared in *Michigan Quarterly Review* and is used by permission of the author. Copyright © 2000 Charles Harper Webb. "Tone of Voice" and "Biblical Also-Rans" are reprinted from *Liver* by permission of the University of Wisconsin Press and the author. Copyright © 1999 Charles Harper Webb. "*Funktionslust*" first appeared in *Virginia Quarterly Review* and is used by permission of the author. Copyright © 1999 Charles Harper Webb.

Bruce Weigl: "One of the Wives of God" and "The Super" are used by permission of the author. Copyright © 2000 Bruce Weigl. "Elegy for Matthews" is reprinted from *After the Others* by permission of TriQuarterly Books/Northwestern University Press and the author. Copyright © 1999 Bruce Weigl.

Roger Weingarten: "Into the Mouth of the Rat" is used by permission of the author. Copyright © 2001 Roger Weingarten.

Dara Wier: "One Enchanted Evening," "Catholic," and "Prayer that the Rod of the Prede Stined Spouse May Blossom" are used by permission of the author. Copyright © 2000 Dara Wier. "Apology for and Further Explanation of an Attempt to Divert Accusations of Equivocation" is reprinted from *Our Master Man* by permission of Carnegie Mellon University Press and the author. Copyright © 1999 Dara Wier.

Valerie Wohlfeld: "Between Zero and Ten" first appeared in *Michigan Quarterly Review* and is used by permission of the author. Copyright © 1999 Valerie Wohlfeld. "Yad" first appeared in *The Forward* and is used by permission of the author. Copyright © 1998 Valerie Wohlfeld. "The Drowning and the Drowned" and "Conundrum" are used by permission of the author. Copyright © 2000 Valerie Wohlfeld.

David Wojahn: "Excavation Photo" is reprinted from *The Falling Hour* by permission of University of Pittsburgh Press and the author. Copyright © 1997 David Wojahn. "Stalin's Library Card" first appeared in *Poetry* and is used by permission of the Modern Poetry Association and the author. Copyright © 1998 David Wojahn.

Carolyne Wright: "The Room" first appeared in *The Iowa Review* and is used by permission of the author. Copyright © 1998 Carolyne Wright. "The Conjure Woman" is reprinted from *From a White Woman's Journal* by permission of Watermark Press and the author. Copyright © 1985 Carolyne Wright. "Note from the Stop-Gap Motor Inn" is reprinted from *Cape Discovery: The Provincetown Fine Arts Work Center Anthology* by permission of Sheep Meadow Press and the author. Copyright © 1994 Carolyne Wright.

C. D. Wright: "Floating Lady Retablo," "Handfishing Retablo" and "Rosesucker Retablo" first appeared in *Conjunctions* and are used by permission of the author. Copyright © 1999 C. D. Wright.

Dean Young: "Today's Visibility" first appeared in *Ploughshares* and is used by permission of the author. Copyright © 2000 Dean Young. "Lives of the Painters" is reprinted from *First Course in Turbulence* by permission of the University of Pittsburgh Press and the author. Copyright © 1999 Dean Young. "Sunflower" first appeared in *Three Penny Review* and is used by permission of the author. Copyright © 1999 Dean Young. "Side Effects" is used by permission of the author. Copyright © 2001 Dean Young.

Kevin Young: "Warhol Attends Roy Cohn's Final Birthday Party at the Palladium, June 1985," "Negative" and "Campbell's Black Bean Soup" are forthcoming from *To Repel Ghosts* and used by permission of Zoland Books and the author. Copyright © 2001 Kevin Young.

A Note on the Type

Poets of the New Century has been set in a digital version of Matthew Carter's Galliard, a type introduced by the Mergenthaler Linotype Company in 1978 under the direction of Mike Parker. A type designer of impeccable pedigree and formidable knowledge, Carter took on the challenge of interpreting a French sixteenth-century face for the then-new medium of phototypesetting, christening it with the name Robert Granjon applied to a type he first cut about 1570. At the time Carter started work on his new type, Granjon's work was little recognized among designers; his italics had been co-opted as partners for the Garamond types and his romans heavily reworked under the name Plantin. Rather than attempt a literal copy of a particular type, Carter sought to capture the spirit of a Granjon original, and in so doing created a type with a distinct heft and a dense color on the page, and a sparkle not found in most Garamond revivals.

Design by Carl W. Scarbrough
Composition by Carl W. Scarbrough and Robert M. Saley